TEACHING FOR LEARNING: APPLYING EDUCATIONAL PSYCHOLOGY IN THE CLASSROOM

GOODYEAR EDUCATION SERIES
THEODORE W. HIPPLE, EDITOR
UNIVERSITY OF SOUTH CAROLINA AT SPARTANBURG

CHANGE FOR CHILDREN
SANDRA N. KAPLAN, JO ANN B. KAPLAN, SHEILA K. MADSEN, BETTE K. TAYLOR

CREATING A LEARNING ENVIRONMENT
ETHEL BREYFOGLE, PAMELA SANTICH, RONALD KREMER, SUSAN NELSON, CAROL PITTS

DO YOU READ ME?
ARNOLD GRIESE

IMAGINE THAT!
JOYCE KING AND CAROL KATZMAN

THE LANGUAGE ARTS IDEA BOOK
JOANNE D. SCHAFF

THE LEARNING CENTER BOOK
TOM DAVIDSON, PHYLLIS FOUNTAIN, RACHEL GROGAN, VERL SHORT, JUDY STEELY, KATHERINE FREEMAN

LOVING AND BEYOND
JOE ABRUSCATO AND JACK HASSARD

MAINSTREAMING LANGUAGE ARTS AND SOCIAL STUDIES
CHARLES R. COBLE, ANNE ADAMS, PAUL B. HOUNSHELL

MAINSTREAMING SCIENCE AND MATH
CHARLES R. COBLE, ANNE ADAMS, PAUL B. HOUNSHELL

NEW SCHOOLS FOR A NEW AGE
WILLIAM GEORGIADES, REUBEN HILDE, GRANT MACAULAY

ONE AT A TIME ALL AT ONCE
JACK E. BLACKBURN AND CONRAD POWELL

THE OTHER SIDE OF THE REPORT CARD
LARRY CHASE

AN OUNCE OF PREVENTION PLUS A POUND OF CURE
RONALD W. BRUTON

REACHING TEENAGERS
DON BEACH

THE READING CORNER
HARRY W. FORGAN

A SURVIVAL KIT FOR TEACHERS AND PARENTS
MYRTLE T. COLLINS AND DWANE R. COLLINS

THE WHOLE COSMOS CATALOG OF SCIENCE ACTIVITIES
JOE ABRUSCATO AND JACK HASSARD

TEACHING FOR LEARNING
MYRON H. DEMBO

WILL THE REAL TEACHER PLEASE STAND UP? 2ND EDITION
MARY C. GREER AND BONNIE RUBINSTEIN

A YOUNG CHILD EXPERIENCES
SANDRA N. KAPLAN, JO ANN B. KAPLAN, SHEILA K. MADSEN, BETTE K. GOULD

TEACHING FOR LEARNING: APPLYING EDUCATIONAL PSYCHOLOGY IN THE CLASSROOM

MYRON H. DEMBO
UNIVERSITY OF SOUTHERN CALIFORNIA

GOODYEAR PUBLISHING COMPANY, INC.
SANTA MONICA, CALIFORNIA

Library of Congress Cataloging in Publication Data

Dembo, Myron H
Teaching for learning.

(Goodyear education series)
Includes index.
1. Learning, Psychology of. 2. Classroom management.
I. Title.
LB1051.D37 371.1'02 76-29390
ISBN: 0-87620-885-5 (paper)

Y-8855-2 (paper)

Current Printing (last digit):
10 9 8 7 6 5 4 3 2 1

Printed in the United States of America

Text design: The Design Quarter/Tom Lewis/Francine Miller
Illustrations and cover design: Tom Gould
Copy and Production Editor: Janice Gallagher

*To my mother, Lillian Dembo,
and father, Harry Guy Dembo, and
to the educator who had
the greatest impact on my
life, John Meehan*

CONTENTS

PREFACE

My primary assumptions in writing this book are that (a) teachers need more detailed information about specific aspects of the teaching-learning process rather than an encyclopedic knowledge of all content in educational psychology, and (b) teachers need to know how to use educational psychology to make better teaching decisions.

The following components of the book are my attempts to translate these assumptions into a textbook that is an alternative to the many textbooks already in the field. First, I have based the book on an instructional model identifying the major variables in the teaching-learning process: individual differences, teacher behavior, instructional objectives, theories and principles of learning, methods of teaching, and evaluation of student behavior and achievement. After presenting the model in Chapter 1, I discuss individual differences in Chapters 2 and 3. Chapter 4 demonstrates how teachers interact with and affect the behavior of different students. Chapter 5 covers the issues and procedures involving the use of instructional objectives, while Chapters 6, 7, and 8 consider the conceptual and practical aspects of theories of learning and the resultant methods of teaching for attaining classroom objectives. Last, Chapters 9 and 10 outline ways to measure and evaluate student progress. I selected this organization with the thought that if you understand the interrelatedness of the variables in teaching and learning you will find it easier to establish effective learning conditions in the classroom.

Second, I have tried to focus on the most relevant theories, principles, and research findings for each of the variables. In some cases I have decided to organize the material differently from existing textbooks. For example, developmental concepts are discussed primarily under individual differences, and Piagetian theory is covered under cognitive learning theory. Learning theories and methods of teaching are organized by their theoretical orientations — behaviorism, cognitivism, and humanism — to help you understand the theory behind the practice.

Third, I have begun each chapter with a brief orientation to acquaint you with the issues and concerns of the chapter.

Fourth, I have interspersed questions throughout the text that ask you to take a stand on various issues or require you to think about your personal experiences in school. These questions encourage you to examine personal beliefs about the teaching-learning process. Follow-up activities at the end of each chapter maintain this self-inquiry process.

You will encounter the pronouns "he" and "she" used interchangeably throughout the text. I have done this to avoid the awkward "he or she" and to remove any taint of sexism from this book.

After you read the book drop me a line (600 Phillips Hall, University of Southern California, Los Angeles, CA 90007) and let me know your reactions. I welcome both your praise and criticism.

I would like to thank some individuals who played important roles in helping me complete this project: the University of Southern California for granting me a sabbatical leave during the Fall 1973 semester to work on the book; A.J.H. Gaite of the University of Oregon for his helpful reviews of the manuscript; Dave Grady, education editor at Goodyear, for his support throughout the project; Janice Gallagher, copy and production editor, who contributed significantly to the final product; and my wife, Nancy, and children, Debbie and Lisa, for their patience and understanding while the book was written. (Now I will be free to take you on Sunday excursions — but after the football games!)

M.H.D.

ACKNOWLEDGMENTS

Excerpt from pp. 63–64 in *Educational Psychology,* Second Edition, by Frederick J. McDonald. © 1965 by Wadsworth Publishing Company, Inc., Belmont, Calif. 94002. Reprinted by permission of the publisher.

Excerpts from pp. 41, 48–49, 112 in *How Children Fail* by John Holt. Copyright © 1964 by Pitman Publishing Corp. Reprinted by permission of Pitman Publishing Corp.

Excerpts from p. 47 in *The Antecedents of Self-esteem* by Stanley Coopersmith. © 1967 by W.H. Freeman and Company. Reprinted by permission.

Excerpts from pp. 15, 63 in *The Professional Education of Teachers* (2nd ed.) by A.W. Combs, R.A. Blume, A.J. Newman, and E.L. Wass.© 1974 by Allyn & Bacon, Boston, Mass. Reprinted by permission.

Excerpt from p. 304 in *Culture Against Man* by Jules Henry.© 1963 by Random House, Inc. Reprinted by permission.

Excerpt from p. 319 in E. Paul Torrance, *Rewarding Creative Behavior: Experiments in Classroom Creativity*. © 1965. Reprinted by permission of Prentice-Hall, Inc., Englewood Cliffs, N.J.

Excerpt from pp. 3–5 in *Classroom Questions* by Norris M. Sanders. Copyright © 1966 by Norris M. Sanders. By permission of Harper & Row, Publishers, Inc.

Excerpts from pp. 31–32 in "Kappans Ponder the Goals of Education" by Harold Spears.© 1973 by *Phi Delta Kappan*. Reprinted by permission.

Excerpt from pp. 106–107 in *Learning by Discovery: A Critical Appraisal* edited by Lee S. Shulman and Evan R. Keisler. Reprinted by permission of the editors.

Excerpt from p. 57 in *Human Teaching for Human Learning* by G.I. Brown. © 1971 by The Viking Press, Inc. Reprinted by permission.

Excerpt from pp. 97–99 in "So You Want To Change to an Open Classroom?" by R.S. Barth. *Phi Delta Kappan* 53.© 1971 by *Phi Delta Kappan*. Reprinted by permission of *Phi Delta Kappan* and the author.

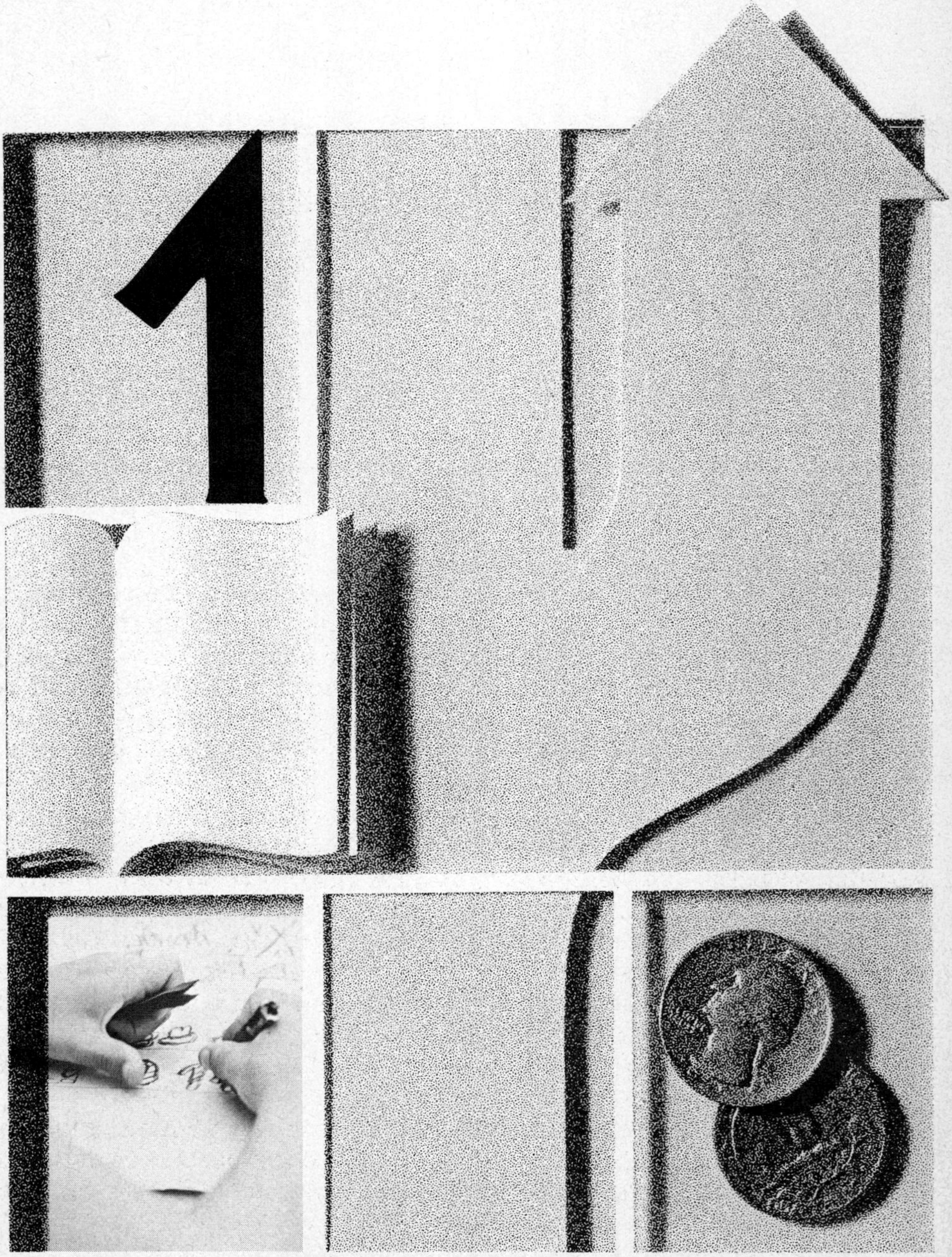
1

THE TEACHER AS DECISION MAKER

ORIENTATION

Teaching and learning are related but independent processes. Sometimes teaching leads to learning, but not always. Although the teacher may facilitate learning, the student takes charge of his learning. Smith (1960) defines teaching as "a system of actions intended to induce learning" (p. 230); learning is often defined as a process by which behavior is either modified or changed through experience or training.

If a teacher is to facilitate learning in others, she must learn to know the major variables that influence the success of the teaching-learning process. This is no easy task, for the classroom is a complex meshing of simultaneous activities and events. I have organized this book around an instructional model identifying some important decisions a teacher must make during the instructional process so that you, the teacher, will better understand the relation between teaching and learning. This introductory chapter explains the model and discusses how you can use psychological content to improve your teaching effectiveness.

Every teacher espouses hypotheses or beliefs about the nature of the teaching-learning process that influence her classroom behavior. These beliefs lead her to make important decisions that determine students' freedom of movement, of speech, of access to materials, and that set the conditions for other behaviors under which students live and learn at school (Prescott, 1957). Careful observation of teacher practices in the classroom can provide insights into a teacher's belief system and will reveal that not all teaching decisions are supported by empirical research or are consistent with sound educational theory or practice.

Let's look at a comment from a student observer who questioned a teacher about a particular teaching behavior:

> She reads to the class because she feels that lecturing "over their heads" is not good and that they will learn nothing from it. She feels that if students understand what she says, they will learn much better. After reading to the class, she asks questions to test their comprehension.

This teacher's beliefs about learning prompt her to read to the class. What classroom experiences led her to this decision? If she lectured "over their heads" in the past, what was the cause of her behavior? Did the students not understand important knowledge? Was her vocabulary too difficult for the students' level of development? The answers to these questions should help to explain why her lecturing was ineffective. Although she feels that her students will learn better by being read to than by being lectured at, this solution to the problem may prove to be as ineffective as her original strategy.

McDonald (1965) provides a good example of how a teacher's decisions can shape what a student will learn:

> A fourth-grade teacher was introducing a unit on "Pioneer Life." He asked the students what they wanted to study about "Pioneer Life" and what kinds of questions they should raise concerning the subject. As the discussion proceeded, the children suggested the usual categories for studying a history unit — namely, the pioneer's food, shelter, and clothing. One child mentioned that he had seen a Western movie in which a man accused of horse stealing was immediately hanged. This comment on the movie evoked considerable interest in the group, and one of the children asked why the man was hanged right away. The teacher dismissed this question as irrelevant to a discussion on pioneer life. The decision not to utilize this question in effect set the stage for the kinds of things that the pupils would talk about. Had the teacher chosen to capitalize upon this question, topics concerning pioneer conceptions of justice and due process of law, the function of law-enforcing bodies, and the validity of citizens' arrests could have been developed.

> These topics did not emerge in the ensuing discussion, nor were they included as relevant points in the outline of topics to be studied under the headline of "Pioneer Life." The teacher's decision at this point, then, determined the character of what the children could learn. (pp. 63-64)

McDonald asks whether this teacher would have profited by examining his decisions in the light of his teaching hypotheses.

These examples illustrate the importance of examining and testing teaching hypotheses or beliefs so that you can make necessary modifications in educational procedures and practices. This book will help you

1. examine the effects of teacher decisions on learning
2. examine personal beliefs about the teaching-learning process
3. evaluate beliefs and practices in order to modify teaching behavior

Educational psychology includes research findings, theories, concepts, and principles that you can use to formulate and test personal beliefs about teaching and learning. Note the emphasis on the word "use." Many people believe that the more knowledge a teacher possesses the more effective he will be in the classroom. Cohen (1973) discusses this belief as "to know good is to do good" (or the "myth-stake"). Unfortunately, research studies have failed to demonstrate a relationship between measures of classroom teaching behaviors and the teacher's knowledge of psychological information (Aspy, 1972a; Silverman & Kimmel, 1972). Perhaps one reason for this finding is that many teachers simply memorize psychological material without attempting to internalize and apply it in any meaningful way. Surely, we would be dissatisfied with an attorney who knew the law but had difficulty defending his clients because he couldn't work with ambiguities in the law.

Teaching is not an exact science. The teacher must apply his knowledge to the complex world of the classroom and make decisions that lead to improved student performance. Teaching will then lead to learning.

To help you internalize the psychological information presented in this book, I have interspersed questions throughout the text and provided follow-up learning activities at the end of each unit with suggestions for further reading. Take time to consider the questions and activities and discuss them with your classmates. Avoid the tendency to be a passive learner by simply underlining sentences with a Magic Marker. Remember, in a short time you will have to apply educational psychology in the classroom — why not begin now?

WHAT TYPES OF INSTRUCTIONAL DECISIONS DO TEACHERS MAKE?

Before studying separate aspects of the teaching-learning process you should understand the major variables in the process. The use of an instructional model will best accomplish this purpose.

Lembo (1969) identified an adequate instructional model as *diagnostic*, *prescriptive*, and *normative*. It is diagnostic in that it provides for the identification of the learner's present level of functioning or cognitive ability, the appropriate kinds of instructional objectives and activities for his level of cognitive abilities and style of learning, and the problems resulting from instructional activities. The model thus points out the direction for remediation when learning does not occur.

A good instructional model is also prescriptive in that it provides some procedural guidelines for establishing learning conditions.

Last, a good instructional model is normative in that it provides general criteria for determining whether or not learning conditions have been met.

Figure 1.1 is an instructional model meeting these criteria. It has been adapted from Hunter (1971), who has applied it to the education of both preservice and inservice teachers.

An important aspect of this model for the teacher is that it integrates the important variables in the teaching-learning process: the students whom she teaches, the objectives she hopes to attain with them, and the methods and behaviors she uses to this end. Because each variable is separated, you can study each variable and relate psychological findings to your teaching decisions during instruction. The model also emphasizes that the teacher's behavior causes learning and directs her to different areas in which she must become proficient.

Let's look at the variables in the model and the decisions that a teacher must make. Each component is numbered for easy identification.

DECISIONS RELATED TO THE LEARNING TASK

One of the important decisions to make in teaching is to decide upon an instructional objective; that is, what is to be learned (#3)? A number of earlier decisions must intervene during this process, such as the teacher's familiarity with the content area and particularly her ability to determine what the learners already know about the content (#1).

Some psychologists refer to this assessment as determining the learner's entry behavior. Hunter (1971) identifies two parts to an adequate assessment. The first is the continuum that exists in most content areas — easy to more difficult. For example, a child who can multiply by a single number may not be able to multiply by two or three numbers. Starting at the proper level of difficulty is an important condition of any instructional program.

The second dimension of a learning task is its level of complexity in the cognitive (knowledge), affective (interests, attitudes), and psychomotor (physical) domains. The *Taxonomy of Educational Objectives — Cognitive Domain* (Bloom et al., 1956) breaks down the decisions about the levels of complexity: Will the learner (1) merely possess knowledge, (2) understand or summarize it, (3) apply it, (4) analyze it, (5) synthesize it with other knowledge, or (6) evaluate it?

DECISIONS RELATED TO THE BEHAVIOR OF THE LEARNER

Another decision for you to consider before determining the instructional objective is the behavior of the learner (#2). What must he do to learn? This decision also has two parts: (1) The behavior must be relevant to the objective (a student can't learn to debate merely by reading books on debating, nor can he solve chemistry problems simply by memorizing formulas); and (2) the behavior must be relevant to the learner (if a child is a poor reader, relying solely on a social studies textbook for factual material is not an appropriate teaching behavior).

The synthesis of the first two teaching decisions — what the student will learn and how he will learn it — constitutes the instructional objective of a lesson (#3). The determination of this objective in advance will help you decide at a later time whether or not you have been successful in changing the learner's behavior.

The model identifies some important responsibilities for you to consider before you even begin teaching a lesson. Too often teachers start out with instructional techniques or strategies before they know what they are trying to teach or identify objectives before they analyze the individual abilities of the students. Planning objectives without first assessing the needs and abilities of the learners is a risky procedure that often leads to inappropriate, irrelevant, or unnecessary teaching (Giusti & Hogg, 1973).

DECISIONS RELATED TO THE BEHAVIOR OF THE TEACHER

Another major decision is the answer to the "how" question in the instructional process (#7). How will the teacher facilitate learning? Teachers differ greatly in their styles of teaching. These behaviors involve degree of planning, amount of control of student behaviors, method of presentation of material, types of grouping, and so forth.

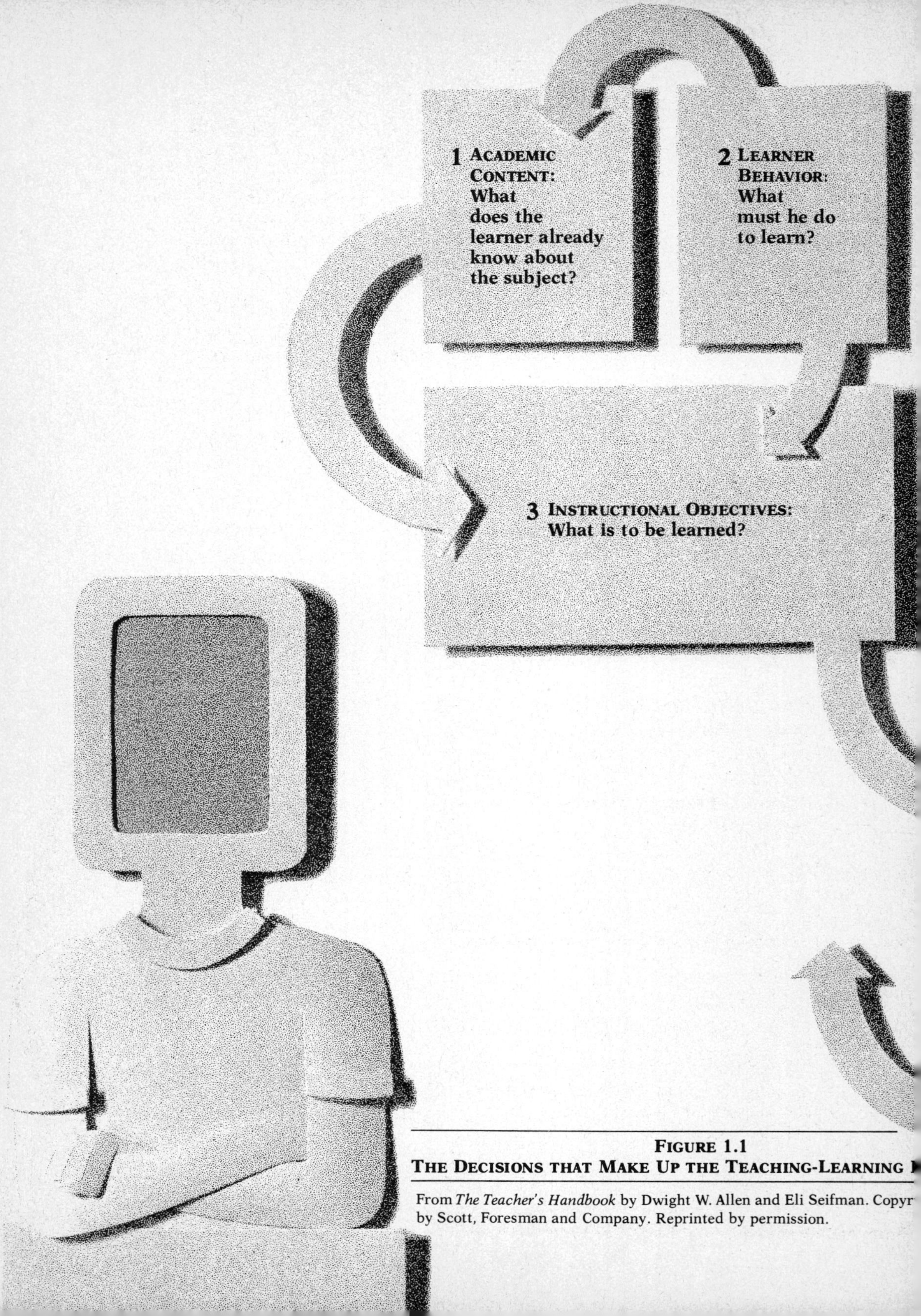

FIGURE 1.1
THE DECISIONS THAT MAKE UP THE TEACHING-LEARNING

From *The Teacher's Handbook* by Dwight W. Allen and Eli Seifman. Copyr
by Scott, Foresman and Company. Reprinted by permission.

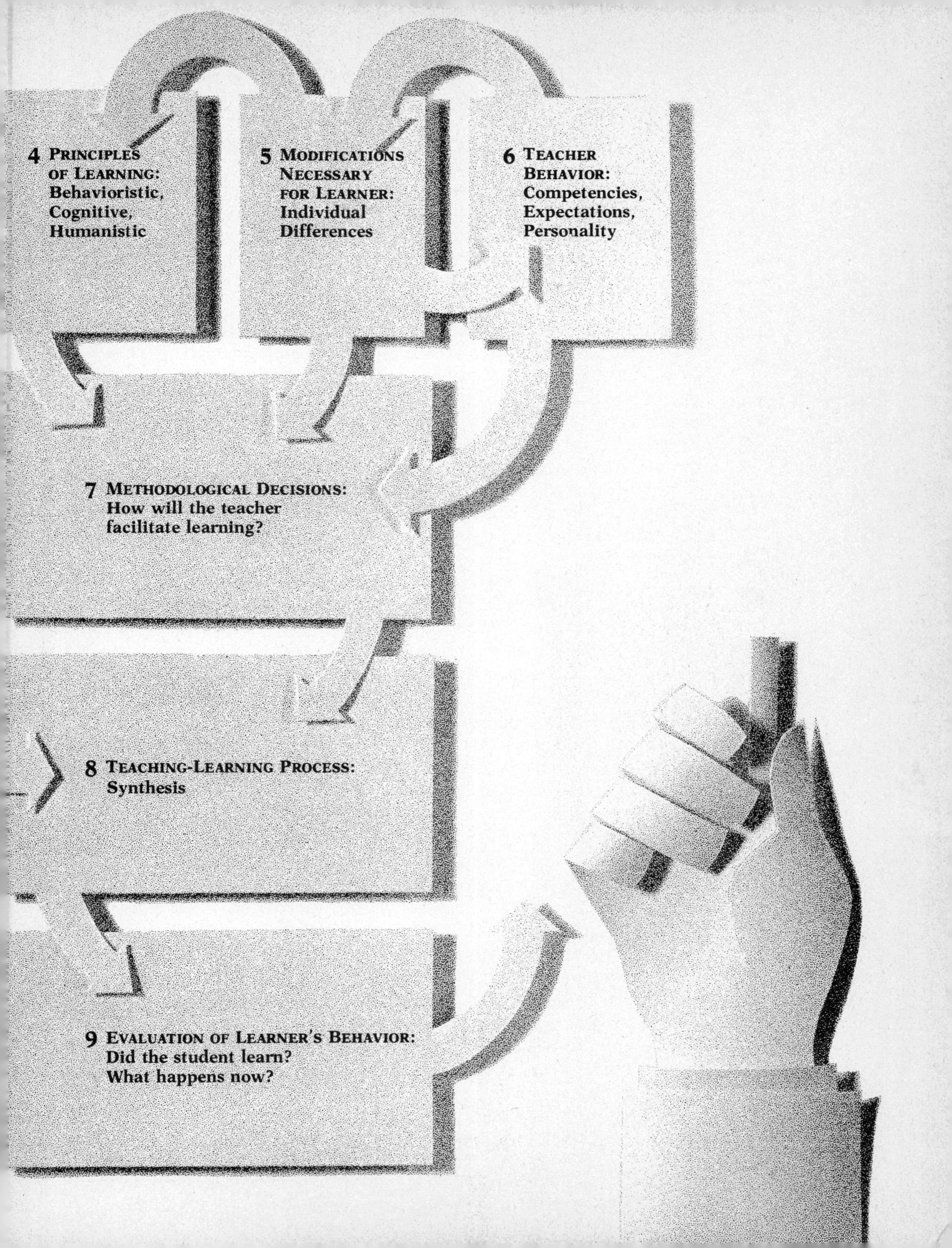
4 PRINCIPLES OF LEARNING: Behavioristic, Cognitive, Humanistic
5 MODIFICATIONS NECESSARY FOR LEARNER: Individual Differences
6 TEACHER BEHAVIOR: Competencies, Expectations, Personality
7 METHODOLOGICAL DECISIONS: How will the teacher facilitate learning?
8 TEACHING-LEARNING PROCESS: Synthesis
9 EVALUATION OF LEARNER'S BEHAVIOR: Did the student learn? What happens now?

The model identifies a number of variables that should influence a teacher's instructional methodology (#7), theories and principles of learning (#4), individual differences of learners (#5), and teacher behavior (#6).

Theories and principles of learning (#4) can inform the teacher about the variables that are necessary and contributing conditions to teach students to improve their performances (Lembo, 1969). Gagné (1970) points out that not all learning is the same and that the instructor needs to teach differently to effect different kinds of learning. Repetition is an important principle in learning multiplication tables but is less useful in learning to solve mathematical equations. Knowledge of the theories and principles of learning can improve a teacher's decisions in selecting appropriate teaching methodologies. It will also help a teacher better understand the assumptions behind various educational procedures and practices.

Another variable to consider in deciding how to teach is the individual differences of students (#5). I pointed out earlier that this information is also important when deciding what is to be learned (#3).

Teachers have to make some modifications because of their students' stage of development. Piaget (1964), a Swiss psychologist, suggests that a child's ability to learn certain concepts is related to his stage of cognitive development. Experienced teachers discover that sometimes procedures that were effective at one grade level are less effective at another. Many differences abound even among students of a specified age or stage of development. There are differences in styles of learning, personalities, aptitudes, and motivation in first-grade as well as in twelfth-grade students. Teachers find that they must continually modify their lessons for particular students to attain instructional objectives.

The last variable influencing how to teach is teacher behavior (#6). Like students, teachers also differ greatly in their teaching styles, personalities, personal concerns and adequacy, expectations, and so on. Educational research has identified important relationships between teacher and student differences and consequently between instructional style and learning performance (Sperry, 1972). For example, teachers hold differential expectations for various students (Brophy & Good, 1970). They do not treat all students alike in the classroom. Some students are called on more frequently, asked more thought-provoking questions, or reinforced more often. If a teacher expects a student to achieve at a lower level than another student, this expectation colors her behavior toward this first student.

Although evaluation (#9) is a separate variable, it manifests itself during the planning of objectives and continues throughout the instructional process. As a teacher you must know how to measure student behavior at various points: before the start of instruction (to organize an appropriate instructional program for students), during each segment of instruction (to facilitate student progress), and at the end of instruction (to determine how well instructional objectives were met and to decide where to go from there).

You should pay particular attention to the evaluation of learning outcomes at the end of instruction: Did the students learn anything from the instructional lesson or unit? If you failed to develop any specific objectives at the beginning of the lesson you may be hard pressed to answer the question. When the expected does not occur, you must ask yourself: What went wrong? Were the objectives appropriate for the students? Was my teaching method appropriate for the objectives? Should I teach all or part of the lesson? Should the class move on to another topic? With this self-questioning technique a teacher can properly evaluate learning and revise his teaching.

DECISIONS, DECISIONS . . .

We can now summarize the major decisions that make the teaching-learning process work. Keep in mind that each decision does not operate independently but interacts with the others in an ongoing manner (Hunter, 1971).

#1 *What learning task can the student handle at the entry stage in his learning?*

#2 *What learner behavior is relevant to the task and to the learner's characteristics?*

#3 *What is the primary instructional objective of the lesson?*

#4 *What principles of learning can a teacher apply to the learning task?*

#5 *What modifications does a particular learner require?*

#6 *How can a teacher use his competencies and personality to translate teaching decisions into effective action?*

#7 *What is the best method to accomplish the instructional objective?*

#8 *How will a teacher synthesize the preceding decisions into the teaching-learning process?*

#9 *How successful was the teaching-learning process? What happens now?*

The succeeding chapters in this book provide psychological information pertaining to each of the variables identified by the instruc-

1
SEPT

tional model. This information, if assimilated properly, can guide a teacher's decisions and actions. I will delve into individual differences (Chapters 2 and 3), teacher behavior (Chapter 4), instructional objectives (Chapter 5), theories and principles of learning, methods of teaching (Chapters 6, 7, and 8) and evaluation of student behavior (Chapters 9 and 10).

WHAT PROBLEMS DO BEGINNING TEACHERS ENCOUNTER?

All teachers are faced with some problems. Bluming and Dembo (1973) state that teachers rarely leave their profession because they are not adequately trained in their discipline. However, many are discouraged by aggravations that interfere with normal teaching situations and find themselves unable to make effective decisions about the problems that arise in their classrooms.

What are the concerns of a beginning teacher? Broadbent and Cruickshank (1965) found that first-year elementary and secondary school teachers were troubled most by methods of teaching, evaluation of students, and discipline. Studying elementary teachers, Franc (1973) reported problems in the following areas: instruction, control and attention, use of material, and use of time. Katz (1970) described the developmental stages of preschool teachers and identified the primary concern during the first year as survival — "Can I get through the day in one piece? Without losing a child? Can I make it to the end of the week? To the next vacation?" Ryan (1970) wrote an interesting book about the problems of beginning high school teachers entitled *Don't Smile Until Christmas.* The following reading is part of his concluding chapter.

The First Year of Teaching

The shock of the first year of teaching is difficult to discuss because each beginner's experience is unique. It is a product of the interaction of his own psyche and the milieu of his school. Amid the familiar surroundings of classrooms and students loom events and individuals for which the beginner is unprepared. Young teachers report a variety of causes for their shock. They find high school students are hard to reach; they underestimate the difficulty of motivating them and overestimate their own skills as disciplinarians. They do not anticipate the

From K. Ryan, "The First Year of Teaching." In K. Ryan (ed.), *Don't Smile Until Christmas* (Chicago: The University of Chicago Press, 1970), pp. 172–175.

amount of time and work necessary to keep up with students. The volume of administrative tasks surprises them. They are unprepared to handle classes *and* take roll, write tardy slips, read notices from the office, and execute the dozens of ever-present administrative details. The emotional and physical drain of teaching five periods a day leaves them little energy for anything else. They are hurt by unprovoked hostility from their students. The invisible barriers which keep their students from understanding concepts and ideas stagger them. They are crushed by the students' disdain for the subject matter they so cherish. Some are overwhelmed by the discovery that they do not like adolescents. Some . . . don't like what they see themselves become as a result of the teaching experience. Others . . . are disappointed by many of their colleagues; they come expecting a community of scholars and find ordinary people toiling at the job.

Of course, the first year of teaching is not always unpleasant. Some beginners are tremendously relieved to discover that their fantasies of failure do not come true. They are surprised to find out that they can teach, that they like what they are doing, and that students do respect them. For some, anticipated sources of trouble turn out to be their strengths: they *do* have good command of their subject matter; they *can* be fair to all the students and avoid playing favorites. For some, teaching is their very first job, and they get a tremendous satisfaction out of finally being autonomous adults, being treated like adults, and *even* getting paid for it. But whether the first year of teaching is a sad one or a joyous one, it is a year of intense learning for all.

* * *

The first year of teaching can be an emotional roller coaster during which the beginning teacher learns a good deal about his emotional makeup. There is a quality of being carried along by the force of one's newly tapped emotions. The rude remark of a student can call up a red anger that the beginner never knew he possessed. His own cutting remark to a student can momentarily bring a cruel sense of triumph and, later, unaccustomed shame. His inability to get a student interested in a particular lesson can generate an unfamiliar frustration. Many situations, which he will learn to live with later, take on a special significance in this initial stage. As a beginner he is *vulnerable*. He is trying to prove to himself, to his students, and to his superiors that he is a teacher. Any evidence which either supports or weakens this contention triggers a strong emotional response.

A veteran teacher, experienced in supervising beginning teachers, summarized one of their major difficulties: "They think their students are just like them, only smaller." The first-year secondary school teacher is usually amazed at how much he has forgotten about high school students in four or five years. Much of the first year is spent in rediscovering the nature of high school students and in acquiring the intangible but all important sense of the teaching-learning process.

There is so much to learn. The beginning teacher must determine what his students know and what they do not know. What are realistic expectations for them? How much can they do? What is the proper vocabulary for different levels of students? To what type of humor are they responsive?

The new teacher must also learn how to organize ideas and at the same time deal with the dynamics of thirty students. He must be able to listen and at the same time anticipate the next question. And he must learn to check the students' understanding.

The beginning teacher must develop a good pace for his instruction. He must be able to tell when the students need variety and when they have had enough instruction to work productively on their own.

Another skill that must be developed is the knack of interesting students in a particular task. What kinds of students respond to different kinds of material? What are the best sources for interesting material in his field?

Finally, the new teacher must learn to budget time. How much time should be spent on preparation? How much on paper grading? How can "administrivia" be dispensed with quickly but efficiently?

There are no hard-and-fast answers to these questions. At present, each teacher has to get the feel for these matters for himself, and on the job.

After reviewing studies on teachers' concerns, Fuller (1969) divided teacher concerns into three phases: preteaching, early teaching, and late teaching. The first phase (preteaching) seems to be devoid of any particular teaching problems. The prospective teacher is concerned with getting good grades and completing required courses for her teaching credential but is not really concerned about the specifics of teaching.

When student teaching starts, the student moves into the early teaching phase and is preoccupied with the personal demand of teaching: Does my supervising teacher like the way I handle the class? Do my students like me? What do my colleagues think of me? How can I better control the class?

During the late teaching phase, with a few years of teaching experience behind her, the teacher changes her focus to pupil gain and self-evaluation as opposed to focusing on personal gain and evaluation by others.

The following excerpt from a "Diary of a Beginning Teacher"

records the personal concerns of a teacher in the early teaching phase. As you read the diary, make a list of the various topics mentioned and discuss them with students in your class. What problems might give you the most trouble?

Excerpts From a Diary of a Beginning Teacher

September 7. *I'm exhausted today. I gave them all back their papers which, thank goodness, took up part of the class time. I also assigned them four questions to do for homework. I didn't write the questions on the board, which was a mistake; I ended up repeating everything five or six times.*

I feel so pushed, preparing and correcting papers; hope things calm down soon.

September 9. *I tried playing a game with them in class today. It didn't go very well. One of the biggest problems was that I didn't have a firm enough control over the class to do it. I had them asking each other questions. They were divided into two teams and all that. I even set up a panel of judges who decided whether the answer to a question was right.*

I also gave them a pop quiz at the beginning of the period. I tried it in one class at the end, but that didn't work as well; they were too excited from the game to settle down.

One real catastrophe today. The map fell on my head during fourth period. The class went wild, luckily the assistant principal was right outside the room, and came in and rescued me.

September 13. *I gave the quiz today and they did pretty well and then I finished up discussing geography — I hope. I only gave them twenty of the spelling words and left off the longest and most difficult. They were very upset because they said they had all learned that one.*

The day has finally come. Despite all of the work and how tired I am, I think I am really going to like teaching.

September 26. *I'm having a problem getting the classes to keep quiet now. For a while they were pretty good, but now they're beginning to get to me. Even the good students are starting to talk during class. I don't think its because they're not interested because the talk is almost always about what I'm discussing, but still they're talking without permission. If it was only a little I wouldn't mind, but it's beginning to get to the point*

Adapted from Jean Morris, "Diary of a Beginning Teacher," *National Association of Secondary School Principals Bulletin* 52 (October 1968): 6–15. Reprinted by permission of the publisher.

where I can't go on because of the talking.

September 27. *The assistant principal came and visited one of my classes today. Before class I was talking at my desk with one student and all of a sudden I heard this deathly silence hit the class. (I guess that's not the right way to say it, but anyway.) I looked up and there he was. I started the class. I'd ask a question and there was absolute silence. Nothing. It was terrible! It's bad when they're all talking at once, but it's horrible when they're afraid to move.*

September 29. *I've been getting bored, teaching the same thing over and over and so today I did different things in different classes. I discussed with some, gave some a quiz and had others writing. I tried discussing with my sixth-period class but they're just impossible after about ten minutes. I got really mad at them and told them to take out their books and study quietly for ten minutes and then I would give them a quiz. While they studied, I made up the quiz and it was a dilly — only four people passed. I suppose it isn't good educational psychology to do that but it made me feel much better, and at that point it was either them or me.*

October 14. *I have now firmly and purposely gotten my classes separated. That is, I am no longer doing the same thing five times a day. At first it was a big help being able to prepare only one lesson each night. But I realized that it was terribly boring for me, and my boredom would be reflected in the kids. Once I felt that I had my bearings, I decided to change all that. Well, it's taken me this long to carry out my plan. Although I use much of the same material in all of my classes, I do not use it all at the same time or in the same manner. I can really see the difference in the classes.*

October 19. *Tonight was the PTA open house. I was pleased at how well it went. I guess that parents are not really ogres after all. But it was an awfully long day. I really do love teaching and I look forward to all of my classes, but I often feel that I am not doing my best for these kids. Teach and learn — and have I learned a lot in these seven weeks!*

November 4. *Teacher's Convention — WHAT A FARCE!*

November 9. *Every day I learn so much. I hope that the children are learning some too, but they couldn't possibly learn more than a fraction of what I have. I think there is hope for me yet. I already know so much more than I did in September. Sometimes I feel the huge mountain of things yet to learn pressing down on me but I think I've made a signifi-*

cant dent in the mountain. I may live through the year. But then again, it seems overwhelming.

November 30. *Beautiful day! Introducing a new unit and the kids were great — love it. Everything went well.*

December 8. *Ugliness! Nothing went well at all. Jabber, jabber, jabber — I don't know. Sometimes I get so upset and depressed it's horrible. They don't listen or follow instructions, or learn anything. I guess it's a normal feeling for new teachers.*

December 12. *Almost the end of the period before vacation. I guess not really but it seems like it must be. Happiness!! They announced that all evaluation meetings are cancelled until after Christmas. Hurray! Except for the faculty meeting Thursday.*

KEY POINTS

1. *All teachers have personal hypotheses or beliefs about the teaching-learning process.*
2. *Teacher beliefs lead them to make important classroom decisions that affect how students learn in school.*
3. *Teachers need to (a) examine the effects of their decisions on learning, (b) examine personal beliefs about the teaching-learning process, and (c) evaluate the effectiveness of beliefs and practices and modify teaching behavior when necessary.*
4. *Educational psychology includes content that the teacher can use to formulate and test personal beliefs about teaching and learning.*
5. *The teacher must both understand and apply psychological knowledge.*
6. *An instructional model that identifies the major variables in the teaching-learning process includes the variables of individual differences, teacher behavior, instructional objectives, theories and principles of learning, teaching methods, and evaluation of student behavior.*
7. *Some teachers become discouraged because they are unable to make effective decisions about the problems that arise in their classrooms.*

8. *Beginning teachers appear to be most concerned with their personal adequacy in meeting the demands of teaching.*

SUGGESTIONS FOR FURTHER READING

Bluming, M., & Dembo, M. *Solving teaching problems: A guide for the elementary school teacher.* Pacific Palisades, Calif.: Goodyear, 1973. This book provides specific suggestions for handling instructional, discipline, and administrative problems.

Greenwood, G., Good, T., & Siegel, B. *Problem situations in teaching.* New York: Harper & Row, 1971. The authors provide a number of case incidents that can be used for group discussion.

Kohl, H. *36 children.* New York: New American Library, 1967. A personal account of a teacher's feelings during the beginning days of a school year.

Schmuck, R., Chesler, M., & Lippitt, R. *Problem solving to improve classroom learning.* Chicago: Science Research Associates, 1966. The authors use a model to illustrate how classroom problems can be solved.

FOLLOW-UP ACTIVITIES

1 Think about teaching problems. Discuss some teaching problems that your teachers have or have had. Did they realize a problem existed? What strategies did they use to attempt to solve the problem? What types of teaching problems do you think will give you the most trouble? Why do you feel this way?

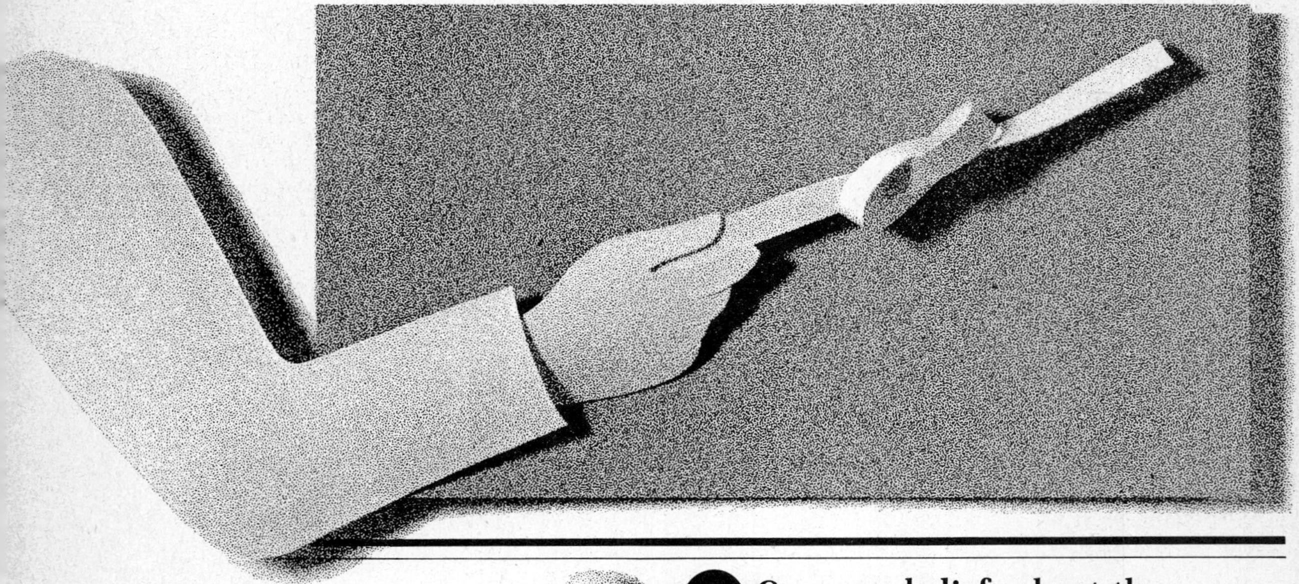

2 Compare beliefs about the teaching-learning process. (a) List three facts about teaching and learning that you believe are true and useful. (b) Select the fact that you have the greatest confidence in and justify your confidence. (c) Select a classmate and determine whether or not each of you can agree with the other's fact.

3 Discover journals in education related to specific grade levels and subject areas. Browse through some recent issues of journals in your teaching area. Read one article, summarize it, and mention how you might use the ideas discussed in the article. Don't hesitate to criticize the author if you disagree with his philosophy or identify application problems in his ideas.

The following list of journals will show you what is available in your area of interest.

African Studies Bulletin
Agricultural Education Magazine
American Biology Teacher
American Business Education
American Music Teacher
American Speech
American String Teacher
American Vocational Journal
Arithmetic Teacher
Art Education
Athletic Journal
Audiovisual Instructor
Business Education World
Coach and Athlete
Coaching Clinic
Education and Training of the Mentally Retarded
Educational Theatre Journal
Elementary English
Elementary School Guidance and Counseling
English Language Teaching
English Studies
Forecast for Home Economics
French Review
Geographical Teacher
German Review
Gifted Child Quarterly
Hearing and Speech News
History Today
Improving College and University Teaching
Industrial Arts and Vocational Education
Industrial Arts Teacher
Instrumentalist
Journal of Industrial Teacher Education
Journal of Negro Education
Journal of Nursing
Journal of Reading
Journal of Research on Science Teaching
Journal of School Health
Journal of Secondary Education
Journal of Special Education
Marriage and Family Living
Mathematics Teacher
Music Education Journal
Music in Education
Music Journal
National Business Education Quarterly
National Elementary Principal
Physical Educator
Physics Teacher
Reading Specialist
Recreation
Safety Education
Scholastic Coach
School Arts
School Counselor
School Musician
School Musician Director and Teacher
School Science and Mathematics
School Shop
Science Educator
Science Teacher
Swimming Technique
Teaching Exceptional Children
Tennis
Theatre Arts
Theatre World
Today's Speech
Track Technique

4 Use library reference sources to identify information about teaching and learning. Get acquainted with the library facilities at your college. Use *Psychological Abstracts, Research in Education,* or *Current Index to Journals in Education* to locate research articles on a topic or issue of interest. If an article reports a research study, write an abstract of the article following the outline below.

Author(s)
Title of article
Journal in which article
  appears (include date,
  volume number, and
  pages)
Purpose of study
Subjects
Procedures (or methods)
Results
Conclusions

a.) *Psychological Abstracts* is published monthly by the American Psychological Association and contains abstracts of articles appearing in over 500 journals in psychology and related areas. Each issue has different sections covering various topics of psychology. The section on child development and adolescence and the section on educational psychology, which includes abstracts in areas such as attitude and adjustment, testing, special education, counseling and guidance, school learning and achievement, and curriculum programs, are most relevant for the teacher.

The December issue contains both an author and subject index of all articles in the previous eleven issues of the year. A semiannual index is also available. When using cumulative indexes, check the subject index for articles pertaining to the topic. The subject of the article appears in a concise form. After the description of the subject, you will find one or more numbers referring to the abstract included during the preceding year. The information will help you find the abstract in the appropriate monthly issue.

APA
ERIC
RIE
CIJE

b.) Another important reference source has been established by the Office of Education: the Educational Resources Information Center (ERIC), which collects, stores, and disseminates information on education. ERIC abstracts include papers presented at educational conferences, progress reports of research in progress, final reports of federally funded studies, and abstracts of some documents listed in *Psychological Abstracts.* The advantage of the ERIC system is that it includes many documents not usually published in journals and provides the best compilation of current educational research.

All the abstracts in ERIC appear in a monthly publication called *Research in Education.* Each abstract is classified by subject area, author, and institutional and accession (identification) number. To locate an abstract, first select key research terms in your area of interest. If you are interested in teaching procedures, you might look under teaching methods, educational strategies, or teaching techniques.

To help identify appropriate search terms, ERIC has published the *Thesauras of ERIC Descriptors.* This publication includes all terms used to classify ERIC documents. Once the key search terms have been identified, you should then examine the semiannual or annual cumulative indexes for the titles or pertinent references and locate the abstract in a monthly issue of *Research in Education.*

Most educational libraries have the ERIC collection in microfiche — small sheets of microfilm — that require special readers to enlarge the image to normal page size. Therefore, once you identify the accession number of the document from *Research in Education* (for example, Ed 013 371), you can locate the corresponding numbered microfiche of the complete article. If you wish to obtain a copy of the document, you can order it through the ERIC Document Reproduction Services.

c.) Another important resource is the monthly journal, *Current Index to Journals in Education,* compiled by specialists of the ERIC system. Articles from over 500 journals are classified and listed according to the same system developed in the ERIC *Thesauras.*

CIJE is divided into four sections: subject index, author index, journal contents index, and main entry section. The procedures for selecting an entry are similar to those for *Research in Education.* Locate articles in the main entry section by checking the subject index to find the titles and numbers of the articles. If the title of an article is not sufficient to convey the main meaning of the article, the CIJE staff provides a brief annotation under the title.

5 Analyze the teaching-learning process. Make arrangements to observe a teacher presenting a lesson. Keep detailed notes on both the teacher's and the students' behavior during the lesson and analyze the lesson by answering the following questions:

a. Was there a perceivable objective? Did the teaching focus on a particular learning target, or did it include a little bit of everything or anything?
b. Was the objective appropriate for this group of learners? Had the objective already been achieved by the learners, or was it so difficult that there was little possibility of achieving it?
c. Was the objective achieved? Was there evidence of progression toward advancement or attainment of the objective?
d. What did the teacher do that facilitated learning?
e. What did the teacher do that interfered with learning?
f. What problems arose during the lesson? How did the teacher handle these problems?
g. What suggestions do you have for improving the lesson? (Hunter, 1973)

Save your analysis of this lesson because I shall ask you to return to it later in the book.

INDIVIDUAL DIFFERENCES I: COGNITIVE FACTORS

ORIENTATION

One of the most important variables influencing the effectiveness of instruction is student characteristics and abilities. The wide variety of student abilities, interests, and attitudes found within any classroom precipitates to a wide variety of results: Some students will enjoy more success in school and more favorable teacher interaction than will others.

Think back to your elementary and secondary school days. These students were probably acquaintances of yours: the student who was always the first to answer the instructor's question; the student who infuriated the teacher by asking different or unusual questions; the student who came from a different cultural background and had difficulty learning in school; the student who always panicked during exam time; the student who always sat in the back of the classroom, rarely said anything, and had an implicit "contract" with the teacher stating, "You don't bother me and I won't bother you." Try to recall additional examples of students who had

differential success in school and pinpoint the characteristics that appeared to help or hinder them in the classroom.

Teachers (and other people!) respond differently to various traits in others. What characteristics do you like in students? What characteristics do you dislike? Your answers to these questions will influence your behavior when interacting with different students in your class.

IDEAL CHILD CHECKLIST

By completing the Ideal Child Checklist that follows, you will define your likes and dislikes. Think about your ratings as you read Chapters 2, 3, and 4. I will ask you to return to your responses in a later chapter.

How can you guide a child to the highest fulfillment of his potentialities? Indicate how you would act, using the list below. Check (✓) each characteristic or behavior that you would encourage. Mark two checks (✓✓) beside each characteristic or behavior that you would wholeheartedly encourage. Place an (X) by each characteristic or behavior that you would discourage.

Chapters 2 and 3 identify student characteristics and abilities that are related to academic success or failure in school. A better understanding of these factors will naturally arouse you to better decision making during the teaching-learning process in selecting and modifying instructional objectives and improving teacher-student interaction. Chapter 2 considers cognitive factors — intelligence, creativity, and learning styles — and is balanced by Chapter 3 — personality and motivational factors. Chapter 4 — Teacher Behavior and Classroom Dynamics — discusses how teachers tend to interact with different students whose characteristics may provide a teacher with a basis to form judgments and make decisions about them.

INTELLIGENCE

It is time for me to slip in a paradox: The study of intelligence — its general nature and measurement — is one of the most emotional issues in educational psychology. Probably no other area is most discussed and least understood by educators. Yet each year teachers and administrators group children by ability and assign them to special classes and tracks in the curriculum, using children's intelligence test scores as the basis for their decisions.

Ideal Child Checklist

1. *Adventurous, testing limits*
2. *Affectionate, loving*
3. *Altruistic, working for good of others*
4. *Asking questions about puzzling things*
5. *Attempting difficult tasks*
6. *Becoming preoccupied with tasks*
7. *Competitive, trying to win*
8. *Conforming*
9. *Considerate of others*
10. *Courageous in convictions*
11. *Courteous, polite*
12. *Critical of others*
13. *Curious, searching*
14. *Desirous of excelling*
15. *Determined, unflinching*
16. *Disturbing procedures and organization of the group*
17. *Doing work on time*
18. *Domineering, controlling*
19. *Emotionally sensitive*
20. *Energetic, vigorous*
21. *Fault-finding, objecting*
22. *Fearful, apprehensive*
23. *Feeling emotions strongly*
24. *Guessing hypothesizing*
25. *Haughty and self-satisfied*
26. *Healthy*
27. *Independent in judgment*
28. *Independent in thinking*
29. *Industrious, busy*
30. *Intuitive*
31. *Liking to work alone*
32. *Neat and orderly*
33. *Negativistic, resistant*
34. *Never bored, always interested*
35. *Obedient, submissive to authority*
36. *Persistent, persevering*
37. *Physically strong*
38. *Popular, well-liked*
39. *Preferring complex tasks*
40. *Quiet, not talkative*
41. *Receptive to ideas of others*
42. *Refined, free of coarseness*
43. *Regressing occasionally, may be playful, childlike, etc.*
44. *Remembering well*
45. *Reserved*
46. *Self-assertive*
47. *Self-confident*
48. *Self-starting, initiating*
49. *Self-sufficient*
50. *Sense of beauty*
51. *Sense of humor*
52. *Sincere, earnest*
53. *Socially well-adjusted*
54. *Spirited in disagreement*
55. *Striving for distant goals*
56. *Stubborn, obstinate*
57. *Talkative*
58. *Thorough*
59. *Timid, shy, bashful*
60. *Truthful, even when it hurts*
61. *Unsophisticated, artless*
62. *Unwilling to accept things on mere say-so*
63. *Versatile, well-rounded*
64. *Visionary, idealistic*
65. *Willing to accept judgments of authorities*
66. *Willing to take risks*

Developed by E. Paul Torrance.

A number of hotly debated questions continue to dominate discussions about intelligence, the answers to which have important implications for the types of decisions made by teachers and administrators: Is intelligence a unitary trait or a composite of traits? What do intelligence tests measure? Are intelligence tests fair to all students? Is intelligence determined more by heredity or by environment (often referred to as the nature-nurture controversy)? Is intelligence fixed or can it be changed?

Before you continue reading this section, think about how an individual might respond to these questions. What kinds of teaching decisions might ensue?

IS INTELLIGENCE A UNITARY TRAIT OR A COMPOSITE OF TRAITS?

Introductory textbooks usually provide a definition of the concept under discussion to clarify any misconceptions regarding its meaning. Well, an intelligent definition of *intelligence* would probably comprise a booklet. The definition of intelligence varies with each psychologist's philosophy regarding its nature.

Generally, theories of intelligence have been viewed from one of two perspectives (Mueller, 1974). The first perspective takes the position that one general factor accounts for most of our mental ability. Spearman, in 1927, was one of the first psychologists to propose that intelligence involves a high degree of general ability. He hypothesized an intellect composed of a general factor (g) underlying all mental functions and a multitude of specific factors (s) related to a given task or situation.

According to Spearman's theory people differed in the degree of the general factor as well as in the quality of the specific factors involved in a given task, so that a person could be relatively "more intelligent" than another person because of a superior *g* but be less capable in a given area (for example, science) because of deficient or inferior *s* factors in that area. However, since *g* represented only a form of mental ability included in all mental operations, a person who was grossly lacking in general intelligence could be knowledgeable in a specific field (Mouly, 1973). Figure 2.1 illustrates Spearman's theory.

Teachers are often surprised that various intelligence tests ask different questions and wonder how students who take these tests can be compared. Psychologists who support Spearman's theory would explain to them that it does not matter what particular combination of mental tests or performances any given test calls for, since they all tap the same general factor (DiVesta & Thompson, 1970).

Any reading and arithmetic test will result in an overlap of the general abilities common to both tests. The *g* factor in both reading

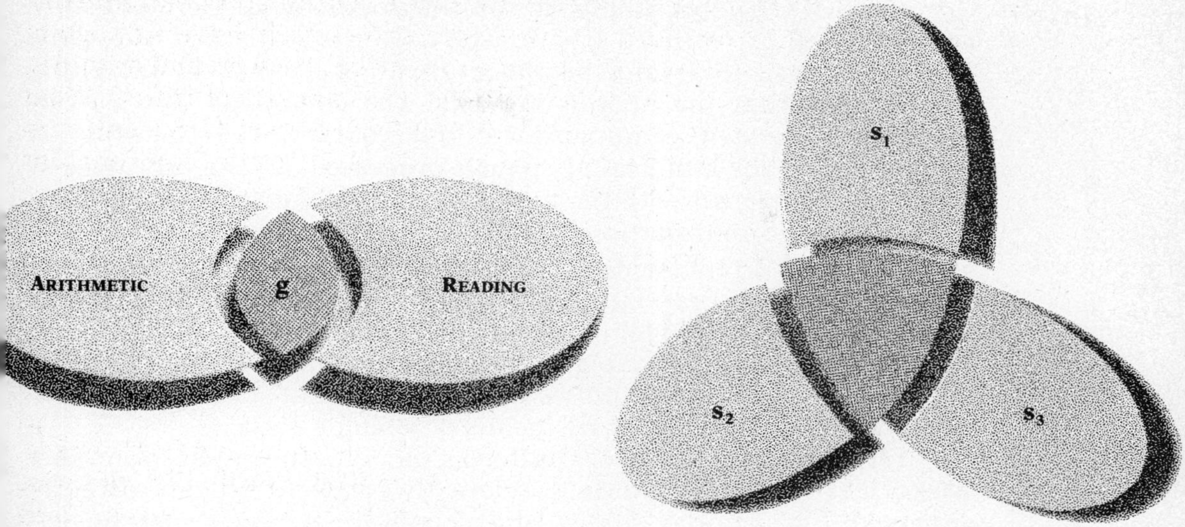

FIGURE 2.1
SPEARMAN'S TWO-FACTOR THEORY. THE SHADED AREA REPRESENTS THE ELEMENT COMMON TO A GROUP OF TESTS. THE REMAINDER OF THE CIRCLE REPRESENTS THE UNIQUE PORTION OF EACH TEST.

and arithmetic tests is vocabulary and word meaning. The measure of intelligence in this case is general ability, although specific abilities that are not common to both tests (that is, computational skills and reading speed) also enter into play.

The second basic approach to intelligence, which has received more attention in recent years, is the study of specific abilities, especially as they relate to behavior success in various subject areas. Thorndike (1927), unlike Spearman, believed that intelligence was the sum of specific abilities. He identified intelligence as (1) *abstract ability* — the ability to deal with ideas and symbols, (2) *mechanical ability* — the ability to deal with mechanisms and tasks involving sensory-motor activities, and (3) *social ability* — the ability to deal effectively with people.

Thurstone (1938) also disagreed with Spearman after his battery of fifty-six tests could find no common intelligence factor. According to Thurstone, there was no general factor; he conceived of intelligence as a number of *primary mental abilities*. His research indicated that mental ability could be grouped into seven factors and that intelligence could be measured by sampling individual performance in seven areas: number, word fluency, verb meaning, associative memory, reasoning, space, and perceptual speed.

One of the most extensive multifactor theories of intelligence was presented by Guilford (1959), who used the statistical technique of factor analysis to develop his Structure of Intellect (SOI) model. He hypothesized that the human intellect was composed of a "three-dimensional" system of numerous intellectual abilities classified on the basis of (1) the material or *content* processed, (2) the processes or *operations* performed with the material, and (3) the forms or *products* of the processed information.

Figure 2.2 represents the three kinds of factors by means of a cubical model. Theoretically, 120 different factors or abilities can be generated from the model (4 contents × 5 operations × 6 products), since any operation can be performed on any content and can result in any product. This model implies that an individual's intelligence cannot be adequately assessed by means of a single score.

The first dimension of Guilford's model, content, has four subcategories: (1) *figural* content refers to concrete objects directly perceived (for example, shapes, diagrams); (2) *symbolic* content pertains to letters, numbers, or other conventional forms; (3) *semantic* content takes the form of verbal meanings or ideas; (4) *behavioral* content is social intelligence — the ability to perceive and interpret the thoughts and feelings of others from their overt behavior.

The second dimension, operations, contains five subcategories: (1) *cognition* is the discovery and recognition of information; (2) *memory* is the retention, recall, and reproduction of information; (3) *convergent thinking* is the process of producing a correct or conventional answer from known and remembered information; (4) *divergent thinking* is the process of thinking in different directions, sometimes seeking variety, from known and remembered information; (5) *evaluation* is the decision-making process relative to the accuracy and appropriateness of the information that has been cognized.

The application of mental operations to the content dimension results in certain kinds of products, the third dimension of Guilford's model. Products are divided into six subcategories: (1) *units* are segregated items of mental work, such as a specific word or image; (2) *classes* are groupings of units of information according to common characteristics; (3) *relations* refer to the relationship between units of information, such as "bigger than" or "next to"; (4) *systems* pertain to the structuring of complex information; (5) *transformations* refer to changes in preexisting information; (6) *implications* refer to inferences or predictions drawn from current knowledge and applied to future actions.

Meeker (1969) has used Guilford's model to assess the curriculum and abilities of children. She believes that when discussing intelligence, educators must ask: Intelligence? In what area? Meeker

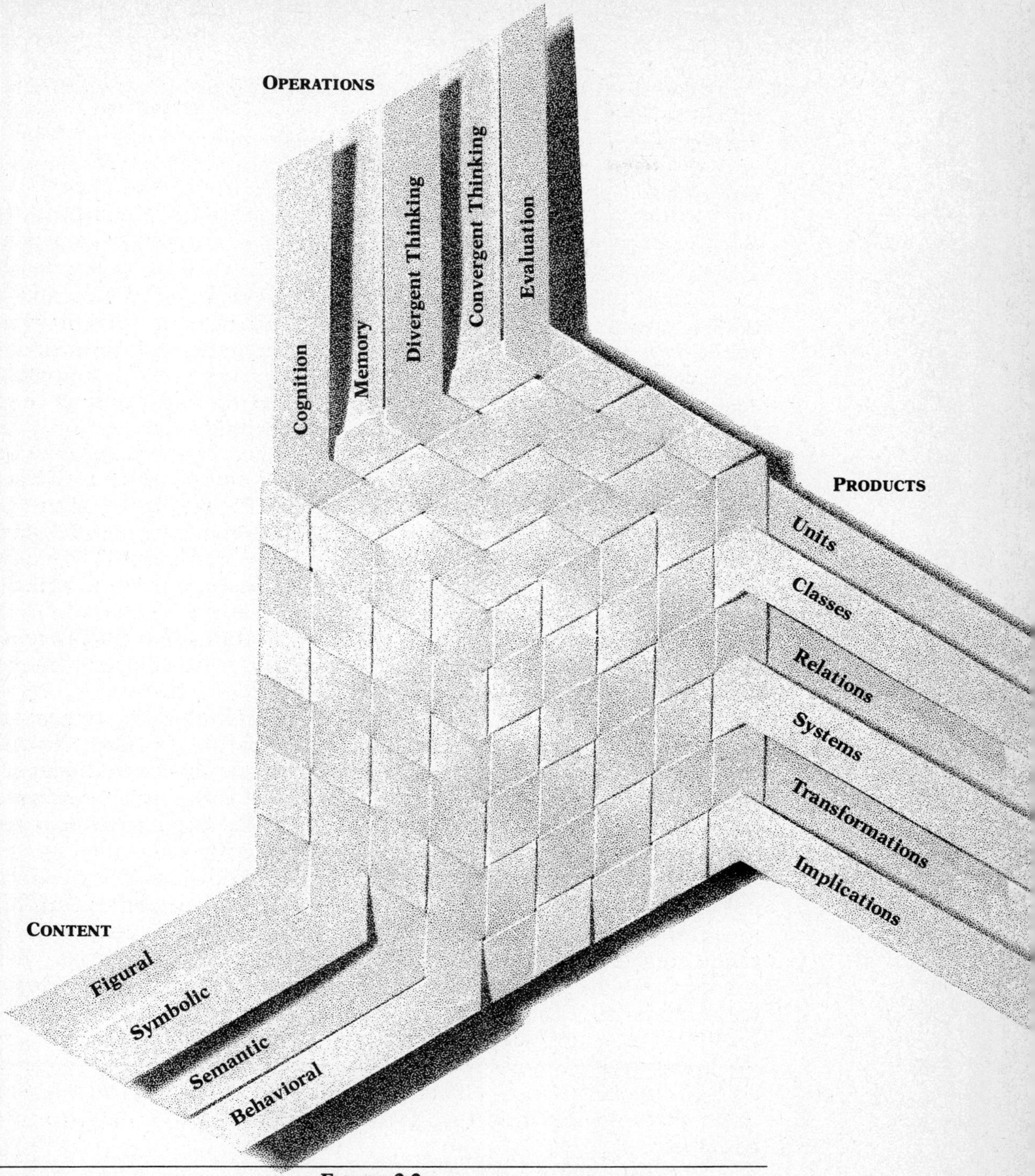

FIGURE 2.2
A CUBICAL MODEL REPRESENTING THE STRUCTURE OF INTELLECT.

From J. P. Guilford, "Three Faces of Intellect." *American Psychologist* 14 (1959): 469–470. Copyright 1959 by the American Psychological Association. Reprinted by permission.

further states that when a child of average ability fails to learn, his IQ score neither explains nor accounts for his failure. According to Meeker we need theoretically based tests that provide the teacher with diagnostic information on which she can make instructional decisions for a given child.

Guilford's model sets forth one way of organizing abilities in a school's curriculum. Examine any traditional school curriculum and you will find that some abilities receive more attention than others. In the field of content, for instance, the stress is on semantic and symbolic abilities, to the detriment of figural and behavioral skills. Three of the five operations — cognition, memory, and convergent production — are stressed over the other two — divergent production (associated with creative thinking) and evaluation. Last, among the six products, a disproportionate amount of emphasis falls on units and classes (Stephens & Evans, 1973).

WHAT DO INTELLIGENCE TESTS MEASURE?

You, among many others, may be confused about what intelligence tests measure. They do *not* measure "innate" or "natural" ability to learn new behavior. An intelligence test measures present ability — specifically, the behavior required by the test at the time the test is given. Thus, when people talk about an individual's "intelligence," they are referring to that person's *test score* (Ausubel & Robinson, 1969).

Rohwer (1971) questions whether a child's intelligence test score is even an accurate reflection of his learning ability. He states that the confusion over children's performances on an intelligence test is based on the faulty assumption that equivalent chronological age implies equivalent learning opportunities. An intelligence test compares what a child has learned over some period of time to what his peers have learned; however, not all children of the same chronological age have had an equal opportunity to learn the material tested by an intelligence test. Because of this inequity, the teacher who concludes that a student with a low intelligence test score simply "lacks the capacity to learn" is making a serious error in interpreting the meaning of the test score.

Individual Intelligence Tests

The first intelligence test was developed in the early 1900s by Alfred Binet, a French psychologist, who was commissioned by the Ministry of Public Instruction in Paris to identify retarded children who could not benefit from a traditional French education. The target of this investigation was the establishment of special schools for children who needed help.

Binet had no particular theory of intelligence but had been working on a series of tests that appeared to be reasonable samples of children's behavior and distinguished abilities at different age levels. He found that at each age level some children performed better than others. The children who performed the best on these tests were also rated by their teachers as "bright." Conversely, those children who performed poorly on the tests were rated by their teachers as poorer students.

Binet based his tests on the comparison of a particular child with his age group. A child who was above average in intelligence could answer more questions than the average child of his age group. If he answered about the same number of questions as the average child in the group, he was considered average in intelligence. The child whose performance was below average for his age group was below average in intelligence.

Thus, Binet established the use of the term *mental age* as a basis of determining the level of a given child's mental functioning. A child might be eight years old, but he would have a mental age of ten if he could answer questions that the average ten-year-old child could answer.

There were many translations of Binet's test in this country. Lewis Terman created one in 1916 at Stanford University that became widely used. His test, known as the Stanford–Binet, is still used today in revised form. Terman defined intelligence as the ability to think in abstract terms, and this definition served as the basis for establishing test items.

The popular term *intelligence quotient*, or IQ, was first used by the psychologist William Stern, who proposed that a child's chronological age should be divided by his mental age, the most important factor being the relationship or ratio of the two numbers. Therefore, IQ = Mental Age (MA) $\div$ Chronological Age (CA) $\times$ 100 (to remove the decimal).

Stern believed that the IQ would be relatively stable throughout an individual's life. For example, if a child of 6 (CA) has a mental age of 8, his IQ equals 133 ($8 \div 6 \times 100$). Stern theorized that at age 12 the child's mental age would be 16 and his IQ would still equal 133.

Later research on the growth of intelligence did not support this linear relationship and psychometrists (measurement specialists) disregarded the IQ formula in determining mental ability.[1] Presently, a table of deviation scores is used in IQ testing. A child's score reflects

[1] We still use the term *IQ* to indicate intelligence or a test score on an intelligence test.

its deviation from the average score of the children of his chronological age in the standardization (comparison) group.

Other reasons for disregarding the use of the IQ ratio have to do with mental age, which loses its meaning for adults. It cannot be used to compare results on different tests, a feat that the deviation score can perform. I present a more detailed discussion of intelligence tests in Chapter 9 when I deal with the evaluation aspect of the instructional process.

INDIVIDUAL DIFFERENCES AND IQ

Most intelligence tests are constructed to have an average score of 100. Approximately two-thirds of a random sample of people score between 85 and 115, 11% score above 120, and 1.6% score above 140. Table 2.1 summarizes this distribution. However, the distribution from one test will differ slightly from that of other tests. The degree of difference depends on the reliability of the test (its ability to generate consistent scores), the traits or factors incorporated in the test, and the standardization (comparison) group that takes the test to establish the distribution.

Probably more can be said about the persons at the extremes of the distribution than about those in the middle. Individuals with IQ's above 120 are frequently identified as gifted, although sometimes the term is reserved for students with IQ's of 130 and above. Students with IQ's below 70 are described as mentally retarded.

Individuals from high-socioeconomic-level homes score higher on intelligence tests than do individuals with low-socioeconomic backgrounds. In addition, Whites tend to score higher than do Blacks and most minority group members. We shall explore some of the explanations for these findings in the next section of this chapter.

Does a high intelligence test score mean anything? According to long-term investigation by Lewis Terman, it does. Starting in the 1920s, Terman and Oden (1925, 1954) studied hundreds of California's gifted students with tested IQ's of 140 or more. They followed the lives of their subjects for twenty-five years to determine whether there existed any relationship between childhood IQ and adult behavior.

They found a relationship between high intelligence and early physical development, the subjects clocking in above average in many physical characteristics, including height, weight, and general health. This data dispelled many false stereotypes of bright children (sometimes reinforced by the mass media) who were supposed to be myopic, frail, obese, or socially rejected by peers.

TABLE 2.1
CLASSIFICATION BY IQ.

CLASSIFICATION	*IQ RANGE*	*% OF POPULATION*
Very superior	140–169	1.6
Superior	120–139	11.3
High average	110–119	18.1
Normal	90–109	48.5
Low average	80–89	14.5
Borderline defective	70–79	5.6
Mentally defective	30–69	2.6

From Terman and Merrill, *Stanford-Binet Intelligence Scale: Manual for the Third Revision, Form L-M* (Boston: Houghton Mifflin, 1960), p. 18. Copyright © 1960, by Houghton Mifflin Company. Reprinted by permission.

Terman and Oden found their subjects to be better adjusted, more popular, and more likely to be leaders than would the average child. These individuals also received higher grades than their peers and skipped grades more frequently. As adults, they proved that "nothing succeeds like success" by earning more money, holding more managerial positions, and contributing far more to literature and science than other adults.

In a more recent and highly controversial study by Jencks (1972) entitled *Inequality: A Reassessment of the Effect of Family and Schooling in America*, the importance of IQ is deemphasized. The researchers state that IQ tests are not good at measuring success in a variety of adult work. Moreover, people who score high on IQ and achievement tests do not perform better than average in most jobs, and in many situations, there is no relationship at all between a man's IQ and his job performance or financial success. They further state that IQ accounts for only one quarter of the income gap between Blacks and Whites, job discrimination being the overriding factor.

Intelligence test scores, in general, correlate fairly high with academic achievement in school and can be used to predict scholastic success. Although we know that a number of nonintellectual variables affect scholastic success — motivation, personality factors, physical health, for example — no other factor is as predictive as intelligence.

This finding is no great surprise, since intelligence or scholastic aptitude tests are constructed to determine a child's scholastic potential. If intelligence influences learning ability, there should be a relationship between IQ and success in school, especially since test makers deliberately incorporate in their intelligence tests tasks related to the school curriculum. Coleman and Cureton (1954) estimated a 90 to 95% overlap between the material included in intelligence tests and that incorporated in academic achievement tests.

ARE INTELLIGENCE TESTS FAIR TO ALL STUDENTS?

The critics of intelligence tests argue that the tests favor the middle-class over the lower-class child by emphasizing verbal rather than mechanical or social ability. The development of verbal ability is a middle-class preoccupation; disadvantaged children will inevitably do poorly on these tests regardless of their innate verbal potential (Ausubel & Robinson, 1969).

The Association of Black Psychologists maintains that current intelligence tests should not be used to test black children:

> The Association of Black Psychologists fully supports those parents who have chosen to defend their rights to allow their children and themselves to be subjected to achievement, intelligence, and performance tests which have been and are being used to: (a.) label Black people as uneducable; (b.) place Black children in "special" classes and schools; (c.) perpetuate inferior education in Blacks; (d.) assign Black children to educational tracts (sic); (e.) deny Black students higher educational opportunities; (f.) destroy positive growth and development of Black people. (Williams, 1970a, p. 5)

The two preceding arguments decry the detrimental effects of labeling intelligence. Many believe that teachers use intelligence test scores, consciously or unconsciously, to label students as poor. If a teacher notices that a student has a low intelligence test score, she will hold a low expectation for his classroom performance and will be less likely to provide remedial instruction for him. She may even act in ways that contribute to the fulfillment of her expectation, such as calling on him less. Chapter 4 will give you more detail on teacher expectations.

Williams (1970b) discusses the cultural bias of intelligence tests. According to him, any response to the Stanford-Binet question "What's the thing to do if another boy hits you without meaning to do it?" is dependent upon the child's environmental background. In some black communities, the response "Walk away" would be a suicide. However, "Hit him back" does not receive any credit on the Stanford-Binet test. This is only one of the examples used to support the argument that many of the test items on standard intelligence tests are not relevant to black (or other minority group) experiences.

Another argument against intelligence tests is that they are often a basis for discriminatory practices in school, especially in the placement of poor and minority children in special classes for mentally retarded or slow students. Mercer (1971) studied the distribution of ethnic group members in classes for the mentally retarded in the public schools of Riverside, California. While the percentage of children in ethnic groups tested by psychologists closely approximated the ethnic distribution of the entire school population, a disproportionate number of Mexican–American and black children had IQ's below 80. More Mexican–Americans than Anglo–Americans were recommended for and finally placed in classes for the mentally retarded.

Mercer believes that neither genetic factors nor environmental deficiencies could account for low IQ scores among minorities. However, children from low socioeconomic groups or from ethnic minorities are more vulnerable to being labeled mentally retarded because clinical measures (primarily intelligence tests) are interpreted from a culture-based perspective.

In the early fifties, two professors from the University of Chicago, Davis and Eells, were certain that the typical IQ test accentuated socioeconomic status (SES) differences by choosing items that were unfair to children of low SES. They attempted to develop a "culture-free" test — the *Davis-Eells Games*. This test was totally pictorial, required no reading, and was administered orally by an examiner. Davis and Eells hoped that it would remove the bias by emphasizing practical problems presumably common to all cultural and socioeconomic groups. Unfortunately, their test proved unsuccessful because first, the lower SES students scored lower on the test than middle-class students, and second, the test failed to predict scholastic achievement as well as other IQ tests.

Mouly (1973) does not think that IQ tests are biased. He argues as follows: The original purpose of the intelligence test was to measure a person's actual ability, for example, performance on particular aspects of intellectual functioning, mainly on tasks that relate to his success in school. Granted that our schools may be too verbally oriented, too traditional, or too abstract. However, intelligence tests still predict, with a reasonable degree of accuracy, students' performance in today's schools. The fault, therefore, is not in the test, but in the way people use it.

Well, what do you think? Are intelligence tests unfair to "culturally deprived" children? How? Can Mouly's argument be refuted?

IS INTELLIGENCE DETERMINED MORE BY HEREDITY OR BY THE ENVIRONMENT? IS INTELLIGENCE FIXED OR CAN IT BE CHANGED?

Since the early 1960s considerable federally funded support has been directed toward establishing preschool programs (for example, Head Start) for children from poverty-stricken and low socioeconomic areas. It was determined that these children had been deprived of the stimuli that effect intellectual and cognitive development. General sensory deprivation resulted from lack of sufficient auditory and visual stimulation, and poor verbal skills stemmed from arrested language development in children's speech at home. In addition, these children lacked motivation to succeed in school. Bernstein (1960), an English sociologist, received considerable attention when he pointed out that lower-class children use an informal language to convey concrete needs and immediate consequences, while middle-class children use a more formal language to communicate concepts that are essential to academic tasks.

The goal of these preschool programs was to *compensate* for the inadequacies of *deprived* children through a planned enrichment program of various sensory experiences and language skills. Thus, "culturally deprived" and "compensatory education" became widely used terminology in educational circles. Numerous books and journal articles were written from 1960 to the present on the problems of and possible solutions for educating "disadvantaged" children.

The proponents of compensatory education believed that improved environmental conditions could influence children's intellectual and academic development and were out to equalize individual differences that existed prior to children's entering school. In fact, J. McV Hunt (1961), a crusader for Head Start, argued that "with a sound scientific educational psychology of early experience, it might become possible to raise the level of intelligence . . . by thirty points . . . " (p. 267).

When the graduates of Head Start programs were evaluated at the end of the first grade and compared to students who had not attended Head Start, the U.S. Commission on Civil Rights (1967) concluded: "None of the compensatory education programs appears to have raised the achievement of participating pupils, as a group, within the period evaluated by the commission" (p. 138).

Many individuals did not agree with the conclusions of the report. With so many types of Head Start programs, they argued, there was no justification for pooling all of them in the investigation of the general success of preschool programs — especially in the light of evidence that some were more effective than others (Spicker, 1971).

Other individuals contended that Head Start was too little and too late. The impact of environmental deprivation begins well before the preschool age. An effective program would have to be initiated in the home soon after birth.

In 1969 a highly controversial article was written for the *Harvard Educational Review* by Arthur R. Jensen, professor of educational psychology at the University of California, Berkeley. In this article, "How Much Can We Boost IQ and Scholastic Achievement?" Jensen covered a number of topics: the contribution of heredity and environment to intelligence and scholastic performance; an evaluation of the efforts to raise IQ and scholastic performance of poor children; his position on social class and racial differences in intelligence; and his research on associative learning ability, socioeconomic status, and intelligence. The resulting article was 123 pages — the longest ever published in the journal. The publication of the article has provoked more than one hundred pro or con articles and books.

In his article, Jensen concluded that the main reason compensatory education programs have failed is that they concentrated on environmental experiences as the determining factor in intellectual development. He presented data to support the position that about 80% of the differences in IQ occur because of genetic differences, with environmental factors contributing to a small portion of the differences among individuals. The most controversial part of Jensen's article was his claim that genetic factors probably account for the fact that, on the average, American Blacks have lower IQ scores than either American Whites, Orientals, or Indians. Because of genetic differences, certain groups — Blacks, for example — might benefit from instruction that stressed associative (memory or rote) learning over conceptual learning. Jensen (1969) stated that Level I ability (associative) was distributed about the same in all social class groups, while Level II ability (conceptual) was distributed differently in lower and middle SES groups. Middle and low SES children were equivalent in Level I ability but middle SES children were superior to low SES children in Level II ability.

Jensen suggests that low SES children do poorly in school because schools tend to emphasize conceptual skills (Level II). He believes that schools can best provide equal education for all children by recognizing that different types of learning abilities exist among different groups and by providing different methods of instruction to capitalize on the existing abilities of each learner. Jensen's recent articles continue to caution the educational establishment that equality of educational opportunity will not necessarily lead to equality of performance.

A correlation between two variables is a statistical indication of their relationship. It is determined by a mathematical formula that we shall not discuss in this book. However, it is important for you to be able to interpret the meaning of a correlation.

If two variables increase proportionately (for example, children's age and weight), their correlation is positive. A negative correlation signifies that as one variable increases the other decreases (for example, a car's increase in age and decrease in price).

The symbol used to denote a correlation is r. r ranges from -1 to $+1$. The closer r is to minus or plus, the higher the correlation. The closer to zero, the smaller the correlation. We almost never obtain a perfect negative or positive correlation (-1 or $+1$), but we do find that variables correlate to some degree. For example, we might refer to $r = .50$ as a moderately positive correlation, to $r = .95$ as a high positive correlation, and to $r = -.91$ as a high negative correlation. Correlations near zero denote no or minimal relationship between the variables. If no sign (+ or −) is given in front of the correlation, it is assumed to be positive.

Finally, correlations do not imply causality. That is, two variables may correlate (for example, smoking and lung cancer) but one variable is not necessarily the cause of the other. There is a high positive correlation between the number of liquor stores and churches in urban areas. I would hope that one is not the cause of the other!

Additional support for a strong genetic explanation of intelligence came from William Shockley (1971), a Nobel Prize winner and professor of engineering science at Stanford University; Richard Herrnstein (1971) of Harvard, who presented his position in an article in the September 1971 issue of *The Atlantic;* and H. J. Eysenck (1971), an eminent English psychologist, who published *The IQ Argument.*

The strongest data favorable to the heredity viewpoint are the correlational studies (degree of association) between identical twins raised together and apart; fraternal twins; siblings reared together;

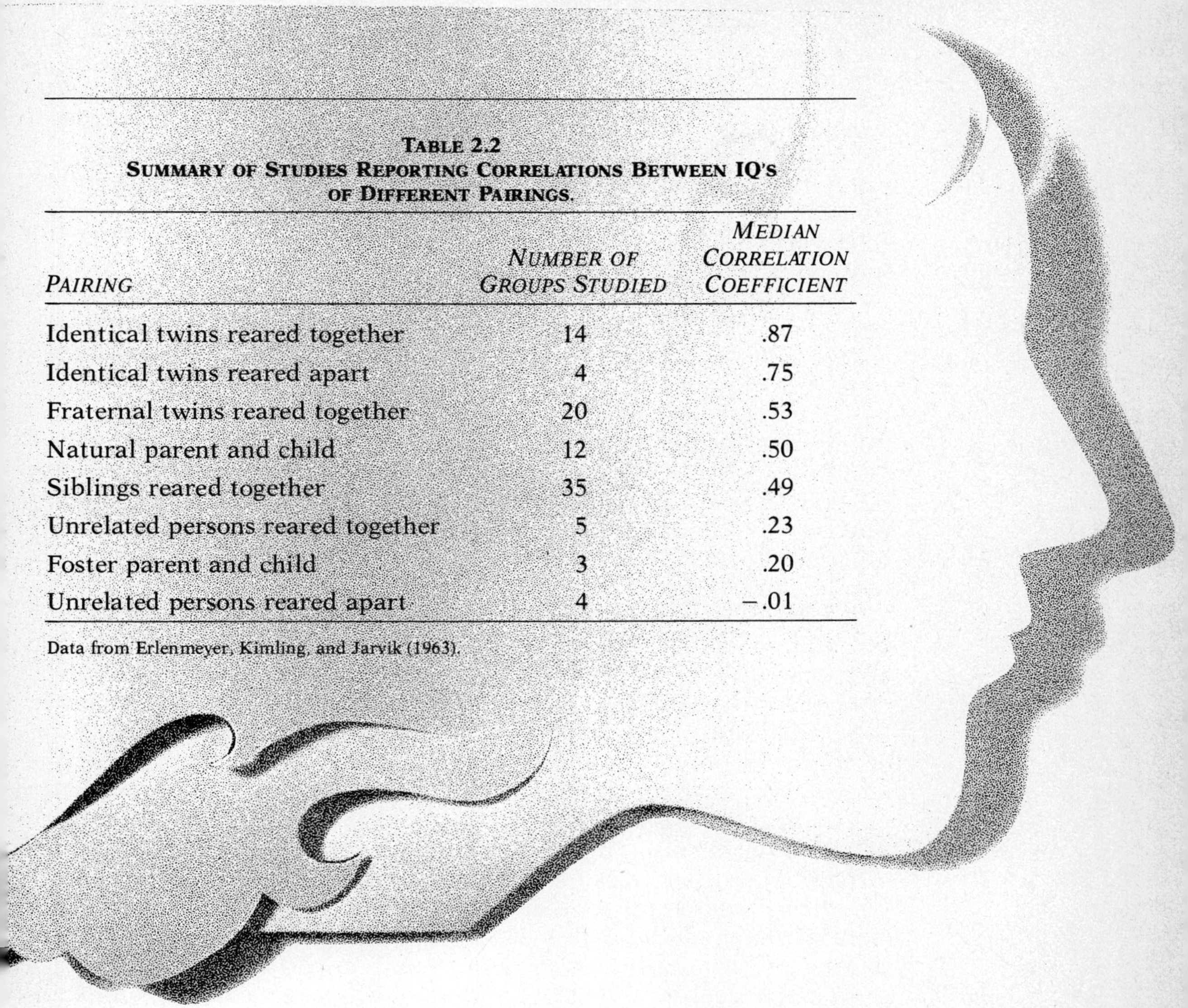

TABLE 2.2
SUMMARY OF STUDIES REPORTING CORRELATIONS BETWEEN IQ'S OF DIFFERENT PAIRINGS.

PAIRING	*NUMBER OF GROUPS STUDIED*	*MEDIAN CORRELATION COEFFICIENT*
Identical twins reared together	14	.87
Identical twins reared apart	4	.75
Fraternal twins reared together	20	.53
Natural parent and child	12	.50
Siblings reared together	35	.49
Unrelated persons reared together	5	.23
Foster parent and child	3	.20
Unrelated persons reared apart	4	−.01

Data from Erlenmeyer, Kimling, and Jarvik (1963).

parent and child; and foster parent and child.

Identical twins develop from the same egg and have identical genetic make-up. Fraternal twins develop from separate eggs and, although they share a common environment, are genetically no more similar than nontwin siblings. Erlenmeyer-Kimling and Jarvik (1963) have organized the results of fifty-two studies from the literature on intelligence to show that the similarity between pairs of people increases as their genetic relationship increases (see Table 2.2).

When we compare identical twins reared together and fraternal twins reared together, we note that, in holding environment relatively constant and manipulating heredity, the IQ correlation changes from .87 for identical twins to .53 for fraternal twins. At the same time, the comparison of the IQ correlation for identical twins reared together (.87) and apart (.75) shows that holding heredity constant and manipulating environment produce a much smaller change. The similarity of IQ scores of identical twins reared apart (.75) is much greater than fraternal twins reared together (.53), suggesting that heredity more strongly influences IQ than environment.

In addition to the twin data, adopted-child studies have revealed that the intelligence scores of the child relate more to the educational level of the true mother, who did not raise the child, than to that of the foster mother, who did raise the child (Honzik, 1967).

These findings have not gone unchallenged by environmentalists, who argue that the actual manipulation of environmental variables in such studies may have been relatively minor. Children may be reared apart but exposed to essentially similar environments. There is not enough difference in the environments to produce a significant effect on their IQ. Furthermore, children reared in the same family can be exposed to different environments.

There is evidence (Newman, Freeman, & Holzinger, 1937) that, given large enough environmental differences, identical twins reared apart can diverge by 15 points or more in IQ scores. Gage (1972) asks: "Are the environmental differences between Negroes and whites in the United States also large enough to produce average IQ differences of about 15 points" (pp. 311–312)? His own answer is that no one knows. We must remember that all the research on identical twins reared apart and on other rearing combinations has been done with white subjects only. This research, therefore, deals only with the environmental differences to which whites are subjected.

Environmentalists also point to the studies reporting a substantial change in IQ scores when children are exposed to a more enriching or stimulating environment and to the studies reporting a progressive decline of IQ in a nonstimulating environment. For example, the longer children remain in orphanages (Skeels et al., 1938; Skeels, 1966), the lower their IQ's become in comparison to children reared in stimulating environments.

Bloom (1964) speculates from a number of different studies that extremes in environmental conditions may make a difference of as much as 20% in the intelligence test scores at age 17. If this is so, two individuals with the same intellectual potential might, because of different environments, earn scores of 100 and 120, respectively, on IQ tests administered at age 17.

The debate about the influence of heredity and environment on intellectual development continues. While educators hear the arguments on both sides, they should carefully consider the following observation made by a leading educational psychologist:

> The psychologist and geneticist may wish to speculate about how to improve the genetic pool — the educator cannot and should not. The educator must be an environmentalist — bridled or unbridled. It is through the environment that he must fashion the educational process. Learning goes on by providing the appropriate environment. If heredity imposes limits — so be it. The educator must work with what is left, whether it be 20 percent of the variance or 50 percent. (Bloom, 1969, p. 50)

Another Explanation

There is another explanation offered for the failure of many preschool programs to improve the intelligence level and scholastic achievement of children. Labov (1974), a linguist, blames differences in learning outcomes between white and black students on the school's failure to understand and respond to the students' culture. He states that educators have spent too much time determining what kind of disadvantages or defects certain children are suffering from.

Labov has studied the language pattern of black youths and reports that they use an English vernacular that is grammatically complex and capable of expressing abstract concepts. Unfortunately, teachers perceive this form of language as an inferior product of environmental conditions. He further points out that programs like Head Start, which are designed to overcome lower- and middle-class language differences, aggravate the black students' learning in school.

Labov does not say that children from ghetto areas do not need additional verbal skills, some of which are characteristic of middle-class verbal behavior: precision in spelling, practice in handling abstract symbols, the ability to state explicitly the meaning of words, and a broader vocabulary. But he questions whether all middle-class verbal habits are functional and desirable in school:

> Before we impose middle-class verbal style upon children from other cultural groups, we should find out how much of it is useful for the main work of analyzing and generalizing, and how much is merely stylistic or even dysfunctional. In high school and college, middle-class children spontaneously complicate their syntax to the point that instructors despair of getting them to make their language simpler and clearer. (Labov, 1974, p. 160)

In summary, Labov believes that the school should change its orientation. Rather than seeking ways to modify the child's behavior, educators should consider how the school can better accommodate its instructional program to the strengths of the child (Gall & Ward, 1974).

MENTAL ABILITIES WITHIN CULTURAL GROUPS

A series of investigations was undertaken by Lesser and his colleagues (Lesser, Fifer, & Clark, 1965; Stodolsky & Lesser, 1967) to study the patterns of various mental abilities in children from different cultural backgrounds and social classes. In their first investigation, they studied four mental abilities — verbal, reasoning, number facility, and space conceptualization — in first-grade children in four cultural groups in New York City: Chinese, Jews, Blacks, and Puerto Ricans).

The tests were carefully constructed to include only objectives and experiences common to all social and cultural groups in an urban area. In addition, the tests were individually administered by an examiner belonging to the same cultural group as the child and required no reading or writing. The tests consisted primarily of pictures and games that each child was asked to manipulate or to label. Each child was familiarized with the testing procedures and directions and was given time to become acquainted with the testing situation. In other words, the researchers attempted to improve upon the testing situation of previous cultural-group studies so that their results would engender greater confidence.

The findings were quite interesting. On all mental abilities, middle-class children performed better than lower-class children, a result consistent with similar research on different SES levels. However, these differences in social class did not influence the patterns among the abilities. Each cultural group exhibited a particular pattern of strengths and weaknesses that was the same regardless of social class.

Figure 2.3 presents the patterns of the mental abilities by cultural groups. The ranking on the four measures of mental abilities, from high to low, was as follows: verbal ability — Jews, Blacks, Chinese, and Puerto Ricans; reasoning — Chinese, Jews, Blacks, and Puerto Ricans; numerical ability — Jews, Chinese, Puerto Ricans, and Blacks; spatial ability — Chinese, Jews, Puerto Ricans, and Blacks. Within each cultural group, the scores were almost exactly parallel for the middle and lower classes. Only the Puerto Rican children departed slightly from this trend.

FIGURE 2.3
PATTERNS OF NORMALIZED MENTAL ABILITIES BY CULTURAL GROUP.

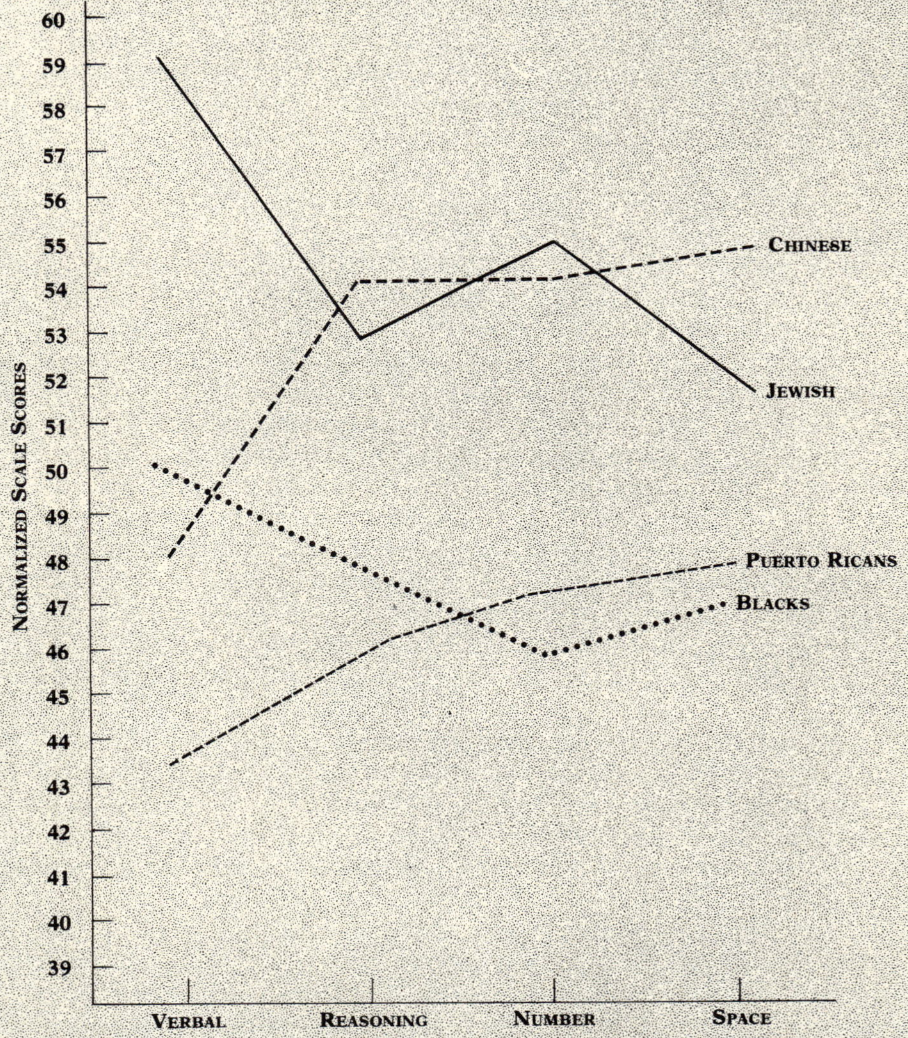

From G. Lesser, G. Fifer, and D. Clark, "Mental Abilities of Children From Different Social-Class and Cultural Groups." *Monographs of the Society for Research in Child Development* 30, serial no. 102 (1965): 64. Copyright © 1965 by The Society for Research in Child Development, Inc. Used by permission.

Typically, studies of culture and mental abilities do not separate social class and cultural or ethnic groups but, instead, treat them equally. The investigators do not know whether the differences found among children of various groups arise from social class or from cultural background. In the Lesser study, the investigators demonstrated that these two variables do not have the same effect on the pattern of mental abilities; social-class conditions failed to alter patterns of mental ability associated with cultural group membership.

The investigators believe that the differences are manifested because each cultural group attaches differential importance and emphasis to different mental abilities. These differences are influenced by "the reinforcement parents provide for different types of intellectual performances, opportunities inside the home to learn various skills, the value placed on different forms of intellectual performances, work habits developed in the home, and the parents' intellectual aspirations for the child" (Stodolsky & Lesser, 1967, p. 580). If you have had contact with members of any of the cultural groups in the study, can you identify specific behaviors that could account for the pattern of mental abilities found by the investigators?

Stodolsky and Lesser (1967) suggest that an implication inherent in these findings is the need for a change in educational methods to suit the learning strengths of different ethnic or cultural groups. This matching of methods with strengths could be accomplished in two ways: First, by assessing the particular patterns of mental abilities and by building an instructional strategy to capitalize on the child's intellectual strengths. For example, when teaching mathematical functions to children strong in spatial conceptualization but weak in numerical facility, the teacher would use more graphical than numerical presentations. Second, by identifying the child's intellectual skills to modify or develop the specific skills necessary to learn the task.

If children possess intellectual skills that do not fit into traditional educational methods, they may never develop to their full potential. An important issue here is differences versus deficiencies. As Labov mentioned earlier, differences are not always deficiencies. However, if school programs and materials fail to take differences into account, these differences may, indeed, become deficiencies.

The implication in Lesser's work is echoed by Jensen, who has consistently stated that certain mental abilities are not necessarily a result of discrimination and unequal environmental conditions. Although the specific nature of the research of Jensen and Lesser differs to some degree, their conclusions are remarkably similar. The key difference is that Lesser attributes cultural differences to familial factors and Jensen to genetic factors. Jensen's findings have been criticized and attacked, while Lesser's work has received considerably less attention from both the academic community and the public.

After reviewing the disparity between school achievement and mental ability, Coleman (1966) concluded that the role of the schools is "to make achievement independent of background and to overcome the differences in the starting point of children from different social groups . . ." (p. 72). Stodolsky and Lesser (1967) question the "equal-footing" basis of Coleman's argument by asking: "Should schools provide equal opportunities to promote equal development of all groups and individuals or equal opportunities for the maximum development of each group or individual? Can the school aim to do both" (p. 583)? Another way of asking the same question is: Should schools strive for equal development or equal opportunity for all children?

Stodolsky and Lesser (1967) believe that if we attempt to develop instructional programs around the intellectual strengths of children from different cultural groups, we should be willing to accept the possible consequence that, in certain areas, we may magnify individual differences among students rather than reduce the differences among various groups.

In discussing the different analyses and solutions for improving the intellectual development and educational achievement of children, we have touched on three major views. First, those who support compensatory education programs feel that minority students or students from low income homes do not get the same opportunities as students from middle-class homes to develop school-related skills. They come to school less prepared to function successfully, and the task of the school is to provide these skills for deprived students.

Second, Jensen holds that genetic factors account for many differences in performance. Unless schools consider these factors when planning instructional programs, they cannot improve and equalize the achievement of culturally and socially different children. Both Jensen and Lesser suggest that the schools will never remove *all* differences among students.

Third, Labov believes that differences in achievement stem not from the lack of basic skills but from the orientation of the schools. Because they are geared to the abilities of middle-class children they fail to consider the learning style and language of children from different cultural and social classes. Labov concludes that the school must adjust its methodologies to the individual's pattern of mental abilities.

How much weight do you give to environmental and genetic factors in learning? How do you think the schools can best help low-achieving students? Give them middle-class skills and knowledge? Design educational programs to match their own skills and knowledge?

CREATIVITY

Guilford (1959) was among the first psychologists to suggest that intelligence and creativity were not synonymous. In the Structure of the Intellect model (see Figure 2.2), Guilford distinguished between convergent and divergent thinking. Convergent thinking produces a well-determined answer to a routine problem, while divergent thinking generates new ideas and solutions to problems that have more than one correct answer.

Convergent thinking would produce the answer "16" to the question "What is the square of 4?" Divergent thought production might entail finding unusual uses for a knife. The latter form of thinking is associated with creativity.

Guilford identified four characteristics of divergent thinking: (1) *fluency* — coming up with a large quantity of ideas, words, and ways of expressing things; (2) *flexibility* — thinking up a variety of ideas and new ways of dealing with situations; (3) *originality* — thinking of uncommon, clever, and novel ideas and images; (4) and *elaboration* — packing detail into the response. Many creative thinking tests use these criteria in evaluating the responses of students.

Let me make a distinction here between *gifted* and *creative* children. Earlier, I reported Terman's study of gifted children who scored at the top three percent on the Stanford-Binet scale. The results from a number of studies (Getzels & Jackson, 1962; Wallach & Kogan, 1965) indicate that although persons above average in intelligence are more likely to be creative, it does not mean that average or highly intelligent persons are necessarily creative. In fact, Torrance (1962) states that "if we were to identify children as gifted simply on the basis of intelligence tests, we would eliminate from consideration approximately seventy percent of the most creative" (p. 5). Figure 2.4 indicates the possible combinations of mental characteristics used in creativity studies.

Getzels and Jackson (1962) compared high school students who scored high on creativity tests (upper 20%) but relatively low on IQ with students who scored high on IQ (upper 20%) but low on creativity tests (Cells b and c respectively of Figure 2.4). Although the highly creative group had a mean IQ score 23 points below the high IQ group, there were no significant differences in academic achievement between the two groups. Getzels and Jackson also found that teachers

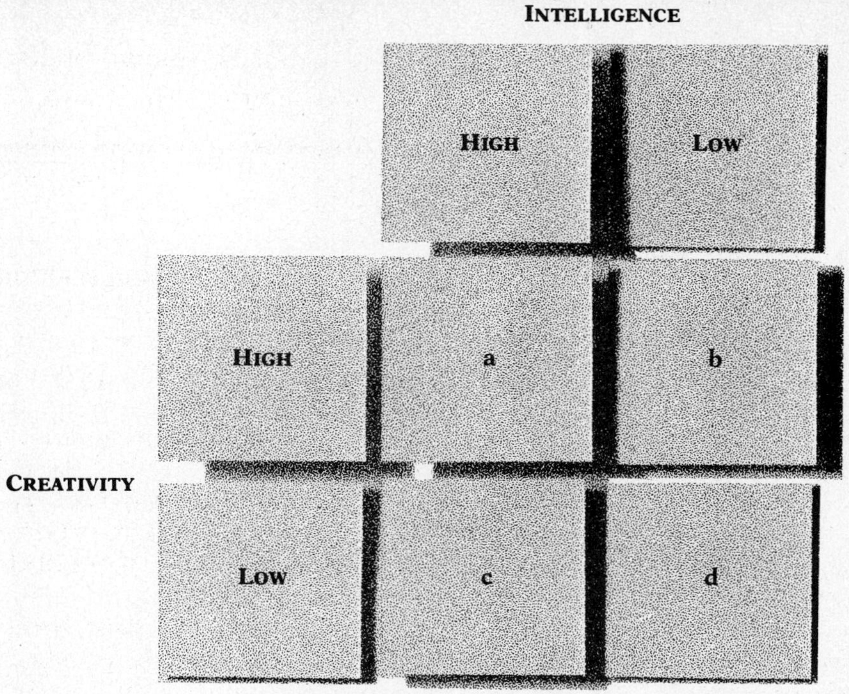

FIGURE 2.4
COMBINATIONS OF MENTAL CHARACTERISTICS USED IN CREATIVITY STUDIES.

preferred the students with high IQ to those with high creativity. Why do you think this might be so?

Students with high grades in school may or may not be creative students. Many noncreative high IQ individuals perform very well in school or on the job but never generate any original ideas. There are also students who do poorly in school and fit into the little-motivation slot but have a high degree of creative talent. Torrance (1972) studied fourth-grade students who were on the honor roll and reported that they achieved lower scores on tests of creative thinking than their peers who were not on the honor roll.

Recognizing the possible discrepancy between academic achievement and creativity, the administrators of the National Merit Scholarships made twenty-five scholarships available annually for applicants who could not meet the grades or IQ requirement but who had displayed high creative abilities in the arts and sciences. The following behaviors were selected as evidence of creative behavior:

THE CREATIVE SCIENCE SCALE

1. *Giving an original paper at a scientific meeting sponsored by a professional society*

2. *Winning a prize or award in a scientific talent search or science fair*
3. *Constructing a scientific apparatus on one's own initiative*
4. *Inventing a patentable device*
5. *Having a scientific paper published in a scientific journal*

THE CREATIVE ARTS SCALE

1. *Winning one or more speech contests*
2. *Having poems, stories, or articles published in a public newspaper or magazine, or in a state or national high school anthology*
3. *Winning a prize or award in an art competition*
4. *Receiving the highest rating in a state music contest*
5. *Receiving one of the highest ratings in a national music contest*
6. *Composing music that is given at least one public performance*
7. *Arranging music for a public performance*
8. *Having a minor role in plays (not church- or school-sponsored)*
9. *Having leads in school- or church-sponsored plays*
10. *Winning a literary award or a prize for creative writing*
11. *Having a cartoon published in a public newspaper or magazine (Barron, 1969)*

The behavioral characteristics of creative children often cause them a great deal of difficulty and discomfort in the classroom. Torrance (1972) states:

> In most classrooms, highly creative children are handicapped by their creativeness and are regarded as behavior problems. Frequently, such children are diagnosed as having learning disabilities. For these reasons, I have suggested that highly creative children be designated as a new category of handicapped children in the field of special education. (p. 25)

The following are some behavioral characteristics of creative children as summarized from Torrance (1962, 1972):

Work characterized by humor, lack of rigidity, and playfulness

Willingness to attempt difficult tasks

Long attention span, concentration, and interest

Likely to express unconventional ideas and engage in imaginative activities

More sensitive and independent than the average child

Lack of preoccupation with what the classroom group thinks

Sometimes labeled by their peers as having "silly" or "crazy" ideas (particularly boys)

Cropley (1967) recounts an incident that illustrates how a creative child's response can cause difficulty in the classroom. In an elementary school the teacher asked his class to draw a head. While the teacher was catching up on some paper work, a child who had previously been troublesome came up to the teacher and asked whether to draw the outside or the inside of the head. The teacher, busy at the time, of course exploded in anger.

Despite some popular stereotypes of creative children, they are no more likely to exhibit neurotic or psychopathological behavior than your normal "dull" person (Dellas & Gaier, 1970). However, you should be cautious in identifying unconventional students as creative. The student who exhibits some of the qualities of the divergent thinker may not be creative. I shall now discuss how to identify creative thinking, other than by watching those mental wheels turn.

Tests of creativity are quite different from intelligence or achievement tests in which conventional or convergent kind of thinking brings forth a single correct response to a well-defined test item. Creativity tests assess the individual's facility in producing fresh or unique associations, ideas, or solutions to problems. Figure 2.5 shows three samples of the kind of questions used in tests of creativity.

The two standardized measures of creativity most widely used are *Guilford's Tests of Divergent Production* and *Torrance's Tests of Creative Thinking*. The Guilford tests measure specific divergent thinking ability and are more appropriate for high school students. The Torrance tests simultaneously measure a number of creative thinking abilities and are oriented more toward elementary school children. The scoring for the Guilford tests is a little more difficult than for the Torrance batteries (Gorman, 1974). Manuals and scoring guides with many examples are available with these instruments, so that, with a little practice, you can learn to master the scoring techniques if you are interested.

FIGURE 2.5
SAMPLE TESTS OF CREATIVITY AND PROBLEM-SOLVING ABILITY.

1
Flanagan's Ingenuity Test:

As part of a manufacturing process, the inside lip of a deep, cup-shaped casting is machine threaded. The company found that metal chips produced by the threading operation were difficult to remove from the bottom of the casting without scratching the sides. A design engineer was able to solve this problem by using one of the following. Can you determine which solution he chose?

a) i— — — — —p h— —h
b) m— — — — —n c— — —e
c) f— — — — —r w— — —i
d) l— — — — —d b— — —k
e) u— — — — —e d— — —n

2
Guilford's Sample Insight Problem:

A man went out to hunt a bear one day. He left and hiked due south for ten miles, then due west for ten miles. At this point, he killed a bear. He dragged the bear back to his camp, a distance of exactly ten miles. What was the color of the bear? Why?

3
Pattern Arrangement Test:

Arrange the glasses shown in the sketch to form an alternating pattern of one filled and one empty by moving just one glass. (The pattern may begin with either a filled or an empty glass.)

Answers

1
The correct answer is (3), upside down, or ˙uʍop ǝpısdn

2
Answer: "white." Only at the North Pole could these directions have been possible. Is it creativity or a good convergent knowledge of geometry and geography that one employs in finding the "correct" answer?

3
Pour the contents of glass #6 into glass #3.

From R.C. Sprinthall and N. A. Sprinthall, *Educational Psychology: A Developmental Approach* (Reading, Mass.: Addison-Wesley, 1974), p. 374. Reprinted by permission of the publisher.

Creativity also comes through in paintings, projects, stories, and class discussions. You should be cognizant of the divergent thinker and encourage him or her in the classroom.

Learning Styles

I have spent considerable time discussing the identification and measurement of mental abilities. Educators use these identification and measurement techniques to identify individual differences among students but neglect the area of learning or cognitive styles of students, which is a more practical area for improving day-to-day instruction. Cognitive styles are the consistent ways in which an individual responds to a wide range of perceptual and intellectual tasks. Sigel and Coop (1974) state that cognitive style is an integrative concept in that its definition bridges the personality-cognitive dimension of the individual.

Think about your own learning style for a moment. Suppose you had to prepare for an examination next week on this chapter. How would you prepare for such a task? Does your learning style

1. *involve studying with other students, or do you work independently?*
2. *include studying for short periods during the week, or would you wait for the night before the exam to begin studying?*
3. *involve taking notes on the chapter during your initial reading, or do you rely on your Magic Marker underscores?*
4. *depend on the type of exam — essay or multiple-choice — scheduled?*
5. *call for studying under quiet conditions, or do you require a minimum level of noise — a radio tuned to your favorite station?*
6. *require working under pressure? Without tests as a prod, would you study as much?*

What additional aspects of your learning style are important to your learning? Compare them with those of other students in your class.

Table 2.3 includes a number of learning-style factors that may influence a student's academic success. Dunn and Dunn (1972) state that teachers should ask their students to assess themselves on these dimensions.

Table 2.3
Learning Style Diagnosis.

1. Time	When is the student most alert? In the early morning, at lunchtime, in the afternoon, in the evening, at night?
2. Schedule	What is the student's attention span? Continuous, irregular, short bursts of concentrated effort, forgetting periods, etc.?
3. Amount of Sound	What level of noise can the student tolerate? Absolute quiet, a murmur, distant sound, high level of conversation?
4. Type of Sound	What type of sound produces a positive reaction? Music, conversation, laughter, working groups?
5. Type of Work Group	How does the student work best? Alone, with one person, with a small task group, in a large team, a combination?
6. Amount of Pressure	What kind of pressure (if any) does the student need? Relaxed, slight, moderate, extreme?
7. Type of Pressure and Motivation	What helps to motivate this student? Self, teacher expectation, deadline, rewards, recognition of achievement, internalized interest, etc.?
8. Place	Where does the student work best? Home, school, learning centers, library media corner?
9. Physical Environment and Conditions	Floor, carpet, reclining, sitting, desk, temperature, table lighting, type of clothing, food?
10. Type of Assignments	On which type of assignments does the student thrive? Contracts, totally self-directed projects, teacher-selected tasks, etc.?
11. Perceptual Strengths and Styles	How does the student learn most easily? Visual materials, sound recording, printed media, tactile experiences, kinesthetic activities, multimedia packages, combinations of these?
12. Type of Structure and Evaluation	What type of structure suits this student most of the time? Strict, flexible, self-determined, jointly arranged, periodic, self-starting, continuous, occasional, time-line expectations, terminal assessment, etc.?

As you talk to other students about their learning styles and observe the behavior of roommates and friends, the range of differences becomes apparent. I have always been intrigued with the metamorphosis of student behavior during final exam time. Some students sleep during the day and study at night, don't bathe, and don't shave. They change their regular study behavior in many ways, as if the new behavior change will make a difference. Why do students make these changes? Do the changes have certain "psychological" effects on them?

Learning styles can make a difference in academic performance. Riessman (1964) states that when a child doesn't learn, teachers and guidance counselors tend to focus entirely on IQ, emotional blocks, and personality conflicts rather than on his style of learning. Why not simply concentrate on the way the child works and learns? Focusing on all the effective reasons for his *not* learning is looking negatively at the problem.

Hunt and Sullivan (1974) would like teachers to view students in terms of their "accessibility channels" — their cognitive, motivational, value, and sensory orientation. They state: "Describing a student in accessibility terms is nothing more than an attempt to specify the needs of the child in terms that have some meaning for the teacher and makes it more likely that the teacher will reach, get in touch, or tune in with the student" (p. 49).

Let's explore some of the learning styles of students that might help us to "tune in." Remember that individuals with the same intelligence test score can approach educational tasks with different cognitive or learning styles. My aim is to demonstrate that certain learning-style factors influence the degree of learning more than does intelligence. The discussion will be limited to two cognitive styles: the reflective/impulsive and field-dependent/field-independent dimensions. The reader may wish to read Kogan (1971) and Sigel and Coop (1974) for a more detailed treatment of this topic.

Persistence is one of the most important abilities a child must possess to be successful in school. If the child finds it difficult to concentrate on a task for any period of time, the chances are great that she is going to come into conflict with her teacher and will not be successful in the classroom. Psychologists label the most severe cases "hyperactives." These children are handicapped by neurological impairment that manifests itself in minimal brain dysfunction. They cannot resist reacting to noise or motion and are constantly squirming or looking about the room.

On a less serious level, restlessness leads to carelessness in school tasks. Kagan et al. (1964) noticed that some students take a long time to think about a question or problem before they respond, while other students respond almost immediately to the questions posed. They have developed a test called the Matching Familiar Figures Test (MFFT) to obtain measures of student response rates and errors. Figure 2.6 illustrates two tasks from this test. The examiner shows the child the drawing at the top of the page and six highly similar ones. The child must select the drawing that is identical to the one at the top. The examiner records both the child's accuracy and the amount of time he takes to make his response.

As a result of his findings, Kagan proposed a stylistic dimension called *conceptual tempo,* referring to the speed with which subjects make a response to their tasks and the number of errors they make in the response. Rapid responders, who make a fair amount of errors, are called impulsive and slower responders, who tend to make fewer errors, are called reflective. Kagan believes that impulsiveness or reflectiveness is a consistent and relatively stable personality trait that may be evident by the time the child is two years old. Research on conceptual tempo has established the following:

1. *Reading errors are more numerous among impulsive children (Kagan, 1965).*
2. *Impulsive children also make more errors on a variety of inductive reasoning tasks (Kagan et al., 1966).*
3. *Impulsive children more frequently fail the early grades, even when they are similar to their nonfailing peers in verbal intelligence (Messer, 1970).*

Holt (1964) describes the behavior of some of his students that is typical of the impulsive individual:

> It used to puzzle me that the students who made the most mistakes and got the worst marks were so often the first ones to hand in their papers. I used to say, "If you finish early, take time to check your work, do some problems again." Typical teacher's advice; I might as well have told them to flap their arms and fly. When the paper was in, the tension was ended. Their fate was in the lap of the gods. They might still worry about flunking the paper, but it was a fatalistic kind of worry; it didn't contain the agonizing element of choice — there was nothing more they could do about it. Worrying about whether you did the right thing, while painful enough, is less painful than worrying about the right thing to do. (p. 41)

Both overly reflective students and impulsive students are likely to have trouble in the classroom — the impulsive student because he quickly responds to questions and tasks "without thinking,"

FIGURE 2.6

SAMPLE ITEMS FROM THE CHILDREN'S MATCHING FAMILIAR FIGURES TEST (MFFT).

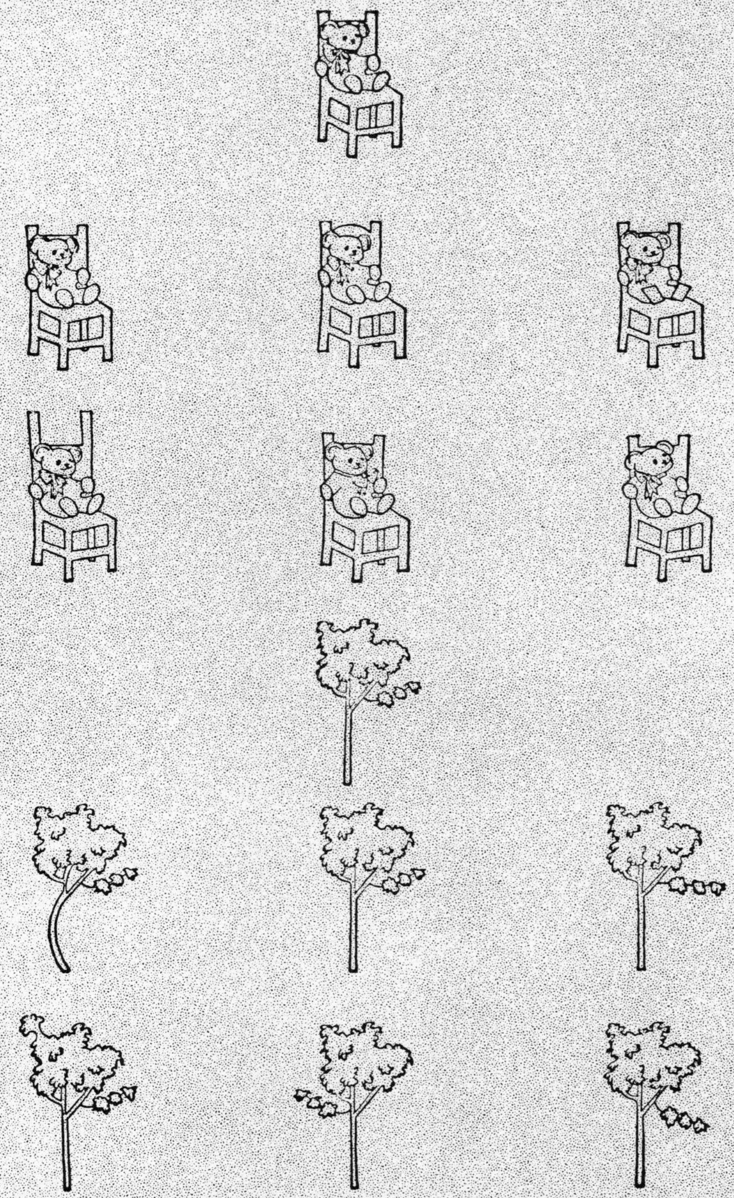

From J. Kagan, "Reflection-Impulsivity and Reading Ability in Primary Grade Children." *Child Development* 36 (1965): 609–626. Copyright © 1965 by The Society for Research in Child Development, Inc. Reprinted by permission.

and the reflective student because he ponders questions endlessly. The important implication here is that impulsiveness, not intellectual deficiency, is partly responsible for poor reading and low intelligence and achievement test scores.

Depending on how the teacher puts them through their paces, both the reflective and impulsive student can have trouble with certain types of tasks. The impulsive teacher will overwhelm the reflective child with a barrage of information or questions that he cannot handle, for example, in speed games. However, the impulsive child, who delivers a volley of responses to straightforward questions, is in his element. His more reflective classmate wastes time mulling over answers that do not require much attention.

The reflective child shines in dealing with questions when there is a great chance of error. He will suppress the incorrect answers that occur to him and will unearth other possibilities that escape the more impulsive child who has already walled himself in.

Kagan (1966) provides an excellent example to illustrate the advantage that the reflective child holds. Suppose a reflective and an impulsive child must remember whether the formula for the circumference of a circle is $2\pi r$ or πr^2. The impulsive child selects one formula quickly, with even odds for selecting the correct formula. The reflective child pauses to evaluate the validity of each formula. During this time, he might remember that the area of a rectangle involves the square of a number and decide that πr^2 applies to the area of a circle; thus, $2\pi r$ is probably the correct formula for the circumference.

How many times have we heard a teacher say, "Why don't you take time to think?" or "Why can't you move a little faster?" What the teacher doesn't realize is that a student's learning style is part of his personality and cannot easily be changed.

One of the most widely investigated forms of cognitive style is the *field-independent/field-dependent* dimension. This dimension is a measure of the extent to which individuals are able to overcome effects of distracting background elements (the field) when they attempt to differentiate the relevant aspects of a particular situation. The more independent the person is of distracting elements, the more analytical, or field-independent, he is. The more dependent or incapable the individual is of freeing himself from the distracting elements, the more global, or field-dependent, he is.

Figure 2.7 presents an example from a Hidden Figures Test used to determine a person's cognitive style in the field-independent/field-dependent dimension.

In a recent paper reviewing the research in this area, Witkin and Moore (1974) pointed out the characteristic orientation of individuals classified as field-dependent and field-independent. Field-

Figure 2.7

A Hidden Figures Test of the Type Used to Assess Field Dependence/Field Independence. The student is asked to identify which of the five simple figures (A-E) is hidden within the embedding context of the more complex patterns.

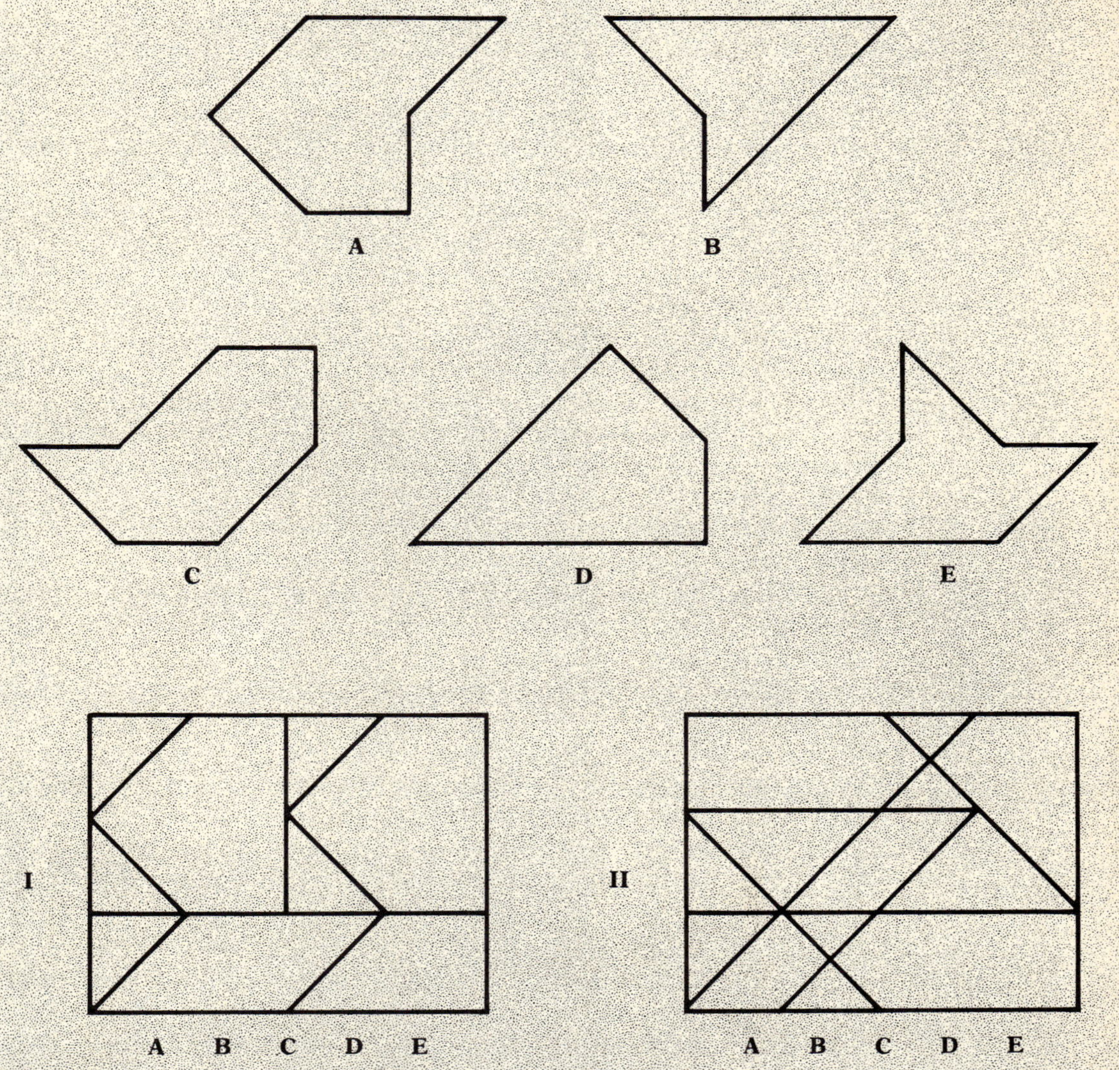

dependent[2] persons are particularly attentive to the social field and will look to others in defining their own attitudes and beliefs. They reflect a considerable degree of social sensitivity. In contrast, field-independent persons show greater interest in the more impersonal, abstract aspects of various stimuli.

These two types of individuals interact differently with the environment. Field-dependent persons are drawn to people, favor occupations like teaching, which require involvement with others, and prefer academic areas like the social sciences, which are more "people-oriented." Field-independent persons prefer occupations like astronomy and engineering, in which working with others is not especially important and favor school subjects like mathematics and the physical sciences, which stress the impersonal and abstract.

Witkin and Moore (1974) also discuss the consequences of these diverse orientations for the type of material ideal for each kind of child. There is no evidence that field-dependent or field-independent persons differ in general learning ability or memory. However, they appear to respond to different stimuli: Field-dependent persons are better at learning and remembering social material and field-independent persons are better at learning and remembering impersonal material.

Another difference — not surprising after learning about their differences in social orientation — is that social reinforcement has a greater impact on field-dependent than on field-independent people. Teachers constantly mention that students respond differently to praise and criticism. Whether or not the student needs social reinforcement may be related to his field-dependent/field-independent character.

Third, field-independent and field-dependent persons respond differently to material in terms of its degree of structure. When the learning material is unstructured, the learner must organize it. Field-independent persons are better able to internalize the structure needed to organize and learn the material. When the material is structured, field-independent and field-dependent people are equally matched in their learning ability.

An important aspect of this cognitive style dimension is that it is culturally influenced. Witkin (1967) has found that field dependence develops from socialization practices — respect for social convention, protectiveness, and close ties between mother and preadolescent child. Ramírez and Price-Williams (1974) have shown that Mexican-American children are more field-dependent, whereas Anglo-American children are more field-independent.

[2]Some psychologists prefer the term "field-sensitive" because the word "dependent" often has negative connotations.

Cohen (1969) presents evidence that most school environments reflect the field-independent style. Mexican-American children, and other children socialized in field-dependent cultures, are thus handicapped in school. Ramírez and Castañeda (1974) believe that teachers should help these children to develop *bicognitively* — to feel at home with both field-independent and field-dependent styles. In Chapter 4, I will show you how to contribute to bicognitive development.

SENSORY MODALITIES

A *sensory modality* is a system for interacting with the environment through one of the basic senses: sight (visual), hearing (auditory), touch (kinesthetic), smell (olfactory), or taste (gustatory). The sensory modalities most important to the teacher are the visual, the auditory, and the kinesthetic.

> The visual modality (sometimes referred to as the spatial modality) functions when a person pays attention to, thinks about, and remembers visual components of his environment. . . . The verbal modality (sometimes referred to as the auditory modality) is at work when an individual attends to the spoken word. . . . The kinesthetic modality refers to the sensations conveyed through the organs of touch — sensations of movement, and muscular tensions. (Bissell, White, & Zivin, 1971, p. 131)

You should emphasize the kinesthetic and visual modalities in the earlier grades and gradually rely on the verbal modality with older children. As children grow older, they acquire greater ability in coordinating and relating information obtained through different sensory modalities.

Children within the same age group also exhibit a disparity in their use of different sensory modalities. The average student is able to use all modalities but may prefer to learn about a new object through either manipulating it, seeing a picture of it, or hearing and answering questions about it. Research on the relationship between an individual's ability in a specific modality and his preference for that modality adds to the complexity of this aspect of individual differences: There is little correlation between the two.

Realizing the possibility of using different sensory modalities in developing a lesson can help the teacher reach students who may have greater strengths in modalities other than the verbal modality. De Hirsch et al. (1966) found that modality strengths and weaknesses of kindergarten children were related to their success in reading at the end of the second grade. Children with visual modality strengths learned more when the teacher taught them to read by using the sight method, while children with auditory strengths learned more with the phonics approach. When the teaching method did *not* match the individual modality strengths of the students, their reading achievement was considerably lower.

Children with strengths in other than the verbal modality usually lose out in school, particularly on intelligence and achievement tests. Smith (1964) believes that verbal thinking has been overemphasized in school, to the neglect of visual or spatial thinking, and suggests ways to match instructional methods with individual strengths of students. The child from a low-socioeconomic background learns more by doing and touching than by reading. While some students shift easily from one modality to another, she is locked into an inflexible learning mode (Riessman, 1964).

Although no standardized procedures are available to measure the sensory modalities of children, Bissell, White, & Zavin (1971) recommend: (1) observing children when they have a choice of learning materials and activities, (2) using IQ tests for information on verbal ability, (3) using the Wepman Auditory Discrimination Test and the Horst Reversals Test (a test designed to assess a child's tendency to make letter and word reversals in reading), and (4) questioning older children about their preferred modality.

The following reading by Shumsky (1968) discusses a number of important learning styles for you to consider while developing teaching strategies and interacting with students.

Individual Differences in Learning Styles

VARIATIONS IN APPROACH TO LEARNING

Children in a given classroom may vary not only in the things they know and in their capabilities for learning, but also in the ways in which they approach and deal with a given task. These variations are usually a function of the way in which they approach most life situations. The timid child will probably approach a new learning task with greater timidity than the bold, assertive kind of child. The highly intense, energetic child will approach a new learning task with more zest than the child who is usually passive and indifferent.

From Adaia Shumsky, "Individual Differences in Learning Styles." In Abraham Shumsky, *In Search of Teaching Style*, ©1968, pp. 156–171. Reprinted by permission of Prentice-Hall, Inc., Englewood Cliffs, New Jersey.

An attempt will be made in the following pages to describe a number of ways in which children show diversity in their handling of learning tasks in the classroom. The examples are by no means inclusive. Rather, they serve the purpose of demonstrating a way by which teachers may observe children to get further insight into the learning process.

TEMPO IN LEARNING

The child's individual rate of learning is often confused with capacity. A child may respond very *slowly* but learn no less than one who reacts and absorbs very quickly. Slow tempo is sometimes associated with cautiousness, sometimes with sluggishness. Rapid reactions may be due to impulsiveness and may be accompanied by either inaccuracies or high quality comprehension. In other words, rate or tempo as such can be highly individualistic or can be associated with a wide range of learning behavior.

In attempting to clarify the role of learning pace in different individuals, the teacher may ask the following questions:

Does the child work slowly, cautiously, and accurately? Or does he work slowly and inaccurately?

Does he work quickly with good quality outcome?

Or does he wish to "get it over with"?

Is he the kind of child who works at a variable pace depending on the nature of the task?

The failure to recognize that children differ in the amounts of time they need to function in the learning process poses a major threat to growth. When we expect all children to complete an assignment or master a task in a given length of time, we not only ignore the fact that people move at different rates, we actually force certain children into adopting undesirable ways of learning.

Johnny, who usually takes long to do a job, is a careful and rather profound thinker. He is not satisfied with one solution but may attempt to look at a problem from more than one point of view. He may find, on second thought, that he needs to qualify, correct, or add to something he had previously thought about. By forcing Johnny into a preset time limit, we may encourage him to take shortcuts and cut corners; thus, we may be encouraging a lower level of operation.

David needs a great deal of time because his responses are deliberate. He will not take a step unless the total plan or concept is conceived. He does not plunge into trial and error. By imposing time pressures on David, we are indeed violating a highly desirable way of thinking. We are encouraging him to be more dependent on guess-work than on reason.

Another child may move slowly because he finds the process of thinking, problem solving, and doing, laborious. This type of child generally stands to gain nothing from speeding up his tempo. Some children need to be prodded to move faster because their attention to meticulous detail is excessive and because they derive little learning benefit from dwelling on insignificant details. Others need prodding because they tend to lose sight of the goal they set out to achieve. They need to be reminded of the goal and the ways to get closer to it.

Some children move so fast they need to be slowed down. They may be satisfied with superficial achievements or they may tend to react impulsively without preplanning.

To enable each child to learn at the pace which would result in optimal learning, flexibility in scheduling, and allowances for individual tempo, variations need to be made in the classroom. This requires flexibility in class organization, curriculum development, and the guidance of the teaching-learning process.

INDEPENDENCE IN WORK

A teacher may want to know how children differ in their capacity to work independently. Who are the children who can work with a minimum of adult direction and prodding? Who are those who need quite a bit of help at the initial stage of a given assignment or task and can later proceed on their own? The teacher needs to know who are the children who need intermittent help (including those who do not ask for it vocally) and who are those who consistently need assistance.

Being aware of variation in children along this dimension can help a teacher make appropriate decisions in the area of grouping. She needs to know which children can make use of self-directed activity while the teacher is busy working with a small group or with an individual. The teacher has to plan in such a way that she will be able to get to those children who may need more help and direction when the group as a whole is working on a given project or assignment.

In assigning homework the teacher may need to know who may or may not be able to complete the work without her presence, how to vary homework assignments so that the children who are more dependent may not have to resort to excessive parental help or complete helplessness. While the teacher is working along with the present levels of development in her class, and adjusting instruction to the needs of the dependent child, she also has to work with this child toward achieving increasing independence.

If independent learning is a major educational goal, then the *ability to plan* becomes one of the major tools to achieve this goal. As

children vary in their capacity to plan, it becomes an important educational responsibility to help them in this direction.

Some children have a good sense of inner organization and can therefore plan better. They may need less direct help in planning. They can also be helpful in working in groups with other children, where they can help others acquire a more adequate capacity to plan. Others may need a great deal of teacher assistance and direction in learning how to distribute time, how to decide what they should do first, and what they should postpone.

The teacher may thus find it necessary to identify those children who can plan long-range work with appropriate time distribution and those who leave things to the last moment. She needs to know who are the children who know how to assign priority to different tasks and those who become confused when expected to attend to more than one responsibility at a time.

In trying to help the children who have difficulty with planning, the teacher must remember that while they are being helped to acquire a better sense of organization, the change may not come easily. They will need to have support in organization and timing provided from the outside by teachers, other adults, and even peers.

ATTENTIVENESS

Children vary in their attentive capacities. Some can be fully attentive for long periods of time, others for short periods of time. Some are more distractable than others; some show various levels of attention at different times. In order to be aware of individual variations in the capacity to be attentive, a teacher may keep in mind the following questions:

> *Who are the children persistent in their capacity to attend, and who are the highly distractable children (either by external factors such as noise, or by inner factors such as daydreams)?*
>
> *Are there children who have adequate attention in nonacademic activities and poor attention in academic work?*
>
> *Are there children who demonstrate good attention capabilities only in areas of special interest to them?*

Information of this nature can help the teacher become aware of the child's contact with her instruction. A teacher may thus know whether she needs to stop at intervals and check whether Johnny is still "with it"; see that Pam, who is easily distracted, works in a spot where distraction is kept at a minimum; watch Sandy's tendency to get lost in daydreams and call her back to reality by asking a question and probing her attention to a certain topic.

Awareness of individual variations in attention span can also help the teacher determine the length of assignments she should give to different youngsters in her room. Paul, who has the capacity for a long attention span, may be given a long assignment, while Josh, who tends to be distracted every few minutes, may need an assignment broken down into smaller units.

In conclusion, attentiveness is an important factor in learning, as it affects the child's capacity to attend to what is said in class by either the teacher or other students. It also affects his ability to remain attentive to a given task, which he is expected to fulfill independently. The teacher's awareness of variations in attention may help her adjust instruction to the specific attention style of an individual child, and when needed, attempt to help the child gradually change in a more positive direction.

REACTIONS TO NEW SITUATIONS

An important way in which children differ is in their reactions to new situations. A child's characteristic response to newness may affect his initial adjustment to a class at the beginning of each year, may affect a move from one school to another and even from one classroom activity to another. In order to become more keenly aware of the different ways in which children respond to new situations, a teacher may observe the children in her class in view of the following questions:

> Does the child tend to accept new situations and new learning as a challenge? Is he slow to warm up only at the very initial stage but usually comes around to handle the task with confidence? Or does he "panic" with the introduction of most new materials and situations?

At the beginning of every new school year Lisa has difficulty in getting to school. She complains about frequent headaches or stomachaches. When Lisa gets to school she enters the classroom shivering and remains very anxious most of the time. She does not seem to make much academic headway because she is too anxious to listen and work. A teacher who does not know that Lisa is having her usual reaction to a new class and a new teacher may label Lisa as "problematic" or "neurotic." The teacher may not know that she can help Lisa by introducing into the new situation as much of the familiar old as she can. She may seat Lisa close to an old friend. She may permit Lisa to begin working on some of the books she had last year. She may find out about a favorite interest Lisa has at home and structure a small group activity around it. She may try to bridge the new experience to the familiar one and thus help Lisa overcome her initial dread of the new classroom.

Burt seems comfortable in new social situations but tends to "freeze" when a completely new subject matter is introduced. His initial reaction to new learning is pessimism and avoidance. Although Burt is a capable youngster he tends to believe he would not get it right. Knowing that Burt tends to react in this manner, the teacher should give him more support during the initial stages of learning new material. She may work with him individually a few times when first introducing long division. This teacher knows that if Burt is helped to face the new concept with less trepidation, he will sail smoothly in a short time.

Teachers are often impressed by the initial enthusiasm of a few children and assume that other children should be equally enthused. If they are not, the teacher takes it to mean that these children are perhaps intellectually less able or even incapable of dealing with the new task. Sensitivity to children's reactions to new situations may often change the teacher's evaluation of the child, may help prevent unnecessary difficulties, and may facilitate learning.

KEY POINTS

1. *Intelligence is defined as a single or multifactor trait.*
2. *Guilford's multifactor theory of intelligence lists 120 different ways to be intelligent.*
3. *Intelligence tests do not measure "innate" or "natural" ability.*
4. *Binet developed the first intelligence test and based it on the concept of mental age.*
5. *Individuals from high-socioeconomic backgrounds score higher on intelligence tests than individuals from low-socioeconomic backgrounds.*
6. *Terman found that gifted children exhibited earlier physical development, better adjustment, and greater occupational success than less gifted children.*
7. *A recent study by Jencks found no relationship between high IQ and job performance or financial success.*
8. *Intelligence scores correlate fairly high with academic achievement in school.*
9. *There is concern over whether intelligence tests adequately measure the academic potential of minority group children.*

10. *Intelligence tests are criticized for emphasizing verbal ability over other types of mental abilities.*

11. *Attempts at developing culture-free intelligence tests have not been successful.*

12. *Head Start programs were established to increase the intellectual development and academic performance of deprived children.*

13. *Jensen questions the ability of such programs to accomplish these objectives because of his belief that genetic factors cause IQ differences.*

14. *Jensen believes that all social class groups have equal Level I ability (associative) but that middle-SES groups have more Level II ability (conceptual) than low-SES groups.*

15. *Correlations of IQ's of twins support the heredity point of view in the nature-nurture controversy.*

16. *Environmentalists point to studies indicating substantial changes in IQ scores when children are exposed to a more enriching or stimulating environment.*

17. *Bloom believes that educators must be environmentalists and work to develop appropriate learning situations no matter how much of a child's IQ comes from genetic factors.*

18. *Labov believes that educators have spent too much time determining how to integrate the child into the school rather than considering how the school can better accommodate its instructional program to the strengths of the child.*

19. *Lesser has shown that children from different cultural backgrounds exhibit cultural patterns of strengths and weaknesses on various tests of mental ability.*

20. *Lesser suggests that varied educational methods will suit the learning strengths of different cultural groups.*

21. *Many educators believe that the task of the school is to overcome the learning deficiencies of lower-class children by providing them with the middle-class skills that spell success in school.*

22. *Divergent thinking is associated with creativity.*

23. *Four characteristics of divergent thinking are fluency, flexibility, originality, and elaboration.*

24. *Although persons above average in intelligence are more likely to be creative, it does not mean that average or high intelligence persons are creative.*
25. *Teachers tend to prefer high IQ students to highly creative students.*
26. *Creative children are characterized by such traits as lack of rigidity, humor, willingness to attempt difficult tasks, and expression of unconventional ideas.*
27. *Cognitive styles are the consistent ways in which an individual responds to a wide range of perceptual and intellectual tasks.*
28. *Conceptual tempo is the relation between the speed with which children make a response to a problem and the number of errors they make in their response.*
29. *Rapid responders, who make many errors, are impulsive; slower responders, who tend to make fewer errors, are reflective.*
30. *Field-independent individuals are able to overcome the effects of distracting elements (the field) when they attempt to differentiate relevant aspects of a particular situation.*
31. *Field-dependent individuals operate in a more global manner and are distracted by background elements.*
32. *Field-independent individuals show greater concern for more impersonal, abstract aspects of stimuli.*
33. *Field-dependent individuals reflect a considerable degree of social sensitivity.*
34. *There is evidence that cognitive style develops from socialization practices.*
35. *Field-dependent children are handicapped in school environments, which tend to reflect the field-independent style.*
36. *Sensory modality preferences and strengths influence success in learning.*

SUGGESTIONS FOR FURTHER READING

Sperry, L. *Learning performance and individual differences.* Glenview, Ill.:

Scott, Foresman, 1972. Part three of the book includes numerous articles on learning style.

Tyler, L.E. *The psychology of human differences.* 3rd ed. New York: Appleton-Century-Crofts, 1965. A detailed discussion of the meaning of the term "intelligence," its development, and its measurement.

Whimbey, A.W., & Whimbey, L.S. *Intelligence can be taught.* New York: Dutton, 1975. The authors argue that intelligence is a skill and can be taught and learned.

The following articles critique the validity of IQ: García, J. IQ: The conspiracy. *Psychology Today.* September 1972, pp. 40–43; 92–94. Mercer, J.R. IQ: The lethal label. *Psychology Today.* September 1972, pp. 44–47; 95–97.

FOLLOW-UP ACTIVITIES

1 Recognize intellectual abilities. How can you emphasize or recognize a wider diversity of intellectual abilities in the classroom?

2 Helping low-achieving students. What do you think of the programs to help low-achieving students? Do you think that Head Start and similar programs for minority and low-socioeconomic students must modify their methods?

3 **Recognize learning styles.** Would you have been more successful in certain classes if teachers had been more cognizant of your learning style? Give specific examples of how teacher awareness could have helped you.

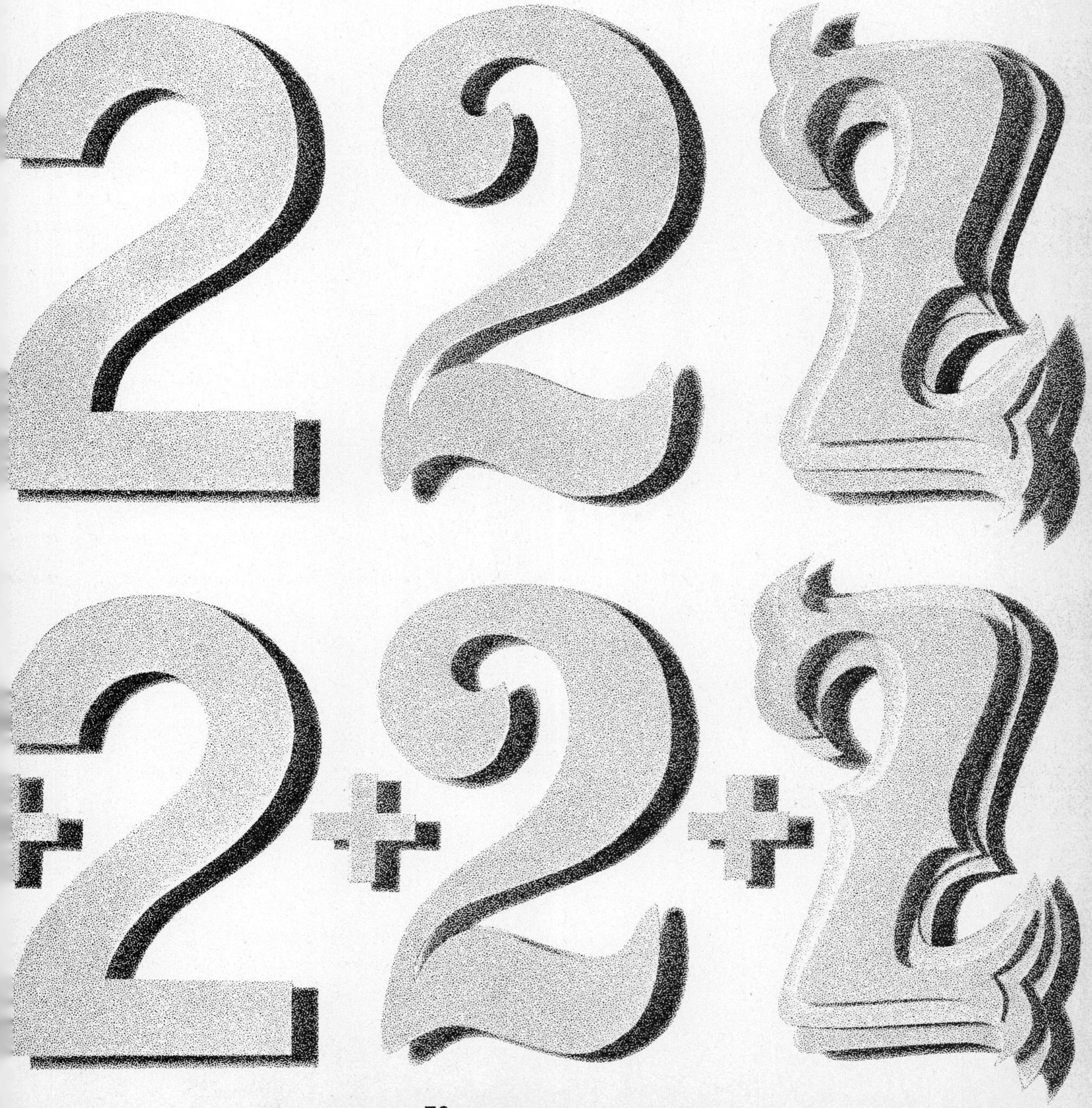

4 Fostering creativity. Goertzel and Goertzel (1962), in *Cradles of Eminence,* studied the lives of eminent twentieth-century Americans and found that most of them experienced a great deal of stress in their lives, particularly in school. The authors concluded that it may not be possible to be both creative and comfortable. Do you accept this view? Is suffering a prerequisite of creativity? What implications do your views have for education?

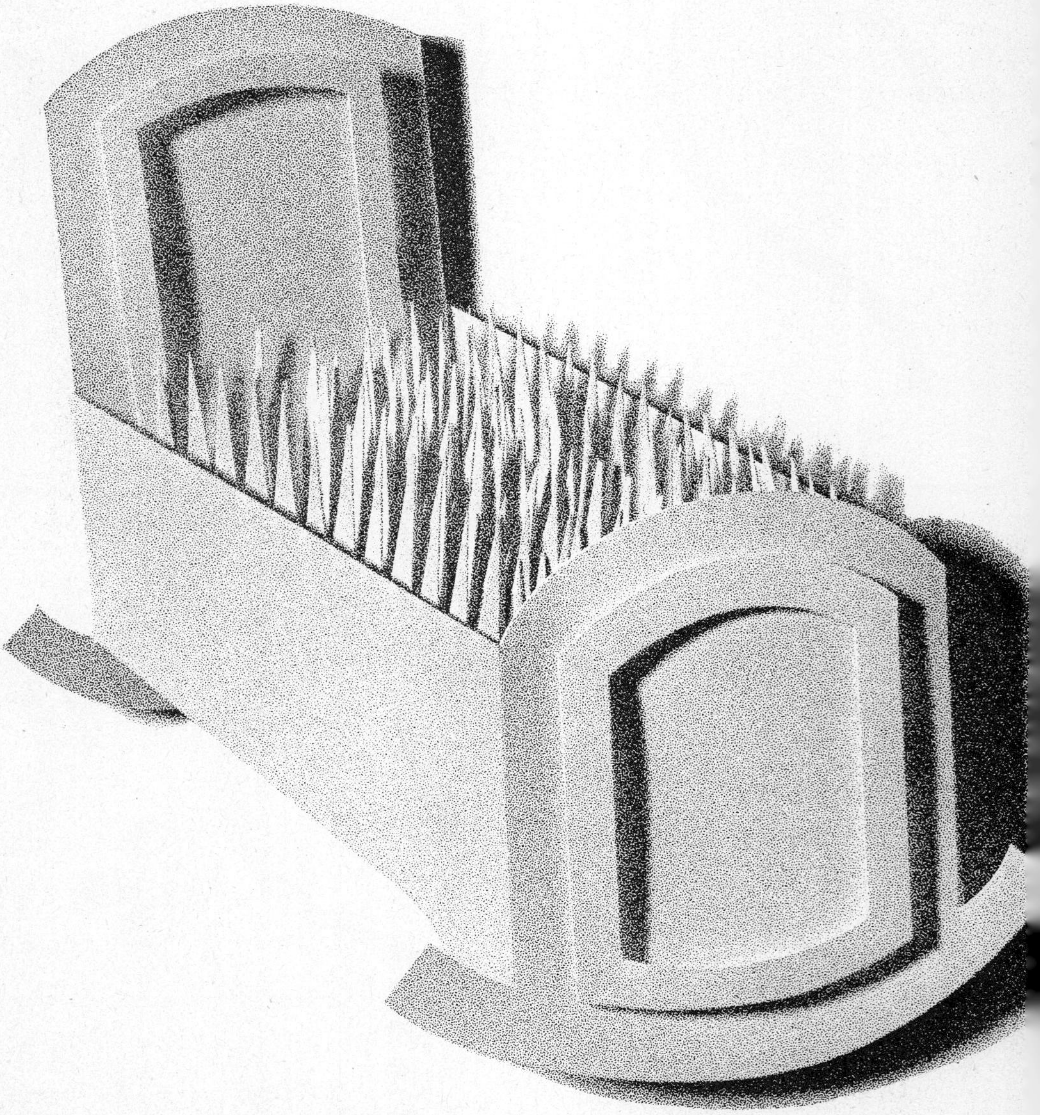

5 Consider Jensen's proposal. Jensen has suggested that Level I and Level II individuals follow different curricula. The former, or associative learning level, provides a closely controlled environment for learning. The latter, or conceptual learning level, leaves the field open for learning. Does this sound like a reasonable proposal? What are some of the implications of Jensen's proposal? You will find Bickham's (1974) article, "The Educational Implications of Arthur Jensen's Research," pertinent to your discussion.

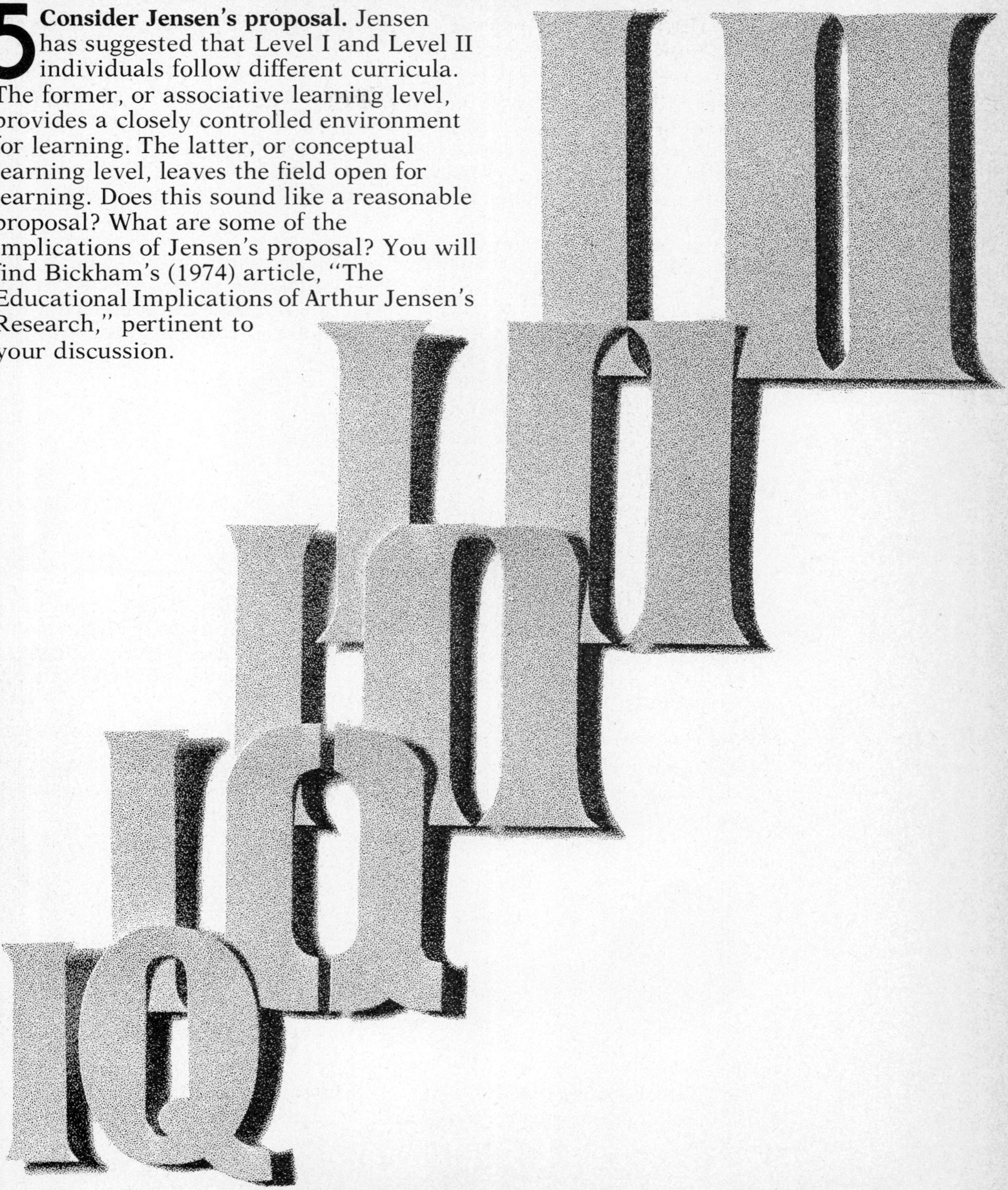

6 Identify differences in learning styles. This observational activity will awaken you to the range of individual differences in the classroom. Listed below are pairs of terms that summarize opposite types of thinking, perceiving, and reacting. Observe students in a public school or college class and pick out — for as many of the opposites as you can — a student who exemplifies each extreme. Then briefly describe that style of behavior. Finally, analyze the appropriateness of the teacher's behavior toward the student (Biehler, 1974b).

Impulsive — gives the first answer, is eager to respond quickly.

Reflective — thinks things over, is deliberate and cautious in responding.

Short attention span — is unable to stick with an assignment or pay attention for more than a few minutes, is easily distracted.

Long attention span—is capable of concentrating on an assignment for an extended period of time, has a high degree of resistance to distractions.

Resistance to change — is unwilling to accept unexpected or unconventional views or evidence.

Flexibility — adapts well to new, different, or unexpected points of view.

Convergent production — seeks or provides the one right answer or a conventional answer.

Divergent production — responds in a nonconventional, unexpected way.

7 Educating special children. Teachers often find students in their classes who are different from the average student: the orthopedically handicapped, blind or partially sighted, deaf or hard-of-hearing, those with speech handicaps or learning disabilities, the mentally retarded, gifted, and creative.

Select one of these differences and report on its nature and the educational procedures that will permit children with such differences to learn. The following books provide appropriate material for your report: *Learning Disabilities* by McCarthy and McCarthy (1969) and *Educating Exceptional Children* (2nd ed.) by Kirk (1972). The following journals carry articles devoted to special children:

Academic Therapy Quarterly
American Annals of the Deaf
American Journal of Mental Deficiency
Educational Technology
Exceptional Children
Journal of Creative Behavior
Journal of Learning Disabilities
Journal of School Health
Journal of Special Education
Journal of Speech and Hearing Disorders
MR/Mental Retardation
Physical Therapy
Rehabilitation Literature
Today's Health
Volta Review (hearing problems)

3

INDIVIDUAL DIFFERENCES II: PERSONALITY AND MOTIVATIONAL FACTORS

ORIENTATION

A student's personality and motivational tendencies shape his academic adjustment and performance. Certain students demand modifications in teaching procedures by their very helplessness. Some students don't believe that they are as good as other students, some students won't take risks and attempt challenging tasks because they are afraid to fail, some students believe that failure is inevitable for them, and some students perform poorly under pressure. In this chapter, I shall identify some important personality and motivational factors that affect classroom behavior and success in learning situations.

SELF-CONCEPT

The self-concept, a person's ideas about herself, is one of the most important single factors affecting behavior (Combs et al., 1971). Educators have become increasingly aware of the impact that an individual's self-concept and self-esteem, the value or judgment she places on herself and her behavior, have on her classroom behavior and achievement.[1] A student's problems in school may have their sole source in her lack of a positive self-concept and self-esteem.

The student "learns" to regard herself negatively because the self-concept develops over a period of time as the child assimilates her experiences with significant people in her life — parents, peers, and teachers. By the time a child reaches school, she has acquired a good deal of information about herself from others and begins to "act like" the type of person she conceives herself to be. Her initial school experiences often reinforce these beliefs. Some students see themselves as successful achievers, but others believe that they are inadequate and inferior to their classmates.

In an extensive investigation of the antecedents of self-esteem among 1700 fifth- and sixth-grade children, Coopersmith (1967) found that positive self-esteem persons viewed themselves along the following general lines:

> I consider myself a valuable and important person, and am at least as good as others of my age and training. I am regarded as someone worthy of respect and consideration. . . . I'm able to exert an influence upon people and events, partly because my views are sought and respected and partly because I'm able and willing to present and defend those views. I have a pretty definite idea of what I think is right . . . and have a fairly good understanding of the kind of person I am. I enjoy new and challenging tasks and don't get upset when things don't go well right off the bat. (p. 47)

At the same time, a similar monologue by an individual with negative self-esteem might proceed as follows:

> I don't think I'm a very important or likeable person, and I don't see much reason for anyone else to like me. I can't do many of the things I'd like to do or do them the way I think they should be done. I'm not sure of my ideas and abilities, and

[1]Many psychologists believe that the self has two aspects — concepts and feelings — and therefore distinguish between "self-concept" and "self-esteem." Self-concept is the total organization of the perceptions an individual has of herself. However, other psychologists fail to make this distinction and refer to "self-concept" as a global term including personal judgment.

> there's a good likelihood that other people's ideas and work are better than my own. Other people don't pay much attention to me and given what I know about myself I can't say I blame them. I don't like new or unusual occurrences and prefer sticking to known and safe ground. . . . I don't have much control over what happens to me and I expect that things will get worse rather than better. (p. 47)

Of course, the characterization of a person with moderate self-esteem falls between these two descriptions, and is more low-keyed in its evaluation of competence and expectations.

The student with poor self-esteem often expects to fail and is likely to throw in the towel. This tendency explains the significant relationship between positive self-concept and high self-esteem, and school achievement. Students possessing positive attributes are generally high achievers, whereas students with negative beliefs and feelings about themselves are usually underachievers and failures in school (Bledsoe, 1964; Brookover et al., 1964).

This relationship between self-esteem and achievement occurs very early in school. In one study (Wattenberg & Clifford, 1964), the investigators gave kindergarten children an intelligence test and a self-esteem test before they began learning to read. Two and a half years later, when the children were in the second grade, they were tested for reading achievement. The results of the earlier self-esteem test were better indicators of current reading achievement than was the children's earlier performance on the IQ test.

The implication of such research is that some children are poor readers because they believe they cannot read. Such children are caught in a vicious cycle. They believe they can't read and so they avoid it. Because they avoid reading, they fail to get practice in the school and don't read well when called upon. Running the gauntlet like this only reinforces their initial belief about their reading ability. This display of behavior is the *self-fulfilling prophecy*. Adults as well as children are victims of the beliefs they hold about themselves.

Three from a number of factors especially mold the child's developing self-concept: school experiences, child-rearing practices, and physical growth and development. You, as a teacher, can exert considerable influence on the direction of a child's self-concept by establishing a constructive learning environment in the classroom and by communicating with your students. The child's concept of his ability grows mainly from his performance on classroom tasks, and you can nourish his self-concept by arranging the conditions for his success. Chapter 4 will guide you in influencing a student's self-concept.

Most self-concept theorists believe that the quality of the

parent-child relationship builds up or tears down self-concept and self-esteem among children and adolescents. Coopersmith (1967) found three child-rearing conditions related to a high self-esteem: parental acceptance of children, parental enforcement of clearly defined behavioral limits and rules, and parental respect for the freedom of their children's actions within the established limits.

Last, the self-concept lessens or grows in response to reactions from others concerning our physical appearance and body size, as well as by activities in which success is reliant on body size and/or physical skills. For example, the awkward child or adolescent who does not possess the agility for games or sports highly valued by his peers will not be accepted with open arms when the time comes to select team members. Do you know what it feels like to be always selected *last* for team competition?

In addition to awkwardness or lack of agility, physical features — height, weight, complexion, or general body proportions — are very much related to feelings about one's self. Evidence indicates that persons who demean their bodies also have negative views about themselves (Jourard & Secord, 1955a).

Adolescent males and females are influenced by mass media stereotypes of the beautiful body. Magazines like *Playboy* and *Playgirl* reinforce ideas about body build. Jourard and Secord (1955b) found that the ideal height and weight for college women were 5 feet, 5 inches, 120 pounds, with a measurement of 35, 24, and 35 inches for the bust, waist, and hips, respectively. The more a woman's dimensions deviated from this ideal, the more she disliked her dimensions.

In studies of men's perceptions of satisfactory body builds, men consistently rated the wide-shouldered, narrow-hipped, athletic-type body build over the obese or thin body build (Brodsky, 1954). In fact, boys as young as six years of age are in close agreement when it comes to assigning certain personality characteristics to particular body build (Staffieri, 1967).

SELF-CONCEPT OF DISADVANTAGED CHILDREN

For a long time it was commonly accepted and supported by research that the self-concept of disadvantaged children was lower than that of advantaged children. Recently more investigators have been finding no differences in self-concept between the two groups, or even higher self-concepts among disadvantaged children (Soares & Soares, 1969). These conflicting results may be attributed to the various definitions and measurements of self-concepts. Miller and Woock (1970) suggest that disadvantaged children may score high, or at least as well as advantaged children, on tests of general self-concept but score lower on tests of self-concept related to achievement, that is, the self measured against the standards and expectations of the school. We must be cautious in attributing negative self-concepts to all disadvantaged children.

SELF-CONCEPT INSTRUMENTS

A number of self-concept instruments are available for teachers' use: the Self-Esteem Inventory (Coopersmith, 1967), the How-I-See-Myself Scale (Gordon, 1968), and the Bledsoe Self-Concept Scale (Bledsoe, 1967). You can check Buros' *Mental Measurements Yearbook* for descriptions of various self-concept tests. Purkey (1970) lists some guidelines for using these tests:

> 1. *When working with young students, items should be read to the students while the children read silently.*
> 2. *Stress the fact that there are no right or wrong answers. The student is to express those ideas he holds true about himself.*
> 3. *All self-report inventories should be administered under conditions which are as unthreatening as possible.*
> 4. *Maintain the confidentiality of the results. (p. 62)*

LOCUS OF CONTROL

Some students blame someone or something else for their poor performance: a poor test, a confusing book, or an incoherent teacher. These students believe external aspects of their environment wield control over their downfall (or over their success). They see themselves as powerless to counteract this trend. Psychologists classify such personality dispositions under one aspect of the construct *locus of control*, which pertains to how an individual perceives the link between his behavior and its consequences and whether or not he accepts responsibility for his actions.

Much of the conceptualization and research in this area stems from the social-learning theory of Rotter (1966), who viewed locus of control as having two dimensions — external and internal. An "external" person feels that he has little control over his fate and fails to perceive a cause-and-effect relationship between his actions and their consequences. An "internal" person holds the reins of his fate securely in his grip and understands that effort and reward are correlated.

The orientation of a student is extremely important. If she does not anticipate her teacher's approval as a response to her efforts, she will not be disposed to strive for success. Children will work harder at tasks if they believe they (rather than chance or the teacher) are responsible for the success they achieve (Rotter, 1966; Lefcourt, 1966). As they work harder and achieve success, they acquire better self-concepts of their ability.

Rotter (1966) has developed a twenty-three-item Internal-External Locus of Control Scale for classification purposes. The following are items included in this scale. In each instance the "a" alternative represents external control:

1. a. *Many times I feel that I have little influence over the things that happen to me.*
   b. *It is impossible for me to believe that chance or luck plays an important role in my life.*
2. a. *Without the right breaks one cannot be an effective leader.*
   b. *Capable people who fail to become leaders have not taken advantage of their opportunities.*
3. a. *Getting a good job depends mainly on being in the right place at the right time.*
   b. *Becoming a success is a matter of hard work; luck has little or nothing to do with it.*

Crandall, Katkovsky, and Crandall (1965) developed the Intellectual Achievement Responsibility Scale, which determines children's beliefs about personal responsibility for their success or failure in academic achievement situations. This instrument is suitable for children from the third grade through high school. The following are some of the items in this instrument:

1. *If a teacher passes you to the next grade, would it probably be*
   a. *because she liked you, or*
   b. *because of the work you did?*
2. *When you have trouble understanding something in school, is it usually*
   a. *because the teacher didn't explain it clearly, or*
   b. *because you didn't listen carefully?*
3. *If a teacher says to you, "Try to do better," would it be*
   a. *because this is something she might say to get pupils to try harder, or*
   b. *because your work wasn't as good as usual?*

There is some evidence that parental behavior is related to the development of control in their children. In several studies (Katkovsky, Crandall, & Good, 1967; Davis & Phares, 1969), it was found that parents who were identified as "warm," "encouraging," and "approving," and who expected children to be independent at an

early age, produced children who developed a more internal locus of control than those children with parents identified as "dominant," "rejecting," and "critical." It appears that the parental factors leading to an internal orientation are similar to the factors leading to the development of positive self-concept and high self-esteem (Solomon & Oberlander, 1974).

The sense of internal control is stronger in white children than in Blacks, and stronger in the middle than in the low SES population (Battle & Rotter, 1963; Crandall et al., 1965). In general, minority group children do not experience a sense of control over their environment. This finding is not surprising, since minority children have come up against many barriers to their efforts to influence their environment. The more an individual finds that he cannot control the sources from which important events in his life spring, the more external a sense of control he develops (Solomon & Oberlander, 1974).

Coleman et al. (1966) found that belief in internal control was the most important indicator of school achievement for black students. Black children who exhibited a sense of internal control enjoyed considerably higher achievement than those who exhibited a sense of external control. The same result occurs in white populations. Coleman also found that the extent of desegregation in the school affected the sense of control: As the proportion of white students in the school increased, black students' sense of control grew stronger.

A considerable amount of research distinguishes between externals and internals. Externals score higher than internals on measures of anxiety, suspicion of others, and hostility. Internals typically perceive themselves to be effective, assertive, and independent (Solomon & Oberlander, 1974). Internals spend more time in intellectual activities and academic pursuits (Crandall, Katkovsky, & Crandall, 1965) and exhibit more achievement motivation: They investigate and plan for college and spend more time doing homework.

ANXIETY

It is not uncommon for teachers to use the term "falls to pieces" or "chokes up" to describe the behavior of some children who consistently perform below par in situations characterized by a high degree of stress. Many college students report these same feelings after taking important examinations or aptitude tests like the Scholastic Aptitude Test (SAT). While some students strive under examination pressure, other students become highly anxious and cannot function at an optimum level.

Anxiety describes the emotional state associated with apprehension or fear. Whenever an individual's assessment of the situational demands leads him to conclude that he may not be able to handle the tasks, he is ripe for the various consequences of anxiety (Hamachek, 1971).

The type and degree of anxiety differs widely among students. For some, anxiety is a generalized fear of the total school situation and for others, a fear of specific aspects of the school environment such as teachers, peers, particular subject areas, or tests. In extreme cases (as in school phobias), the fear is so great that the child may refuse to go to school.

Test anxiety is a specific form of anxiety about academic and intellectual evaluation. Educators are especially concerned about this type of anxiety because it increases through the elementary grades and becomes more strongly (negatively) related to indices of intellectual and academic performance (Sarason, Hill, & Zimbardo, 1964). This relationship probably occurs because evaluation and grades become more important each year in school.

Why do students become anxious? Two sets of factors contribute: factors that are immediately and directly responsible for anxiety reactions and factors that have had an impact during the child's early years of life and whose vibrations spread throughout his life (Phillips, Martin, & Meyers, 1972). The first set of factors relates to such stress conditions in the environment as an ambiguous threat (for example, the child who anticipates his new class in September), a situational constraint, and a feeling of inability to cope. The second set of factors is indirect and includes unpleasant preschool and elementary school experiences, racial-ethnic minority status and/or lower social-class status, a nonsupportive parent-child relationship, and sex identification.

Sarason et al. (1960) undertook an extensive study on school anxiety and test situations and provided a good deal of information about both the direct and indirect antecedents of anxiety. First, they found that bright children, as well as average and slow children, are often anxious about tests and classroom performance. Second, they attributed a major role to parental attitudes in the initial formation of anxiety in children. Mothers of high-anxiety children probably have conflicts about their own adequacy and depend on the opinions of others. They consistently make demands on the child that she feels are difficult to meet and that lead to failure and the development of a poor self-image. When the child begins school she transfers her anticipation of negative evaluation from the parent to the teacher and becomes anxious when the teacher presents her with any type of test.

Last, the researchers found girls to be much more anxious than boys. Before the male chauvinists reading this book raise their banners, they should read the researchers' explanation for this finding. They attributed this difference between the sexes to the boys' defensiveness to admitting anxiety. In boys, such admission is not culturally accepted; it is unmasculine. However, whether or not girls admit to anxiety feelings, their femininity is not called into question.

Anxiety levels can be inferred in a variety of ways. One of the easiest ways is to ask the child how he feels about a particular situation or task.[2] There are also physiological indicators like severe headaches or stomach disorders that have no physical cause. Nail biting, sweating, irregularity in speech or motor coordination, restlessness, and general distraction are also warning signs for the teacher.

Last, tests can be used to identify anxiety. One of the most widely used is the Test Anxiety Scale for Children (TASC), containing thirty questions about test situations to which the child answers "yes" or "no." Some sample questions are: "Do you worry a lot before you take a test?" and "Do you think you worry more about school than other children?"

Anxiety has a number of consequences that can cause the child social as well as academic problems. Most highly anxious children have lower self-concepts, blame themselves for their failures, and daydream, flights of fantasy that compensate for their lack of success (Sarason et al., 1960).

During adolescence, anxiety can lead to feelings of inadequacy, associated with hostility toward school (Phillips, Hindsman, & McGuire, 1960). High anxiety is also associated with relatively low performance for poor and average students at the school and university levels. Poor reading is most closely related to anxiety in the earlier grades, with arithmetic becoming more associated with anxiety toward the end of the elementary grades. At the college level (particularly for the middle range of scholastic aptitudes) high anxiety is associated with lower grades (Spielberger & Katzenmeyer, 1959).

There is also a negative correlation between anxiety and intelligence test scores: the higher the test anxiety, the lower the IQ score. To the argument that people with high anxiety are also less intelligent, and as a result, score lower on IQ tests, Gaudry and Spielberger (1971) respond: High-anxiety students perform as well as low-anxiety

[2]Although this procedure may seem too obvious to mention, I have witnessed that many teachers begin their problem solving by calling in specialists to initiate personality assessments of the child without first discussing the behavior problem with the parent or child. A good rule to follow when confronted with any serious behavior problem is first to talk to the child about his behavior. You may be surprised about the amount of information that you can glean. Also check the child's health records for physical clues to his behavior — for example, poor vision or hearing. When these avenues have been exhausted and the problem still persists, then call on a professional to assist you.

students on nonstressful and more structured tasks. Other researchers have found a more plausible explanation. Highly anxious students react to a normal intelligence test situation as they would to any regular examination seen as a stressful situation, but when intelligence tests or learning tasks are presented under "nontest" situations, high-anxiety students perform as well as or better than low-anxiety students (Sarason et al., 1960; Wrightsman, 1962).

The debilitating effect of anxiety on complex learning tasks has been illustrated in a number of studies. Waite et al. (1958) selected a group of high-anxiety and low-anxiety students equated for IQ. They found that children with high test anxiety began a task with as much skill as children with low test anxiety but deteriorated as the task progressed. By the end of the task, the highly anxious children were performing much worse than the low-anxiety group.

In another study, Dittes (1959) linked self-esteem, anxiety, and academic achievement. He found that when individuals with low self-esteem were faced with an anxiety-provoking situation, they were inclined to make hasty, impulsive judgments. On the other hand, high self-esteem persons in similar situations, were more deliberate and careful in making judgments.

Achievement Motivation

The school experience that creates the most harmful anxiety is repeated failure. Atkinson and Feather (1966) have developed a useful model for explaining the disintegration of a student's motivation for achievement when past learning experiences have yielded feelings of inadequacy and fear of future failure. They posit that the avoidance of the pain caused by failure becomes the student's major orientation in school. Students shun activities that they believe will result in failure and avoid competition whenever possible. For many of these students, admitting to the teacher that they can't accomplish the task is less anxiety-producing than trying and failing.

Holt (1964) provides an excellent analysis of some of the strategies students use to protect themselves in the classroom. The following is Holt's description of the school behaviors that highly anxious children may adopt:

> The strategies of most of these kids have been consistently self-centered, self-protective, aimed above all else at avoiding trouble, embarrassment, punishment, disapproval, or loss of status. This is particularly true of the ones who have had a tough time

> in school. When they get a problem, I can read their thoughts on their faces, I can almost hear them, "Am I going to get this right? Probably not; what'll happen to me when I get it wrong? Will the teacher get mad? Will the other kids laugh at me? Will my mother and father hear about it? Will they keep me back this year? Why am I so dumb?" And so on.
>
> Even in the room periods, where I did all I could to make the work non-threatening, I was continually amazed and appalled to see the children hedging their bets, covering their losses in advance, trying to fix things so that whatever happened they could feel they had been right, or if wrong, no more wrong than anyone else. "I think it will sort of balance." They are fence-straddlers, afraid ever to commit themselves — and at the age of ten. . . .
>
> These self-limiting and self-defeating strategies are dictated above all else by fear. For many years I have been asking myself why intelligent children act unintelligently at school. The simple answer is, "Because they're scared.". . .
>
> . . . Perhaps most people do not recognize fear in children when they see it. They can read the grossest signs of fear; they know what the trouble is when a child clings howling to his mother, but the subtler signs of fear escape them. It is these signs, in children's faces, noises, and gestures, in their movements and ways of working, that tell me plainly that most children in school are scared most of the time, many of them very scared. Like good soldiers, they control their fears, live with them, and adjust themselves to them. But the trouble is, and here is a vital difference between school and war, that the adjustments children make to their fears are almost wholly bad, destructive of their intelligence and capacity. The scared fighter may be the best fighter, but the scared learner is always a poor learner. (pp. 48–49)

What strategies have you used to protect yourself from the possibilities of failure? Have you ever raised your hand early in a class period to answer a question, knowing that the instructor might not call on you later? Have you remained silent when asked a question by an instructor, hoping that if you paused long enough he would rephrase the question once or twice until he either gave you the answer or called on someone else? If you stop to think about it, you will be able to recall numerous incidents of classroom strategies that you used to protect yourself from failing.

I can identify with the following situation, and it may be uncomfortably familiar to you, too: A common practice in language

classes is to require students to take turns translating sentences into English. As the instructor moves down the row asking one student after another to translate, the anxious student is not paying attention to each translation; instead, he is counting down the row to locate the sentence he will have to translate and begins covertly practicing the task. During this time he has missed the translations of all the previous sentences. Learning all the sentences is vital to the concept of the particular lesson, but the student is more motivated to avoid failure than to learn the lesson.

Atkinson and Feather (1966) state that any competitive situation arouses one of two major motivations: the need to achieve success (achievement motivation) and the need to avoid failure. Some students work hard for success without seriously worrying about the possibility of failure; other students think less about succeeding than about avoiding failure. The two researchers have found that a person in whom motivations to achieve are stronger than motivations to avoid failure sets herself goals of intermediate difficulty, while a person with the opposite motivational tendency avoids tasks of intermediate difficulty and prefers easier or more difficult tasks. Achievement-motivated persons like moderate risks in which their efforts are neither doomed to failure nor guaranteed success. Avoiders of failure like very easy or difficult tasks because they are certain of succeeding at an easy task and they can rationalize failing a difficult task — either way they can't lose!

Since high standards of performance are stressed in most classrooms, persons motivated to succeed (M_s) will work harder than persons motivated to avoid failure (M_{af}). Consequently, Weiner (1967) suggests that persons in whom M_s is greater than M_{af} should receive challenging work and persons in whom M_{af} is greater than M_s should initially receive work in which success is fairly certain. As M_{af} individuals enjoy more success in the classroom, they may become more secure and begin attempting more difficult tasks.

The motivation to play it safe can be unproductive and lead to poor academic performance. If a student repeats the same math problems over and over again or repeatedly studies the same history material, he will not increase his mastery of new content. In contrast, children with M_s proceed to difficult or more challenging material following success and master more course material.

The behavior of persons with M_{af} following failure is also not conducive to academic success. They turn to the most dissimilar task the second time around, thus avoiding the problem. Persons with M_s select moderately similar tasks the second time around, thus obtaining further practice in the general area in which they experienced failure. Smith (1969) states:

> Willingness to move to new things following success and to try again following failure are important personality tendencies affecting academic performance. If a child's proclivities are observed and understood to follow from his motivational makeup, the teacher may be able to guide his selection of activities more effectively. (p. 243)

The teacher's task, therefore, is to help the child with M_{af} avoid counterproductive behavior in attempting to achieve academic success.

Children's achievement motives either hack away at or build up their persistence. Smith (1964) found that students with strong M_s leave an exam more quickly than students with strong M_{af} when they perceive the questions as easy, but the reverse is true when they perceive the questions as more difficult. In addition, Crandall (1969) reviewed studies showing that children with higher expectancies of success generally persist longer in attempting to solve problems than children with lower expectancies.

A number of parental practices have been associated with the presence of high achievement motivation in children. Winterbottom (1953) studied the parents of thirty middle-class boys (ages 8 to 10) and found mothers of boys with high achievement motivation (1) set higher standards for their children, (2) expected independence and mastery behavior to occur at an earlier age, and (3) more often used affectionate rewards such as kissing and hugging than did mothers of boys with low achievement motivation.

In a subsequent study, Rosen and D'Andrade (1959) found that in addition to self-reliance training, parents also provided direct achievement training in the goals and standards they set for their children and the methods of control they used to ensure that these standards were maintained. They observed parents interacting with their sons while they were attempting a task. Parents of boys who had shown high need for achievement typically set higher standards for their boys, expected more improvement, and controlled behavior more directly by expressions of warmth and rejection than did parents of boys with low achievement needs.

Need for Affiliation

Not all students are achievement motivated. Some students have a greater affiliation need — a desire to establish and maintain close, friendly interpersonal relations. Younger children often express this need by wanting to be with friends, to sit next to the teacher, and, in general, to be liked. Older children often manifest their affiliation need by being extremely sensitive to the desires of the peer group. Coleman (1961) has shown that capable adolescents sometimes play down the importance of attaining good grades to escape disapproval from friends.

Sutter (1967) measured students' need for affiliation by giving them an exercise to solve, either working alone or in pairs. She found that students high in affiliation need achieved better working in paired settings, while those low in affiliation need achieved better working alone. In addition, highly anxious students learned more effectively alone, while less anxious students learned more in the interpersonal setting. Working in pairs was an anxiety-producing situation for the highly anxious students, who compared themselves to their peers. Working alone did not produce such anxiety.

How many times do teachers place students in groups because they believe that students will benefit from this type of instruction? Yet Sutter's study suggests that some students are better off working alone.

Students with either achievement or affiliation needs respond differently to teacher feedback. French (1958) identified different tendencies in students with a strong motivation to achieve and those with a strong need for affiliation. Students with high achievement motivation performed better when the teacher provided feedback relevant to the task performed; those with high affiliation motivation responded better to feedback of a more personal nature.

LEVEL OF ASPIRATION

Level of aspiration is an important psychological construct that will further enhance your understanding of achievement behavior. This construct is particularly important in education today because of the emphasis on independent work, as in learning centers, and student selection of personal goals.

Research indicates that repeated success or failure can influence a student's goal setting or level of aspiration — the level of performance to which an individual expects to rise on a given task. A student may informally reveal such information when you ask him what grade he is trying for on the next test or how many problems he thinks he will get correct on the next assignment. Success perpetuates goal setting and leads to a higher level of aspiration. Failure tends to lower the aspiration level (Sears, 1940).

Of course, teachers can't guarantee that all students will be successful. On the other hand, you can ensure that no student repeatedly experiences failure. In addition to lowered aspirations, successive or prolonged failure eventually leads students to set unrealistic goals, lose interest in the activity in which they have failed, and develop a negative self-concept.

Mahone (1960) completed a study of vocational aspirations among college students that illustrated the danger of continued failure: Students may unrealistically plunge into tasks that are much too difficult for them. He measured the achievement motivation and fear of failure (from a measure of test anxiety) in his subjects. Test anxiety and achievement motivation are generally not correlated with each other. Subjects may be high in one but not the other, or either high or low in both. Mahone separated his subjects into these different combinations and determined how their vocational aspirations varied. Each subject filled out a vocational questionnaire that indicated his objectives, his concept of the skills required, and an estimate of his own relative skill. These answers were then compared with an assessment of the subjects' actual abilities made by two clinical psychologists, using a number of factors.

The results are shown in Table 3.1. Subjects high in failure

TABLE 3.1
ACHIEVEMENT MOTIVATION, FAILURE ANXIETY, AND REALISM OF VOCATIONAL ASPIRATION.

TESTED LEVEL			*VOCATIONAL ASPIRATIONS*	
ACHIEVEMENT MOTIVATION	*FAILURE ANXIETY*	*NUMBER OF SUBJECTS*	*PERCENTAGE OF GROUP* Realistic	Unrealistic
High	High	31	48%	52%
High	Low	36	75	25
Low	High	28	39	61
Low	Low	40	68	32

Data from Mahone ("Fear of Failure and Unrealistic Vocational Aspiration," *Journal of Abnormal and Social Psychology*, 1960) in Sylvia Farnham-Diggory, *Cognitive Processes in Education* (Harper & Row, 1972), p. 202.

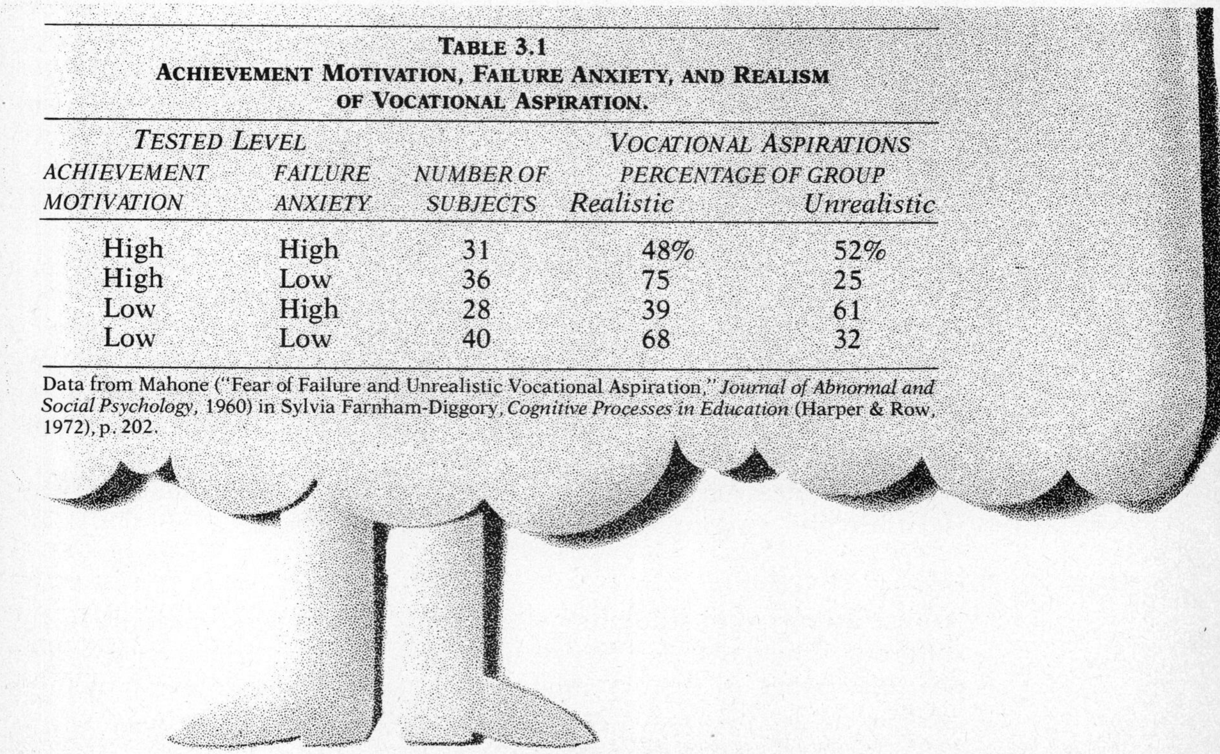

anxiety were unrealistic about their vocational futures: Eighteen percent of the unrealistic subjects were underaspiring and 82% were overaspiring, both groups being unrealistic in opposite directions. Subjects low in failure anxiety were more realistic about their vocational aspirations, particularly if they were also high in achievement motivation.

Mahone's study points out that although students' level of aspiration may not decrease after repeated failure, something as detrimental may occur: They may show a paradoxical increase in aspirations as they dream of success (Farnham-Diggory, 1972).

The following excerpt provides some suggestions for applying motivational techniques in the classroom (Gorman, 1974). Can you think of some other procedures? I will present additional discussions of motivational procedures under various learning theories in Chapters 6, 7, and 8.

WAYS TO MOTIVATE STUDENTS

GENERAL

Use a variety of motivating techniques: personal goals, practical value of a subject, individual interests, felt needs, and praise. Motivating students is often difficult; having a repertoire of techniques will prove valuable. Emphasize intrinsic motives such as curiosity, involvement, and discovery as much as possible. When necessary use extrinsic incentives to a lesser extent.

CURIOSITY

Provoke curiosity in students before starting a topic by pointing up a problem or conflict, or giving a pre-test to make them realize what they don't know about the topic. Arouse surprise and a feeling of contradiction in students by presenting a phenomenon that violates their expectations or runs counter to their experience and former training, e.g., plants that live without sunlight or chlorophyll (fungi). Arouse doubt, uncertainty, bafflement by giving students a problem with no indications for its solution, e.g., how to find one's position (latitude and longitude) in the middle of the desert.

ATTENTION

Arouse attention in students by starting a class with something novel, different, unusual, e.g., a brainstorming demonstration or a copy of an old newspaper in history. Maintain attention and interest through

From R. M. Gorman, *The Psychology of Classroom Learning* (Columbus, Ohio: Charles E. Merrill, 1974), pp. 140-142. Reprinted by permission.

variety and change; never start a class the same way three times in a row.

Level of Aspiration

Provide for different levels of aspiration among students by encouraging them to strive for levels of performance in keeping with their abilities and by having differentiated materials, activities, and projects available for students of different ability and aspiration levels. This is as important for the student's involvement as it is difficult for a teacher. The contract system and the task-oriented nongraded programs can be of help here.

With individual ability levels in mind, set standards and provide tasks of intermediate difficulty that are within the reach of students but still offer some challenge. Provide easier tasks for students who are discouraged because of low or failing grades. Mastering easier tasks will help them set realistic — and gradually higher — levels of aspiration for their work.

Achievement Motivation

On occasion, try to increase the basic achievement motivation of some students through talking with them, having them read about highly motivated persons, putting them in with a group of highly motivated students, etc. Chances of an increase in achievement motivation are greater with above average socioeconomic class students. Make students aware of their successes and the satisfaction they bring through comments such as: "You really did well in that," "Didn't it feel good to get so many right?" etc. Try to divert students' attention away from their failures by not threatening or punishing them or dwelling on their errors.

Reinforcement

Use praise and encouragement often, particularly for average and slower students and those who are more introverted and lack self-assurance. Give personal, encouraging comments on tests and other work rather than just a grade. Inform students regularly on how they are doing in a course, the sooner after a test or assignment the better. Use positive comments as much as possible.

Sex Differences

Sex differences in the area of cognitive functioning have been found to be minimal. I shall discuss sex differences in this chapter because more significant differences appear in the affective area.

Although there are no sex differences in general intelligence or ability, girls excel at verbal tasks and boys at mathematical and visual-spatial tasks. On standardized achievement tests girls score higher than boys in subjects requiring verbal abilities, perceptual speed, and accuracy, and boys surpass the girls in subjects requiring various reasoning and spatial skills. Girls receive higher grades throughout elementary school with boys closing the gap during high school. More boys are nonreaders, comprising 75 to 85% of all reading disabilities in the upper elementary grades (Stanchfield, 1973).

In regard to personality differences, girls are generally more dependent and have a higher degree of anxiety, while boys are more aggressive and have a higher expectation of success. The differences between the sexes in aggressiveness and expectancy of success are the most conclusive finding among these traits. There is considerable disagreement on the other two traits of dependency and anxiety (Maccoby & Jacklin, 1974). It is only on self-report studies on dependency and anxiety that girls score consistently higher than boys. As a result, we do not have conclusive evidence that boys *are* less anxious or less dependent than girls, only that boys consistently report less anxiety and dependency.

The relationship between these personality characteristics and intellectual performance differs for boys and girls. For example, timidity, caution, and other components of anxiety are positively related to IQ for boys but not for girls. Impulsiveness and aggressiveness, which are negatively related to a number of academic measures for boys, may actually aid the achievement of girls.

Maccoby (1966) proposes an integrative hypothesis in which the personality dimension of passivity-activity is curvilinearly related to intellectual performance. Boys and girls occupy different positions on this dimension as indicated in Figure 3.1.

Extremely passive and extremely active boys will perform the worst, but those who occupy the intermediate positions on this dimension will perform optimally. Maccoby suggests that for the best academic performance, most girls need to be less passive and inhibited and most boys need to be less impulsive. She makes a parallel analysis for anxiety, which is also curvilinearly related to academic performance.

> Either very high or very low levels of anxiety interfere with performance on a variety of tasks; intermediate levels facilitate performance. If women and girls have a high base level of anxiety, then increases in anxiety above their base level will frequently carry them past the optimum point of the curve, and

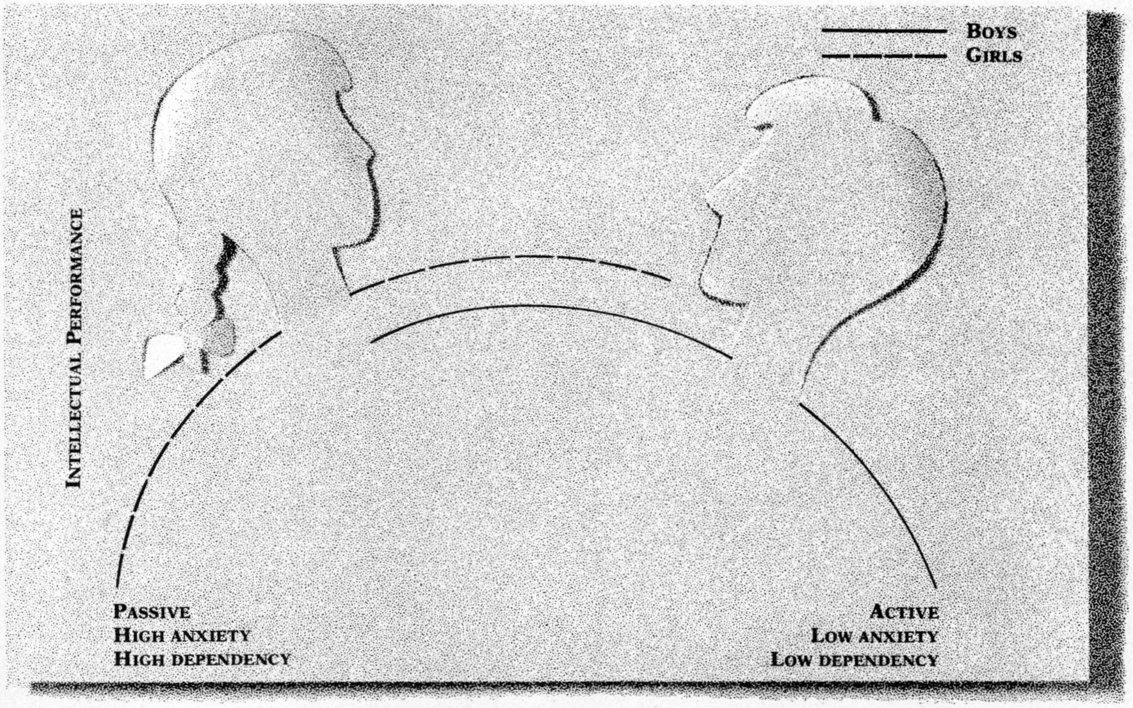

FIGURE 3.1
MACCOBY MODEL OF SEX DIFFERENCES IN PERSONALITY TRAITS AND INTELLECTUAL PERFORMANCE.

From S. Boocock, *An Introduction to the Sociology of Learning.* Copyright ©1972 by Houghton Mifflin Co. Reprinted by permission of the publisher.

> result in inhibition or disorganization of performance. If boys and men have a low base level of anxiety, increases in anxiety will more often either improve performance, or move them through the middle portions of the curve where changes in performance would not be found. (pp. 47–48)

There is very little evidence to support any argument for innate differences between the sexes in the intellectual and personality domains. Not only is there considerable overlap between the sexes on these dimensions, but reported differences like dependency, passivity, or conformity only appear in late-adolescent and college-age women. Even differences in mathematical abilities do not appear until the late elementary grades.

Most psychologists and sociologists view sex differences in terms of role training and social expectations. As early as age two or three, boys and girls have different interests and attitudes, which their parents influence and strengthen.

There appears to be a reversal in the academic performance

and motivation of boys and girls between elementary school, and high school and college. Boys have more difficulty than girls functioning in the typical elementary school classroom. Teachers report that boys are more aggressive and less conforming, have a lower frustration level for boredom, and exhibit a higher activity level and shorter attention span than girls (Stanchfield, 1973).

There are three major explanations for the sex differences found in the elementary grades: maturational differences favoring girls, predominance of female teachers, and conflict between the sex-role expectations for boys in society and the student-role expectations that schools apply to all students (Brophy & Good, 1974). The two latter explanations have received the most support in recent years.

Both girls and boys are inclined to see the school as a female-oriented institution. Boys would naturally be less interested in classroom routines, which eventually would lead to poorer academic success. Students also state that it is more important to do better in subjects or tasks defined as appropriate for their sex (Stein, Pohly, & Mueller, 1969; Stein, 1971). Girls may be socialized to believe that excellence in mathematics is not a proper pursuit. Classroom rules and regulations, especially the emphasis on orderliness and cleanliness, are more in line with the socialization of girls than boys.

However, when boys receive the proper motivation and when teachers associate a subject like reading with male activity by using instructional materials and procedures oriented toward boys, scholastic differences between the sexes have been eliminated (Stanchfield, 1973). Such evidence weakens any support for a maturational explanation for girls' reading achievements. Furthermore, in countries like England and Germany, where there are more male teachers in the elementary school to make reading and school achievement more compatible with the male role, males surpass girls in reading achievement and have fewer problems of reading disability (Preston, 1962; Johnson, 1972).

During the beginning of high school, the academic performance of the two sexes begins to change and middle-class boys take over the starring role. Academic achievement is now a necessary antecedent to vocational success for boys. Vocational success is an important component of the masculine sex-role identity, and the adolescent male is more interested in mastering those tasks that are linked to his vocational goals. The adolescent girl is in a different situation because different social expectations confront her.

Bettelheim (1965) believes that women are socialized to believe that their main fulfillment will come with marriage and children. Whereas it is proper for a male not to show interest in marriage while pursuing academic or professional goals, a female cannot afford to ignore this institution. No matter how successful she is in school or work, she is still judged a failure if she doesn't marry early. As a result, women are subjected to societal pressures that are not directed at men. Women are often made to fear success and failure at the same time.

This trend begins during high school, when girls often fear that achievement will make them unpopular with boys and may not do their best in school (Coleman, 1961). Intellectual interests are seen as a form of aggressive behavior, partly because school success usually requires competition with peers. Since girls are not socialized to be competitive, they inhibit themselves from undertaking intellectual pursuits that might be defined as "unfeminine."

One of the classic studies on the socialization of girls to lower their achievement goals is Komarovsky's *Women in the Modern World* (1953). It contains reports by college girls describing advice they received from parents, brothers, and friends urging them not to set their sights too high and not to reveal their intellectual abilities or goals to potential boy friends until they anticipated a favorable reaction. We must wonder about the number of outstanding women who have been talked out of (by themselves or by others) high educational and occupational achievement (Boocock, 1972).

Research on the college level indicates that some women actually desire to avoid achievement. Horner (1968) found that women showed substantial fear of the social rejection associated with achievement. While 56% of her female subjects ($N = 90$) denied that they could achieve success, less than 10% of her male subjects ($N = 88$) made the same statement. It appears that men have a progressively better opinion of themselves as they grow up, but women do not. When college women are asked how well they will do on a task they are about to undertake or how good their grades will be the next semester, they are less optimistic than college men, even on tasks where they do in fact perform as well as men.

Present evidence indicates nothing in the intellectual or social-emotional makeup of either sex that imposes limits on what members of that sex may hope to become or to achieve (Maccoby & Jacklin, 1974). But external societal expectations impose their own limits on achievement and vocational success. Part of the emphasis of the women's liberation movement is to improve the self-concept of women and to encourage them to pursue goals and ambitions. Although many changes have come about in the social expectations of both men and women, archaic expectations still influence academic performance. To what extent have you been influenced by sex roles? Can you remember specific instances in which your parents or friends responded to you in terms of sex-role stereotypes?

KEY POINTS

1. *A person's self-concept embodies the ideas he has about himself and the value he places on his behavior.*
2. *Students with negative beliefs and feelings about themselves are likely to be underachievers or failures in school.*
3. *The self-concept is influenced by such factors as child-rearing practices, school experiences, and physical growth and development.*
4. *It is wrong to assume that all disadvantaged children have poor self-concepts.*
5. *Locus of control pertains to how an individual perceives the link between his behavior and its consequences and whether or not he accepts responsibility for his actions.*
6. *An external person fails to perceive a relationship between his actions and their consequences.*
7. *An internal person perceives that he is in control of his fate and that effort and reward are correlated.*
8. *Locus of control is an important indicator of motivation and achievement.*
9. *High anxiety has a debilitating effect on academic performance.*
10. *High anxiety often is associated with low self-concept and low academic performance.*
11. *Some students experience the need to avoid failure rather than the need to achieve success.*
12. *Students motivated to achieve success prefer challenging tasks, while students motivated to avoid failure prefer to play it safe.*
13. *Child-rearing practices that focus on raising an independent child are associated with the presence of high achievement motivation in children.*
14. *Some children have a strong need for affiliation – the desire to establish and maintain close, friendly interpersonal relations.*
15. *Research studies demonstrated that students with different*

motives responded differently to classroom teaching practices.

16. *Repeated success or failure influences a student's goal setting or level of aspiration.*

17. *Success raises the level of aspiration and failure lowers it. Successive failure can eventually lead students to set unrealistic goals, lose interest in the activity in which they have failed, and develop a lowered or negative self-concept.*

18. *Females excel at verbal tasks and males at mathematical and visual-spatial tasks.*

19. *Males report less anxiety and dependency than females.*

20. *There is little evidence to support any argument for innate differences between the sexes in the intellectual and personality domains.*

21. *Socialization experiences appear to account for most differences in performance among males and females.*

SUGGESTIONS FOR FURTHER READING

Alschuler, A. S. *Motivating achievement in high school students: Education for human growth.* Englewood Cliffs, N.J.: Educational Technology Publications, 1972.The author describes a training program to increase an individual's need for achievement.

Cofer, C. N. *Motivation and emotion.* Glenview, Ill.: Scott, Foresman, 1972. This book covers both the theoretical and experimental literature on motivation.

Glasser, W. *Schools without failure.* New York: Harper & Row, 1969.

Hamachek, D. *Encounters with the self.* New York: Holt, Rinehart and Winston, 1971. The author discusses the many factors influencing an individual's self concept.

LaBenne, W. D., & Greene, B. I. *Educational implications of self-concept theory.* Pacific Palisades, Calif.: Goodyear, 1969.

FOLLOW-UP ACTIVITIES

1 Evaluate your own level of aspiration. Give examples of how your level of aspiration for various goals has changed after you have experienced success and failure.

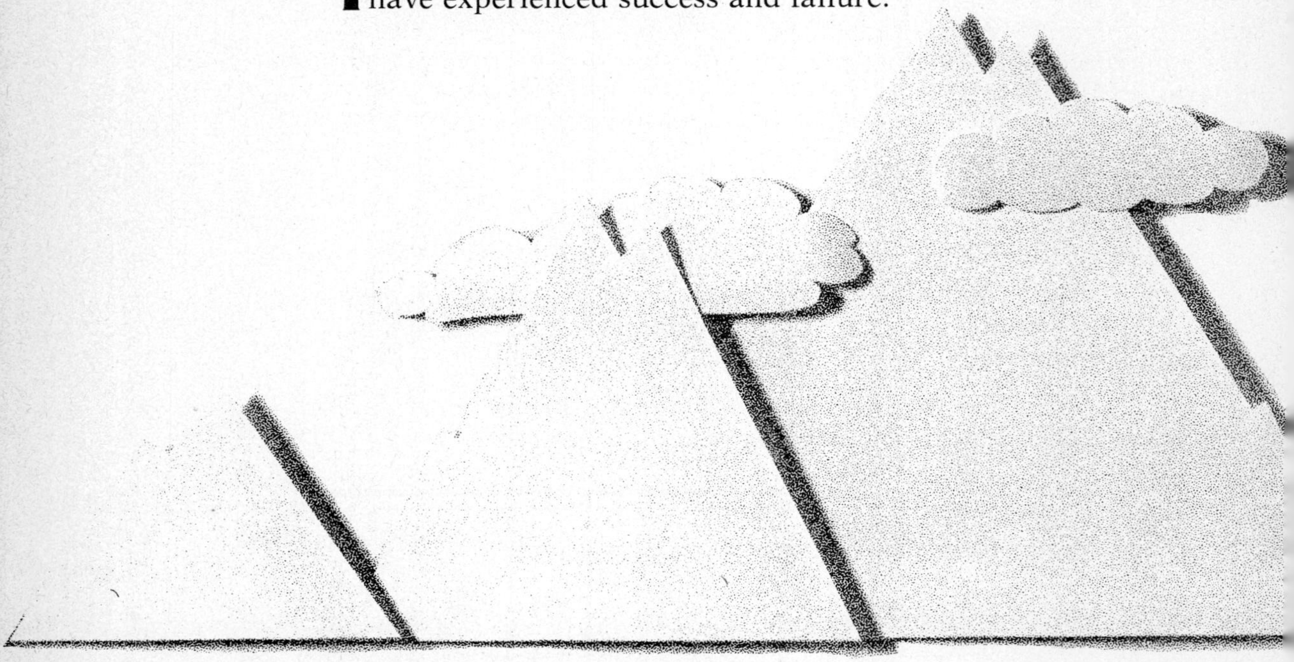

2 Evaluate your own motivation. Analyze your motivation in pursuing different goals. What seem(s) to be the most important factor(s) influencing you?

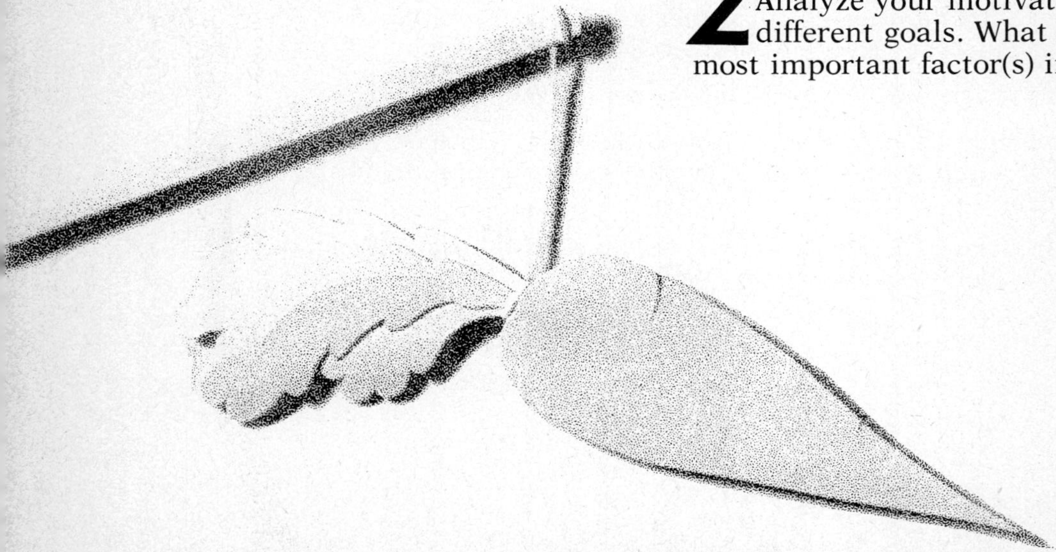

3 Explore anxiety-producing situations in school. "School anxiety" covers anxiety stemming from all situations in school — peer relations, authority relations, test situations, and other in-school anxiety-arousing transactions. Discuss your school experiences and identify situations that you found anxiety-producing. Interview elementary or high school students and determine which situations they find anxiety-producing. What can you do to reduce anxiety in your classroom?

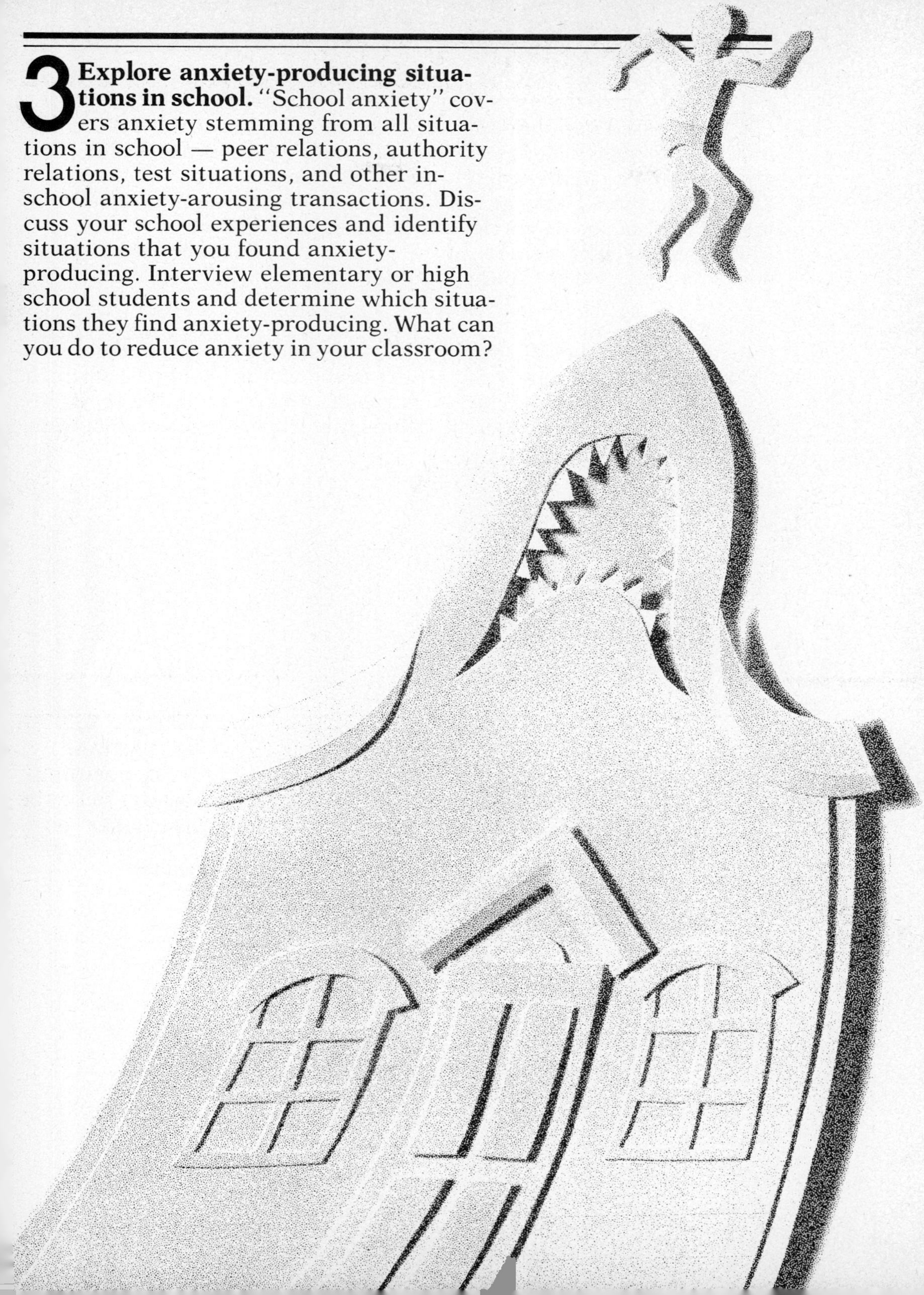

4 Analyze texts to check on sex stereotyping. A number of studies have uncovered sex stereotyping between the covers of books used in public schools. For example, the authors often depict boys as ingenious, creative, brave, and adventurous and depict girls as lonely, frightened, and poorly motivated.

Examine three books at random used at the elementary level in a local school or in the curriculum materials section of your college library. Ask a class member of the opposite sex to examine the same books and provide the following information:

Titles of books
Grade level

Indicate the number of times males and females are the central characters and put a tally mark next to the words listed below which you feel reflect the behavior of characters portrayed in the texts. Include some direct quotes or situations that illustrate sex stereotyping (Biehler, 1974b).

Males		Females
	Number of main characters	
	Adventurous	
	Ambitious	
	Creative	
	Dependent	
	Engaged in home chores	
	Engaged in important, exciting work	
	Helpless	
	Self-confident	

What conclusions do you draw from your analysis?

5 Changing sex-linked differences in behavior. Read some books and articles on sex-role behavior. I suggest *On the Psychology of Women* by Sherman (1971); *Masculine/Feminine or Human* by Chafetz (1974); *Sexism in School and Society* by Frazier and Sadker (1973). Decide which of the following positions is closest to your point of view on sex-linked differences in behavior and defend your position (Gall & Ward, 1974):

a. Everyone, whether male or female, should have an opportunity to develop full intellectual potential. Teachers and others should strive to eliminate traditional sex-role stereotypes, because these biases influence what is learned by boys and girls, and thus prevent them from reaching their full potential.
b. Many differences in the behavior of boys and girls are desirable. They should not be eliminated even if it means some individuals will not achieve their full potential. For example, achievement of a woman's full intellectual potential may not be desirable if it, in turn, necessitates the loss of her sensitivity to others. (p. 263)

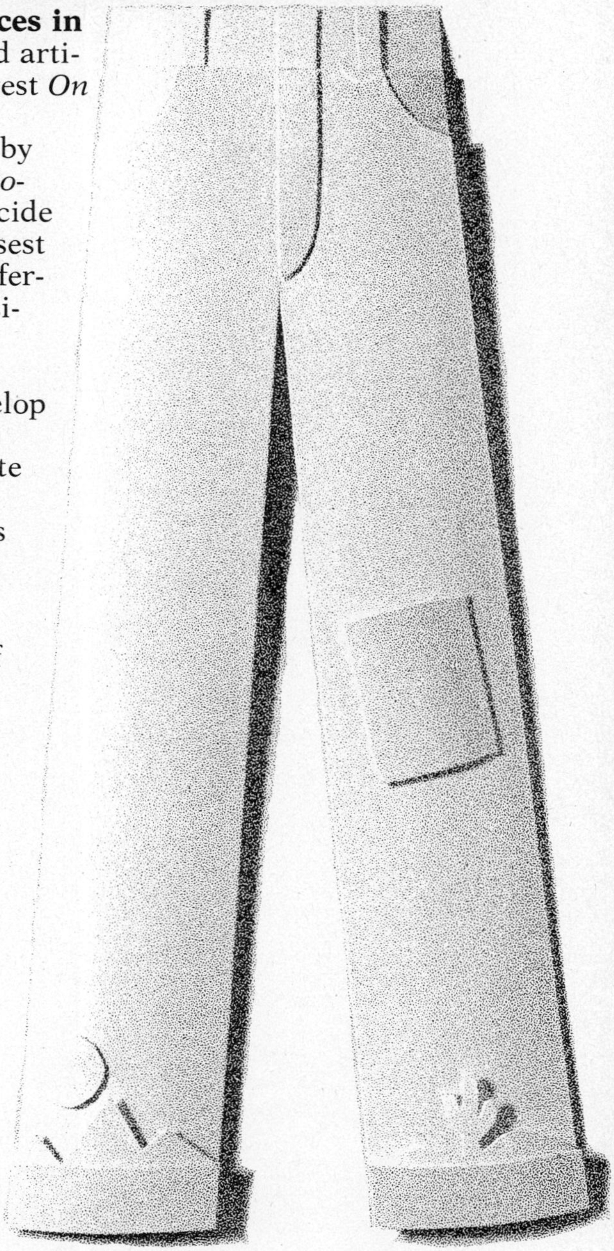

4

TEACHER BEHAVIOR AND CLASSROOM DYNAMICS

ORIENTATION

I discussed student characteristics and the manner in which they are related to academic achievement in the preceding two chapters. Identifying important individual differences is a prerequisite to making decisions about developing and implementing instructional programs, and Chapters 2 and 3 laid the groundwork for such decisions.

This chapter is about how teachers interact with different students and what student characteristics are variables that affect teachers' judgments and decisions. I answer a number of important questions about classroom dynamics in this chapter: How do teachers and students influence each other? Can teachers influence the way students interact with each other? Do teachers prefer certain types of students? If so, how do they react to students who possess characteristics that they either do not like or do not identify with? How can teachers develop classroom climates that foster creativity, positive self-concept, and high-level academic success? Just who is the effective teacher? Can teachers change their behavior?

TEACHERS INFLUENCE STUDENT BEHAVIOR

Tanner and Lindgren (1971) strike the following note in discussing the impact of teacher behavior:

> The teacher is the most powerful person in the classroom, psychologically speaking. His ability to reward and punish is usually greater than that of any individual in the room; he sets the pace; he takes the initiative, or rather, the initiative is his if he wants to take it. The teacher's power is such that even when he does *nothing,* he does something to the class. He even has an effect on the class when he is not present. (p. 25)

Students continually react to the attitudes, values, and personalities of their teachers. Imitation of the teacher is a common method of learning (see Chapter 6 for a more detailed discussion of this type of learning). Bandura and Walters (1963) point out that "models who are rewarding, prestigeful, or competent, who possess high status, and who have control over rewarding resources are more readily imitated than are models who lack these qualities" (p. 107). This description of the attributes of a good model helps us to understand why a teacher is a powerful model.

The important aspect of learning through imitation is that behavior can be acquired simply through observation; the student does not have to practice the behavior, nor does it have to be formally presented. Students constantly pick up subtle expressions, gestures, and attitudes about classroom procedures from their teacher (especially when they are rewarded) without the teacher's referring to the behavior. If the teacher responds to student errors with sarcasm or ridicule, the chances are that his students will respond to each other in a similar manner. Remember that modeling can occur at any time, so students will learn both positive and negative behavior from you.

If students perceive discrepancies between what the teacher preaches and what she practices, they will ignore the sermon and follow the practice. They will also take advantage of discrepancies between what she demands and what she actually allows. If you state that students can't leave the room until the bell rings but fail to enforce your rule, you may find yourself "hanging" in the middle of a sentence at the end of the period, which is a "grave" situation to be in!

Student behavior also reflects the teacher's actions in the following situations: The teacher emphasizes the importance of reading but never reads a book herself; the teacher emphasizes control of one's temper but consistently shouts at her students; the teacher stresses respect for student ideas but ridicules student ideas she thinks are foolish. In all these situations, the students take their cues more from what the teacher actually does than what she says.

The teacher's general instructional competencies can either stifle or encourage student behavior. Taba (1966) has found that the teacher's timing of questions and the sequence in which she poses them cause an ebb or flow in level of pupils' thinking. If you consistently ask factual questions like "In what year was Lincoln elected president?" you seriously limit your students' thinking processes. But your encouragement of divergent thinking will initiate a surge of creativity in your classroom.

Many teachers do not realize the extent to which their influence on students' classroom behavior carries over into other areas. Teachers' leadership behavior in the classroom is one such area. Two classic studies in the 1930s showed that the type of leadership affects the quality of peer interaction and classroom climate. Anderson (1939) hypothesized that dominating or hostile teachers affect students adversely and nonpunitive (integrative) teachers aid the social adjustment of their students. The earmarks of dominative behavior are the use of force, shame, and rigid insistence on conformity. Integrative behavior is exemplified by approval, urging student participation in class, interest in students' activities, and sympathy and understanding.

In general, Anderson found that children in classes with an integrative teacher displayed more integrative-type behavior than children with the dominative teachers. The integrative teachers sparked more spontaneity in their students, which led to greater classroom participation, whereas the dominative teachers generated either a conforming, submissive child or a rebellious, nonworking student.

In another study, Lewin, Lippitt, and White (1939) investigated different styles of leadership in eleven-year-old members of a boys' club working on projects. They experimentally arranged three styles of leadership: authoritarian, democratic, and laissez-faire. The leader of the authoritarian group stated the objectives of the program and directed all the activities of the group. The democratic leader encouraged group decision making, suggested possible alternatives in procedures, and encouraged the boys to work on tasks with partners. The laissez-faire leader offered no direction and did not interact with the boys in making decisions or setting goals. Boys in the authoritarian group were more dependent on the leader, were more attention-demanding, and failed to initiate group activity, especially when the leader was out of the room. In the group led by the democratic leader, there were more work-related conversations, more friendly behavior, and the activity level was fairly stable whether the leader was present or absent. The quality of the work was highest in this group. In the laissez-faire group, more questions, confusion, and discontent abounded.

One of the most interesting findings of the study involved the percentage of time the boys spent in task-related activities with the leader present or absent. In the authoritarian group, the boys were active for 50% of the time when the leader was present but only 15% of the time when the leader left the room; the figure rose to 60% as soon as he returned. Under democratic leadership, work activity was 50% with the leader present or absent and a little less when he returned. Under laissez-faire leadership, the percentage of time spent in activity was the lowest compared with the other forms of leadership when the leader was present but was as high as the democratic group when the leader was absent. Apparently, peer group leaders emerged to take over activities and encouraged the group to move ahead on its own.

It is interesting to note that under authoritarian leadership, the activity level was much lower when the leader was absent, but under democratic and laissez-faire leadership, activity continued with the leader absent. Under authoritarian leadership, the boys either did not know how to proceed on their own or did not want to.

Be cautious in applying these results directly to the classroom because (1) the authoritarian leadership, as described in the experiment, was quite harsh and atypical of teacher leadership, and (2) the subjects were not involved with school activities. Nevertheless, the study does illustrate the impact of different leadership styles. More recent investigations in this area (Trickett & Moos, 1973; Walberg, 1968) continue to support the fact that teachers strongly influence the classroom environment.

Students Influence Teacher Behavior

Although teacher behavior is the focal point of this chapter, we cannot neglect the impact of students on teachers. In fact, many teachers have left the profession because they didn't like the way they were being affected by student behavior. A number of studies illustrate teacher vulnerability to student behavior.

Klein (1971) used college students as confederates and asked them to respond to lectures by a guest professor with positive behavior—smiling, looking at the instructor attentively—negative behavior—frowning, looking out the window—or neutral behavior at various times during each lecture. Klein recorded and analyzed the

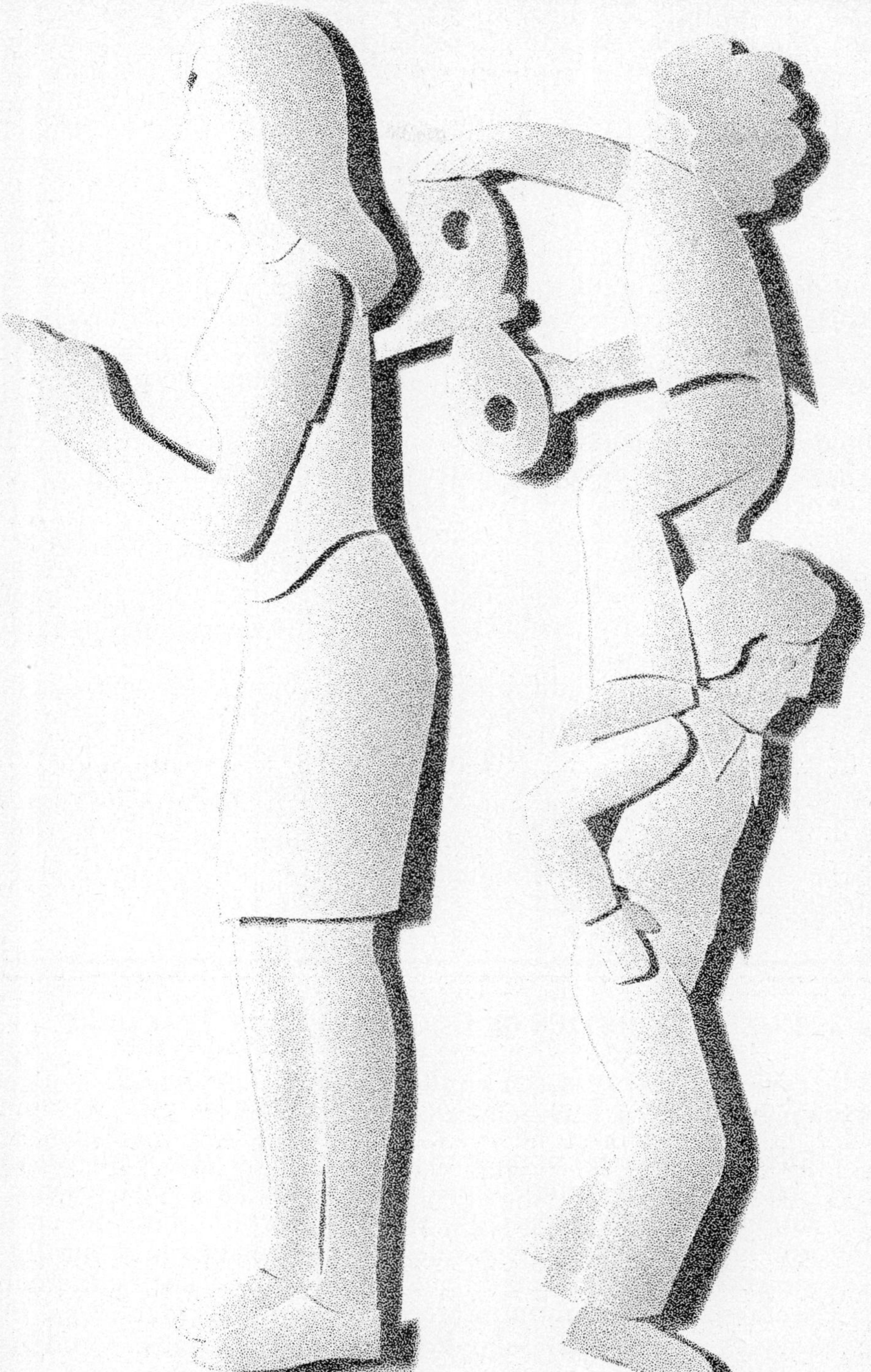

guest professor's verbal and nonverbal behavior in response to these student behaviors. The evidence showed that student behavior conditioned teacher behavior. The professor's behavior reflected that of his students. His behavior was positive when the students' behavior was positive and negative when the students' behavior was negative.

In a related study, Jenkins and Deno (1969) exposed student teachers to classes that had also been instructed to appear either attentive or uninterested. Following the lecture, the student teachers were asked to evaluate their effectiveness on a questionnaire. Not surprisingly, the teachers who received positive feedback thought that teaching was more enjoyable, that they would be more effective teachers, and that their students had learned more from the lesson.

These studies are consistent with personal reports by teachers who use student reaction to a lesson as a prime indicator of teaching success. Rarely will a teacher state that she presented a good lesson if student feedback was negative. However, this reminds me of one statement made by a frustrated student teacher: "Teaching would be great if it weren't for those kids!" This student teacher would have enjoyed lecturing via closed-circuit TV. He wanted to impart knowledge but not to receive feedback from students — perhaps such information was threatening!

Teaching is a dyadic process in which students and teachers form an interlocking unit. One of the best examples of this process occurs when students misbehave in the classroom. The students' behavior influences their teacher's attitude toward them, which in turn influences the students' attitudes toward the teacher. As you read this chapter, you will identify additional illustrations of how the quality of teacher-student and peer interaction raises or lowers the degree of learning in the classroom.

CHARACTERISTICS OF GOOD AND POOR TEACHERS

While reviewing the research on the personal characteristics of good versus poor teachers, Hamacheck (1969) concluded:

> Effective teachers appear to be those who are, shall we say, "human" in the fullest sense of the word. They have a sense of humor, are fair, empathetic, more democratic than autocratic, and apparently are more able to relate easily and naturally to students on either a one-to-one or group basis. Their classrooms seem to reflect miniature enterprise operations in the sense that they are more open, spontaneous, and adaptable to change. Ineffective teachers apparently lack a sense of humor, grow

impatient easily, use cutting, ego-reducing comments in class, are less well-integrated, are inclined to be somewhat authoritarian, and are generally less sensitive to the needs of their students. (p. 342)

At one time, it was assumed that a person was a good teacher if he was a good scholar. The reasoning was simple: If a teacher knew his subject matter, he could teach others. There is some truth to this statement, but subject-matter knowledge does not bridge the gap between teaching and learning. Perhaps the best example of this assertion is found at the college level. Some of the most knowledgeable professors are not the best teachers. How many times have you heard the comments "He knows his stuff, but he can't communicate," "He can't get his material across," or "He talks over our heads"? These comments communicate problems in student-teacher relationships.

In no way do I wish to communicate that knowledge of subject matter isn't important—it is! But when we investigate the studies of grade point average in college, intelligence, and subject matter preparation during teacher training, we consistently find little relationship between these factors and subsequent success in teaching. Such variables as warmth and enthusiasm are more related to achievement gains (Rosenshine & Furst, 1971) and better affective responses from students (Kleinfeld, 1972; McKeachie, Lin, & Mann, 1971).

Many humanistic or perceptual psychologists distinguish the effective teacher from the ineffective teacher by determining what the teacher believes about herself (self-concept) and what she believes about others. Combs et al. (1971) believe that only when teachers feel fundamentally secure about themselves and their abilities can they give attention to the needs of others. They state: "People who feel inadequate cannot afford the time and effort required to assist others as long as they feel deprived themselves" (p. 13). A teacher with feelings of inadequacy might respond to students by developing rigid or authoritarian rules and regulations in the classroom to protect herself.

Do you feel that people like you, or do you feel ignored, unwanted, or rejected? Are you a person who sees yourself as worthy of respect, or do you see yourself as a person whose ideas of dignity and integrity do not matter? Do you see yourself as essentially dependable or reliable, or do you have doubts about your ability to cope with events? Do you identify with others, or do you feel withdrawn, removed, or alienated from them? Watch how you answer—your answers to these questions might influence your success in teaching!

Teaching involves interaction with people, and the perceptions a teacher has about people in general will prompt his behavior toward students in particular. The literature on expectations appearing later in this chapter will clearly illustrate this fact. The teacher who believes that students have the ability to learn will behave in a more positive manner toward them than will the teacher who believes they cannot learn. From the research studies conducted by Combs et al. (1974), it appears that good teachers distinguish themselves from poor ones with respect to the following beliefs about people:

> 1. *The good teacher perceives others as having the capacities to deal with their problems successfully.*
> 2. *The good teacher sees others as being friendly and enhancing.*
> 3. *The good teacher tends to see other people as being worthy rather than unworthy.*
> 4. *The good teacher sees people and their behavior as essentially developing from within rather than the product of external events to be molded and manipulated; he sees people as creative and dynamic rather than passive or inert.*
> 5. *The good teacher sees people as essentially trustworthy and dependable in the sense of behaving in a lawful way.*
> 6. *The good teacher sees people as being potentially fulfilling and enhancing to self rather than impeding or threatening. (p. 63)*

The Authentic Teacher

Beginning teachers often spend so much time planning and concentrating on teaching lessons that they forget that good teaching is not simply a matter of learning techniques and methodology. Patterson (1973) believes that too many teachers try to play a role when they begin teaching rather than being authentic and developing a relationship with students. Teachers find it necessary (or at least they think so) to play a role primarily for fear of having "disciplinary problems" in their classrooms. The authoritarian, aloof, and cold behavior of some teachers is really a façade, constructed to hide their fear of being taken as a "soft touch." "Act tough at the beginning," "Show them who is boss," "Don't let them get away with anything": the typical advice given to beginning teachers. Unfortunately, as one plays a role, he may find the role comfortable, or at least successful, and settle into it. Soon his behavior is organized around a number of teaching myths (Greenberg, 1969). Let's explore some traditional teaching myths that have been handed down through the generations of teachers:

1. The myth of calmness and moderation. *This myth projects the*

teacher as a sterile individual who faces any situation calmly and coolly. He does not lose his temper or display elation or joy. He is neutral on all controversial issues and expresses no personal opinions.

2. The "I love all children" myth. *Teachers must like all children equally. Feelings of anger, hate, or rejection are not in a teacher's repertoire of feelings. Teachers experiencing these natural feelings at times feel guilty because they have been erroneously programmed to believe that good teachers don't have them.*
3. The "I treat all children alike" myth. *Teachers must treat all students equally. This myth is related to the "I love all children" myth, which insists that teachers feel the same way about children, regardless of their individual characteristics.*
4. The "I can hide my true feelings from children" myth. *When a teacher is hurt or disturbed, she can hide her real feelings. This attitude is particularly cultivated toward younger children, who are supposedly not mature enough to know how the teacher really feels about a given incident or situation.*
5. The "children need me" myth. *This myth draws its strength from the belief that young children cannot work independently or assume responsibility for their own learning in the classroom because they are young, frail, and need the support of the teacher.*
6. The "I live to know all the answers" myth. *Teachers have all the answers on every topic. This myth appeals to the inadequate feelings in some teachers and prevents them from admitting that they are wrong or saying, "I don't know, but I can find out for you." Patterson (1973) quotes a sensitive observation concerning this myth made by one of his students.*

If I am real, my students will be able to relate to me as I am — a human being with feelings and ideas, not an authority figure who issues mandates from above. They will realize that I am being my whole "self," and that I can and do make mistakes; furthermore, when I make mistakes, I will be able to admit them. It is only human to make mistakes, but very few teachers are accustomed to letting their students know that they are less than infallible. In my opinion, students would feel more at ease with a teacher who is able to admit errors, and who relinquishes his role of all-knowing authority. The teacher would also become a learner in the eyes of the student if he were able to admit that his ideas are not always absolutely correct. (p. 101)

These are but a few of the many myths some teachers work under. You can probably identify many more. Teaching myths seriously undermine the enjoyment of teaching for many individuals. They prevent teachers from sharing both sorrow and joy with their students. They can prevent teachers from being honest about their own feelings, from encouraging independence, and from developing meaningful relationships with students.

The perpetuation of these and other myths about teachers inspires students to view teachers as different human beings rather than to perceive them as individuals with the same strengths and weaknesses as themselves. A second-grade student once asked a colleague of mine whether he ever ate. Since most teachers eat lunch in special rooms away from students, it is not hard to understand why a young child would ask such a question. I remember another revealing incident that occurred when I was teaching seventh-grade math. One Saturday afternoon the paper boy, who was an eighth grader in the same school, came to collect his money. I came to the door in tennis shorts and without any shoes or shirt. When the student saw me he looked shocked, as if he expected me to wear a shirt and tie as I watched a football game. Can you remember seeing a teacher smoking in public or dressed in some mod outfit when you were in elementary school? How did you react?

Today, many teachers dress informally, participate in many student activities, and develop personal friendships with students without suffering a loss of respect or rapport. In fact, most of these teachers report greater rapport with students. It's normal to be anxious or afraid of certain situations. But the building of barriers between yourself and your students only increases the problems.

THE ATMOSPHERE THE TEACHER CREATES

In the following reading, Purkey (1970) poses many important questions about the part teaching behavior plays in the formation of classroom environment. Although the author discusses a number of factors as they are conducive to developing positive self-concepts in students, they are also pertinent to enhancing creativity and various achievement-related motives in children.

The Atmosphere the Teacher Creates

Six factors seem particularly important in creating a classroom at-

From *Self-concept and School Achievement* by W.W. Purkey, 1970, pp. 50-56. Copyright © 1970 by Prentice-Hall, Englewood Cliffs, New Jersey. Reprinted by permission.

mosphere conducive to developing favorable self-images in students. These are (1) challenge; (2) freedom; (3) respect; (4) warmth; (5) control; and (6) success. A brief discussion of each of these may be helpful.

CHALLENGE

Because of the focus of this book, little has been said about high standards of academic accomplishment. This omission should not be taken to mean that achievement should be minimized. As we have seen, high academic expectations and a high degree of challenge on the part of teachers have a positive and beneficial effect on students. A good way to create challenge is to wait until the chances of success are good, and then say: "This is hard work, but I think that you can do it." The teacher chooses the right moment to put his trust on the line with students. Of course, an important part of challenge is relevance. If the required learning is relevant to the student's world of experience and has some personal meaning to him, then he is likely to work hard—*if* he feels free to try. This brings us to the question of freedom.

FREEDOM

It is difficult for self-esteem to grow in an environment where there is little or no freedom of choice. If the student is to grow and develop as an adequate human being, he needs the opportunity to make meaningful decisions for himself. This also means that he must have the freedom to make mistakes, and even to laugh at his inadequacies. Carlton and Moore (1966, 1968) have shown that the freedom of self-directed dramatization improved the reading ability and enhanced the self concept of elementary-school youngsters. This general emphasis on freedom has been highlighted by Moustakas, who wrote: "Self values are in jeopardy in any climate where freedom and choice are denied, in a situation where the individual rejects his own senses and substitutes for his own perceptions the standards and expectations of others" (1966, pp. 4*f*). When the student has a say in his own development and is given personal decisions to make, he develops faith in his own judgments and thoughts.

Closely related to the notion of freedom of choice is the idea of freedom from threat. Children seem to learn and develop best in an atmosphere characterized by much challenge and little threat. Kowitz has noted, for example, that if the child feels evaluation takes place with "vicious assault upon his self concept" (1967, p. 163), there can be little real freedom. In fact, some students fear failure so much that they avoid achievement whenever they can and, when they cannot, do not try to succeed. In this way, they can avoid the task of trying to achieve. A comprehensive study of the person who fears failure is provided by Birney, Burdick, and Teevan (1969).

What this means to the teacher is that students will learn, provided the material appears to be relevant to their lives and provided they have the freedom to explore and to discover its meaning for themselves. We know that exploration is curtailed in an atmosphere in which one must spend most of his time avoiding or reducing the experience of anxiety brought about by threat to the self. Sarason (1961) has reported that a poor performance by anxious subjects occurred only when the task was presented as a threat. When anxious subjects were told that failure was normal and expected, they actually outperformed subjects who were less anxious. The freedom to try without a tiger springing at you if you fail is essential to a healthy atmosphere in the classroom.

In considering the factors of freedom and challenge, the classroom teacher can ask himself:

Do I encourage students to try something new and to join in new activities?

Do I allow students to have a voice in planning, and do I permit them to help make the rules they follow?

Do I permit students to challenge my opinions?

Do I teach in as exciting and interesting a manner as possible?

Do I distinguish between students' classroom mistakes and their personal failure?

Do I avoid unfair and ruthless competition in the classroom?

Questions like these can help the teacher evaluate himself and the classroom climate he creates.

RESPECT

A basic feeling by the teacher for the worth and dignity of students is vital in building self concepts in them. No aspect of education is more important than the feeling on the part of the teacher that the individual student is important, valuable, and *can* learn in school. Sometimes teachers forget the importance of respect and run roughshod over the personal feelings of students. Using both the official and unofficial school practices which we cataloged in Chapter 3, teachers sometimes lower the feelings of worth of many young people. One of my students told me why he could never get along with his previous English teacher. It was because, although his name is Cribbidge, "She always called me cabbage whenever she called roll, and then laughed." The rule seems to be that whenever we treat a student with respect, we add to his self-respect, and whenever we embarrass or humiliate him, we are likely to build disrespect in him both for himself and for others.

If the teacher genuinely values and respects students, it will be reflected in everything he does. Davidson and Lang (1960) found that when students feel that teachers value and respect them, they are likely to value and respect themselves. Moustakas summed it up this way: "By cherishing and holding the child in absolute esteem, the teacher is establishing an environmental climate that facilitates growth and becoming" (1966, p. 13).

The need for respect is particularly important in working with culturally disadvantaged students. These are the children whose behavior makes them most difficult to respect, but who probably need respect the most. Teachers must make an extra effort to communicate to these young people a feeling of trust, positive regard, and respect. Closely related to respect is the concept of warmth.

Warmth

There is considerable evidence to support the assumption that a psychologically safe and supportive learning situation encourages students to grow academically as well as in feelings of personal worth. Cogan (1958) reported that students with warm, considerate teachers produced unusual amounts of original poetry and art. Christensen (1960) found the warmth of teachers significantly related to their students' vocabulary and achievement in arithmetic. Reed (1962) concluded that teachers characterized as considerate, understanding, and friendly, and with a tolerance for some release of emotional feeling by students, had a favorable influence on their students' interest in science.

Relating more directly to the task of building favorable self concepts, Spaulding's research (1964) supported the findings of previous investigators regarding positive attitudes toward the self. He found significant correlations between the height of the self concept and the degree to which the teachers in his study were calm, accepting, supportive, and facilitative. It is interesting to note that significant negative correlations with the height of pupils' self concepts were found when teachers were dominating, threatening, and sarcastic.

An important part of warmth is commitment. Teaching has been described as a delicate relationship, almost like a marriage, where, in a sense, the teacher and student belong to each other. The student says "There is *my* teacher" and the teacher says "These are *my* students." The process of commitment is illustrated by the story of the chicken and pig who were walking down a country lane: The chicken excitedly told the portly pig of his latest business idea. "We'll prepare and franchise the best tasting ham 'n eggs money can buy, and we'll make a fortune." The pig thought it over for a moment and replied: "It's easy for you to get enthused. For you it's an occupation, but for *me* it means *total* commitment!" Perhaps total commitment is asking too much of teachers, but certainly they need to feel that their work with students is more than an occupation. A warm and supportive educational atmosphere is one in which each student is made to feel that he belongs in school and that teachers care about what happens to him. It is one in which praise is used in preference to punishment, courtesy in preference to sarcasm, and consultation in preference to dictation.

Some practical questions about respect and warmth which the teacher might ask himself are:

> *Do I learn the name of each student as soon as possible, and do I use that name often?*
>
> *Do I share my feelings with my students?*
>
> *Do I practice courtesy with my students?*
>
> *Do I arrange some time when I can talk quietly alone with each student?*
>
> *Do I spread my attention around and include each student, keeping special watch for the student who may need extra attention?*
>
> *Do I notice and comment favorably on the things that are important to students?*
>
> *Do I show students who return after being absent that I am happy to have them back in class, and that they were missed?*

It is in ways such as these that we tell the student that he is important to us.

CONTROL

Coopersmith (1967) has suggested that children who are brought up in a permissive environment tend to develop less self-esteem than those reared in a firmer and more demanding atmosphere. The assumption that clearly established and relatively firm guidance produces more self-esteem in children can also be applied to the classroom. It is important for the teacher to maintain discipline, for the type of control under which a child lives has considerable effect on his self-image. It is yet another way of telling the student that the teacher cares about him and what he does. Classroom control does not require ridicule and embarrassment. The secret seems to be in the leadership qualities of the teacher. When he is prepared for class, keeps on top of the work and avoids the appearance of confusion, explains why some things must be done, and strives for consistency, politeness, and firmness, then classroom control is likely to be maintained. When punishment is unavoidable (and often it *can* be avoided), then it is best to withdraw the student's privileges. Of course, this means that teachers must be sure that there *are* some privileges in school which can be withdrawn. Poor control procedures would include punishing the entire class for the transgressions of a few, using corporal punishment, or using school work as punishment.

In considering classroom control, teachers might ask themselves:

> *Do I remember to see small disciplinary problems as understandable, and not as personal insults?*
>
> *Do I avoid having "favorites" and "victims"?*
>
> *Do I have, and do my students have, a clear idea of what is and what is not acceptable in my class?*
>
> *Within my limits, is there room for students to be active and natural?*
>
> *Do I make sure that I am adequately prepared for class each day?*
>
> *Do I usually make it through the day without punishing students?*

Questions such as these help the teacher to estimate his ability to handle students in a way which maintains discipline and, at the same time, builds positive and realistic self concepts in students.

Some teachers believe that warmth and firmness are in opposition to each other, but this is not so. Warmth is more than the obvious display of affection, it is also expressed by firmness which says to the student, "You are important to me and I care about the ways in which you behave."

SUCCESS

Perhaps the single most important step that teachers can take in the classroom is to provide an educational atmosphere of success rather than failure. Reviewing over a dozen experiments, Wylie (1961) made the tentative statement that students are likely to change their self-evaluations after experimentally induced success or failure. This statement has been echoed in more recent studies. Costello (1964) found that overall, regardless of the task or the ability of the students, praise produces more improvement in performance than blame. Ludwig and Maehr (1967) showed that the approval of significant others caused an increase in self-ratings and an increased preference for activities connected with the criterion task, and that disapproval resulted in a lowered self-rating and a decreased preference for related activities. Moreover, the reaction to the evaluation was followed by a spread of effect, from the areas directly approved by the significant others to related areas of self-regard.

A number of writers have pointed out some of the steps involved in giving honest experiences of success. Page's (1958) research showed that pupils' performance improved significantly when teachers wrote encouraging comments on their written work. A control group, given conventional grades without comment, lost ground. Walsh (1956) explains that it is helpful to show students that they have mastered even the smallest step, rather than vaguely saying "That's nice" about everything.

The sensitive teacher points out areas of accomplishment, rather than focusing on mistakes. Continuing awareness of failure results in lowered expectations, not learning. According to Combs and Snygg (1959) a positive view is learned from the ways people treat the learner. People learn that they are able, not from failure but from success. Questions about success which the teacher might ask himself when he thinks about success experiences for students include:

Do I permit my students some opportunity to make mistakes without penalty?

Do I make generally positive comments on written work?

Do I give extra support and encouragement to slower students?

Do I recognize the successes of students in terms of what they did earlier?

Do I take special opportunities to praise students for their successes?

Do I manufacture honest experiences of success for my students?

Do I set tasks which are, and which appear to the student to be, within his abilities?

What all of this discussion hopes to say to teachers is that a backlog of challenge, freedom, respect, warmth, control, and success develops positive self-images in students and encourages academic achievement. The absence of these factors makes for the person who is crippled psychologically.

Johnson and Johnson (1975) discuss the importance of the type of goal structure a teacher sets up for various learning activities. A goal structure "specifies the way in which students will relate to each other and to the teacher in working toward the accomplishment of instructional goals" (p. 7). There are three types of goal structures: (1) *cooperative*—students work together to accomplish shared goals; (2) *competitive*—

students work against each other to achieve goals that only few students can attain; and (3) *individualistic*—one student's achievement of the goal is unrelated to other students' achievement of the goal. An example of each of these goal structures is students working together to survey political attitudes in the community (cooperative), students taking an examination that will be graded on a curve (competitive), and a student writing a paper on the federal election process (individualistic).

Each type of goal structure promotes a different pattern of interaction among students, thus creating a different learning climate. A cooperative goal structure promotes positive interpersonal relations such as trust, acceptance, sharing, and helping. A competitive goal structure promotes little trust and acceptance and generates more attempts to mislead and obstruct others. An individualistic goal structure promotes interaction with the teacher rather than with peers and minimizes positive affective outcomes.

All three goal structures are effective under certain conditions and are relevant for specific goals and objectives of a lesson. Table 4.1 identifies some of these conditions. The teacher must make "a decision as to which goal structure will promote the desired classroom climate and interpersonal processes to facilitate the accomplishment of the desired cognitive and affective outcomes" (Johnson & Johnson, 1975, p. 62).

Many teachers have been taught to use competition as a basic motivator for academic achievement and overutilize this goal structure. Johnson and Johnson (1975) detail some of the myths about the benefits of competition in the classroom: (1) competition builds the character and toughness necessary to prepare the young for the "real world"; (2) children prefer competitive situations; (3) ambition, motivation, achievement, and success depend on successful competition with other individuals; and (4) society is highly competitive, and a student must be able to function in this type of environment.

The following arguments are presented to refute each of the myths: First, Ogilvie and Tutko (1971) spent many years studying the effects of competition on athletes' personalities and found no evidence of character building. In fact, their data indicated that competition limits growth in some areas: concern for others, need to take care of others, and need for affiliation with others. Second, recent research studies done by Johnson and Johnson (1973) indicate that children prefer cooperative instructional situations to competitive ones. Third, they have found no evidence that competition yields higher achievement than cooperation. Last, they hypothesize that competitiveness is probably overemphasized because individuals find themselves more often in cooperative rather than in competitive situations in society.

TABLE 4.1
APPROPRIATE CONDITIONS CHART

	COOPERATIVE	*INDIVIDUALIZED*	*COMPETITIVE*
PE OF STRUCTIONAL TIVITY	Problem solving; divergent thinking or creative tasks; assignments can be more ambiguous with students doing the clarifying, decision making, and inquiring.	Specific skill or knowledge acquisition; assignment is clear and behavior specified to avoid confusion and need for extra help.	Skill practice; knowledge recall and review; assignment is clear with rules for competing specified.
RCEPTION OF AL IMPORTANCE	Goal is perceived as important for each student, and students expect group to achieve the goal.	Goal is perceived as important for each student, and each student expects eventually to achieve his goal.	Goal is *not* perceived to be of large importance to the students, and they can accept either winning or losing.
JDENT PECTATIONS	Each student expects positive interaction with other students; sharing of ideas and materials; support for risk taking; making contributions to the group effort; dividing the task among group members; to capitalize on diversity among group members.	Each student expects to be left alone by other students; to take a major part of the responsibility for completing the task; to take a major part in evaluating his progress toward task completion and the quality of his effort.	Each student expects to have an equal chance of winning; to enjoy the activity (win or lose); to monitor the progress of his competitor; to compare ability, skills, or knowledge with peers.
PECTED SOURCE SUPPORT	Other students are perceived to be the major resource for assistance support, and reinforcement.	Teacher is perceived to be the major resource for assistance, support, and reinforcement.	Teacher is perceived to be the major resource for assistance, support, and reinforcement.

rom David W. Johnson and Roger T. Johnson. *Learning Together and Alone: Cooperation, Competition, and Individualization,* p. 62.

Many critics have pointed out the detrimental effects of competition in the classroom. Holt (1964) writes about the classroom behavior of students who have a fear of failure in competitive situations. They spend most of their time devising strategies to protect themselves in the classroom. According to Holt's experience, competition does not encourage learning but motivates students to do their all to avoid failure.

Some of the most striking examples of the effects of competition have been presented by Henry (1963), who believes that the teacher is a powerful agent in reinforcing competition. He states that teachers encourage students to find faults or errors in their peers' work. When a child makes a mistake, hands wave in all directions, calling the error to the attention of the teacher. Encouraging this behavior gives rise to situations in which one student's success is another student's failure. This behavior easily leads to a climate Henry identifies as the "witch hunt syndrome."

The following excerpt illustrates his concern. Students in a fifth-grade class are taking turns reading stories they have made up. Charlie's is called "The Unknown Guest":

> One dark, dreary night on a hill a house stood. This house was forbidden territory for Bill and Joe, but they were going in anyway. The door creaked, squealed, slammed. A voice warned them to go home. They went upstairs. A stair cracked. They entered a room. A voice said that they might as well stay and find out now; and their father came out. He laughed and they laughed, but they never forgot their adventure together.
>
> *Teacher:* Are there any words that give you the mood of the story?
> *Lucy:* He could have made the sentences a little better. . . .
> *Teacher:* Let's come back to Lucy's comment. What about the sentences?
> *Gert:* They were too short.
>
> *(Charlie and Jeanne have a discussion about the position of the word "stood" in the first sentence.)*
>
> *Teacher:* Wait a minute; some people are forgetting their manners. . . .
> *Jeff:* About the room: the boys went up the stairs and one "cracked," when they were in the room. Did they fall through the stairs, or what?
>
> *(The teacher suggests Charlie make that a little clearer. . . .)*
>
> *Teacher:* We still haven't decided about the short sentences.

Perhaps they make the story more spooky and mysterious.

Gwynne: I wish he had read with more expression instead of all at one time.

Rachel: Not enough expression.

Teacher: Charlie, they want a little more expression from you. I guess we've given you enough suggestions for one time. (*Charlie does not raise his head, which is bent over his desk as if studying a paper.*) Charlie! I guess we've given you enough suggestions for one time, Charlie, haven't we? (Henry, 1963, p. 304)

If you desire positive interaction among students, you should encourage cooperation. Aronson (1975) provides an excellent example of the use of cooperation in newly integrated classrooms that resulted in higher achievement, decrease in social insults, higher self-esteem, and improved attitudes toward school. He divided students into small groups and developed tasks in which they had to cooperate with each other to succeed. He accomplished this by giving each member of the group information that the other group members needed to complete the task. Each student had to learn his information and teach it to others. Aronson calls this procedure the "jigsaw-puzzle method": Each student had a piece of information, and it took all of the group members to put the puzzle or task together.

Student Characteristics and Teacher Response

Let us now review some salient group and individual characteristics to learn more about how these characteristics influence teachers' judgments and decisions. I have touched on the topic in Chapters 2 and 3, but it merits further attention. No attempt is made to suggest that all teachers behave in the same way. The purpose of the discussion is to make you more aware of your possible responses to individual differences.

SOCIOECONOMIC STATUS

Socioeconomic status (SES) has an important bearing on both teachers' perceptions of students and their treatment of students in the classroom. Yee (1963) found that SES was *the* important variable determining teacher attitude toward students. Goodwin and Sanders (1969) asked first- and sixth-grade teachers to rank the importance of seven variables in predicting a child's school success. They ranked SES as the most important for predicting success for the first-grade pupils, followed in order by IQ, standardized tests, age, sex, anecdotal notes, and grade-point average (GPA). At the sixth-grade level, the teachers ranked in order of importance standardized tests, SES, IQ, age, and anecdotal notes. Yee's study indicated that elementary school teachers rely more on SES than IQ scores for predicting academic performance.

There is also evidence that teachers treat higher social class students differently than lower social class students. They exhibit more reinforcing behavior, especially nonverbal reinforcement—a pat on the back or a smile—to middle-class children than to lower-class children (Friedman & Friedman, 1973). Studies on ability grouping (Goldberg, Passow, & Justman, 1966; Husén & Svensson, 1960) show that children from higher social classes are usually placed in higher tracks and children from lower social backgrounds in lower tracks than their measured ability predicts.

Rist (1970) reported the results of his observational study of one class of ghetto children from the beginning of kindergarten through the second grade. The teacher placed the children in reading groups that reflected the social composition of the class. As early as the eighth day of kindergarten the teacher designated the higher social class children as "fast learners" and the lower social class students as "slow learners"! Rist pointed out that not one of the various sources of information the teacher had access to about the children was directly related to their academic potential.

What is it about social class differences that influences teacher judgments about students? It appears that teachers develop certain criteria that to them are important indicators of expected success or failure. These criteria might be classified as important "middle-class" values—ease of communication with adults; a higher degree of verbalization in standard American English; the ability to become a leader; a neat and clean appearance; coming from a family that is educated, employed, living together, and interested in the child; and the ability to participate well as a member of a group (Rist, 1970).

RACE AND CULTURAL DIFFERENCES

Teachers often have different attitudes toward the academic potential and future success of students from different races and cultural groups. Teachers generally hold more negative attitudes about most minority group students than they have about white middle-class students. This is especially true for black, Mexican-American, and Puerto-Rican students (Datta et al., 1968; Leacock, 1969).

If you have taken courses in anthropology or read books like Hall's *The Silent Language* or *The Hidden Dimension* you are already aware of important cultural differences in social interaction, time, space, and materials. Hall (1969) has also written about cultural differences in listening behavior, a topic of particular interest to teachers. He states that there exists in black culture a series of responses governing the use of the eyes, the hands, the orientation and position of the body, and the tone of voice. Many of these characteristics are frequently misread by Whites. Hall notes an informal rule in black culture: "If you are in the room with another person or in a context where he has ready access to you, there are times when there is no need to go through the motions of showing him you are listening because that is automatically implied" (p. 380). This behavior causes some difficulty when Blacks and Whites interact. While Whites expect some visible or audible sign that one is listening, Blacks, according to Hall, have no such expectation. So when a polite black child casts his eyes downward as a sign of respect, instead of looking straight at his teacher, he might hear his teacher angrily state, "Johnny, look at me when I talk to you!"

Listening behavior is but one example of cultural differences that a teacher from another culture could misinterpret. It is imperative that a teacher interacting with children from a different culture learn about cultural influences. Can you identify any incidents from your own experiences in school when problems arose that were partially attributed to misunderstandings about cultural differences?

STUDENTS' SEX

The impact of school on sex-role behavior has received considerable attention in recent years. In Chapter 3 we discovered differences in the academic achievement patterns of males and females and learned that cultural expectations played an important role in influencing academic motivation and behavior. I now want to explore how students' sex shapes student-teacher relationships.

Many writers have suggested that female teachers favor girls over boys, either because they prefer girls or because they have difficulty controlling boys who have trouble responding to the demands placed on them in elementary school classrooms. These critics call for more male teachers to counteract the "feminization" of the elementary schools (Vairo, 1969; Kendall, 1972).

The line of reasoning used by many of the individuals against feminizing schools is that the characteristics of the elementary schools are similar to those characteristics of the female sex role in our society. Lee (1973) summarizes this relationship in Table 4.2 and breaks down the argument into its components:

1. *There is an extremely high percentage of female teachers at the elementary grade level (about eighty-five percent).*
2. *Elementary schools appear to promote and favor passive, docile, and teacher-centered behaviors on the part of children.*

3. *These behaviors are included in the traditional sex-role repertoire of girls, but are largely alien to the boys' repertoire of sex-typed behaviors. (p. 80)*

Using this logic, we would reach the conclusion that the blame for the apparent feminine characteristics of the elementary schools must fall upon the female teacher.

Research evidence suggests that teachers criticize boys more frequently (Jackson & Lahaderne, 1967) and give them lower grades than their actual achievement dictates (Carter, 1952; Hess et al., 1969). Several studies also have indicated that female teachers are more favorably disposed toward girls and female qualities than boys and male qualities (Arnold, 1968; Jackson, Silberman, & Wolfson, 1969). There is also evidence that teachers overestimate the achievement potential and intelligence of girls, underestimate the abilities of boys, and hold lower expectations for boys than for girls of equal ability (Doyle, Hancock, & Kifer, 1972).

Before castigating the female teacher for the feminization of the elementary schools and her apparent bias against males, let us look at some other explanations offered for the current state of affairs.

Lee (1973) suggests that rather than asking whether the schools have been feminized by female teachers, it is more appropriate to ask whether both female and male teachers have been "schooled." We cannot discount the possibility that the schools socialize their personnel to suit their own goals, placing constraints on the behavior of teachers and thereby accounting for certain institutional demands often erroneously identified with the feminization of the schools.

One such institutional demand is the compulsory attendance laws requiring schools to educate students who may not be very enthusiastic about school. Pupil control becomes an important aspect of school life and teachers bear the onus of imparting the disciplines and regulations that smooth the path of school routines. Teachers' ability to maintain control of their classes is one measure of their success, so they strive for docile, obedient, quiet behaviors and attitudes on the part of students.

Another demand of institutional life is the grade-level organization of the school, binding the teacher to a prescribed amount of material to impart to students over a nine-month period. Strict adherence to schedules and socialization of children to respect and obey the schedule are the teacher's preliminary task. We thus have a strong case against institutional demands as the instigators of the same behavior commonly attributed to the female teacher.

But what about the question of female bias against male students? Brophy and Good (1974) recently reviewed all the literature on

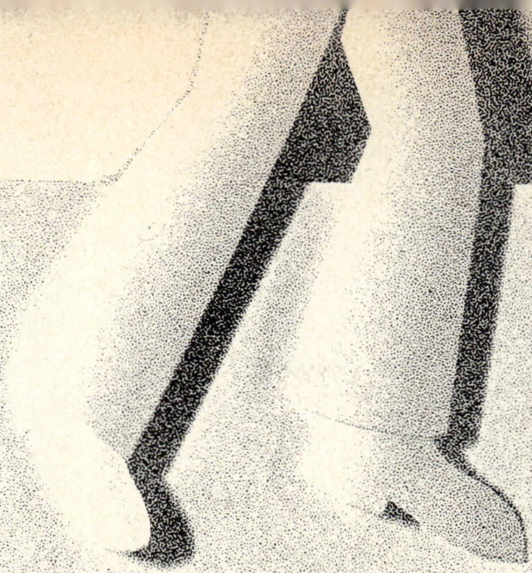

TABLE 4.2
A COMPARISON OF SOME SCHOOL CHARACTERISTICS WITH SEX-ROLE CHARACTERISTICS OF AMERICAN GIRLS AND BOYS.

CHARACTERISTICS OF SCHOOL

Politeness, neatness, obedience, and cleanliness are promoted.

Strong emphasis on language and symbols. Deemphasis on things.

Speaking is discouraged, listening is encouraged. Learning is sedentary and passive, not active.

Teacher is dominant figure.

Strategies for figuring out the teacher offer more success than strategies for learning.

CHARACTERISTICS OF GIRLS AND BOYS

Girls: Polite, tactful, neat, conforming.
Boys: Physically aggressive.

Girls: Verbally competent.
Boys: Object-oriented, competent in physical activities.

Girls: Submissive, passive, dependent.
Boys: Independent, aggressive, strong interest in gross motor behavior.

Girls: Submissive.
Boys: Dominant, aggressive.

Girls: Person-oriented, affiliative.
Boys: Object-oriented.

From P. C. Lee. "Male and Female Teachers in Elementary Schools." *Teachers College Record,* 1973, *75,* 79–98. Reprinted by permission.

the weight that sex differences carry in student-teacher interaction and suggested that the feminine qualities in the elementary school cannot be blamed totally on female teachers. Their evidence indicates that boys have more interaction with their teachers than girls do. It is true that teachers more often warn or criticize boys for misbehavior than they do girls. But many of these same studies indicate that boys often receive more praise and reinforcement for their behavior than girls.

In reviewing the studies of interaction between male teachers and male students, Brophy and Good found no evidence that male teachers were more sympathetic to boys or were better able to diagnose their needs than were female teachers. In other words, the presence of a male teacher in the classroom without any other changes in methods or procedures will not make a difference in the behavior or achievement of boys, other than perhaps having some benefit for fatherless boys. Brophy and Good (1974) state that "male teachers treat boys and girls differently in quite the same ways that female teachers do" (p. 229). They suggest that educators have overemphasized the impact of the large majority of female teachers in the elementary grades and have not adequately investigated the way sex roles are controlled by the institutional expectations of the school.

How do you feel about this issue? Have Brophy and Good deemphasized the importance of male models in the schools? Did you have female teachers throughout the elementary grades? What type of impact did they have on you?

Before we leave the topic of sex differences, there is still another issue to consider. Many authors (Frazier & Sadker, 1973) describe how the combination of courses, materials, and student-teacher interaction makes the majority of female students passive, shy, and dependent but provides male students with learning experiences that help them become self-assured, competitive, and independent. Content analysis of textbooks used in various subject areas reveals that females are portrayed in stereotyped ways. Sadker (1974) states: "A female student desiring to read about another female who is intelligent, creative, powerful, interesting, or charismatic will have to wade through many books before meeting one" (p. 277).

Some critics insist that the curriculum and activities in the school promote sex-role stereotyping. Why must a girl take homemaking rather than shop if she is more interested in making furniture than cookies? Thomas and Stewart (1971) found that guidance counselors responded more positively to females who held traditionally feminine career goals than to those who were interested in traditionally masculine fields.

School athletic programs have also come under attack. For

years, obtaining financial support for girls' athletics has been a struggle. However, Title IX of the Higher Education Act of 1972 no longer allows discrimination on the basis of sex in any school program or activity receiving federal financial assistance. This legislation is currently having considerable influence on the athletic budgets at colleges and universities, which are now increasing women's athletic programs. Similar changes are occurring also at the high school level.

STUDENT PERSONALITY

In the beginning of Chapter 2 I asked you to identify certain characteristics of students that you would encourage. One of the purposes of this exercise was to have you pin down the many student characteristics that you like and dislike. The important point I want to make here is that although you may not particularly like a student, you don't want to treat him in ways detrimental to his academic achievement.

What type of student do teachers favor? Feshback (1969) studied female student teachers' preferences for particular kinds of pupils. She asked her subjects to read stories about elementary students engaged in routine classroom activities and to rate each child in the stories according to his probable popularity among peers, his intelligence, his grades, his generosity, and whether or not the student teachers would prefer him as a student in their class. Student teachers preferred rigid, conforming, and orderly students. Next in popularity were dependent, passive, and acquiescent students, followed by flexible, nonconforming, and untidy students. The student teachers least preferred the independent, active, and assertive students.

An interesting sidelight is that the teachers projected personal preferences onto other students' judgments of peer popularity. They assumed that the classmates of the children described in the stories would prefer the same rigid, conforming, and orderly pattern of behavior in their peers. The teachers also endowed the students they preferred with higher intelligence and grades.

A later study by Good and Grouws (1972) using a sample of both male and female student teachers came up with the same results. Their findings jibed with the results of earlier investigations: Instructors gave higher grades to conforming and rigid students, even though they had lower aptitude and reading scores on final examinations than students who received lower grades (Kelly, 1958); they gave higher grades to students they liked and lower grades to students they disliked, even though their standardized achievement test did not justify the grades received (Hadley, 1954).

Other evidence of differential teacher behavior toward different students springs from a series of studies initiated by Silberman (1969) and continued by Good and Brophy (1972) and Jenkins (1972).

Silberman asked teachers to nominate one student in their class to each of four attitude groups: (1) *attachment* (If you could keep one student another year for the sheer joy of it, whom would you pick?); (2) *indifference* (If a parent were to drop in unannounced for a conference, whose child would you be least prepared to talk about?); (3) *concern* (If you could devote all your attention to a child who concerned you a great deal, whom would you pick?); and (4) *rejection* (If your class was to be reduced by one child, whom would you be relieved to have removed?). He then observed in each class to determine the characteristics of the chosen students and how their teachers interacted with them. Table 4.3 summarizes different student characteristics and accompanying teacher behavior.

It is interesting to note that the students in both the concern and rejection groups appear to be quite similar, with the exception that teachers view the rejection-group students as more of a discipline problem than concern-group students. Yet teachers exhibit sharply contrasting behavior toward these students. They are supportive of and attentive to the academic needs of students in the concern group but are rejective of and primarily attentive to controlling the conduct of students in the rejection group.

The research studies in this section relate a teacher's attitude toward a student to the personal qualities of the student and the way in which he reacts to the teacher. The investigations initiated by Silberman (1969) show that achievement, race, and sex are not the only characteristics determining a teacher's attitude toward a student. Another important factor is the extent to which the student rewards the teacher: The teacher's general satisfaction in working with the student marks her behavior toward him.

SPEECH CHARACTERISTICS

Is it possible to say anything about a student's personality and abilities from the way he talks? The research indicates that if a teacher judges a child's language inferior, she also rates that child more negatively in other characteristics. Williams, Whitehead, and Miller (1972) investigated the concept of vocal stereotyping by examining the relationship between teachers' expectations of student academic performance and teachers' attitudes toward student speech. Using students from three ethnic groups, the study found that teachers expected students whose speech they judged to be nonstandard to perform academically worse than students whose speech they judged to be standard.

Guskin (1970) found that education majors listening to tape-recorded readings by a ten-year-old black boy and a white boy rated the black speaker's language and personality more unfavorably than

TABLE 4.3
TEACHER BEHAVIOR TOWARD DIFFERENT TYPES OF STUDENTS.

STUDENT CHARACTERISTIC	*TEACHER BEHAVIOR*
ATTACHMENT	*ATTACHMENT*
Tend to be high achievers who conform and respond warmly to the teacher.	Teachers like these students but don't show any overt favoritism in interacting with them.
INDIFFERENCE	*INDIFFERENCE*
Tend to be passive and have low salience in the classroom.	Teachers have low rate of interaction with these students and respond with indifference or apathy toward them.
CONCERN	*CONCERN*
Tend to be low achievers and make considerable demands on the teacher.	Teachers perceive demands of these students as legitimate and have high rates of interaction with them.
REJECTION	*REJECTION*
Tend to be low achievers and exhibit behavior problems.	Teachers are turned off by these students and have high rates of interaction with them in dealing with their behavior rather than their academic work.

Adapted from Silberman (1969) and Brophy and Good (1974).

the white speaker's. The raters did not actually see the black student nor did they observe any of his social interaction. They could not have formed their impressions of his personality from any other factor but his language ability while reading a story. Undoubtedly, they associated his black dialect with negative attributes.

F. Williams (1970) has found that teachers' ratings of children's speech enter two main judgmental dimensions—confidence-eagerness and ethnicity-nonstandardness—and apply to language samples of black, Mexican-American, and white ethnic groups.

STUDENT ACHIEVEMENT

The evidence in this area is that teachers interact differently with students of different achievement levels. Good (1970) found that first-grade students whom teachers perceived as high achievers received more questions and praise from their teachers than did students perceived as low achievers. Kranz, Weber, and Fishell (1970), who studied student-teacher interaction in eleven elementary classrooms, recorded interaction in the course of teaching and learning the curriculum and found that teachers consistently interacted more with the top third of their class. Mendoza, Good, and Brophy (1972) have documented this same type of interaction at the high school level.

In addition to the quantity of interaction with students of different achievement levels, there are a number of studies relating the quality of teacher-student interaction to the achievement level of the student. Rowe (1969) found that teachers waited significantly longer for higher-achieving students than for lower-achieving students before giving the answer or calling on another student.

Brophy and Good (1970) studied the classroom behavior of four first-grade teachers toward high- and low-achieving students. Although they found minor differences in the frequency of teacher interaction with students at different achievement levels, they were confronted with significant differences in the quality of teacher contact with these students. Their data illustrate how differential expectations for student achievement take their toll on teachers' classroom behavior. The high achievers were the objects of consistent favoritism. They were *more* likely to be praised for a correct answer and *less* likely to be criticized for a wrong answer than low achievers. The teachers repeated or rephrased a question for the highs but not for the lows when they could not immediately answer it. Last, the teachers neglected feedback to the lows but not to the highs.

The teacher behavior toward high- and low-achieving students is inconsistent with recommended teaching practices. After all, low achievers need more reinforcement from their teachers than high achievers, especially after a correct answer. If you want to encourage low-achievers to respond in class, limiting criticism following an incorrect response is good strategy. Yet, this did not happen. The teachers were more supportive of the students who needed it least and critical of the students who most needed encouragement. Such treatment of high and low achievers maintains the same levels of success and failure for these students.

To demonstrate the effect of differential expectations toward achievement Palardy (1969) studied the reading achievement results produced by two groups of first-grade teachers. Palardy identified one group of teachers who believed that boys could not learn to read as well as girls in the first grade and another group of teachers who believed that boys could learn to read as well as girls. He collected his information from one item in a questionnaire asking numerous questions about students, so that the teachers were unaware of the nature of the study.

The teachers selected for study had the same teaching experience, used the same reading books, had the same type of students, and organized their classes in the same way for reading instruction. All the students in these classes took reading readiness tests in September resulting in initial differences among the classes. However, the boys' reading achievement scores obtained in March were varied. Boys in classes in which the teacher believed they could achieve as well as girls scored significantly higher on the reading tests than boys in classes with teachers who did not believe they could do as well as girls.

TEACHERS' EXPECTATIONS AS SELF-FULFILLING PROPHECIES

The previous studies indicate that teachers' expectations can lead to self-fulfilling prophecies. When teachers' expectations determine the ways they treat students, over time these expectations influence how much students learn.

Rosenthal and Jacobson's *Pygmalion in the Classroom* (1968) stimulated a great deal of interest and controversy about this phenomenon. They administered a nonverbal intelligence test to all children in an elementary school. The test was disguised as one designed to predict academic "blooming" or intellectual gain during the school year. Rosenthal and Jacobson provided each teacher with the names of children in her class with encouraging scores on this test of intellectual blooming. Actually, these children were selected randomly from the teachers' class lists, not on the basis of any test. There should have been no real reason to expect unusual gain from them.

Eight months later all chidren in the school were retested with the same IQ test, and the designated "bloomers" *did* demonstrate significant intellectual growth. The effects showed up more strongly in the first two grades.

Many subsequent studies attempting to induce similar teacher expectations failed to show any impact on student behavior (Fleming & Anttonen, 1971; Claiborn, 1969). Although the findings of *Pygmalion in the Classroom* were widely publicized and discussed, many individuals criticized the methodology of the study (Snow, 1969; Thorndike, 1968). Brophy & Good (1974) pointed out that studies that attempt to induce teacher expectations by providing teachers with phony information have generally not yielded significant results. However, naturalistic studies (observing actual teacher behavior in the classroom) do show the effects of expectancy.

Good and Brophy (1973) identify the steps in the self-fulfilling prophecy:

1. *The teacher expects specific behavior and achievement from particular students.*
2. *Because of these different expectations, the teacher behaves differently toward the different students.*
3. *This teacher treatment tells each student what behavior and achievement the teacher expects from him and affects his self-concept, achievement motivation, and level of aspiration.*
4. *If this teacher treatment is consistent over time, and if the student does not actively resist or change it in some way, it will tend to shape his achievement and behavior. High-expectation students will be led to achieve at high levels, while the achievement of low-expectation students will decline.*
5. *With time, the student's achievement and behavior will conform more and more closely to that originally expected of him. (p. 15)*

This model charts a course for teacher expectations to be self-fulfilling: They must be translated into behavior that will communicate the expectations to the student and shape his behavior in the direction of the expected behavior. This process does not always happen because a teacher may either not form a concise expectation about a student, or continually change his expectations. Even when a teacher does have a consistent expectation for a particular student, if she doesn't communicate that expectation to him the expectation cannot be self-fulfilling. In still another situation, a student who rejects a teacher's conception of himself will act in ways that force the teacher to change her behavior toward him. Teacher expectations about a student have no direct impact on student behavior unless they are communicated to the student and ultimately shape his behavior.

Rist's (1970) observational study provides a good example for understanding Good and Brophy's model. Rist studied teacher behavior toward a small group of kindergarten children that she followed through the second grade. As early as the eighth day of school, the teacher identified the fast learners from the slow learners and seated them at three tables, with the higher social class children seated at table 1 next to the teacher and the lower social class students seated at tables 2 and 3, further from the teacher. Rist provides evidence that the teacher formed her expectations on the basis of such factors as physical appearance, information about the children's family background, language ability, and classroom interaction.

The teacher began communicating her expectations, first, by her seating arrangements, and second, by her treatment of the students in the class. Rist (1970) reports: "Within a few days, only a certain group of children were continually being called on to lead the class in the Pledge of Allegiance, read the weather calendar each day, come to the front for 'show and tell' periods, take messages to the office, count the number of children present in the class, pass out materials for class projects . . ." (p. 419). While the students at table 1 (high social class) interacted regularly with the teacher and received more praise and encouragement, the students at tables 2 and 3 (low social class) had considerably less communication with the teacher, were less involved in class activities, and received less instruction by the teacher. Rist also noted that the blackboard was long enough to extend parallel to all three tables, but the teacher typically worked on the board in front of the students at table 1 and ignored the plight of the children at table 3, who often had difficulty seeing the material on the board.

At the end of the school year, the teacher was asked to comment on the children in her class. She said the following about the children at table 1:

> I guess the best way to describe it is that very few children in my class are exceptional. I guess you could notice this just from the way the children were seated this year. Those at table 1 gave consistently the most responses throughout the year and seemed most interested and aware of what was going on in the classroom. (p. 425)

Of those children at the remaining two tables, the teacher commented:

> It seems to me that some of the children at table 2 and most of

> the children at table 3 at times seemed to have no idea of what was going on in the classroom and were off in another world all by themselves. It just appears that some can do it and some cannot. I don't think that it is the teaching that affects those that cannot do it, but some are just basically low-achievers. (p. 425)

One of the most interesting findings of the study was that the children seated at the first table internalized the attitudes and behavior of the teacher toward the children at the remaining two tables. The children at table 1 ridiculed and belittled the other students. It did not take long for the students at tables 2 and 3 to start calling one another "stupid," "dummy," or "dumb-dumb." We see that the teacher's powerful role in the classroom not only dictates self-fulfilling prophecies but also imposes a social organization on the class. The children at tables 2 and 3 did not begin the year ridiculing and belittling each other. It was the teacher who established the patterns of different behavior that the class adopted.

The seating arrangement that emerged in kindergarten based on the teacher's expectations of academic performance continued into the first grade. Not one of the students identified as slow learners and seated at tables 2 and 3 in kindergarten was assigned to the table for the fast learners in the first grade.

The first-grade teacher relied heavily on the readiness materials completed in kindergarten to detemine academic ability. The criterion established by the school district for determining readiness for the first grade was the completion of kindergarten material. The kindergarten teacher spent most of her time with the "chosen" students at table 1, who completed more material at the end of the school year than the remaining students, so that they were the only group prepared for the first-grade reading material. The other students spent the first few weeks of school doing kindergarten work that they had not completed the year before. This condition ensured that the students at tables 2 and 3 would not be placed in the fast-learners group in the first grade.

School policy also had powerful effects on the continuation of the rigid ability groups formed since kindergarten. The labeling of students as fast or slow by the eighth day of kindergarten stuck to them through the second grade and perhaps throughout their entire elementary school experience.

Not all teachers behave in different ways toward high or low achievers, black and white students, males and females, nor do their expectations lead to self-fulfilling effects. These teachers do not allow their expectations to interfere with their treatment of students. They are more likely to be warm, friendly, and confident in relating to students, unlike hostile or rejecting teachers who are more likely to arouse undesirable negative expectancy effects in their students. "Teachers who have appropriate teaching experiences and develop effective techniques are likely, among other things, to develop effective ways to communicate positive expectations to students, while teachers who have less favorable experiences are likely to begin to communicate consistently negative expectations to some or all of their students" (Brophy & Good, 1974, p. 121).

Can you think of incidents in your schooling when teacher expectations led to self-fulfilling prophecies? Identify the behaviors under each of the following categories: How were they formed? How were they communicated? What type of behavior was exhibited?

USING CUMULATIVE RECORDS

One of the indirect ways teachers learn about student abilities is through the permanent files that contain various kinds of information about each student in the school. These cumulative records usually include health information, family data, test results, report card grades, and teachers' comments.

The availability of these records to teachers and their use by teachers are often-debated issues. Teachers need to know information about individual students to better meet their needs. Yet, teachers must be on their guard against negative expectations implanting themselves in their behavior. If you read that a student was difficult to handle or a slow learner, wouldn't such information influence your attitude or behavior? How do you stand regarding the availability and use of cumulative records?

TEACHER BEHAVIOR AND CREATIVITY

In Chapter 2 I asked you to consider why teachers might prefer high-IQ students rather than highly creative students, even when there were no differences in the academic achievement levels between the two groups. Feshback's (1969) research on teachers' preferences for various types of students provides some explanation for this occurrence, since the very type of behaviors that teachers least prefer—nonconforming, independent, active, and assertive—are the behaviors that creative children exhibit.

Three additional factors contribute to teacher selection of high-IQ students (Cropley, 1967). First, the teacher who values convergent thinking and conformity in classroom activities often finds it difficult to distinguish between divergency and misbehavior. The creative student's humor and independence run close to the behavior of the student who is simply troublesome. Since classroom discipline is a major concern for the teacher, she may find it difficult to tolerate certain divergent behavior. Second, the unexpected responses and unusual questions the creative child comes up with interfere with the teacher's planned lesson by taking the class off the track from the main issue or topic. Third, the creative student's learning style may not fall within the teacher's range of experience. He is willing to take risks by probing and guessing at solutions to problems even when he isn't sure of the answer. Most teachers instruct their students to "think before answering," so the creative child's problem-solving behavior is inconsistent with his teacher's style.

There is some evidence in support of matching divergent students with divergent teachers and convergent students with convergent teachers to aim for higher achievement and improved teacher-student relationships (Yamamoto, 1963). These studies suggest that convergent students and teachers prefer a well-organized, disciplined, and achievement-oriented classroom with the teacher providing strong leadership in directing the class. Divergent teachers and students are less achievement- and structure-oriented and prefer greater student involvement and decision making in the class (Brophy & Good, 1974).

Teachers who want students to express divergent ideas often behave in ways that hinder such expression. Many teachers begin a lesson with the idea of leading students to the "right answer." In fact, Holt (1964) believes that one of the first things children learn in school is to give teachers the answers they want, because teachers reinforce the producers—students who find the correct answers—rather than the thinkers—students who attempt to understand why an answer is correct.

The following dialogue illustrates faulty discussion techniques on the part of the teacher:

T: You read poetry for your . . . ?
1st St: Enjoyment.
T: What else?
2nd St: Entertainment.
T: Yes, another word?
3rd St: Recreation.
T: Yes, but what does it make you feel?

4th St: Good.
T: Yes, it's good for you, and don't you also read it for pleasure? (*T writes the word "pleasure" on the board.*) (Leacock, 1969, p. 52)

Under the guise of an open discussion, this teacher has led her class to the answer she wanted; to avoid any confusion concerning the appropriateness of the answer, she has even written it on the board. Students in such classes soon learn that their ideas are not as important as their teacher's ideas. Leonard (1968) states that this fill-in-the-blank behavior hinders children's creative potential. His report on his observation of elementary classrooms, in which he compares kindergarten children to those in fourth-grade classes, states that it is almost as if one were viewing specimens of two different species. The kindergarten children are natural and responsive, while the fourth graders are inhibited and controlled. From your own observations of children's attitudes and behavior in school, would you agree with Leonard's observation? What happens to these same children when they reach high school?

Teachers can take steps to enhance creative behavior in the classroom. Torrance (1965), one of the leading experts on creativity, recommends the following:

1. Treat questions with respect. *Use poor questions as an opportunity to teach how to ask good ones. Try to help the child or teach him how to find answers to questions. One of the most important rewards for the curious child is to find the answers to his questions.*
2. Treat imaginative ideas with respect. *Do not make fun of the child's ideas or conclusions from his experiences. Show him how to test his ideas for reasonableness against what he already knows. Try to establish, in the class, habits of considering and testing ideas.*
3. Show your pupils that their ideas have value. *Have them write down their ideas (or dictate them in the lower grades); adopt some of them or try them out in classroom activities; display them on the bulletin board. Above all, give them time to think.*
4. Occasionally have pupils do something "for practice" without the threat of evaluation, *to try something out, and later do a similar task for the record, for keeps.*
5. Tie in evaluation with causes and consequences. *In criticizing defects in ideas or in punishing naughty or dangerous be-*

> *havior, explain the response in such a way as to foster the ability to see causes and consequences of behavior. Do not say, "This is good" or "This is bad." Say, "I like this because . . ." or "This could be made better by . . ." (p. 319)*

Carin and Sund (1971) believe that the type of questions that teachers ask plays an important role in encouraging creativity. Examples of divergent questions appear in Table 4.4. Although the list is by no means complete, it will aid the teacher in improving her questioning behavior. From this model she can build her own creative question format list for her class on academic discipline and encourage students to develop creative questions during their studying.

TEACHER BEHAVIOR AND LEARNING STYLES

A number of investigations have explored the effects of matching and mismatching students and teachers on the basis of their cognitive styles. DiStefano (1969) found that students with different cognitive styles (field dependent/field independent) matched to each other viewed each other positively, whereas teachers and students who were mismatched viewed each other negatively. In another interesting study, James (1973) asked teachers at the end of a mini-course to assign grades to the six students in their classes. The most extremely field-independent teacher gave all three of his field-independent students higher grades than his three field-dependent students. The most extremely field-dependent teacher assigned the three highest grades to this three field-dependent students.

Matching students and teachers on cognitive style also increases students' academic performance. Furthermore, the results show that if children are introduced to an unfamiliar cognitive style, they can function effectively in both cognitive styles. This is what Ramirez and Castañeda (1974) found in their program to help Mexican-American children develop bicognitively. In this program, they assessed the cognitive styles of both children and teachers, trained teachers to teach bicognitively, and developed curriculum and classroom environments reflecting both cognitive styles.

Table 4.5 identifies field-sensitive (dependent) and field-independent student behaviors. Table 4.6 identifies different teaching methods used by teachers for each cognitive style. Generally, field-independent teachers encourage independent student achievement and competition between individual students. In contrast, field-sensitive teachers are more interpersonally oriented and prefer situations that allow them to use personal, conversational techniques while interacting with students.

TABLE 4.4
CREATIVE RESPONSE QUESTIONS FORMAT.

PROCESS	*QUESTION*
1. Evaluate	What is your reaction to: a play, concert, story, social event, etc.?
2. Evaluate	If you were going to make something better, i.e., a play, car, couch, skis, bicycle, painting, poem, experiment, solve a problem, what changes would you make?
3. Design an approach to solve a problem	a. How would you go about solving this problem? b. In what ways would you artistically convey your feelings about . . . the film, play, picture, painting, course problem? c. What picture would you draw to show what science, mathematics, home economics, or social studies means to you?
4. Design an experiment	How would you design an experiment to find an answer to the problem?
5. Hypothesize	What do you think will happen if . . . ?
6. Test hypotheses	Which of these hypotheses is best, and why?
7. Infer	What inferences and conclusions can you make from the statement: People who smoke have more lung cancer than people who do not smoke? What inferences can you make from these statements? (1) Smoking causes lung cancer. (2) People who smoke have a biological susceptibility to lung cancer.
8. Invent	How many ways can you think of using a tin can, clothes hanger, roller skates, spool of thread, cardboard box, can opener, surfboard, etc.?
9. Invent	What things do you think are most in need of invention?
10. Design an approach to solve a problem	If you were going to teach _____ to the class below you, how would you do it to insure they really learned?
11. Design an approach to solve a problem	If you were going to convey in an artistic way the message of peace, Christmas, good will to men, non-smoking, non-use of drugs, etc., what would you do?
12. Design an approach to solve a problem	What kinds of problems should we study?

Carin and Sund (1971).

TABLE 4.5
BEHAVIOR OF FIELD-INDEPENDENT AND FIELD-SENSITIVE STUDENTS.

FIELD-INDEPENDENT BEHAVIORS

Relationship to peers
1. Prefers to work independently
2. Likes to compete and gain individual recognition
3. Task-oriented; is inattentive to social environment when working

Personal relationship to teacher
1. Rarely seeks physical contact with teacher
2. Formal; interactions with teacher are restricted to tasks at hand

Instructional relationship to teacher
1. Likes to try new tasks without teacher's help
2. Impatient to begin tasks; likes to finish first
3. Seeks nonsocial rewards

Characteristics of curriculum that facilitate learning
1. Details of concepts are emphasized; parts have meaning of their own
2. Deals with math and science concepts
3. Based on discovery approach

FIELD-SENSITIVE BEHAVIORS

Relationship to peers
1. Likes to work with others to achieve a common goal
2. Likes to assist others
3. Is sensitive to feelings and opinions of others

Personal relationship to teacher
1. Openly expresses positive feelings for teacher
2. Asks questions about teacher's tastes and personal experiences; seeks to become like teacher

Instructional relationship to teacher
1. Seeks guidance and demonstration from teacher
2. Seeks rewards which strengthen relationship with teacher
3. Is highly motivated when working individually with teacher

Characteristics of curriculum that facilitate learning
1. Performance objectives and global aspects of curriculum are carefully explained
2. Concepts are presented in humanized or story format
3. Concepts are related to personal interests and experiences of children

From M. Ramírez and A. Castañeda. *Cultural Democracy, Biocognitive Development, and Education.* New York: Academic Press, 1974.

TABLE 4.6
FIELD-INDEPENDENT AND FIELD-SENSITIVE TEACHING STYLES.

D-INDEPENDENT TEACHING STYLES

onal behaviors
Is formal in relationship with students; acts the part of an authority figure
Centers attention on instructional objectives; gives social atmosphere secondary importance

ructional behaviors
Encourages independent student achievement; emphasizes the importance of individual effort
Encourages competition between individual students
Adopts a consultant role; teacher encourages students to seek help only when they experience difficulty
Encourages learning through trial and error
Encourages task orientation; focuses student attention on assigned tasks

iculum-related behaviors
Focuses on details of curriculum materials
Focuses on facts and principles; teaches students how to solve problems using short cuts and novel approaches
Emphasizes math and science abstractions; teacher tends to use graphs, charts, and formulas in teaching, even when presenting social studies curriculum
Emphasizes inductive learning and the discovery approach; starts with isolated parts and slowly puts them together to construct rules or generalizations

D-SENSITIVE TEACHING STYLES

onal behaviors
Displays physical and verbal expressions of approval and warmth
Uses personalized rewards that strengthen the relationship with students

uctional behaviors
Expresses confidence in child's ability to succeed; is sensitive to children who are having difficulty and need help
Gives guidance to students; makes purpose and main principles of lesson obvious; presentation of lesson is clear with steps toward "solution" clearly delineated

(continued)

M. Ramírez and A. Castañeda, *Cultural Democracy, Bicognitive Development, and Education.* New York: emic Press, 1974.

3. Encourages learning through modeling; asks children to imitate
4. Encourages cooperation and development of group feeling; encourages class to think and work as a unit
5. Holds informal class discussions; provides opportunities for students to see how concepts being learned are related to students' personal experiences

Curriculum-related behaviors

1. Emphasizes global aspects of concepts; before beginning lesson, ensures that students understand the performance objectives; identifies generalizations and helps children apply them to particular instances
2. Personalizes curriculum; teacher relates curriculum materials to the interests and experiences of students as well as to her or his own interests
3. Humanizes curriculum; attributes human characteristics to concepts and principles
4. Uses teaching materials to elicit expression of feelings from students; helps students apply concepts for labeling their personal experiences

Both types of teachers were trained to organize learning environments conducive to each cognitive style. A field-sensitive environment encouraged group projects, close work with the teacher, and material in tune with the ethnic and social background and interests of the students. The field-independent environment was geared to independent activities, minimal participation of the teacher, curriculum materials, charts, and diagrams, and student work that emphasized individual achievement. Ramirez and Castañeda (1974) state:

> The ideal classroom for bicognitive development is one that allows children to work on individual projects and on group projects that afford close contact with the teacher and classmates. A program of study is developed for each student so that he or she has opportunity to work with both field-sensitive and field-independent peers. In this environment it would be possible for both field-sensitive and field-independent children to act as tutors. Classroom walls would be decorated with both field-sensitive and field-independent materials. (p. 145)

When we discussed the reflective-impulsive dimension of cognitive style in Chapter 2, I proposed that a mismatch between the conceptual tempo of a teacher and student could cause problems for the student. Yando and Kagan (1968) studied the relationship between the conceptual tempo of teachers and students. They found that while reflective teachers were able to foster reflectiveness in their students, impulsive teachers had little impact on their students' tempo of response.

Present evidence suggests that the matching or mismatching of students and teachers on conceptual tempo may have important effects on student learning. For this reason, a teacher must recognize his own tempo and relate this information to how he perceives his students' tempos.

Have you noticed teachers rewarding or criticizing certain behaviors related to a reflective or impulsive conceptual tempo? Do you tend to be more reflective or impulsive? Has your conceptual tempo influenced your interaction with certain teachers?

Witkin (1973) raises the question of whether it is too simplistic to speak only of "good teachers" and "bad teachers." Describing teachers in terms of their effects on different students seems more appropriate to him. Students also are not only "good" or "bad" but "good" or "bad" in relation to the teacher.

You can probably remember students in elementary or high school whose behavior and performance underwent a metamorphosis with certain teachers and classroom procedures. Some students definitely favor a highly opinionated teacher; others prefer a teacher who presents a more balanced treatment of issues. Some students get along with a nondirective teacher who places the responsibility of learning on them; others want more guidance and direction from the teacher. Some students like a "lecturer-teacher" and are disappointed if they leave class without many notes; others like an "emcee-teacher" who constantly opens the class for discussion. This list can easily be extended ad infinitum.

By the time a student reaches college, her preferences for certain types of teachers and classroom procedures are set. Earlier you were asked questions about your learning styles. I would now like you to think about the type of teaching style you like best—student- versus content-oriented, businesslike versus unplanned, learner- versus teacher-oriented, and so on. What type of style motivates you? Turns you off? Why do these teaching styles have such an impact on you?

Teacher Behavior and Anxiety

Children want to succeed in school. But sometimes anxiety is so intense that it interferes with academic performance. Three of the factors mentioned in Purkey's reading, "The Atmosphere the Teacher Creates" — warmth, respect, and success — are vital to the anxious child.

If a child respects his teacher highly and wants her to like him, he must be reassured that he is capable and that his teacher will still like and accept him regardless of his academic performance. Sometimes teachers find this a burden because they will have negative reactions to the highly anxious child. They should not compare such a child to another child who is succeeding or question him rigorously in front of the class to find out the nature of his difficulties or simply tell him, "You'll do better next time." They should help him to improve. Ignoring the child's performance is not the answer either, because the anxious child's dependency needs are great. Perhaps the worst thing the teacher can do is simply to neglect him, for such behavior reinforces his ideas that his poor performance affects the teacher's attitude toward him (Sarason et al., 1960).

Anxious children perform better in more structured learning situations (Gaudry & Spielberger, 1971). It appears that a student's anxiety waxes or wanes with the nature of the task required of him. Students who prefer and excel in highly structured classrooms tend to be personally insecure and fear failure; if they know exactly what is expected of them, they can control their anxiety. This precludes independent study, discussion groups, and other types of student-directed learning activities as wise learning strategies for anxious students.

Exam situations strike fear into the hearts of highly anxious students. McCandless (1967) offers some advice to teachers for providing a student with clues about performing in such situations.

> 1. [*Tell him to*] *read all the questions before answering any given question.*
> 2. [*Advise him to*] *answer the questions for which he is sure he knows the answers, leaving those about which he is unsure until last.*
> 3. *Encourage him to express his worry about examinations in general.*
> 4. *Tell him that if he does not understand a question, he should ask its meaning (a good reassurance technique is to say, "If you don't understand what the question means, then probably at least half the class doesn't understand").*
> 5. *If group testing situations bother him, let him take the examination individually, if this is possible.*
> 6. *Underplay the general importance of examinations by saying, "They are necessary. We have to check to see whether you know the material. This test is such a check, and only a check." (p. 546)*

In attempting to help the low-achieving, anxious child, we should not forget the influence of his parents. Some psychologists believe that parents (particularly the mother) initially contribute to the child's anxiety.

Brookover et al. (1965) initiated a successful program to raise the academic achievement of underachieving junior high pupils by enhancing their self-evaluations and expectations. Over 90% of the pupils asked valued their parents' opinion of their ability over the opinion of friends and teachers. As a result of this finding, Brookover et al. set up a series of discussions over a period of one year to inform parents about ways they could encourage the self-concept and academic ability of their children. By the end of the ninth grade, the pupils whose parents were in the program significantly improved their grade-point averages and self-concepts. These pupils were pleased to perceive that their parents also had a higher expectation of their ability.

This program has important implications for dealing with parents. In too many situations, parents are contacted by the school only when their children are in some difficulty. The one-sided negative input lowers parental concepts of their children's potential, which in turn has detrimental effects on their children. We also need to communicate positive information to parents and work more closely with them while helping their children.

TEACHER BEHAVIOR AND ACHIEVEMENT-RELATED MOTIVES

In Chapter 3 we read about Atkinson and Feather's (1966) explanation of the different behaviors exhibited by students with a motive to achieve and by those with a motive to avoid failure. Atkinson (1965) identifies two approaches to the problem of inadequate motivation: deficient motivation because of either personality problems or inadequate challenge. In the first case, the motive to avoid failure is stronger than the motive to achieve. Second, even if the motivation to achieve is strong, the challenge may be inadequate. The tasks presented to the individual may be too easy or too difficult for him.

Looking at the theory and research stemming from achievement motivation, it is apparent that the teacher has to respond differently to students with high and low achievement motivation. Weiner's (1967) advice (giving persons in whom M_s is greater than M_{af} challenging work and giving persons in whom M_{af} is greater than M_s work for which success is within grasp) is a good start in motivating these types of individuals. You may have to divide tasks into smaller units to ensure a greater probability of success for the failure-threatened child.

Maehr and Sjogren (1971) consider other educational procedures in the light of students' achievement motivation. Ability grouping is one such procedure in which achievement motivation is not necessarily correlated with ability. The disparity exists partly because many students with M_s are not at home with school regulations or classroom procedures that do not allow them to set goals and take responsibility for their own learning. They may also have problems with their teachers similar to those faced by highly creative children.

Students who are placed in groups that are homogeneous in ability are probably heterogeneous in achievement motivation. If educators accept the findings of O'Connor et al. (1966), they should consider achievement motivation as important as ability in future grouping procedures. These investigators noted that achievement-oriented students demonstrated greater academic performance and more interest in schoolwork when placed in an ability-grouped class. Students who feared failure stayed at the same level of academic achievement when placed in an ability-grouped class but had less interest in schoolwork. Students with high achievement motivation were more challenged in a homogeneous ability group because of the competition and, in such groups, they show higher preferences for and stronger persistence at tasks than students with low achievement motivation in ability groups.

Independent-study programs are another educational procedure ideal for students with high achievement motivation who are inclined to assume responsibility for their achievement behavior. They are better able to handle independent-study programs than low achievement-motivated students (Heckhausen, 1967). This finding confirms McKeachie's (1961) research: Students with high achievement motivation perform better than low achievement-motivated students in classrooms where teachers emphasize more self-instruction.

Together, the results of ability grouping and independent-study research have implications for differential performance of students in open classrooms (see Chapter 8) where students are given a good deal of responsibility for directing their own learning. Students with different achievement motivation will select different goals and tasks for themselves, the success-oriented students seeking out challenging tasks and the failure-threatened students seeking out very easy or difficult tasks. More monitoring of task selection and performance of low achievement-motivated students in these classes is called for.

CHANGING TEACHER BEHAVIOR

Throughout this chapter I have emphasized important ways in which teacher behavior raises or lowers the degree of student learning in the classroom. Can teachers develop or change their behaviors to adopt more effective ways of interacting with students? I am optimistic that this goal is feasible, but I do not underestimate the difficulty of the task.

Schmuck and Schmuck (1974) have identified a number of barriers facing teachers. The nature of teachers' preservice education is such that many programs are packed with required courses and fail to include opportunities for actual observation and participation in school settings. Many individuals begin student teaching with little understanding of the demands of teaching.

Another barrier is experience, strange as this may seem. Most young adults enter the teaching profession with high hopes and aspirations. They want to make learning meaningful; they want to be democratic, authentic, and helpful. They must grapple, however, with ambivalence in their impulses toward their students because the experienced teachers often set the standards for "appropriate" behavior, which, in many respects, is inconsistent with novice teachers' behavior. It's easy to say, "The hell with experienced teachers." But the inexperienced teacher's need for support, security, and affection is strong during the first year of teaching, and she hesitates to challenge the norms of the teachers in the school.

The inconsistencies between beliefs and practices may give birth to feelings of inadequacy and reduced self-esteem in the beginning teacher. Walberg (1967) believes that many teachers panic at the onset of these feelings. They forget some of the behaviors and values they acquired during teacher training and resort to their own most elementary ideas about teaching (many of which come from their memories about their own student days) or look to the experienced teachers as models for effective teaching. Soon the values and attitudes of the school staff are dominant.

One of the most widely used attitude instruments in education is the Minnesota Teacher Attitude Inventory (MTAI). This instrument measures attitudes of teachers toward teacher-student relationships and predicts how satisfied a person might be as a teacher. A number of studies (see Charters, 1963) have recorded that trainees in education who took the MTAI preferred classrooms exhibiting democratic and humanistic characteristics. But after these same students taught in a classroom for a short period, they changed their ideologies and were less concerned with students than with discipline and meeting academic standards.

Hoy (1968) reported a like finding. He developed Pupil Control Ideology, an instrument similar to the MTAI, designed to measure a teacher's values about education. The two extremes of the conceptual dimension measured by the instrument are labeled "custodial" and "humanistic." A teacher who scores toward the custodial extreme believes that students need control and discipline and that the school must assume authority in developing regulations and procedures regarding student behavior. The teacher with a humanistic orientation believes that power should be shared by students, teachers, and administrators and that students can take responsibility for much of their own behavior.

The results of investigations using the Pupil Control Ideology prove that teachers become more custodial as they teach. Hoy (1968) tested teachers after they had completed four years of teacher training. Some of them did not teach the following year. After one year he tested the two groups again and found that the group who had taught were more custodially oriented, while the group who had not taught their first year out of college had *not* changed their humanistic orientation over the one-year period.

I have spent time on this issue, not to discourage you but to sensitize you to the influence of the staff you work with. Let your confidence and enthusiasm enable you to influence and contribute to the professional development of your colleagues so that the door of educational authority swings both ways.

Teachers can change or improve their interaction with students, but like any form of human behavior, change does not always come about easily. If a teacher does not want to change, how can he be convinced to change his mind and then his ways? The source of feedback to the teacher is extremely important in effecting change. Tuckman and Oliver (1963) demonstrated this fact in a study in which they divided a large group of teachers into smaller groups and provided each group with feedback about their teaching from one of three sources: students only, vice-principal only, and both students and vice-principals. The feedback was in the form of ratings and comments (from his students or vice-principal or both) on his knowledge of the subject, ability to explain, ability to maintain discipline and interest, extent of sympathetic understanding, and fairness. Tuckman and Oliver measured the amount of change in the students' ratings of the same teachers after a twelve-week interval. Student feedback alone resulted in positive, desirable change in the teachers, as did feedback from the students and the vice-principals. However, feedback from the vice-principals alone resulted in teacher changes in a negative direction; this negativity showed up when the students rated their teachers after the twelve-week study. Tuckman and Oliver (1968) interpret their results:

> It can only be surmised that teachers are defensive toward (or even hostile to) administrators who, in the absence of much basis for judgment, attempt to tell them how to teach. Of interest, though, is the fact that within the educational milieu, the only source of feedback to teachers, typically, is their supervisors. The data collected here indicate that such feedback is doing more harm than good, with the best source of feedback, students, overlooked.

Another problem in changing teacher behavior is posed by Combs et al. (1974), who tell us that a teacher's behavior is a function of her perceptions of the situation. To maximize her effectiveness, a teacher must see the entire classroom situation, including herself, as it really exists.

Reaching this level of awareness requires that the teacher stretch her mind; so many things happen so quickly that it is almost impossible to know about everything in the classroom. Aspy (1972b) points out that "it is important to understand that seeing is *not* perceiving" (p. 12). Perception is selective. In teaching many things are not even seen; other situations are seen but not perceived. For example, we learned in Chapter 1 that the beginning teacher is most concerned with personal adequacy: Her perceptions are oriented toward behavior related to this concern rather than toward other dimensions of the classroom.

The key to self-improvement is to become aware of both behavior and its consequences. Much of the content in this chapter has dealt with this relationship. How can you obtain specific information about your teaching behavior? Try these: asking a colleague to observe your behavior and to provide feedback, using video- or audiotape equipment during class sessions and studying your behavior at leisure, and initiating informal conversations with students or anonymously administered student questionnaires.

Observation instruments enable a teacher or observer to look for specific behaviors during student-teacher interaction. Simon and Boyer (1970) have compiled over ninety different systems. One of the most widely used instruments is Flanders' System of Interaction Analysis. Table 4.7 presents this observational system. Notice that teacher talk is classified as either indirect (1–4) or direct (5–7). Indirect teacher influence maximizes student opportunities in the classroom, while direct teacher influence minimizes opportunities for the students. Student talk is also classified into two categories: re-

TABLE 4.7
CATEGORIES FOR INTERACTION ANALYSIS.

TEACHER TALK
INDIRECT INFLUENCE

1. *Accepts Feeling:* accepts and clarifies the feeling tone of the students in a non-threatening manner. Feelings may be positive or negative. Predicting or recalling feelings are included.
2. *Praises or Encourages:* praises or encourages student action or behavior. Jokes that release tension, not at the expense of another individual, nodding head or saying, "Um hm?" or "Go on" are included.
3. *Accepts or Uses Ideas of Student:* clarifies, builds, or develops ideas suggested by a student. As teacher brings more of his own ideas into play, shift to category five.
4. *Asks Questions:* asks a question about content or procedure with the intent that a student answer.

DIRECT INFLUENCE

5. *Lecturing:* gives facts or opinions about content or procedure; expresses his own ideas, asks rhetorical questions.
6. *Giving Directions:* gives directions, commands, or orders with which a student is expected to comply.
7. *Criticizing or Justifying Authority:* makes statements intended to change student behavior from nonacceptable to acceptable pattern; bawls someone out; states why the teacher is doing what he is doing; extreme self-reference.

STUDENT TALK

8. *Student Talk —Response:* talk by students in response to teacher. Teacher initiates the contact or solicits student statement.
9. *Student Talk —Initiation:* talk by students that they initiate. If calling on student is only to indicate who may talk next, observer must decide whether student wanted to talk. If he did, use this category.
10. *Silence or Confusion:* pauses, short periods of silence, and periods of confusion in which communication cannot be understood by the observer.

There is no scale implied by the numbers above. Each number is classificatory; it designates a particular kind of communication event. To write these numbers down during observation is to enumerate, not to judge a position on a scale.

sponse to the teacher and initiation of talk. The final classification, silence or confusion, includes situations that do not fall into the other two categories.

An observer using this system records the number of the category representing the type of interaction going on in the classroom while the teacher is communicating with students. The observer does this every three seconds. By summarizing the data, the observer determines the proportion of direct to indirect teacher talk, the amount of teacher talk to student talk, the proportion of responses in each category, and the patterns of responses. A teacher can tape-record his own behavior and code it according to Flanders's system in his free time. After analyzing the total interaction, he can determine whether his behavior warrants modification. A teacher may find that he does not reinforce students enough (2) or ask questions that encourage students to initiate their own ideas (9). Specific directions and training for using the system appear in a number of references (Flanders, 1970; Kryspin & Feldhusen, 1974).

KEY POINTS

1. *Students model many of their teachers' behaviors and attitudes.*
2. *A teacher's leadership style influences classroom climate and student behavior.*
3. *Teachers' perceptions of their teaching effectiveness and satisfaction are a reflection of students' classroom behavior.*
4. *A teacher's beliefs about himself and others will distinguish an effective teacher from an ineffective teacher.*
5. *Some teachers organize their behavior around a number of teaching myths.*
6. *Challenge, freedom, respect, warmth, control, and success are important factors in creating a classroom climate conducive to developing positive self-concepts in students.*
7. *Teachers can improve student interaction in the classroom by establishing different goal structures–cooperative, competitive, or individualistic.*
8. *Some teachers overutilize competitive goal structures.*

9. *Some teachers prefer higher social-class students and have less favorable attitudes toward minority students.*
10. *Schools have been criticized for being too feministically oriented.*
11. *Male teachers treat boys differently from girls but in the same way that female teachers do.*
12. *More conforming and orderly students find more favor with many teachers than do independent and assertive students.*
13. *A teacher's attitude toward a student grows out of the student's personal qualities and the degree of satisfaction the teacher obtains from working with him.*
14. *Some teachers are biased by the speech characteristics of students.*
15. *Some teachers vary their behavior with students of different achievement levels.*
16. *Teachers' expectations lead to self-fulfilling prophecies in students.*
17. *Teachers must create learning environments that harmonize with the learning styles of their students.*
18. *Teachers can enhance creative behavior by asking more divergent questions and by treating student questions and ideas with respect.*
19. *Anxious students perform better under more structured learning situations.*
20. *Students with a motive to avoid failure should be given work at which the probability of success is high.*
21. *Students who have a motive to succeed should try their hand at challenging work.*
22. *Experienced teachers socialize beginning teachers to the norms of the school.*
23. *There is a tendency for teachers to develop less positive attitudes toward students as they gain more experience working with them.*
24. *Observational instruments are available to help the teacher assess and evaluate his own behavior.*

Suggestions for Further Reading

Good, T., & Brophy, J. *Looking in Classrooms.* New York: Harper & Row, 1973. An excellent source of information on how to prepare yourself for observing a classroom.

Jackson, P. *Life in Classrooms.* New York: Holt, Rinehart and Winston, 1968. An insightful analysis of classroom life.

Rowen, B. *The Children We See: An Observational Approach to Child Study.* New York: Holt, Rinehart and Winston, 1973. This book discusses how to observe children and includes case studies to illustrate developmental problems.

FOLLOW-UP ACTIVITIES

1 Remember your teachers. Students have different experiences with teachers during their school career. They remember some teachers with excitement and fondness and others with resentment and hate. Think about the teachers who had the greatest impact on you (either positive or negative) and examine their behavior. Tell your class or group about these teachers.

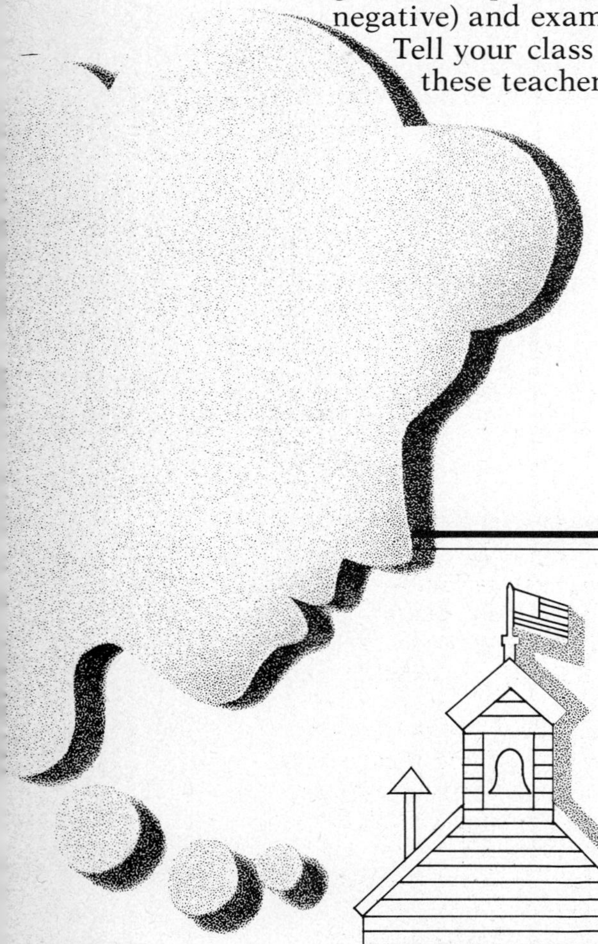

2 Identify college professors who excite or stifle creativity. Chambers (1973) has listed significant factors displayed by college professors that facilitate and inhibit creative development. These factors are summarized below. Discuss these factors as they relate to your own professors. Identify one professor who facilitates and one who inhibits creative development and discuss the specifics of their behavior and the impact on students in the class.

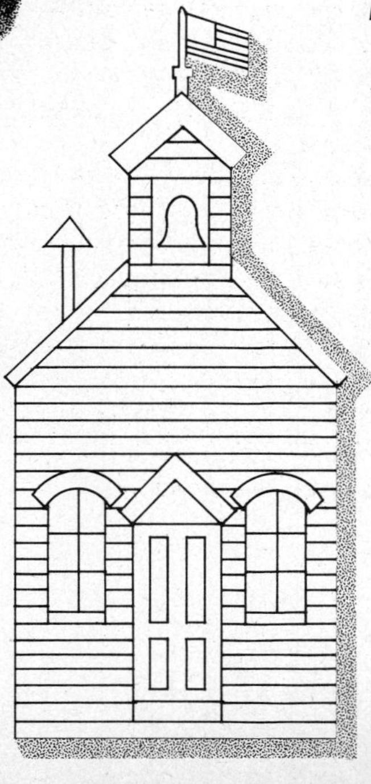

Significant Facilitating Factors

Treated students as individuals; offered encouragement

Encouraged students to be independent

Teacher served as a model

Teacher spent considerable amount of time with students outside of class

Teacher indicated that excellence was expected and could be achieved

Teacher's enthusiasm

Students accepted by teacher as equals

Teacher directly rewarded students' creative behavior or work

Teacher was interesting, dynamic lecturer

Teacher was not good in classroom, but excellent on one-to-one basis

Significant Inhibiting Factors

Teacher discouraged students (ideas, creativity, etc.)

Teacher was insecure (hypercritical, sarcastic)

Teacher lacked enthusiasm

Rote learning was emphasized

Teacher was dogmatic and rigid

Teacher did not keep up with field; generally incompetent

Teacher had narrow interests; was a narrow person

Teacher was not available outside the classroom

Adapted from Chambers (1973), pp. 331–332.

3 Report an incident of rewarding creative thinking.

Torrance (1970) suggests the following exercise for understanding how teacher behavior affects creative responses in children. Observe a class on any educational level and describe an incident in which the teacher or the pupils in the class showed respect for an unusual question, a silly question, a difficult question, an annoying question, and so on.

a. What was the question, who asked it, and what were the general conditions under which it was asked?
b. What was your immediate reaction?
c. What was the immediate reaction of the class, if observable?
d. In what way was respect shown for the question?
e. What, if any, were the observable effects (immediate and/or long-range)?

Repeat the same observation for an imaginative or creative idea expressed by a student.

5 Observe a classroom.

Observe a classroom. Focus on a few students (perhaps two high achievers and two low achievers) and keep a record of their interaction with the teacher and their participation in the class. It might be interesting to include in your report the following type of information (Good & Brophy, 1973):

a. How often do low, middle, and high achievers raise their hands?
b. Do all students approach the teacher to receive help, or do some students seldom approach the teacher?
c. How long does the reading group last for each group of achievers?
d. Are the students involved in their work? How long do they work independently at their desks?
e. How often are students in different groups praised? (p. 49)

4 Analyze expectations influencing behavior. In Figure 4.1 below, Finn (1972) identifies a network of expectations brought to bear on student behavior along with some indication of the direction in which they operate. Use this diagram to discuss the expectations of your peers, parents, friends, and teachers on your self-expectations and achievement. Have your self-expectations been consistent throughout your educational career? In what way did they change? What influences or situations led to the changes? Do you think your educational experience will have an impact on how you behave in the classroom? In what way?

FIGURE 4.1

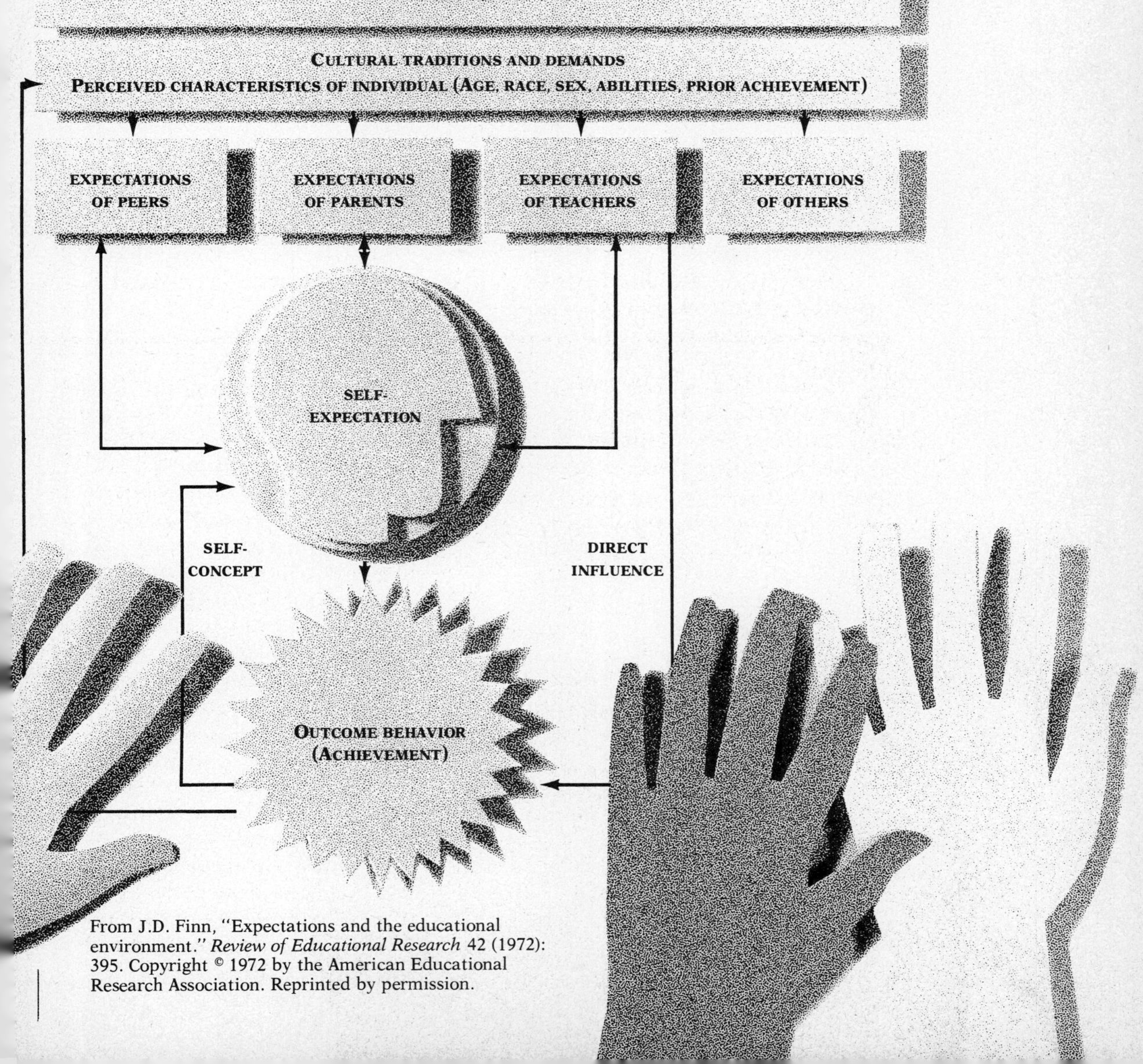

From J.D. Finn, "Expectations and the educational environment." *Review of Educational Research* 42 (1972): 395. Copyright © 1972 by the American Educational Research Association. Reprinted by permission.

6 Respond again to the Ideal Child Checklist. Let's return to the Ideal Child Checklist you completed in Chapter 2. Rate the student characteristics in the same manner as you did before, entering your responses by checking (✔) each behavior that you would encourage, putting two checks (✔✔) beside each behavior that would especially encourage, and placing an (**X**) by each behavior that you would discourage. *After you complete the rating,* go back to your previous responses (from Chapter 2). Were there changes in your second rating? If so, what changes did you make? Why?

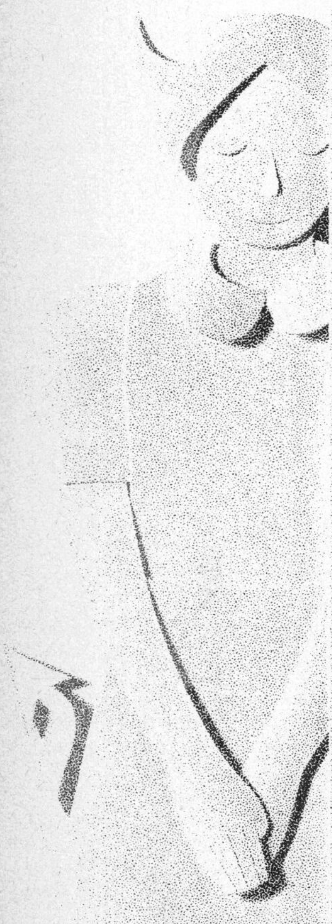

Ideal Child Checklist

1. Adventurous, testing limits
2. Affectionate, loving
3. Altruistic, working for good of others
4. Asking questions about puzzling things
5. Attempting difficult tasks
6. Becoming preoccupied with tasks
7. Competitive, trying to win
8. Conforming
9. Considerate of others
10. Courageous in convictions
11. Courteous, polite
12. Critical of others
13. Curious, searching
14. Desirous of excelling
15. Determined, unflinching
16. Disturbing procedures and organization of the group
17. Doing work on time
18. Domineering, controlling
19. Emotionally sensitive
20. Energetic, vigorous
21. Fault-finding, objecting
22. Fearful, apprehensive
23. Feeling emotions strongly
24. Guessing, hypothesizing
25. Haughty and self-satisfied
26. Healthy
27. Independent in judgment
28. Independent in thinking
29. Industrious, busy
30. Intuitive
31. Liking to work alone
32. Neat and orderly
33. Negativistic, resistant
34. Never bored, always interes
35. Obedient, submissive to authority
36. Persistent, persevering
37. Physically strong
38. Popular, well-liked
39. Preferring complex tasks
40. Quiet, not talkative
41. Receptive to ideas of others
42. Refined, free of coarseness
43. Regressing occasionally, ma be playful, childlike, etc.
44. Remembering well
45. Reserved
46. Self-assertive
47. Self-confident
48. Self-starting, initiating
49. Self-sufficient
50. Sense of beauty
51. Sense of humor
52. Sincere, earnest
53. Socially well-adjusted
54. Spirited in disagreement
55. Striving for distant goals
56. Stubborn, obstinate
57. Talkative
58. Thorough
59. Timid, shy, bashful
60. Truthful, even when it hurts
61. Unsophisticated, artless
62. Unwilling to accept things mere say-so
63. Versatile, well-rounded
64. Visionary, idealistic
65. Willing to accept judgments authorities
66. Willing to take risks

Developed by E. Paul Torrance.

7 Evaluate the pros and cons of students' right to see their educational records and recommendations. The Family Educational Rights and Privacy Act, or Buckley Amendment to the Elementary and Secondary Education Act of 1975, refuses federal funds to any institution that denies parents or students over the age of 18 the right to review the students' educational records. It also prohibits institutions from releasing file documents to other parties without the consent of the parent or student. What are the pros and cons of this amendment?

Another important consequence of this amendment is that college students can request open access to confidential letters of recommendation about themselves. Of course, the person writing the recommendation would be told that this was the case. College students can waive their rights of access to these letters. The decision whether or not to waive these rights is usually made when students apply to a college or university or when they establish a file in the placement office. What would you decide about access to letters of recommendation? What are the advantages and disadvantages of open access? Will letters of recommendation remain an important source of information about students, or will college officials and employers rely more on test scores and grades?

5

INSTRUCTIONAL OBJECTIVES

ORIENTATION

From time to time you probably take a drive in your car without any particular destination in mind. Sometimes you wind up in unexpected places! Taking some courses can be a similar experience. I'm sure that sometime during your college career you asked the following questions: "Where is this instructor taking me?" "What is this class about?" "What am I supposed to be learning in this class?" One of the important aspects of a teacher's decision making is first determining what is to be learned and then communicating this information to students.

The purpose of this chapter is to consider some of the important issues related to this decision: How does a teacher select objectives? How specific does he need to be in identifying the objectives of a course or lesson? How should objectives be communicated to students?

WHAT SHOULD STUDENTS LEARN IN SCHOOL?

Educators clash over what students should be learning in school. Ebel (1972) believes that schools have taken on too much responsibility in trying to solve all the problems of students. The main job of the schools is teaching useful knowledge and skills. Although feelings, attitudes, and interests can facilitate or inhibit learning, they are by-products rather than the main products of an educational program. Ebel argues that schools are not adjustment centers where self-concept and personal problems merit major emphasis in the curriculum.

Other educators believe that, given the "constant change" in knowledge, *how* students learn is more important than *what* they learn. They encourage the development of intellectual skills that equip students to acquire information, formulate hypotheses, and solve problems.

Still another large group of educators believe that the schools are responsible for providing experiences to enhance the personal and social development of students. Rogers (1969) and Holt (1964) insist that the schools must train students to take responsibility for their own learning. Their point of view implies that students should play a major role in determining what they want to learn.

Throughout the history of American public education, the thrust of the schools' goals and objectives has often changed in direction and in intensity. One of the most dramatic shifts has taken place within the last fifteen years. After the launch of Sputnik in 1957, the public education system in this country came under attack for not training the scientists and mathematicians needed to maintain leadership in technology. Commissions were established to study and evaluate public education. One of the most noted investigations of this period, the Conant Report (1959), recommended that capable high school students take four years of mathematics and foreign languages and at least three years of science. During the late 1950s and early 1960s, students in these academic areas were given priority for scholarships and loans.

During the latter part of the 1960s, we began to hear new criticisms of public education. This time the issue was the rigid, impersonal, and authoritarian nature of the schools. The emphasis on rigorous programs in science and mathematics had waned. Educators and psychologists began urging the need for more humanistic schools concerned with personal and social development in addition to academic competency. The era of humanism waxed.

One of the important controversies in curriculum development is over the ascendancy of cognitive versus affective dimensions of learning. Brown (1971) has been involved in developing an educational process called *confluent education* whereby the affective and cognitive dimensions are interrelated. He believes that teachers cannot isolate intellectual experiences from emotional experiences and that they should make use of the relationship rather than deny it. Many other educators also believe that knowledge must be related to feelings and attitudes. If it is not, knowledge will have less impact on behavior change.

In responding to the question of whether schools should direct their attention from teaching skills and knowledge to fostering the development of positive self-concepts and high self-esteem, Coopersmith and Feldman (1974) state: "The resolution is not a choice of which to emphasize but a question of how to develop procedures that increase skills and at the same time promote development of a positive self-concept and self-esteem" (p. 149). They report the results of a study in which teachers and parents ranked the educational goals and objectives these two groups had established for their school and children. Building positive self-concept ranked among the top three goals for both teachers and parents. Objectives involving motivation and decision making ranked higher than spelling, physical education, science, or history. Other studies (Spears, 1973) on educational goals and objectives indicate that both the cognitive and affective dimensions are considered important educational outcomes.

Recently the public has been raising new issues of appropriate educational goals and objectives. Many communities desire health education to counteract the influence of drugs, alcohol, and tobacco; career education is now considered an important part of a student's education in some communities.

An interesting development has occurred in Oregon. Beginning in 1978, the state of Oregon will include in its graduation requirements a number of "survival" competencies that all students will have to demonstrate mastery of in addition to their basic academic requirements (Parnell, 1974). These survival competencies pertain to the students' ability to function effectively on the job, as citizens, as learners, as consumers, as individuals, and as family members. Table 5.1 includes examples of these competencies.

The survival competencies are products of the recognition by educators and citizens that today's world — credit cards, installment buying, television, and numerous other modern developments — requires more individual competencies than were required fifty years ago and that the educational program must be expanded to prepare students to meet these challenges.

SPECIFICITY OF EDUCATIONAL OBJECTIVES

Learning goals are generally expressed in terms of educational objectives written at different levels of specificity for various purposes. At one level are general objectives describing long-range projections for

Table 5.1
Sample Competencies and Performance Indicators From Oregon Graduation Requirements.

Competencies	*Sample Performance Indicators*
Select appropriate governmental or political agencies to contact for assistance with basic problems or concerns.	Given an opportunity to select an issue for which he feels support or concern, the student will write a letter explaining his opinions to the appropriate elected representative at the local, state, or national level.
Describe adverse and beneficial effects of common uses of chemicals.	Given three cans or bottles of pesticides, the student will read and explain warnings on the labels. Given samples of some common household chemicals (detergents, bleaches, insecticides, etc.), the student will briefly describe their harmful effects.
Demonstrate a basic understanding of the financial aspects of motor vehicle ownership and maintenance.	Given a description of the Oregon financial responsibility law, the student will list three basic insurance coverage provisions. Given the terms "down payment," "monthly payments," and "annual percentage rate of interest," the student will define each term.
Demonstrate correct use of banking services that aid in personal money management.	Given a simulated activity, the student can demonstrate ability to write a check, balance a check book, and reconcile a bank statement.
Estimate the consequences for family finances before signing a legal document.	Given a problem situation, the student can predict the consequences of a large installment purchase for future family spending.

From D. Parnell, "The Oregon Walkabout." *Phi Delta Kappan* 56 (1974): 205–206. Reprinted by permission of the author and *Phi Delta Kappan*.

the direction of education on a local, state, or national level. These objectives are usually formulated by special committees or commissions studying the aims and goals of education. *Central Purposes of American Education* (1961) includes a discussion of general educational objectives. Objectives of this type outline their goals in phrases similar to the following: "to develop better citizens," "to foster creative ability," and "to promote our cultural ideals." These statements provide us with the philosophical guidance for determining the nature of the curriculum in our schools (Kibler et al., 1974).

At a much higher level of specificity are explicit instructional (sometimes called performance or behavioral) objectives, which are precise statements of what the student will be able to *do* as a result of instruction. They are stated in terms of behaviors that can be observed and measured to determine whether the objectives have been attained. The objectives in Table 5.1 are examples of behavioral objectives.

Some objectives do not fit neatly into either the general or explicit instructional objective category and are placed at different levels between the two. Table 5.2 provides examples of three different types and levels of objectives. It would not be difficult to add additional levels of implicit objectives to this schema.

One of the crucial issues in instructional planning is the specificity of educational objectives — the teacher's determination of precise goals for a lesson, unit, or course. Some teachers don't feel it necessary to identify all outcomes of a lesson before starting to teach or are satisfied with general descriptions of learning outcomes (implicit instructional objectives). At the opposite end of the continuum are teachers who believe that all outcomes must be stated in behavioral terms that identify specific performances the students are to exhibit at the end of the lesson (explicit instructional objectives). Many educators stand up for explicit instructional objectives because they aid in teaching, learning, and evaluation (Popham & Baker, 1970; Gronlund, 1970). Before I discuss how to write and use explicit instructional objectives,[1] I would like to differentiate them from other procedures teachers often use in planning.

The first question raised by many teachers in planning for instruction is "What shall I do?" This question focuses on the necessary teacher activities in the presentation of the lesson. A similar question is "How shall I teach?" The teacher asking this question considers lecturing, discussion strategies, textbook activities, and numerous other procedures in her repertoire of teaching behavior. Although this question should not be taken lightly, it is premature because the teacher hasn't decided what behaviors or outcomes the students

[1] I shall refer to *explicit* instructional objectives when discussing instructional objectives in this chapter.

Type and Level of Objective	*Example 1*
Educational	The student should be able to communicate effectively.
Implicit Instructional	The student will learn appropriate writing skills.
Explicit Instructional (Behavioral or Performance)	Given a reference manual, the student will write a job application letter in correct form that has no grammatical or spelling errors.

Example 2	*Example 3*
The student should develop into a good citizen.	The student should develop mathematical intellect.
The student will understand the principal functional elements in American elections.	The student will know multiplication facts sufficient to comprehend pertinent word problems.
Without the aid of references, the student will list at least five major steps in American elections and describe the function of each step.	Without the use of tables or a slide rule, the student will solve correctly 90 percent of 20 word problems requiring multiplication of two-digit numbers.

Table 5.2
Sequential Examples of Educational, Implicit Instructional, and Explicit Instructional Objectives.

From Table 2.1 (p. 36) in *Facilitating Student Learning: An Introduction to Educational Psychology* by William L. Goodwin and Herbert J. Klausmeier.

should exhibit as a result of the lesson. Does she want students to learn facts? Analyze events or situations? Solve problems? The answer to the question "What shall I do?" can best be sought *after* determining the desired student outcomes. The following statements focus on teaching activity rather than learning outcomes and are sometimes mistaken for instructional objectives:

to demonstrate to students how to use lab equipment

to work individually with students on their independent reading assignments

to point out the causes of the Civil War

These activities are means to an end, not an end in themselves, because they do not identify what the student will demonstrate as a result of the lesson.

Another approach to writing objectives is identifying the activity or process of the students — stating the objective in terms of a learning *process* rather than as a learning *product*. The following two phrases clarify this difference. Which one states an instructional outcome?

1. *Gains knowledge of the election system*

2. *Identifies the steps in the election process*

If you selected the second phrase, you are correct. This statement tells the teacher what the student should be able to do after instruction. The first statement describes the acquisition of knowledge (learning process) rather than the type of behavior the student will demonstrate after the instruction (learning product). The use of the words "gains," "acquires," and "develops" are clues that an objective is focused on the learning activity rather than on student outcomes.

Another approach that is mistakenly identified as an instructional objective strategy is the listing of the course content. A course description is not the same as describing the course objectives because this description also fails to identify the student performances at the end of the course. Suppose you were told at the beginning of an economics course that you were going to learn about the following:

The demand curve

Investment demand

Price level

The listing of content is often ambiguous because the procedure does not identify what you are supposed to do with the topics.

Writing Instructional Objectives

The instructional objectives in Table 5.2 identify the three major components of this type of objective:

1. *The* behavioral term *expressing the type of task required by the student ("write," "list," "solve").*
2. *The* situation *or* condition *under which the behavior is to be performed ("given a reference manual," "without the aid of references," "without the use of tables or a slide rule").*
3. *The* criterion *or* level of performance *that will be used to evaluate the success of the performance or product ("no grammatical or spelling errors," "at least five major steps," "90%").*

THE BEHAVIORAL TERM

The most important component of an instructional objective is the specific term that describes the observable act the student is to perform. This description is in the form of an action verb. Mager (1962) states that many ambiguous words used in writing objectives are open to a wide range of interpretations. Listed below are words that express outcomes. The words in the left-hand column are ambiguous and can be interpreted in many ways, while the words in the right-hand column are action verbs and are open to fewer interpretations.

Ambiguous	*Precise*
to know	to write
to understand	to recite
to really understand	to identify
to appreciate	to differentiate
to fully appreciate	to solve
to grasp the significance of	to construct
to enjoy	to list
to believe	to compare
to have faith in	to contrast

What does a teacher mean when she states that she wants a student to "know" something? Does she want him to remember certain information, to solve problems, to create new ideas? To "know" can mean many things. The same holds true for words like "appreciate" or "grasp the significance of." How do we determine whether a student appreciates or grasps the significance of some information or value? Until we describe specifically what the student will be *doing* when demonstrating that he "appreciates" or "grasps the significance of," we really don't know exactly what the student is to learn from the experience. The more we use words similar to those listed in the right-hand column, the more we communicate to the student the exact behavior expected of him. The statements below provide concise information on student outcomes:

The student presents *an impromptu speech.*

The student draws *a diagram of the combustion engine.*

The student writes *the name of each of the states in the United States.*

THE SITUATION OR CONDITION

The important aspect of this component is to describe the "givens," limitations, or restrictions that are imposed on the student as he strives for the learning outcome. Here are some examples of some conditions that narrow the focus of instructional objectives:

given a map of the United States

without the use of notes

after reading Chapter Four in the textbook

after viewing Hamlet

THE CRITERION OR LEVEL OF PERFORMANCE

This component is a statement of the minimal level of performance that will be accepted as evidence that the learner has achieved the objective. The following are some levels of performance that further delineate an instructional objective:

all four steps stated in the textbook

without an error

at least 90% correct

must include three of the four reasons

must be correct to the nearest percent

must be completed within thirty minutes

Now try to write an instructional objective for teaching students to determine the area of a square. The exact wording will vary, but you should have written something like the following: "Given a square with the length of side marked, the students will determine its area using the formula $A = s^2$."

Try writing another objective for teaching students the correct use of colons in writing. You are also interested in having them identify the rule used. You should have written something like the following: "Given a set of rules for the use of colons and a set of sentences that require colon insertion, the students will place each colon properly and identify the rule appropriate to each placement without any errors."

In some cases, the situation or level of performance or both might be omitted from lists of instructional objectives, as in this objective: "The students state the capital of each of the states." Although these objectives are not as complete as they might be, they still serve an important function in communicating instructional intent to students.

Plowman (1971) details some instructional objectives in different subject areas:

> *Math:* Given an illustration of an acute angle overlaid by a protractor, the student will indicate the measure of the angle in degrees.
>
> *Social Studies:* After studying an affluent and a poor community, the student will identify at least two examples of deprivation (parental, social, cultural, or nutritional) in each community.
>
> *Art:* After visiting an art museum, the student will identify two paintings he likes and two he does not like and give reasons for his choices. Reasons given are to reflect the individual's own values or a set of external standards discussed in class.

Instructional objectives benefit the teacher because she knows exactly what student behavior is desired upon the completion of a lesson. She is then in a better position to select appropriate teaching methods for the designated student outcome. We shall learn in Chapters 6 through 8 that some teaching methods are more effective than others for attaining certain objectives. Knowing the type of expected outcome is important in making decisions to direct students to that outcome.

Instructional objectives help the teacher during evaluation, because she can construct test questions directly from her objectives. Constructing tests in this manner takes the guesswork out of the evaluation process.

There is some evidence to suggest that if teachers initially give students the objectives of a lesson or course they will spend more time focusing on the designated outcomes. Long and Huck (1972) studied subjects who received explicit objectives and subjects who received none. Those students armed with objectives knew what to attend to during a lecture. Mager and McCann (1961) reported that students who were given detailed statements of the instructional objectives significantly reduced the time required for training, as compared to students who were instructed without objectives.

There are many studies that have not found students to learn more because of instructional objectives. Duell (1974) suggests that instructional objectives may be most helpful when they direct the student to learn information that he would not otherwise consider important. But, if explicit objectives do not always lead to greater learning gains, they may lead to more efficient learning. Let's look at the possible benefit to students.

Students often ask instructors how to prepare for an examination or request information about what they are supposed to know. A typical teacher response is: Everything! The instructor may respond in this way because he hasn't constructed the exam and is not sure what he will ask, or he hasn't thought about classifying the information presented to the class in terms of degree of importance. Deterline (1968) points out that students take lecture notes, read textbooks, take part in discussions, write papers, and study — all as part of an attempt to process a mass of information and "learn it." During this process it is not unusual for a good deal of misunderstanding to take place between a student and teacher. Can you remember a situation when a student argued with a teacher about "what the teacher wanted" after receiving his examination? The following dialogue from Deterline (1968) illustrates a typical problem:

> *Student:* I don't think this question is fair.
>
> *Teacher:* Why not?
>
> *Student:* Because it is about something that doesn't seem to be very important. You spent only a short time on it, and the book covers it in only a half a page. I concentrated on this other topic because it seems to me to be so much more important. You spent three class periods on it, and it fills almost eight pages in the book, but you only asked two questions about it. What should I do before the next test in order to study the right things? (p. 8)

Can you think of a "misunderstanding" you had with an instructor concerning what was to be learned in a course? Deterline (1968) believes that instructional objectives will alleviate these problems: Studying is more relevant, the student spends his time more wisely on appropriate content, and each student is in a better position to determine his progress and the amount and type of preparation needed for examinations.

Would you like to begin a course by receiving a complete list of all the objectives for the semester, knowing that your examinations would be limited to these objectives? Are there some limitations to this approach?

Educators disagree about the importance or necessity of explicit instructional objectives. Eisner (1969) argues for the legitimacy of what he calls expressive objectives. An expressive objective:

> identifies a situation in which children are to work, a problem in which they are to engage; but it does not specify what from that encounter, situation, problem, or task they are to learn. An expressive objective provides both the teacher and the student with an invitation to explore, defer, or focus on issues that are of peculiar interest or importance to the inquirer. (pp. 15 – 16)

A teacher who wants to take her class to the zoo for no other purpose than to allow the students to explore the environment knows that each student will achieve different learning outcomes from the experience. In this situation, the teacher is more concerned with an expressive objective than with an instructional objective.

In the following article, Adams (1972) raises some additional questions concerning the use of instructional or behavioral objectives. As you read the article identify the questions and think about how the proponent of behavioral objectives might respond to these questions.

Some Questions Concerning Behavioral Objectives

The clear-cut formulation of behavioral objectives is becoming increasingly fashionable. Furthermore, some educators seem to feel that without a thorough understanding of overt formal objectives one cannot accomplish anything in teaching.

The use of these objectives in teaching focuses on dehumanized output (the terminology of comptuer programming), even though measures of educational output (i.e., results) have been shown to have little validity. Nonetheless, Department of Defense and business successes with such rational, decision-making models are thought worthy of being applied to education. In fact, behavioral goals, usually deliberately stated with vagueness, may or may not be worthwhile.

From D. M. Adams, "Some Questions Concerning Behavioral Objectives," *Journal of Teacher Education* 23 (1972): 25–26. Reprinted by permission.

But let's look at what often happens if a teacher balks at using behavioral objectives. He is, at least in many quarters, accused of promoting unclear thinking and of doing a great disservice to the quality of instruction. The underlying assumptions of using such objectives are not to be questioned, even if they do prove to be empty and pretentious.

We need to ask ourselves some very basic questions about whether we really can clearly identify the objectives of education. After all, any learning progress has thousands of conscious and unconscious objectives, and to slice it up into terms of concrete, overt goals may take all the life out of it.

Another series of questions needs to be asked regarding measurement. It may very well be that our concern with evaluation results in the subtle (or not so subtle) feeling that anything that cannot be measured is unimportant and/or a threat. This would mean that unmeasured or unmeasurable experiences are allowed (or forced) to slip away when we deal only with measurable production. Is the idea that only those things that we can measure are the most important just so much pseudoscientific nonsense? Should the things we do come mainly from our primitive measuring instruments? It seems to me that nothing is more absurd and dangerous than thinking that we measure all results worth achieving; what we in fact end up measuring may be trivial, insipid, and useless.

Is learning short-circuited by the very methods that lead to and stem from behavioral objectives? I shudder to think of the deadening effect of identifying (and reemphasizing) all worthwhile educational results in these terms. The outcome would be worse than teaching for so-called objective tests. Furthermore, the attempt to channel learning according to preconceived objectives may very well waste the best human powers to learn.

Somehow it seems dishonest to have carefully thought out behavioral notions about exactly what and how someone is supposed to learn. A teacher, by his natural authority, may tell the students what makes sense to him; but if they don't want to follow, why should they have to? Maybe we also need to rethink the notion of manipulating others for their own good rather than simply coming up with more comprehensive and seductive techniques.

Much that is creative, imaginative, and innovative seems to be hampered and fenced in by demands for identifying and teaching toward behavioral objectives. Perhaps we should also take a long, hard look at whether this make-believe framework of precision really helps. This does not mean that it is automatically necessary to rule out completely the use of behavioral objectives; they may, at times, prove useful. But with the same degree of fairness, we should not assume that a teacher is wasting his time if he doesn't make use of objectives; because, after all, when one deals with real people, many unanticipated, intuitive, and spontaneous things happen. And these things, in the long run, may be the most important.

Gage and Berliner (1975) have collected some of the criticisms of behavioral objectives and replies by their proponents. Analyze the statements below, along with Adams' arguments, and figure out your position in the controversy.

Criticisms

1. *Only trivial objectives can be put in behavioral terms.*
2. *Behavioral objectives are antihumanistic and mechanical.*
3. *Unanticipated outcomes of instruction may be the most important.*

Replies

1. *If enough ingenuity is applied, important objectives can be stated in behavioral terms.*
2. *It may be more humane to let students know what they should be learning.*
3. *If so, let them occur, but this fact does not rule out the desirability of anticipated and measured outcomes.*

DEVELOPING OBJECTIVES

In some schools, the teacher is provided with a curriculum guide including objectives and a topical outline for a particular course. But in other situations, the teacher has to develop objectives by herself.[2] In any situation the task is complex, because as the teacher learns more about each student in her class she finds that the variability in student ability, attitudes, and interests prohibits the use of the same objectives for all students.

WHERE STUDENTS ARE NOW

In the process of developing objectives the teacher must determine the students' present behavior or knowledge — this is most important. Of course, it is possible to generate lists of objectives for a course without

[2]Recently, various organizations have established objective exchanges to which teachers can write for lists of objectives in various subject areas. I list a number of these organizations at the end of the chapter.

considering what the students already know. But what good does it do to develop objectives that students do not have the necessary skills or knowledge to strive for? In such situations, it would be better to establish objectives at a lower level of difficulty that the students could reach within a reasonable time.

Teachers make many mistakes in failing to consider student characteristics when establishing objectives. A common error is requiring students to read textbooks at two or more grade levels above their reading ability to attain certain objectives. These students fail because their reading deficiency impedes them in benefitting from this mode of instruction. The behavior (to read) identified by the instructional objective is inappropriate for the students. As a teacher learns more about the characteristics of students and the knowledge they possess in a given subject area or topic, he will be better equipped to develop instructional objectives consistent with the ability level of his students.

Informal teacher tests assess student readiness better than the standardized achievement tests given periodically throughout a student's academic career. Standardized achievement tests have not been developed for specific instructional objectives and do not provide the type of information the teacher needs (see Chapter 9 for a more detailed discussion of teacher-made and standardized measurement instruments).

ACADEMIC CONTENT

Academic content provides important raw material for shaping implicit or explicit instructional objectives. There are at least two ways to view academic content. The first is the level of difficulty. Hunter (1971) states: "A continuum exists in most content areas, with certain knowledge of skills prerequisite to achievement of more difficult or more complex knowledge and skills" (p. 149). A student must be able to count before he can add; he must be able to add before he can multiply. Reading a paragraph depends upon reading a sentence, which depends upon understanding the meaning of words, which depends upon identifying letters.

Suppose a teacher wants to teach subtraction to a group of students who have already had some introduction to the topic. After analyzing the skills needed for subtraction, she determines that borrowing is a key operation in many subtraction situations. She develops an informal test comprised of the following items to determine what her students already know. The examples below indicate some of the levels of difficulty in subtraction (Spencer & Smith, 1969, p. 165).

Easy	Skill	Examples of problems
	1. number facts up to ten	$8 - 5$
	2. number facts above ten	$11 - 7$
	3. no borrowing	$22 - 2$
	4. with borrowing	$40 - 3$
	5. two numbers no borrowing	$57 - 37$
	6. two numbers with borrowing	$51 - 18$
Difficult		

The second dimension of academic content is the dimension of complexity. One of the most helpful guides in selecting and defining objectives on this continuum is the *Taxonomy of Educational Objectives,* comprising two handbooks. The handbook on the cognitive domain (Bloom et al., 1956) classifies objectives involving intellectual tasks; the handbook on the affective domain (Krathwohl et al., 1964) classifies objectives involving attitudes, values, and interests. Each of the taxonomies organizes objectives into a hierarchical framework of behaviors that are more complex or internalized than the previous category. In the cognitive domain, the categories are arranged along a continuum from simple to more complex: knowledge, comprehension, application, analysis, synthesis, and evaluation.

In the affective domain, the continuum is based on the degree of internalization that each behavior exhibits. That is, the classification begins with an attitude or value from the level of awareness, proceeding to the point where it guides or directs a person's actions: receiving, responding, valuing, organization, and characterization of a value or value complex.

> For example, a person's value regarding the welfare of his fellow man can develop from (1) an awareness of the need that some people have for a better life, to (2) a financial contribution to the United Fund, to (3) a commitment to work in a local tutoring program, to (4) incorporating the ideal of the greatest welfare of all men into his political, religious, and economic system of values, all of which then reflect a more humanitarian

> outlook, to (5) pursuing a career in social work out of a deep concern for the welfare of less advantaged members of our society. (Gorman, 1974, p. 367)

Tables 5.3 and 5.5 include brief descriptions of each of the major categories in the cognitive and affective domains. A more detailed treatment of the various categories and their subcategories appears in the handbooks with illustrative examples and test questions.

The committee that produced the handbooks in the cognitive and affective domains has not produced one for the psychomotor domain. If you are interested in a classification in this area, refer to Harrow (1972).

Tables 5.4 and 5.6 provide examples of illustrative general instructional objectives and behavioral terms (action verbs) for writing objectives at various levels of the cognitive and affective domains of the taxonomy.

If an English teacher wants to write an objective at the evaluation level of the cognitive domain, the illustrative general (implicit) instructional objectives in Table 5.4 provide him with information about the type of educational activity occurring at this level (for example, judges the logical consistency of written material). In the next column he observes illustrative behavioral terms for writing instructional objectives (for example, appraises, compares, concludes). Using this information he might write as a performance objective:

> After reading *Profiles in Courage,* the student will contrast the political behavior of one individual in the book with one of his own United States senators.

In another situation, an elementary school teacher deplores students' intragroup hostility and wants her students to be more cooperative. She would like to include this behavior in her list of instructional objectives. In Table 5.6, summarizing the affective domain, she notices an illustrative general objective—enjoys helping others—at the responding level of the taxonomy. She selects "helps" from the behavioral terms column and writes the following instructional objective:

> After discussing the importance of cooperation in the classroom, the student will help peers having homework problems.

Note that some behavioral terms are used at several levels of the taxonomy. The term "identifies," for example, can be used as follows (Gronlund, 1970):

> *Knowledge:* Identifies the correct definition of a term.
> *Application:* Identifies proper grammar usage.
> *Analysis:* Identifies the parts of a sentence. (p. 79)

TABLE 5.3

MAJOR CATEGORIES IN THE COGNITIVE DOMAIN OF THE TAXONOMY OF EDUCATIONAL OBJECTIVES (BLOOM, 1956)

DESCRIPTIONS OF THE MAJOR CATEGORIES IN THE COGNITIVE DOMAIN

1. *Knowledge.* Knowledge is defined as the remembering of previously learned material. This may involve the recall o wide range of material, from specific facts to complete theories, but all that is required is the bringing to mind of t appropriate information. Knowledge represents the lowest level of learning outcomes in the cognitive domain.

2. *Comprehension.* Comprehension is defined as the ability to grasp the meaning of material. This may be shown translating material from one form to another (words to numbers), by interpreting material (explaining or summar ing), and by estimating future trends (predicting consequences or effects). These learning outcomes go one step beyo the simple remembering of material, and represent the lowest level of understanding.

3. *Application.* Application refers to the ability to use learned material in new and concrete situations. This may inclu the application of such things as rules, methods, concepts, principles, laws, and theories. Learning outcomes in t area require a higher level of understanding than those under comprehension.

4. *Analysis.* Analysis refers to the ability to break down material into its component parts so that its organizatio structure may be understood. This may include the identification of the parts, analysis of the relationships betw parts, and recognition of the organizational principles involved. Learning outcomes here represent a higher intellect level than comprehension and application because they require an understanding of both the content and the str tural form of the material.

5. *Synthesis.* Synthesis refers to the ability to put parts together to form a new whole. This may involve the production unique communication (theme or speech), a plan of operations (research proposal), or a set of abstract relati (scheme for classifying information). Learning outcomes in this area stress creative behaviors, with major emphasis the formulation of new patterns or structures.

6. *Evaluation.* Evaluation is concerned with the ability to judge the value of material (statement, novel, poem, resea report) for a given purpose. The judgments are to be based on definite criteria. These may be internal criteria (organ tion) or external criteria (relevance to the purpose) and the student may determine the criteria or be given th Learning outcomes in this area are highest in the cognitive hierarchy because they contain elements of all of the ot categories, plus conscious value judgments based on clearly defined criteria.

TABLE 5.4
EXAMPLES OF GENERAL INSTRUCTIONAL OBJECTIVES AND BEHAVIORAL TERMS FOR THE COGNITIVE DOMAIN OF THE TAXONOMY.

LLUSTRATIVE GENERAL INSTRUCTIONAL)BJECTIVES	*ILLUSTRATIVE BEHAVIORAL TERMS FOR STATING SPECIFIC LEARNING OUTCOMES*
:nows common terms, knows specific facts, knows 1ethods and procedures, knows basic concepts, knows rinciples	Defines, describes, identifies, labels, lists, matches, names, outlines, reproduces, selects, states
'nderstands facts and principles, interprets verbal 1aterial, interprets charts and graphs, translates verbal 1aterial into mathematical formulas, estimates future onsequences implied in data, justifies methods and rocedures	Converts, defends, distinguishes, estimates, explains, extends, generalizes, gives examples, infers, paraphrases, predicts, rewrites, summarizes
pplies concept and principles to new situations, applies aws and theories to practical situations, solves 1athematical problems, constructs charts and graphs, emonstrates correct usage of a method or procedure	Changes, computes, demonstrates, discovers, manipulates, modifies, operates, predicts, prepares, produces, relates, shows, solves, uses
:ecognizes unstated assumptions, recognizes logical fallacies in reasoning, distinguishes between facts and inferences, evaluates the relevancy of data, analyzes the rganizational structure of a work (art, music, writing)	Breaks down, diagrams, differentiates, discriminates, distinguishes, identifies, illustrates, infers, outlines, points out, relates, selects, separates, subdivides
Vrites a well-organized theme, gives a well-organized peech, writes a creative short story (or poem, or music), roposes a plan for an experiment, integrates learning om different areas into a plan for solving a problem, ormulates a new scheme for classifying objects (or vents, or ideas)	Categorizes, combines, compiles, composes, creates, devises, designs, explains, generates, modifies, organizes, plans, rearranges, reconstructs, relates, reorganizes, revises, rewrites, summarizes, tells, writes
udges the logical consistency of written material, judges he adequacy with which conclusions are supported by ata, judges the value of a work (art, music, writing) by se of internal criteria, judges the value of a work (art, 1usic, writing) by use of external standards of excellence	Appraises, compares, concludes, contrasts, criticizes, describes, discriminates, explains, justifies, interprets, relates, summarizes, supports

eprinted with permission of Macmillan Publishing Co., Inc. from *Stating Objectives for Classroom Instruction* by Norman E. Gronlund. © Copyright, Norman E. :onlund, 1970.

TABLE 5.5
MAJOR CATEGORIES IN THE AFFECTIVE DOMAIN OF THE TAXONOMY OF EDUCATIONAL OBJECTIVES (KRATHWOHL, 1964).

DESCRIPTIONS OF THE MAJOR CATEGORIES IN THE AFFECTIVE DOMAIN
1. *Receiving.* Receiving refers to the student's willingness to attend to particular phenomena or stimuli (classroom activities, textbook, music, etc.). From a teaching standpoint, it is concerned with getting, holding, and directing the student's attention. Learning outcomes in this area range from the simple awareness that a thing exists to selective attention on the part of the learner. Receiving represents the lowest level of learning outcomes in the affective domain.
2. *Responding.* Responding refers to active participation on the part of the student. At this level he not only attends to a particular phenomenon but also reacts to it in some way. Learning outcomes in this area may emphasize acquiescence in responding (reads assigned material), willingness to respond (voluntarily reads beyond assignment), or satisfaction in responding (reads for pleasure or enjoyment). The higher levels of this category include those instructional objectives that are commonly classified under "interests"; that is, those that stress the seeking out and enjoyment of particular activities.
3. *Valuing.* Valuing is concerned with the worth or value a student attaches to a particular object, phenomenon, or behavior. This ranges in degree from the more simple acceptance of a value (desires to improve group skills) to the more complex level of commitment (assumes responsibility for the effective functioning of the group). Valuing is based on the internalization of a set of specified values, but clues to these values are expressed in the student's overt behavior. Learning outcomes in this area are concerned with behavior that is consistent and stable enough to make the value clearly identifiable. Instructional objectives that are commonly classified under "attitudes" and "appreciation" would fall into this category.
4. *Organization.* Organization is concerned with bringing together different values, resolving conflicts between them, and beginning the building of an internally consistent value system. Thus the emphasis is on comparing, relating, and synthesizing values. Learning outcomes may be concerned with the conceptualization of a value (recognizes the responsibility of each individual for improving human relations) or with the organization of a value system (develops a vocational plan that satisfies his need for both economic security and social service). Instructional objectives relating to the development of a philosophy of life would fall into this category.
5. *Characterization by a Value or Value Complex.* At this level of the affective domain, the individual has a value system that has controlled his behavior for a sufficiently long time for him to have developed a characteristic "life style." Thus the behavior is pervasive, consistent, and predictable. Learning outcomes at this level cover a broad range of activities, but the major emphasis is on the fact that the behavior is typical or characteristic of the student. Instructional objectives that are concerned with the student's general patterns of adjustment (personal, social, emotional) would be appropriate here.

TABLE 5.6
EXAMPLES OF GENERAL INSTRUCTIONAL OBJECTIVES AND BEHAVIORAL TERMS FOR THE AFFECTIVE DOMAIN OF THE TAXONOMY.

ILLUSTRATIVE GENERAL INSTRUCTIONAL OBJECTIVES	*ILLUSTRATIVE BEHAVIORAL TERMS FOR STATING SPECIFIC LEARNING OUTCOMES*
Listens attentively, shows awareness of the importance of learning, shows sensitivity to human needs and social problems, accepts differences of race and culture, attends closely to the classroom activities	Asks, chooses, describes, follows, gives, holds, identifies, locates, names, points to, selects, sits erect, replies, uses
Completes assigned homework, obeys school rules, participates in class discussion, completes laboratory work, volunteers for special tasks, shows interest in subject, enjoys helping others	Answers, assists, complies, conforms, discusses, greets, helps, labels, performs, practices, presents, reads, recites, reports, selects, tells, writes
Demonstrates belief in the democratic process, appreciates good literature (art or music), appreciates the role of science (or other subjects) in everyday life, shows concern for the welfare of others, demonstrates problem-solving attitude, demonstrates commitment to social improvement	Completes, describes, differentiates, explains, follows, forms, initiates, invites, joins, justifies, proposes, reads, reports, selects, shares, studies, works
Recognizes the need for balance between freedom and responsibility in a democracy, recognizes the role of systematic planning in solving problems, accepts responsibility for his own behavior, understands and accepts his own strengths and limitations, formulates a life plan in harmony with his abilities, interests, and beliefs	Adheres, alters, arranges, combines, compares, completes, defends, explains, generalizes, identifies, integrates, modifies, orders, organizes, prepares, relates, synthesizes
Displays safety consciousness, demonstrates self-reliance in working independently, practices cooperation in group activities, uses objective approach in problem solving, demonstrates industry, punctuality, and self-discipline, maintains good health habits	Acts, discriminates, displays, influences, listens, modifies, performs, practices, proposes, qualifies, questions, revises, serves, solves, uses, verifies

The use of a particular action verb does not necessarily place the objective at a particular level of the taxonomy. Although there is some overlap in terms, many terms are more directly relevant to one category than to another (for example, criticizes [evaluation] and solves [application]).

One of the important uses of the taxonomy is to make the teacher aware that it is possible to write objectives for and measure more complex skills than the recall of basic facts. Sanders (1966) has written a book entitled *Classroom Questions: What Kinds?* to show teachers how to improve their questioning behavior using the taxonomy. He points out that many teachers overemphasize questions at the knowledge and comprehension levels and omit higher-level questions. He provides examples for leading students to higher levels of thinking through an improvement in the quality of questioning.

The following example from Sanders (1966) illustrates the relationship between various intellectual skills, the subject-area content (in this case, the concept of gerrymandering in social studies), and the questions and activities used:

Memory[3]: What is meant by "gerrymandering"? (The student is asked to recall the definition presented to him earlier.)

Interpretation: Each county in the diagram of the mythical state has about the same population and is dominated by the designated political party "A" or "B." The state must be divided into five voting districts of about equal population. Each district must contain three counties.

A	B	B	A	A
A	A	B	A	B
A	A	B	A	B

What is the greatest number of districts that Party A could control if it is in charge of the redistricting and chooses to gerrymander? What is the greatest number of districts that Party B could control if it is in charge of the redistricting and chooses to gerrymander? (The students have previously been given a definition of gerrymandering.)

Application: The mayor recently appointed a committee to study the fairness of the boundaries of the election districts in our community. Gather information about the present districts and the population in each. Determine whether the present city election districts are adequate. (The student is

[3]Sanders has slightly modified the cognitive domain by using the term "memory" for knowledge and "interpretation" for comprehension.

expected to apply principles of democracy studied in class to this new problem.)

Analysis: Analyze the reasoning in this quotation: "Human beings lack the ability to be fair when their own interests are involved. Party X controls the legislature and now it has taken upon itself the responsibility of redrawing the boundaries of the legislative election districts. We know in advance that our party will suffer."

Synthesis: (This question must follow the application question given above.) If current election districts in our community are inadequate, suggest how they might be redrawn.

Evaluation: Would you favor having your political party engage in gerrymandering if it had the opportunity? (pp. 3–5)

Guidelines for Selecting Objectives

Whether the teacher uses implicit or explicit instructional objectives, he has access to a number of guidelines for selecting objectives for classroom instruction (Gronlund, 1970):

1. Do the objectives indicate learning outcomes that are appropriate to the instructional area? *This question asks whether the teacher is informed about all the important outcomes in a particular subject area. What do the curriculum experts in the area suggest in terms of content? Although the teacher will never find complete agreement among these specialists as to what should be taught, a review of their recommendations will help to ensure that important objectives are not excluded.*

2. Do the objectives represent all logical learning outcomes of the instructional area? *Here the concern is whether the objectives are comprehensive and representative. Are cognitive objectives stressed over affective objectives? Can both types of objectives be taught in the same lesson? A lesson dealing with both the responsibilities and value systems of elected officials would stress both domains. The* Taxonomy of Educational Objectives *is a teacher's guide to developing an adequate balance of learning outcomes.*

3. Are the objectives attainable by these particular students? *The answer to this question depends on the teacher's knowledge of individual differences in the classroom. Some students may not be ready for particular learning experiences and would meet with failure in their attempts.*

4. Are the objectives in harmony with the philosophy of the school in which the instruction is to be given? *This criterion is often difficult to measure because most schools do not clearly articulate their philosophy of education. Some teachers are faced with the dilemma of whether to teach content that they feel is important, even though it might conflict with the attitudes of the community. How detailed should the biology teacher be about sex education in a community that believes that schools should not be the conveyors of such information? The solutions to problems of this type are not laid out in the district's manual for teachers (if such a manual exists). The issue is whether a teacher should depart from the basic philosophy of a school in developing objectives.*

5. Are the objectives in harmony with basic principles of learning? *The next two chapters of this book provide help in answering this question. Are the objectives sequenced properly? Do the objectives reflect the needs and interests of the students? Do the objectives reflect learning behaviors that students will retain for a long period of time? These kinds of questions do not have ready answers, but they do suggest that you should consider the learning process when you select and formulate objectives.*

KEY POINTS

1. *Educators disagree about what students should learn in school.*
2. *Learning goals are expressed in terms of educational objectives that are written at different levels of specificity.*
3. *An explicit instructional or behavioral objective is a precise statement of what a student will be able to* do *as a result of instruction.*
4. *A behavioral objective usually includes a* behavioral term *expressing the type of task required of the student, the* situation *or* condition *under which the behavior is to be performed, and the* criterion *or* level of performance *that will be used to evaluate the success of the performance or product.*
5. *Not all educators agree on the need to explicitly state goals before instruction.*
6. *There is some concern that explicit objectives may dehumanize the educational process, force teachers to emphasize experiences that are the easiest to measure, and hinder creativity.*

7. *The assessment of a student's present knowledge plays an essential part in the process of preparing objectives.*
8. *Academic content can be assessed in two dimensions: degree of difficulty and level of complexity.*
9. *Teacher-made tests help the teacher determine the student's present knowledge. The* Taxonomy of Educational Objectives *helps her write objectives at different levels of complexity.*
10. *The following questions can be used as guidelines for selecting objectives for classroom instruction (Gronlund, 1970):*
    a. *Do the objectives indicate learning outcomes that are appropriate to the instructional area?*
    b. *Do the objectives represent all logical learning outcomes of the instructional area?*
    c. *Are the objectives attainable by these particular students?*
    d. *Are the objectives in harmony with the philosophy of the school in which the instruction is to be given?*
    e. *Are the objectives in harmony with basic principles of learning?*

SUGGESTIONS FOR FURTHER READING

Eisner, E. W. Educational objectives: Help or hindrance? *The School Review,* 1967, *75*, 250–260. A position paper by one of the leading critics of behavioral objectives.

Mager, R. F. *Preparing instructional objectives* (2nd ed.). Belmont, Calif.: Fearon, 1975. An excellent programmed-instruction book on writing objectives.

Plowman, P. *Behavioral objectives.* Chicago: Science Research Associates, 1971. This book provides examples of explicit instructional objectives in many academic areas.

The following organizations maintain lists of instructional objectives in numerous academic areas. Interested teachers may write and obtain information about them.

Instructional Objectives Exchange
P.O. Box 24095, Los Angeles, California 90024

UNIPAC Objectives
Institute for the Development of Educational Advancement (IDEA)
University of California, Suite 950
110 Glendon Avenue, Los Angeles, California 90024

FOLLOW-UP ACTIVITIES

1 Discuss the goals of education. Discuss the degree to which you agree or disagree with each of the following goals of education (Gall & Ward, 1974):

a. The main job of the schools is to impart useful knowledge and skills.
b. Because knowledge and skills become dated so quickly, the schools should concentrate on training students how to think.
c. The schools should assume the responsibility of teaching skills and attitudes that concern the student's personal and social development.
d. The students, not their teachers, should determine what they will learn in school. (p. 54)

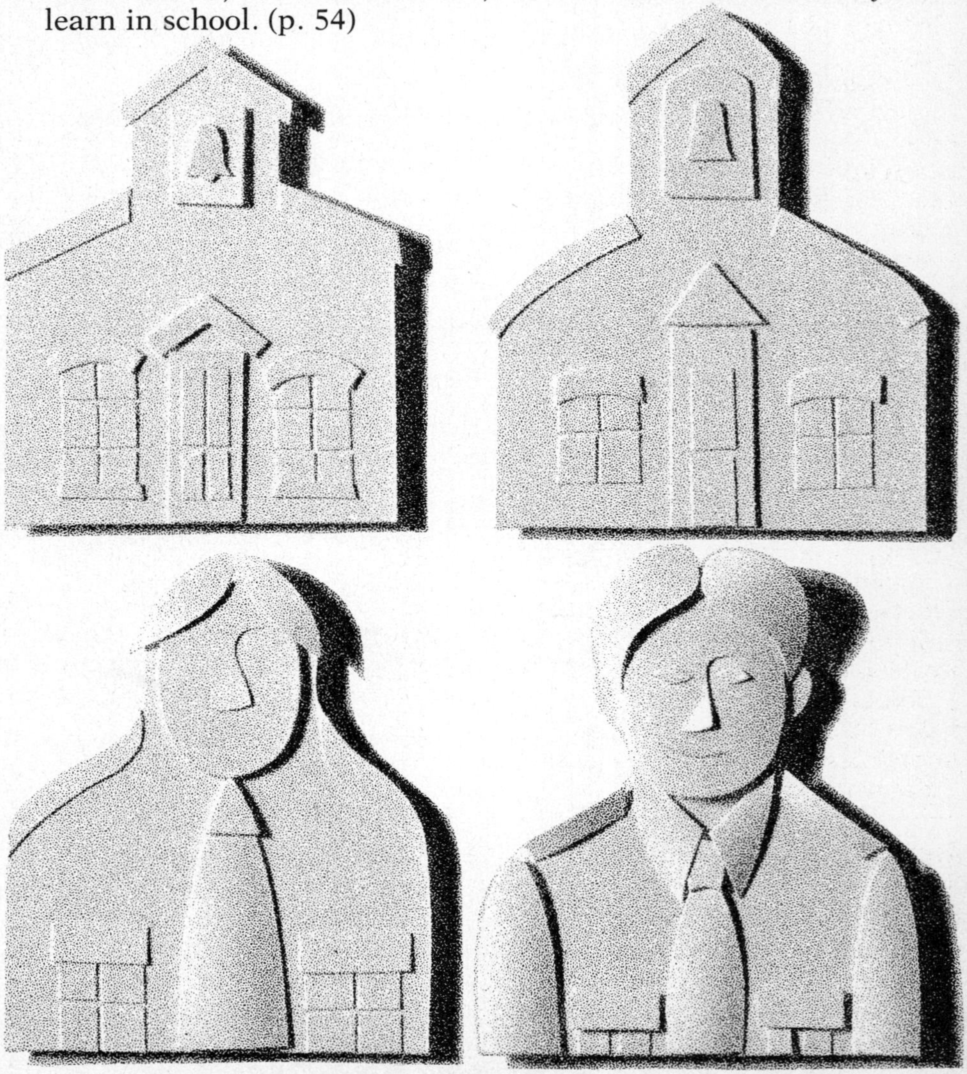

2 Rank the goals of education. Spears (1973) undertook a survey of American educators to determine how they would rank-order the importance of eighteen educational goals. The ranking, from most to least important, was as follows:

Develop skills in reading, writing, speaking, and listening
Develop pride in work and a feeling of self-worth
Develop good character and self-respect
Develop a desire for learning, now and in the future
Learn to respect and get along with people with whom we work and live
Learn how to examine and use information
Gain a general education
Learn how to be a good citizen
Learn about and try to understand the changes that take place in the world
Understand and practice democratic ideas and ideals
Learn how to respect and get along with people who think, dress, and act differently
Understand and practice the skills of family living
Gain information needed to make job selections
Learn how to be a good manager of money, property, and resources
Practice and understand the ideas of health and safety
Develop skills to enter a specific field of work
Learn how to use leisure time
Appreciate culture and beauty in the world (pp. 31–32)

Would you have ranked these goals in about the same order? Note that subject-matter skills headed the list, while appreciation of beauty and culture ranked least in importance. Rank the goals yourself on the basis of what you hope to gain from your college education and compare your list with those of other students in your class.

3 Interview teachers regarding their use of objectives. Interview teachers and ask them whether or not they use instructional objectives and to what degree of specificity. What reasons do they give for and against developing explicit objectives?

4 Write explicit instructional objectives. Select a topic in your teaching field and write an objective for each level of the taxonomy of educational objectives in both the cognitive and affective domains.

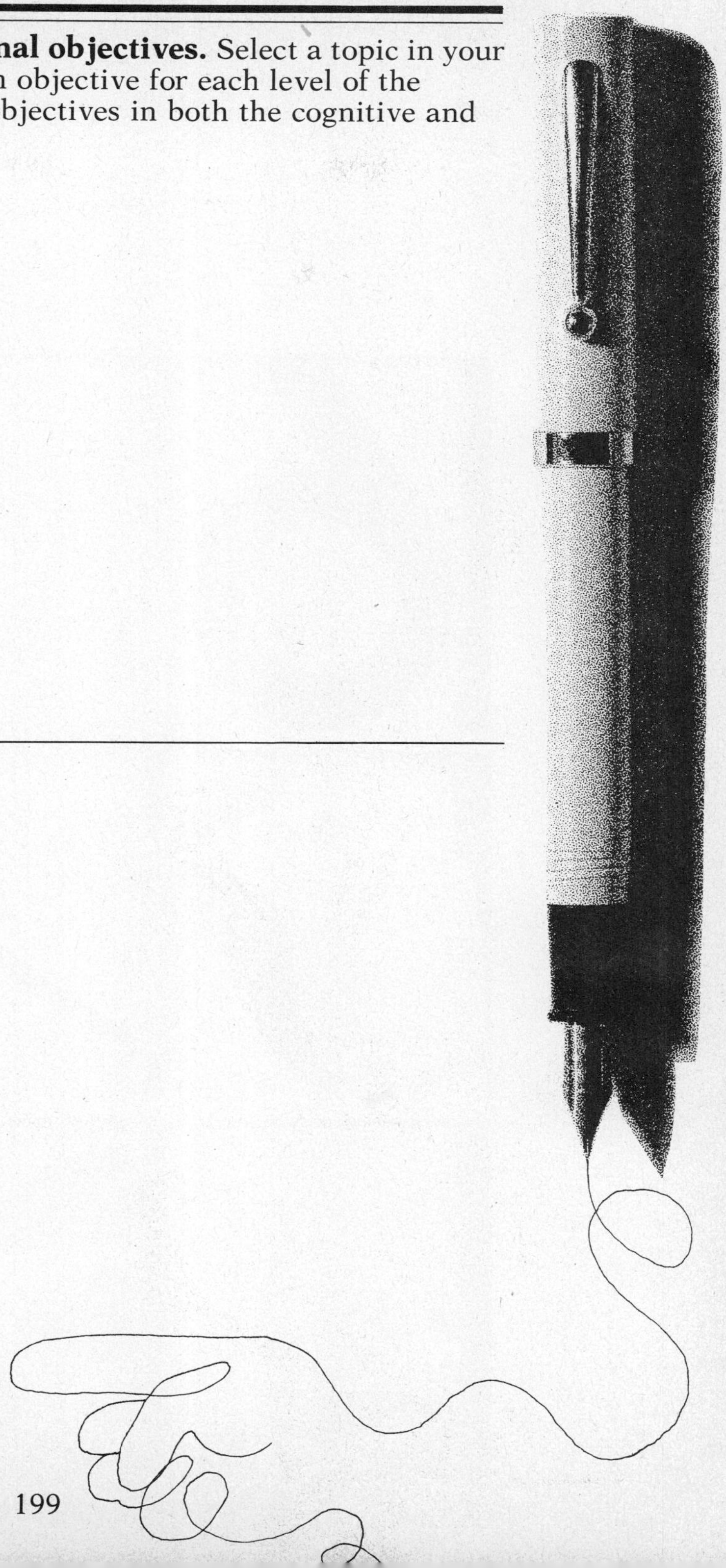

Cognitive

Knowledge

Comprehension

Application

Analysis

Synthesis

Evaluation

Affective

Receiving

Responding

Valuing

Organization

Characterization

6
Sr

BEHAVIORISTIC PSYCHOLOGY: LEARNING THEORIES AND APPLICATIONS

Orientation

The primary responsibility of a teacher is to help students learn. Her selection of educational goals, instructional procedures, and classroom organization receives its impetus from her conceptualization of the learning process. In Chapter 4, I discussed how a teacher's teaching-learning beliefs influence the nature of teacher-student interaction. We shall now see these same beliefs have a similar impact on her instructional decisions.

All teachers have a belief or theory about learning that is the very fabric of their teaching strategy. By watching a teacher behave in the classroom, we can usually infer her basic assumptions about the learning process, although the teacher may not be able to articulate them herself. The teacher who directs and controls all student activities is operating under a different set of beliefs than the teacher who establishes conditions in which students make their own decisions about what and how they will learn.

I believe that one of the objectives of teacher education is to help teachers see the relationship between beliefs and practices. Throughout the history of education, practices have changed as we have learned more about the learning process. Years ago teachers had it drummed into their heads that the best way to ensure learning was through repetition, a principle from a particular learning theory that dominated educational thinking for some time. Students spent their time copying spelling words, historical information, and mathematical formulas over and over again, until they learned the information. Teachers began to change some of their teaching methods when presented with different views that questioned the effectiveness of repetition for many types of learning objectives.

Before proceeding, let's identify some of your beliefs about learning. Check whether you agree or disagree with the statements on the next page (Seaberg, 1974, pp. 7–8). Statements 1, 4, and 6 would be supported by behavioristic psychologists, statements 3 and 7 by cognitive-developmental psychologists, and statements 2, 5, and 8 by humanistic psychologists. Did your responses fall into any particular pattern? Let's briefly review each of these theories before going into detail on them.

Contemporary behaviorists (often called *S-R* psychologists) view environmental factors in terms of *stimuli* and resultant behavior in terms of *responses*. They attempt to demonstrate that behavior is controlled by environmental contingencies of external reward or reinforcement, which are links between behavioral responses and their effects (or stimuli).

Teachers who accept the behavioral perspective assume that the behavior of students is a response to their past and present environment and that all behavior is learned. The classroom troublemaker "learns" to be disruptive because of the attention (reinforcement) he gets from his peers; the withdrawn student "learns" that his environment does not reinforce gregariousness and becomes reserved and silent.

We can analyze any behavior in terms of its reinforcement history. The logical extension of the behavioral principle of learning is as a method to change or modify behavior. The teacher's responsibility, therefore, is to construct an environment in which the probability of reinforcing students for correct or proper behavior is maximized (Mathis & McGaghie, 1974).

Cognitive psychologists delve into the internal processes by which an individual deals with the complexity of his environment. They also try to define the resulting cognitive structures that he con-

Agree	*Disagree*	*I Believe That:*
______	______	1. Learners need grades, gold stars, and other incentives as motivation to learn and to accomplish school requirements.
______	______	2. Learners can be trusted to find their own goals and that they should have some options or choices in what they do in school.
______	______	3. Children proceed through separate stages of intellectual or cognitive development.
______	______	4. Children should be graded according to uniform standards of achievement which the teacher sets for the class.
______	______	5. Children should set their own individual standards and should begin to evaluate their own work.
______	______	6. To ensure the transmission of the cultural heritage, the program of the school should be organized along subject-matter lines that are carefully sequenced.
______	______	7. Children learn best when the complexity of the subject matter is related to their level of cognitive development.
______	______	8. School experience should help the learner understand himself and find meaningful relationships with his fellow man.

structs in his mind: the ways in which he perceives and conceptualizes his physical and social world. An important assumption of cognitive theory is that an individual's behavior is always based on cognition, the act of knowing about the situation in which behavior occurs.

Cognitive-developmental psychologists study the steps in children's thinking and believe that it is quite different from adult thinking. They stress that the teacher must understand the nature of thought processes in planning for instruction.

Humanistic psychologists believe that how a person "feels" is as important as how he behaves or thinks. They describe behavior according to the believer rather than the observer and are especially concerned with "self-actualization" — the growth of persons in whatever area they choose. The humanistic teacher must create an educational environment that fosters self-development and understanding leading to self-actualization.

In the next three chapters we shall investigate theories of learning and their instructional applications in educational settings. You will then be in a position to develop your own beliefs about the educational process.

There are a few points I would like you to keep in mind while reading these three chapters: (1) there is no *one* behavioristic, cognitive, or humanistic theory. Individuals within each of these systems differ on various points; (2) not all educational practices are backed by one specific theory; and (3) you might either wind up strongly favoring one theory or believing that each theory has applications for at least some types of learning. There is nothing for you to read between the lines, nothing to make you adopt any one position.

EARLY DEVELOPMENTS

THORNDIKE

For the first several decades of this century the learning theory of E. L. Thorndike (1874–1949) dominated educational practice in the United States. His theory became known as *connectionism* because he posited that learning was a process of "stamping in," or forming, connections between a stimulus and response.

Thorndike developed his theory from extensive research on the effect of reward on the behavior of various animals. One of his major studies used cats that he placed in a "puzzle box" — a small cage with a door that would open if the cat pulled a string hanging inside the cage. The cat's task was to get out of the cage to obtain food (reward) placed outside the cage. Usually the cat went through the process of walking around, clawing at the floor, jumping at the sides of the cage, and other similar movements until, by chance, he pulled the string opening the door of the cage. Thorndike repeated the experiment several times: The cat still stalked around his cage but pulled the string much sooner. After several trials the cat centered his behavior around the string, eventually pulled the string immediately, and collected his reward (food).

Thorndike explained the process of learning as follows: After the cat hit upon the correct response and was rewarded for it, a connection was gradually strengthened between the situation (stimulus) and the response.

From animal learning, it was only a step upward (maybe more!) to human learning, which Thorndike saw as comprising the same elements. His research with various animals gave him his most important principle of learning, the *law of effect:*

> When a modifiable connection is made between a situation and a response and is accompanied or followed by a satisfying state of affairs, the strength of that connection is increased. When an annoying state of affairs goes with or follows a connection, the strength of that connection is decreased. (Thorndike, 1913, p. 71)

The main factor influencing all learning was reward, or a "satisfying state of affairs." In his later writings, Thorndike eliminated the negative or "annoying" part of the law of effect because he found that punishment did not necessarily weaken bonds and did not have the opposite effect of reward.

The *law of exercise* was his second important learning principle. In general, it stated that the more a stimulus-response connection was practiced or used, the stronger it would become; the less it was used, the weaker it would become. He also modified this law in his later writings because he found that practice without reward was ineffective. Connections were only strengthened by rewarded practice.

Thorndike's learning theory led to a number of educational practices. His general advice for teachers was: "Put together and exercise what should go together, and reward desirable connections" (Thorndike, 1913, p. 70).

Thorndike showed one bond between stimulus and response occurring in mathematics. Constant repetition of multiplication tables with the teacher providing the reward formed bonds between the stimulus (What is 7×7?) and the response (49). In reading, repetition was also emphasized by having students learn the most frequently used words at various grade levels.

The more S-R bonds an individual had, the more intelligent he was considered to be, since he had more bonds at his disposal in problem situations. The law of effect led to the use of concrete rewards such as gold stars placed on students' papers and emphasis on verbal praise. The law of exercise led to much repetition, practice, and drill in all subjects.

PAVLOV

During the time Thorndike was conducting his research, a Russian physiologist, Ivan Pavlov (1849–1936) had accidentally come upon an interesting learning phenomenon while working with dogs in his laboratory. If a bell was sounded a few seconds before a hungry dog was presented with food, after several trials the dog would salivate simply at the sound of the bell. Pavlov identified the food as an *unconditioned stimulus* and salivation as an *unconditioned response* (an example of a stimulus that produces some observable response without prior learning). The bell, which originally had no particular meaning for the dog, took on meaning, or became a *conditioned stimulus,* because of its association or pairing with the food, eliciting a *conditioned response* — salivation.

This kind of learning is called *classical conditioning* or stimulus substitution, since the conditioned stimulus, after being paired with the unconditioned stimulus often enough, can then be substituted for it. Figure 6.1 presents a schematic representation of classical conditioning.

Pavlov found that when a dog was conditioned to salivate at the sound of a bell, it would also salivate at other similar sounds, such as that of a siren, even though the new stimuli were never used in training. Once a particular conditioned stimulus was associated with a response, other similar stimuli also were able to elicit the response. He called this phenomenon *stimulus generalization..*

WATSON

John B. Watson (1878–1958) was the first psychologist in the United States to use Pavlov's research findings as a basis for a learning theory. Watson believed that learning was a process of conditioning reflexes (responses) through the substitution of one stimulus for another. According to Watson, humans are born with a few reflexes and emotional reactions of fear, love, and rage. All other behavior is established by building new S-R connections through conditioning.

In one of his most famous experiments, he conditioned an eleven-month-old child to fear a white rat that he had made friends with. Watson made a loud noise (unconditioned stimulus or US) whenever the rat was presented to the boy, which resulted in a fear response (unconditioned response or UR). Within a short time, the boy

Figure 6.1
A Schematic Representation of Classical Conditioning.

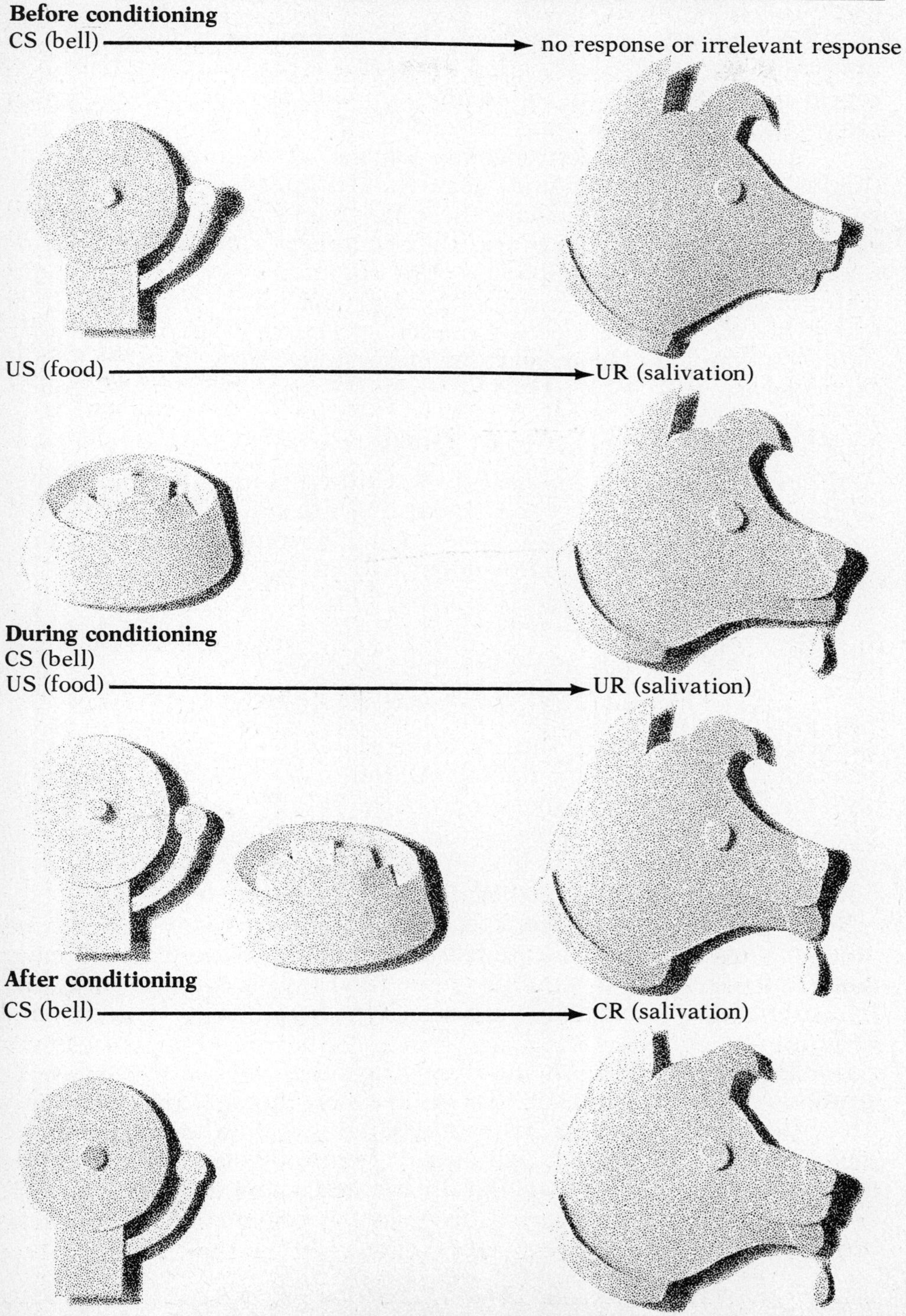

became fearful (conditioned response or CR) at the sight of the rat (conditioned stimulus or CS).

Watson also demonstrated that the boy's fear could also be unlearned by the process called *extinction.* This is accomplished by repeating the CS without following it up with the US: presenting the rat without making the loud noise.

Many students' attitudes are learned through classical conditioning. They learn to acquire negative attitudes toward foreign languages because they associate these languages with the unpleasant experience of being asked to translate sentences aloud in class. Being asked difficult questions in class (US) elicits anxiety (UR). Students who are conditioned to fear foreign languages may generalize their fear to blanket other subjects of the school's curriculum or the institution of school. The same learning process operates in other school experiences.

GUTHRIE

Another American psychologist, E. R. Guthrie (1886–1959), expanded further on Watson's approach to learning. He stated his major learning principle as the *law of association:* "A combination of stimuli which has accompanied a movement will on its recurrence tend to be followed by that movement" (Guthrie, 1952, p. 13). In other words, if you do something in a certain situation, the next time you are in that situation you will tend to do the same thing again.

Guthrie believed that learning occurred in one trial. The learner did not have to repeat the S-R sequence over and over again, nor did he need reward. Guthrie's theory was more general than the principle of classical conditioning. All that was necessary for learning was the contiguity or association of stimuli and responses. It didn't matter whether the responses were elicited during training by an unconditioned stimulus or in some other way; as long as the stimuli and response occurred together, learning would occur.

Guthrie believed that a teacher should provide the stimuli for student responses to facilitate learning. She might point to a French word and the students would provide the English equivalent. Learning would occur because of the association between the stimulus and response.

Guthrie's advice for modifying behavior was to rearrange the stimulus-response sequence. If a child comes home after school and drops his coat on the floor instead of hanging it up, the parent should make him put his coat on, go outside, come through the door, and hang up his coat. In this way, the child learns a new stimulus-response sequence: Hanging up his coat becomes the response to the stimulus of entering the house.

So far in our discussion of S-R psychologists we have viewed learning from the perspective of forming connections or associations between a stimulus and response. We have identified two different vantage points within this approach: learning through the simultaneous occurrence of stimulus and response (Pavlov, Watson, and Guthrie) and learning through the act of being rewarded (Thorndike).

Since the early explanations of learning by these psychologists, many individuals have contributed to these perspectives. Few have made as much impact on educational practice as B. F. Skinner (1904–), who is considered *the* contemporary spokesman for the behavioristic position.

SKINNER'S OPERANT CONDITIONING

Like Thorndike, Skinner views reward or reinforcement as the most important element in the learning process. We tend to learn a response if it is immediately followed by reinforcement. Skinner prefers the term "reinforcement" to "reward" because reward is a subjective interpretation of behavior associated with a pleasurable event, whereas reinforcement is a neutral term, defined simply as an effect that increases the probability of a response. The use of "reinforcement" removes any subjective interpretation from the concept and, like his other concepts, is discussed in terms of observable and measurable events.

Skinner believes the purpose of psychology is to predict and control behavior. Since all behavior is learned, it follows that a teacher or psychologist can apply the same principles of learning to change behavior (Skinner, 1953).

He identifies two types of responses in the learning process: *respondents* and *operants*. Respondents are elicited by specific stimuli such as Pavlov's bell. Earlier we read about Pavlov's classical conditioning theory and found that an individual can learn by the pairing or association of stimuli. In a respondent situation, an individual learns merely by being in the situation. The environment acts on him.

Although humans learn some behavior by classical conditioning, Skinner thinks that most human behavior takes the form of operant responses that the individual emits. Such behaviors as writing a letter, picking up a book, and driving a car are operants — responses that an individual makes to no known stimulus.

Initially, an individual's responses in a given situation are random, but after a period of time certain responses (operants) become

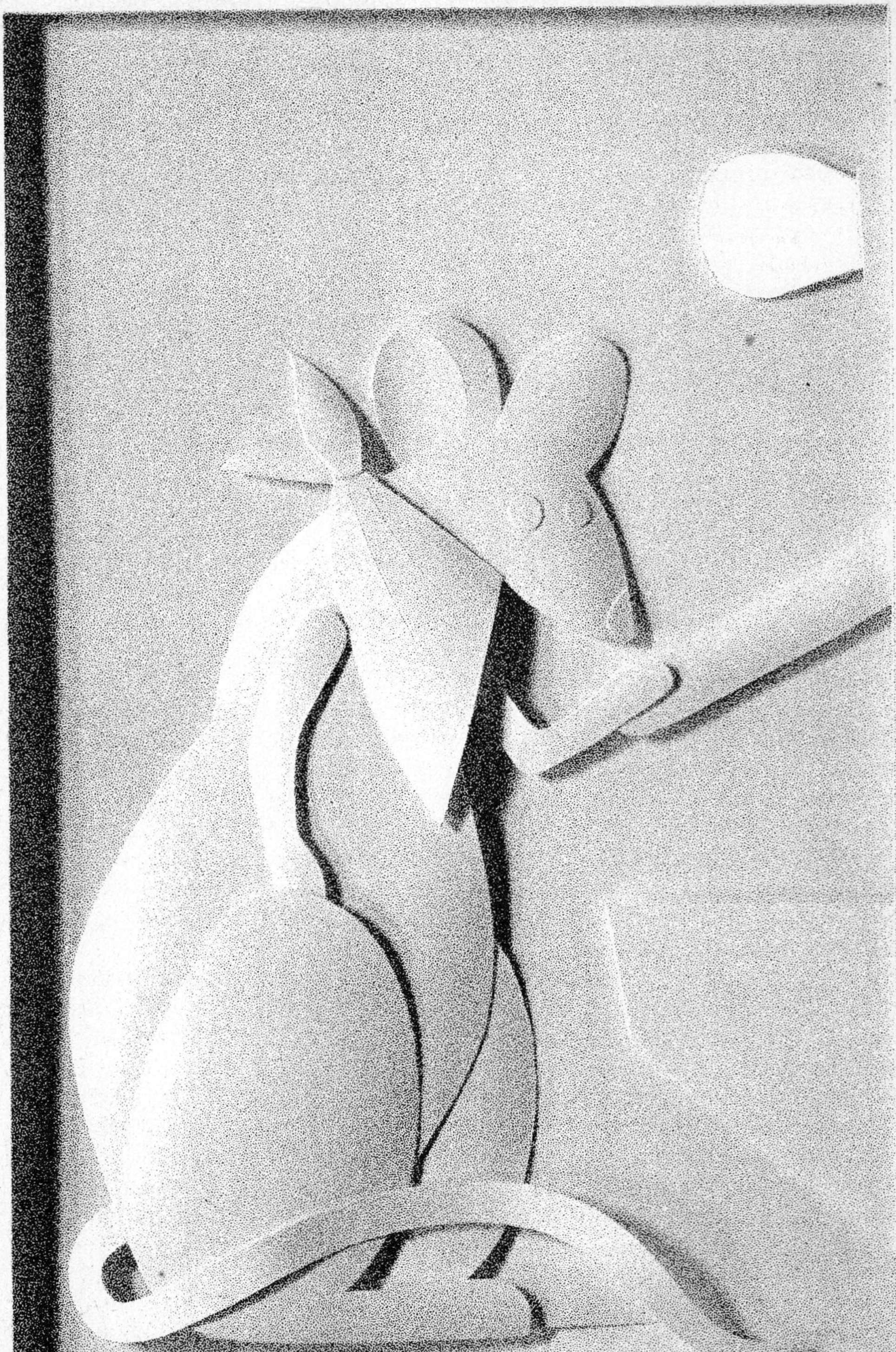

more dominant than others because of selective reinforcement. Skinner calls this process *operant conditioning* — a learning situation in which a response is made more probable or frequent as the result of immediate reinforcement. A kindergarten student during the first week of school emits a number of responses: He talks with other students, pays attention to the teacher, walks around the room, and bothers other students. As the teacher begins reinforcing certain responses by smiling when the student pays attention, for example, some of the responses begin to occur more frequently. Of all possible responses that could be emitted in a given situation, some responses become more dominant than others.

An important difference between Pavlov's classical and Skinner's operant conditioning is that in classical conditioning, the consequences of a behavior carry no weight in the learning of that behavior. Reinforcement is unnecessary because the stimuli bring about the desired response.

Operant conditioning, although closer to Thorndike's theory than to Pavlov's, is different from Thorndike's explanation of learning. Thorndike felt that reward strengthened a bond that existed between a stimulus and response, whereas Skinner feels that what is strengthened is not an S-R bond but the probability that the same response will occur again.

Operant conditioning can be adequately explained without the presence of a stimulus initiating a response. However, we can talk about a response being brought under the control of a discriminative stimulus (S^d), a cue or signal that increases the probability of a response. This situation is best illustrated in Skinner's early research with rats placed in a small apparatus called a Skinner box, which is equipped with a lever, light, food tray, and food-releasing mechanism. A rat can be trained to push the lever only when the light (S^d) is turned on by providing a reinforcing stimulus (S^r), food. If the rat pushes the lever when the light is off, he receives no reinforcement. The light is a cue that makes the response of lever pushing more likely to occur. Later, the rat can be taught to push the lever only when the light is off.

Events occurring before and after a student makes a response can determine when and where that response will occur again. The teacher wants students to learn certain responses under specific conditions. When a student receives the stimulus (4 + 3 = ____) and responds (7), reinforcement follows. We say that *discriminative* learning has taken place. An important part of teaching is presenting stimuli so specific that only one response is correct. If reinforcement is contingent only upon the correct response, more learning transpires (Lefrancois, 1972b). The use of *prompts* in a new teaching situation to

Teacher presents preceding stimulus (S^d)	*Child responds*	*Teacher presents consequent stimulus* (S^r)
1. "When did Columbus discover America?"	"In 1492."	"Good."
2. "How many times will 3 go into 12?"	"Three."	"No, that's wrong."
3. a. Teacher shows the letter M and asks: "What sound is this?"	No response.	No consequence.
3. b. Teacher then says, "This is mmmm; say 'Mmmm.' "	"Mmmm."	"Good, you're getting it."

get a response going is illustrated in example 3 of the above examples of teacher-student interaction, which illustrate three important steps in the teaching process (Becker, Engelmann, & Thomas, 1971, p. 2).

The basis of operant conditioning in teaching is to ensure responses to stimuli events. Unless the learner emits responses to stimuli, it is impossible to guide his behavior toward a behavioral goal. The teacher plays an important role in the classroom by controlling and directing the learning activities. He must first determine the most logical order of presenting the material in small steps and then try to provide reinforcement immediately after the learner responds. Behaviorists urge the use of explicit objectives in teaching, since the teacher must know what he is trying to accomplish before he plans a sequence of behaviors toward a goal.

Biehler (1971) maps out a few routes along which teachers can travel to improve their reinforcement capabilities: returning and discussing all exams promptly, questioning students regularly and reinforcing correct answers, checking student work continually, and generally making an attempt to reinforce all behavior conducive to developing good attitudes toward learning.

CONSEQUENT STIMULI

A number of consequences can occur after a response. First, we have already discussed positive reinforcement — the presentation of a stimulus that, when added to a situation, increases the probability of a response occuring. Second, an individual can receive *negative reinforcement* — the termination of an unpleasant stimulus (such as isolation) that, when taken away from a situation, also increases the probability of a response occurring. In the case of isolation, it may be maintained until the student promises to cease misbehaving. Third, he can receive *punishment* — the presentation of an unpleasant stimulus (such as contradiction or reprimand) that decreases the probability of a response occurring at all.

Note that positive and negative reinforcement attempt to increase the probability of a response, whereas punishment attempts to suppress the response. When a reinforcing stimulus is no longer presented after a response and the response weakens, the *extinction* process occurs. Often the teacher has to use punishment to discourage wrong responses, but he must decide when to use reinforcing and punishing consequences for effective teaching.

Let's begin with reinforcing consequences. In the studies of operant conditioning with animals, primary reinforcement (food or water) is a factor. These reinforcing stimuli work toward the satisfaction of the animals' physiological needs. Most reinforcement in educational environments is secondary or learned. It is reinforcing because it has been paired with (or is exchangeable for) a primary reinforcer. Money, for instance, is not reinforcing to an infant, but later becomes influential in affecting behavior when she learns that it can be exchanged for candy.

Gentile, Frazier, and Morris (1973) identify three classes of secondary reinforcers: *social reinforcers* (social acceptance, smiles), *tokens* (physical objects like money, grades, prizes, points), and *activities* (free play, listening to music, trips). The premise behind using activities is Premack's (1959) principle: Given two activities, the more preferred may be used to increase the rate of the less preferred. In other words, an interesting activity on which a person spends a good deal of time can reinforce behavior in an activity in which the person is less interested and on which he spends less time. If a child likes to build model airplanes but does not like to read, telling the child he can work on his project after he successfully completes his reading assignment accomplishes reinforcement of his reading behavior.

Havighurst (1970) points out that people react to different types of reinforcers. Some students are motivated by being praised verbally in front of their peers; others shun such attention. A reinforcing event is not inherently effective, so it's wise for a teacher to make a list of possible reinforcers for various students in the class. The expression "different strokes for different folks" best summarizes the preceding point.

Teachers who learn about behavior modification invariably ask, "How do I know what will be reinforcing to a student?" The only sure way is to observe the student and to recognize which stimuli increase the frequency of the response that follows. In a class of thirty or more students, the burden entailed is staggering. Instead, ask the students to fill out a potential-reinforcing-stimuli-or-events questionnaire that includes such questions as: 1) What special things do you like to work with or play with in the classroom? 2) What are three jobs in this classroom you like to do most? 3) If you went to a store to buy three games that you like, what would they be (Blackham & Silberman, 1971)? You can modify these questions for the age level of the students in the classroom.

Age difference should be a factor in the teacher's selection of reinforcers. You can use a five-cent eraser as a reinforcer for a young child, but an adolescent demands a tangible reinforcer of greater value. Activities like helping the teacher, using a tape recorder, or doing puzzles are potentially reinforcing activities for elementary students; for junior high and high school students, more appropriate reinforcing activities are talking to a friend, reading a teen magazine, or listening to a record. Make a list of some potential reinforcing stimuli and events for the age level of students you will be working with.

SCHEDULES OF REINFORCEMENT

A schedule of reinforcement describes the contingency of when or how often a response is reinforced. Through experiments with rats, pigeons, and then humans, Skinner has been able to identify some important relationships between the way in which reinforcement is administered and the rates of learning, response, and extinction.

Reinforcement can be continuous or intermittent; the teacher reinforces correct responses each time or periodically. An experimenter or teacher using an intermittent schedule of reinforcement has two choices: reinforcing a proportion of responses (a ratio schedule) or reinforcing responses following a lapse of time from the previous reinforcement (an interval schedule).

Table 6.1 outlines the alternatives available for schedules of reinforcement. There are two types of ratio and interval schedules: fixed and variable. A fixed-ratio schedule is based on presenting the subject with a reinforcer after she emits a specified number of responses. In a 4:1 ratio, the subject is reinforced after each set of four responses. The teacher who tells her students that they can go to

TABLE 6.1
SCHEDULES OF REINFORCEMENT.

I. Continuous schedules
II. Intermittent schedules
  A. Fixed schedules
    1. Fixed-ratio schedules
    2. Fixed-interval schedules
  B. Variable schedules
    1. Variable-ratio schedules
    2. Variable-interval schedules

recess after completing four more problems is using a fixed-ratio schedule of reinforcement.

A variable-ratio schedule is based on presenting the subject with a reinforcer after an average number of responses. The exact number of responses may vary, from one reinforcer after every three responses to one reinforcer after every twenty responses. In this schedule the subject never knows the exact number of responses required for reinforcement. Venturing outside the realm of education, we find another example: Slot machines work on a variable-ratio schedule of reinforcement.

Interval schedules are also fixed or variable. A fixed-interval schedule is based on a constant unit of time between reinforcements. Grading students on a ten-week period is an example of a fixed-interval schedule of reinforcement.

A variable-interval schedule provides intermittent reinforcement following the first correct response after a specified lapse of time. As in the variable-ratio schedule, the subject never knows when the next reinforcer is due. The subject might be reinforced according to the following sequence: after five minutes, three minutes, ten minutes, one minute. The child who constantly nags his mother for a cookie until the mother finally gives in is being reinforced on a variable-interval schedule because the exact time period from cookie to cookie varies in direct proportion to the amount of nagging the parent can take in a given day.

Each of the different schedules produces its own patterns of response. The continuous schedule of reinforcement is most effective in increasing the frequency of responses. However, the rate of extinction for behavior reinforced continuously far outstrips the rate for behavior reinforced intermittently. You should start out by reinforcing appropriate behavior continuously and then move to a variable schedule to maintain the behavior.

Lower response rates accompany fixed-interval schedules because of the time lapse involved. The response rate picks up at the end of the time interval, as confirmed by college students' cramming for their final examinations. Fixed-ratio schedules are more conducive to constant response rates, while variable-ratio schedules are most effective for maintaining high response rates.

Undesirable behavior is often unwittingly reinforced. When a teacher occasionally gives in to her students' pleading for certain activities, she is reinforcing them intermittently — a variable-interval reinforcement schedule that contributes to the perpetuation of behavior.

Here are some reinforcement rules to keep in mind:

1. *In teaching a new task, reinforce immediately rather than permit a delay between response and reinforcement.*
2. *In the early stages of a task, reinforce every correct response. As learning occurs, require more correct responses prior to reinforcement; gradually shift to intermittent reinforcement.*
3. *Reinforce improvements or steps in the right direction. Do not insist on perfect performance on the first try.*
4. *Don't reinforce undesirable behavior.*

PROCEDURES FOR DEVELOPING NEW BEHAVIORS

In addition to the use of reinforcement to strengthen behavior, there are other methods of influencing behavior patterns. Two important methods are shaping and modeling.

SHAPING

Most of what is learned in school is a complex sequence of behavior rather than a simple response. This complex behavior can be taught through the process of shaping or *successive approximations* — small bits of behavior that come close to the terminal response. First you decide on the desired terminal behavior, or the end product you want. Then you analyze the task: What steps must the student master and in what order? After you pinpoint the student's present level of proficiency, you are ready to reinforce each approximation to the desired response.

Frazier (1969) reported on the use of shaping to improve studying behavior in a residence home for children. The steps needed to attain this goal were broken down into the following components:

1. *Coming to class on time*
2. *Participating in studying behavior and responding to the teacher*
3. *Performing well on tests*
4. *Completing homework*
5. *Improving performance as time progressed*

The students earned points for exhibiting each of these behaviors. Students exchanged their accumulated points for various toys and prizes in a store set up for this purpose. Students who earned enough points could participate in the many preferred activities available.

This behavior modification program increased the level of school attendance from around 50% to 86% after a few months. More important, the students became more cooperative in class and utilized their study time more effectively.

One of the most widely known classroom management programs is Hewett's (1967) engineered classroom. Hewett's concern is for emotionally handicapped children, who have not acquired the necessary classroom behavior to learn. They are unable to pay attention, follow directions, and get along with others. Hewett's program is designed to teach these behaviors by organizing them in a graduated hierarchy of seven levels. Table 6.2 summarizes the seven levels of the hierarchy, the child's problems at each level, the type of learner rewards available, and the degree of structure inherent at each level.

The major advantage of the system is that it allows the teacher to assess the student's educational deficiencies and to establish a program for each student on the basis of this assessment. Notice that the nature of the rewards and the degree of teacher structure vary with the developmental readiness of the student. In keeping with this learning theory approach, the engineered classroom establishes an educational program by *shaping* appropriate behavior, step by step,

Tab

Hierarchy Level	*Attention*	*Response*
Child's problem	Inattention due to withdrawal or resistance	Lack of ir volvemen unwilling to respon learning
Educational task	Get child to pay attention to teacher and task	Get child respond t tasks he and whic offer pro of succes
Learner reward	Provided by tangible rewards (e.g., food, money, tokens)	Provided gaining s attention
Teacher structure	Minimal	Still limi

From Frank Hewitt, "Educational Engineering With Emotionally Disturbed Children," *Exceptional Children* 33 (1967):461. Reprinte with permission of The Council for Exceptional Children.

…CRIPTION OF THE HIERARCHY OF EDUCATIONAL TASKS.

…DER	*EXPLORATORY*	*SOCIAL*	*MASTERY*	*ACHIEVEMENT*
…bility to …ow …ctions	Incomplete or inaccurate knowledge of environment	Failure to value social approval or disapproval	Deficits in basic adaptive and school skills not in keeping with IQ	Lack of self motivation for learning
… child to …plete tasks … specific …ting points … steps …ing to a …clusion	Increase child's efficiency as an explorer and get him involved in multisensory exploration of his environment	Get child to work for teacher and peer group approval and to avoid their disapproval	Remediation of basic skill deficiencies	Development of interest in acquiring knowledge
…ided …ugh task …pletion	Provided by sensory stimulation	Provided by social approval	Provided through task accuracy	Provided through intellectual task success
…hasized	Emphasized	Based on standards of social appropriateness	Based on curriculum assignments	Minimal

up the educational hierarchy toward the mastery level.

A rather sophisticated reinforcement system is used in the program. Each morning the students get individual record cards divided into 200 squares. As the teacher and classroom aide recognize individual accomplishments they check off squares on the card. They give check marks for starting the assignment, following through, and working cooperatively with other students. The completed work record cards, to be used on a weekly basis, are exchange tickets for candy, small toys, special privileges, and other reinforcers.

Hewett's program is an excellent example of a token reinforcement program. The term *contingency* reinforcement describes this system, because reinforcement depends upon the occurrence of certain responses that have been communicated, in advance, to the students.

MODELING

Modeling is a form of learning that cannot adequately be explained either by classical or operant conditioning. I mention it here because it is a useful procedure for learning new behaviors. In modeling, an individual (observer) learns by witnessing the behavior of another person (model). Much human behavior is learned through modeling, or imitation, as it is sometimes called, rather than through direct instruction. A few years ago a plane was hijacked; within a short time it appeared that hijacking had become a national pastime. Fads such as streaking, language patterns, and dress styles are learned by observing the behavior of others.

Modeling can occur immediately. For this reason, it merits the label "no-trial learning" because the observer can often correctly imitate the behavior in his first attempt. Bandura (1969) hypothesizes that the observer records and stores the sensory events or symbolic responses at the time he views the model's behavior. The sensory events or symbolic responses are cues for the observer when he later imitates the behavior.

We probably learn to imitate because we are reinforced for doing so. Most of a child's early learning experiences involve direct reinforcement by models (parents). It's not uncommon to hear a child proudly proclaim that he or she is doing something just like Mommy or Daddy.

Modeling can also occur without direct reinforcement. Such is the case when a famous actor does a T.V. commercial asking you to use a certain product. The reward is a vicarious reinforcement — the pleasure you feel he receives from his use of the product. If you use the product or engage in the same behavior, you too will receive the same reinforcement. The high school baseball player who watches Pete

Rose swing a baseball bat attempts to copy his swing because he "feels" Rose's satisfaction as the baseball star trots around the bases after a home run. In both incidents, the observer imitates behavior without direct reinforcement. Research indicates that if an observer experiences the consequences of a model's behavior in terms of reinforcement or punishment, he will respond as if he has been directly rewarded or punished.

In one study (Bandura, 1962), three groups of children observed a model who behaved aggressively toward an inflated plastic doll. In one condition the model was reinforced for his behavior, in another punished, and in a third condition suffered no consequences. When the children were observed in a play situation, the model-rewarded group responded significantly more aggressively than the model-punished group. The children vicariously assumed the behavioral consequences of the model's behavior.

Bandura (1969) has organized imitative behavior into three categories: the *inhibitory-disinhibitory* effect, the *eliciting* effect, and the *modeling* effect. The inhibitory-disinhibitory effect makes a response less frequent or allows it to occur by influencing the response consequences of a model. Generally, we become inhibited when we observe others experience unpleasant consequences for engaging in behavior similar to ours. Bandura (1967) demonstrated how children could disinhibit their fear of dogs. He had children watch a film in which a child who did not fear dogs was playing with a dog in a party setting. He found that the children lost their fear of dogs after viewing the film.

A model can also have an eliciting effect on an observer by facilitating a response repertoire already present in the observer. Facilitation occurs when an unlikely response becomes more probable: Observing a friend donate time to collect for the annual cancer drive in your community may elicit the response of volunteering your services for various charitable activities. Zimmerman and Dialessi (1973) demonstrated how a model's behavior can facilitate or prompt responses by exposing children to a model who asked a particular type of question. The children responded by asking similar questions. The researchers did not teach the children to ask questions, which they knew how to do, but the researchers did alter the types of questions the children produced.

The final category, modeling effects, develops new responses through the observation of a model. This category has important implications for education. Children learn much new behavior from observing the behavior of parents, siblings, or peers. The small boy who watches his older brother move a kitchen chair to the cupboard to reach a cookie will probably attempt the same behavior later on.

Modeling can be used to teach academic and motor skills. It is especially useful when reliance on operant conditioning procedures would be less efficient or even dangerous. Would you want to be in a car where the instructor was using a trial-and-error method of learning, waiting to reinforce the driver's correct response? In teaching by modeling the instructor demonstrates how to perform the task or skill; the student observes his behavior and attempts to imitate the teacher or model. The student is able to learn complete sequences of behavior in a much shorter time by modeling than he can by successive approximations or shaping.

Clarizio (1971) provides an excellent example of how a teacher used modeling to develop students' interest in English literature. The teacher made it a practice to read an interesting book as the students entered the room. Sometimes he laughed out loud, frowned, smiled, or exhibited other behaviors that conveyed interest in the book. Some student always commented about the teacher's interest in the book. The teacher reinforced the student's interest by telling the class a little bit about the book or by reading some of the more humorous or exciting passages. He also asked students to talk about interesting books they had recently read. As an English teacher, he not only talked about the enjoyment gained from reading but demonstrated his own enjoyment and interest in reading. Can you think of other ways for a teacher to model important learning behaviors?

A good deal of classroom behavior is learned by vicariously experienced rewards and punishments. Kounin (1970) has found that interaction between a teacher and student has an impact on other students who view the incident. When the teacher reprimands a student for inappropriate behavior, the whole class experiences the effect. You can encourage classroom social control by discussing how one should behave in the classroom and pointing out how individual students and groups help to maintain this behavior. The identification and reinforcement of positive models provide clues for other class members. However, this same learning process works against the teacher if students see others getting away with misbehavior.

PROCEDURES FOR CONTROLLING OR ELIMINATING BEHAVIOR

Students acquire a variety of inappropriate behaviors that are detrimental to the classroom environment. I shall now discuss procedures to control or eliminate students' behavior patterns. These procedures include (1) reinforcing competing behaviors, (2) extinction, (3) satiation, (4) changing the stimulus environment, and (5) punishment (Gardner, 1974).

REINFORCING COMPETING BEHAVIORS

The key to changing undesirable behavior is the successful strengthening of desirable behavior that will compete with and eventually replace undesirable patterns of behavior. Reinforcing a student for cooperating with the teacher is incompatible with his refusing to follow directions; reading is incompatible with sitting passively; working at one's desk is incompatible with wandering around the room. Gardner (1974) states:

> It is easy to punish inappropriate behavior as it occurs; it is more difficult to identify and to provide systematic reinforcement for appropriate competing modes of responding. The major question should be "what should the child be doing at the time he is behaving inappropriately?" Once this is established and demonstrated to the child, such behaviors or reasonable alternatives can more easily be strengthened through reinforcement. (p. 136)

Becker et al. (1967) demonstrated that selective reinforcement of desired behaviors can replace a variety of undesirable ones. A group of children attending elementary school exhibited a high degree of undesirable behaviors — pulling hair, ignoring the teacher's requests, fighting, and walking around the room. After explaining the classroom rules to the children, the teacher ignored the inappropriate behavior but praised any behavior that enhanced learning. In a short time the social reinforcement for appropriate behavior led to a significant reduction in the behaviors that were incompatible with effective classroom learning.

EXTINCTION

It is possible to weaken behavior by removing the reinforcing events that maintain the behavior. Behaviorists recommend that extinction be used in conjunction with other techniques. Clarizio (1971) details the use of extinction with modeling and social reinforcement. A second-grade teacher faced a problem with overage children in the classroom who continually blurted out answers without raising their hands. The teacher ignored all called-out answers and acknowledged only those children who raised their hands, with such comments as "Billy has his hand up and is waiting to answer the question" or "Mary has her hand up and is being considerate to the class." The teacher soon noticed a marked increase in hand-raising behavior. In addition, many students who had not participated in class discussions

I will not yell
I will not yell
I will not yell
I will not yell
I will not yell
I will not yell
I will not yell
I will not yell
I will not yell
I will not yell
I will not yell
I will not yell
I will not yell
not yell
not yell

began raising their hands and had more opportunities to contribute to the class discussion.

Many teachers find extinction difficult to use because they must learn to ignore certain misbehaviors. Sometimes they admonish students about the improper behavior and then ignore the behavior for the remaining time. On an intermittent schedule of reinforcement, the teacher's behavior is likely to cause the misbehavior to occur at a higher level than if extinction had not been attempted. Of course, there are many types of behavior teachers cannot ignore, especially behavior that is injurious to students. If the misbehavior consistently occurs, extinction procedures may not be advisable.

Extinction works primarily when the reinforcement is attention. If a student is getting attention elsewhere, say from peers, other changes in teacher-student interaction will have to discourage the behavior.

Last, keep in mind that during the early stages of extinction, misbehavior may worsen before it improves. The kindergarten student who gets his way with his teacher by having a tantrum will become extremely frustrated when the teacher pays no attention to his behavior. However, he will quickly get the message.

The message for teachers regarding the use of extinction is: Be consistent, ignore certain misbehavior, and combine extinction with other methods such as reinforcement of competing responses.

SATIATION

Another method for weakening behavior is satiation, a procedure that encourages a person to engage in the problem behavior over and over again, until he is tired of it. The father who catches his young son smoking cigarettes and makes him smoke the whole pack is using satiation. The teacher who is constantly interrupted by a student's humming has recourse to the same technique. She stops the class and asks the student to hum a few songs. If the student stops, she encourages him to continue until he appears to be quite tired of his own behavior.

The satiation tactic is not feasible when the behavior is harmful and when pursuit of the behavior results in additional reinforcement. In the humming incident just described, the student might outlast the teacher trying to satiate him because of peer reinforcement.

Krumboltz and Krumboltz (1972) point out that when the repeated behavior differs from the undesirable behavior, satiation is inappropriate. The old-fashioned discipline method of requiring the student to write 100 times "I will not yell in school" is one such situation. A better means of satiation is to ask him to come in after school and yell for fifteen minutes or more. Asking him to come in and write "I will not yell in school" will make him tired of writing, not yelling.

Like the other procedures discussed in this section, the satiation procedure may have only temporary effects on behavior, especially if the behavior has been maintained for some time. The teacher should instead try reinforcing appropriate behaviors that will replace the undesirable behavior.

CHANGING THE STIMULUS ENVIRONMENT

Some behavior can be controlled by changing the stimulus condition that influences the behavior. If a student is distracted by the noise outside the classroom, shutting the window might alleviate the distraction. If a difficult task is frustrating to a student, the teacher may want to replace the task with a less difficult one.

Instead of changing the stimulus conditions influencing inappropriate behavior, the teacher may find it helpful to present cues that inhibit problem behaviors. When two students are not working, she may sit down by the students or walk by them.

Last, the teacher can prompt desired behavior that competes with problem behavior. She may ask the student who finishes his work and gets into mischief to help pass out some material to the rest of the class.

Each of these procedures can prevent the occurrence of inappropriate behavior and provide the teacher with an opportunity to prompt desirable behaviors that can be reinforced (Gardner, 1974).

PUNISHMENT

The use of punishment to weaken behavior is a technique that should be judiciously applied in the classroom. Punishment can suppress undesirable behavior for short periods of time and should be accompanied by reinforcement. Clarizio (1971) states: "Punishment reminds the student what not to do. The reward of appropriate alternative behavior tells the student what to do" (p. 100). The student who continually fights with other students and is sent to a corner of the room should be reinforced during the day when he displays cooperative behavior. The teacher must find the time to teach alternative behaviors to take the place of the behavior suppressed by punishment.

There is evidence to suggest that punishment upon the child's initiation of inappropriate behavior is more effective than deferred punishment (Walters, Parke, & Cane, 1965). Once the child has completed the misbehavior, self-reward or peer reward maintains the behavior and to some extent counteracts the inhibiting effects of punishment. In other words, the child has already accomplished what he set out to do! As a child you probably heard your mother say something similar to "Just wait until your father comes home!" This threat probably didn't change your behavior much during the day, but you probably did learn one thing — to avoid your father's arrival.

Punishment is not a panacea, I must caution you. First, its effect is often temporary, and once it is discontinued the same behavior that initiated the punishment is likely to occur again. Second, the person undergoing constant punishment learns to avoid situations. He may not want to attend class, or, if he can't physically escape, he may psychologically escape by turning the teacher off. Third, punishment can produce fear or anxiety so that the teacher, the classroom, or educational materials can become aversive (negative) stimuli because of their association with unpleasant consequences. The anxiety response occurs through the process of classical conditioning. Last, as I mentioned earlier, punishment doesn't direct the student to alternative behavior.

There are two basic forms of punishment: the presentation of a distressing stimulus — being yelled at, ridiculed, or threatened — and the withdrawal of a positive reinforcer — taking away a toy or preventing a child from playing with his peers. Most teachers are very familiar with the first method and use it with various degrees of success. In light of the limitations discussed earlier in this chapter, you might wonder why teachers continue to nag, yell, scream, and hit. They have probably been positively reinforced for this behavior!

Let's look at how this might work in getting students to stay in their seats. When the teacher sees a student out of his seat she begins her tirade: "Get back in your seat. How many times . . . blah . . . blah . . . blah . . . !" The student returns to his seat; the teacher has been reinforced. This behavior sequence leads to an increase in yelling and a decrease in ignoring out-of-seat behavior. Soon the process recommences. The teacher often feels bad about yelling so much, but she learns that yelling suppresses behavior — albeit only for a while (Poteet, 1973).

Sometimes a teacher's behavior instills undesirable behavior in students, unbeknownst to the teacher. In an interesting study, Madsen et al. (1968) found that the more frequently teachers asked young children to sit down after getting out of their seats at inappropriate times, the more frequently they stood up. It appeared that while the teachers intended their remarks as mild reprimands, their social attention was reinforcing to the students. The undesired behavior increased rather than decreased.

Many teachers prefer the withdrawal of a positive reinforcer, used under the proper conditions, as a more effective use of punishment. One technique in this category is *timeout,* a procedure that temporarily removes the child from a reinforcing situation and places him in a location where the reinforcement is minimal or unlikely to occur. This location might be a seat in the back of the room or a special section in the room where he cannot observe the activities of the class. The effectiveness of the timeout procedure hinges on the premise that removal from the class is punishment. If the child is sent out of the class to stand in the hall, where he can talk with other students passing by or observe interesting activities, the procedure is ineffective. The student who misbehaves to get out of completing a task will enjoy being removed from class activities. In these situations, timeout becomes a rewarding experience. Can you think of other incidents in which a teacher thought he was punishing a student when the event was actually reinforcing to the student?

In enforcing timeout procedures, the teacher should not yell or scold but simply tell the student to move to the designated area. In addition, he must be consistent by isolating the student immediately upon the infraction of the class rule. In some situations the teacher may tell the student to return whenever he is ready to follow the class rules; in other situations the teacher might set a time for the student to remain in the designated area.

Remember that punishment is often pitted against peer approval. If a student's peer group reinforces misbehavior and the student values peer approval, the loss of privileges has little effect on the student's behavior.

When using punishment be sure that it is immediate, carried out in a calm manner, paired with reinforcement of incompatible behavior, and consistent (Becker et al., 1971).

BASIC STEPS FOR BEHAVIOR MODIFICATION

I recommend the following steps to the teacher undertaking to analyze and modify behavior:

1. Define and state operationally the behavior to be changed. *Don't generalize, such as "the kid fools around in class" or "has a bad attitude." Explicitly define the behavior to be changed — leaving a seat without permission, yelling out answers in class. Know exactly what you want the student to do, so that you can reinforce the appropriate behavior.*

2. Obtain a reading of the operant level of the behavior that you are considering changing. *Before you treat a specified behavior, note its frequency. You can then determine after the treatment whether the behavior was modified. For example, how many times does the student leave his seat in a given hour*

or day? A general recommendation is to use a graph depicting the frequency for each observation period.

3. Arrange the learning or treatment situation so that desirable behavior will occur. *Before starting reinforcement for appropriate behavior, check to determine whether the individual can come through with the desired response. It is often helpful to prompt the desired behavior by a verbal request or by establishing a situation in which the behavior is likely to occur: "Let's clean up this room so we can have some space to work."*
4. Identify potential reinforcers. *A stimulus has no inherent reinforcing property. Also, what is reinforcing at one time may not be reinforcing at another time.*
5. Shape and/or reinforce desired behavior and, if necessary, use procedures to weaken inappropriate behavior. *Initially, the desired behavior should be reinforced each time until it has assumed proper strength. Once this occurs, you can change the reinforcement schedule. If the student is unable to respond with the desired behavior, successive approximations of the behavior must be identified and appropriately reinforced.*
6. Maintain records of the reinforced behavior to determine whether the strength or frequency of the response has increased. *By comparing the progress of the treatment or learning session with the initial or baseline rate, you will know whether the reinforcement contingencies had an effect on modifying behavior. If the reinforcement had no effect on the behavior, you must then determine why and make the necessary adjustments.*

Two pitfalls along the path of behavior modification are misidentifying reinforcers and demanding too much too soon by not beginning with small steps toward the target behavior. A child who is not able to work independently at his seat without annoying other students will not become a model student in one or two days. It's important that he be reinforced when he completes one or two problems, sits quietly for short periods of time, and exhibits other behaviors that approximate the terminal behavior.

Check the references at the end of this chapter for examples of behavior modification programs in the classroom. Although these sources demonstrate that behavior can be changed, some educators question the application of various behavioral change methods in the schools. In the following reading, Cote (1973) identifies some of the issues involved in using behavior modification. Be prepared to voice your own opinions after analyzing his position.

Behavior Modification: Some Questions

Behavior modification is made to order for the classroom teacher. It is, first of all, impressive in its effectiveness. Second, one can come to a reasonably thorough understanding of the basic principles without too much difficulty. Third, behavior modification can be used even in dire classroom situations. These are some of the main reasons why behavior modification is gaining general acceptance in the educational community. Unfortunately, this acceptance may have been given too hastily.

The problem in short is this: How does one who has as his (her) goal the development of children into bright, creative, free, and open individuals reconcile this goal with a program that controls and manipulates behavior? Behavior modification can indeed control behavior to such a degree that we can create, maintain, and eliminate almost any behavior that we can define and measure. Behavior modification can take freedom of response from the child and place it into the hands of the controlling teacher. With younger or slower children external control can turn into a "bucket of worms." The more a child has to struggle to make a decision, the happier he will be to have the teacher make it for him. The temptation to misuse this power over behavior may be too great. The fact that behavior modification works well adds to the problem.

I am aware of the standard responses that advocates of behavior modification make to the question of control, yet I am never quite satisfied by them. Proponents of behavior modification say: "But teachers control behavior anyway, only they do it in a sloppy, random manner." This response begs the question. The fact that some methods of control are more effective than others does not relieve us of the problem of questioning how much control we should exert in the first place. Furthermore, the issue has little to do with how the technique eases a teacher's burden or appears to raise objective measures of performance. The issue has to do with one human being (big) deliberately and willfully planning, managing, and determining the responses of another human being (small).

Truthfully, I have not resolved this issue in my own thinking. In the past I have used, and I continue to use, versions of behavior modification. I am well aware of how well behavior modification can raise objective measures of performance of a class. I am also aware that with certain pupils the results approach the miraculous. Neverthe-

From R.W. Cote, "Behavior Modification: Some Questions." *The Elementary School Journal* 24 (1973): 45-47.

less, I have a strong "gut" reaction about manipulating children in this fashion (for their own good or otherwise).

Still another issue is involved here, an issue as important as those already raised. We use behavior modification generally when a child's motivation and achievement are low. What, however, is a child telling us when he behaves in a manner that we deem calls for behavior modification? The answer is obvious. The child is telling us that something is wrong. But is something wrong with the child or with the system that is attempting to educate him? Probably something is wrong with both. But we manipulate the child to fit the environment because that course is easier than creating an environment to fit the child. However, the child may be acting more like an accurate weather vane than a troublesome pupil. He may be telling us that something is radically wrong with the way we are trying to educate him. We ought not to ignore this message. What we may be seeing when we look at a poorly motivated, low achieving child is someone whose self-activating, self-developing program has been engaged. The child's innate drives toward self-mastery are being thwarted, and he is reacting (consciously or unconsciously) in the only manner open to him. He could be trying to tell us that we are not helping him grow. Worse yet, he could be telling us that we are holding him back. The question we should be asking ourselves here is this: Is it moral to use a system of control to adjust a child to a learning environment that his behavior tells us does not work? Should we change the environment instead of changing the child? I am not advocating open classrooms, or structured classrooms, or no classrooms. In time, the right mixture will evolve. I am merely asking whether behavior modification (and other emergency systems) are holding back that evolution.

While this problem appears to have a long life before it, some clarification is possible. We can safely say that various forms of behavior modification suffer from overexposure. Behavior modification as a topic of conversation seems to generate more emotional responses than rational ones. A highly placed government official has felt a need to cast aspersions on behavior modification in public. (His responses, however, have been high in emotion and low in rationality and can be dismissed on that basis.) A psychologist who for years was unknown outside the academic world of psychology has in recent months become something of a media star. He has made behavior modification a household word with late night television viewers. The fact that behavior modification lends itself to mechanization has helped many companies to prosper by producing any amount of educational gimmickry. These gimmicks are bought by school systems that are desperate to raise reading achievement. The general result has been to saturate us with discussions of the use, the need, and the applicability of behavior modification. We must bring some professional perspective to this issue.

Pioneers in the use of behavior modification in the classroom were looking for a last-ditch remediative technique for poor performers.Students of behavior management are aware that the first widespread uses of behavior modification were largely institutional. The approach was used with psychotic and severely retarded individuals. Behavior modification was never intended for large groups of children who are performing at, or just below, grade level. It is a system to generate intrinsic motivation for children whom school (as we define it now) has little power to motivate. While the system initially makes the rewards external, the end goal is to take the child to the point where he can reinforce himself for his achievements. Behavior modification was never intended to force children to respond to a dull, lifeless, uninviting environment, be it a single classroom, a school, a school district, or the entire American educational complex. A danger of behavior modification is that it takes the pressure off the profession to find new stimulating activities, programs, or alternatives to classrooms. The pressure is off because through behavior modification we can get children to respond even in a depressing environment that is self-defeating to them.

Educating young children can be compared to inviting them to a feast. Some children, for one reason or another, have lost their appetite. They need an appetizer. Behavior modification is just that — an appetizer. Once the children are hungry again, the gimmicks can be dropped. We must keep our goal of a gimmick-free environment for learning before us. We must spend less time with the appetizers and more with the main course. If and when behavior modification is used as an enticement, it becomes imperative that we consider some of the issues raised here and make a rational response to them.

The proponents of behavior modification refute the limitations and concerns raised by its critics. Responding to the freedom-and-creativity issue, Givner and Graubard (1974) state:

> Creativity can come only after the basic building blocks have been laid. A child cannot be creative if he does not have the tools to be creative with. One goal of a behavior modification system is to give the child these basic skills to cement together a repertoire with which he can interact with his environment and create a new environment and new behaviors. (p. 152)

In his article "The True Humanist: The Behavior Modifier," Nolan (1974) identifies four bulwarks of behavior modification:

1. *It extends the system of rewards to those who rarely, if ever, received them.*
2. *It removes the punitive aspects from the educational process.*
3. *It systematizes what we have always done so that we do it more effectively.*
4. *It demands better teaching by forcing the teacher to analyze carefully the learning behavior of each student. (p. 337)*

What are your beliefs about behavior modification? Under what circumstances would you use it?

PROGRAMMED INSTRUCTION

Programmed instruction applies operant conditioning principles to human learning in school settings. It works as a self-instructional package that presents a topic in a carefully planned sequence and requires the learner to respond to questions or statements by filling in blanks, selecting from a series of answers, or solving a problem. Immediate feedback occurs after each response. The program can be incorporated in books, teaching machines, or computers (Computer Assisted Instruction). Those who advocate programmed instruction stress that it improves classroom learning, presenting even the most difficult subjects in small steps so that all students can succeed at their own rates.

The 1950s generated much excitement about programmed instruction. Some educators believed that this new form of instruction would revolutionize teaching, making learning more efficient and freeing the teacher from dull tasks. On the other hand, many teachers feared that machines would replace them in the classroom and that they would lose their jobs.

Throughout the late 1950s and early 1960s, many articles dealing with the research and issues of programmed instruction appeared in the professional journals. By 1970, it was obvious that the revolution was more than "fashionably late." Educators concluded that programmed textbooks and teaching machines could teach, but for the most part, their future role lay in supplementing the teacher's instructional program.

Sidney Pressey (1926) is credited with developing the first teaching machine. Pressey's machine was not used to instruct students. It was primarily a multiple-choice testing device that informed students whether or not their answer was correct as soon as it was given. Educators showed little interest in this type of device.

In 1954, B. F. Skinner published a paper, "The Science of Learning and the Act of Teaching," about his laboratory techniques that modified the behavior of both animals and humans. He stated in detail the principles of operant conditioning and described methods for automating instruction. This paper provided the theoretical basis and provoked the enthusiasm for programmed instruction.

Earlier you read about the learning principles of reinforcement, immediacy of reinforcement, discriminative stimuli, extinction, and shaping as they applied to operant conditioning. Bugelski (1964) applies these principles to programmed instruction:

> Skinner would say that because the learner must emit (compose) the answer (not merely recognize it out of a choice of two or four) operant conditioning is present. Because the emission of the answer is controlled by the question, we have a discriminated-stimulus situation. The learner does not emit answers at random — they are the kinds of answers that are desired under this, and only this, stimulus situation. If the answer is correct, the learner has reinforcement and immediacy of reinforcement; he knows he is right; he has immediate knowledge of results. Wrong answers presumably become extinct because of failure of reinforcement. Finally, the sequence of questions results in the shaping of the learner. (p. 212)

Teaching machines were to correct the following limitations of current educational practice: First, a long period of time between an act and its reinforcement is common in the classroom. If you accept the premise that the immediacy of reinforcement is an important variable in learning, wouldn't you be concerned about handing back test papers two or three weeks after examination or about being unable to provide feedback to all your students every time you ask a question? Second, Skinner criticizes the relative infrequency of the use of reinforcement in many classrooms. We found evidence in Chapter 4 of the differential use of reinforcement by teachers. Enough research evidence is available to support the claim that some students are rarely reinforced for their responses (Brophy & Good, 1970). Last, there is a lack of organized instructional sequence in the teaching of complex skills. Teachers do not carefully arrange material (stimuli to shape the learner's behavior) toward instructional objectives.

Programmed instruction attempts to improve learning by (1) breaking down material into small units, (2) forcing the learner to respond to these small units, (3) providing immediate knowledge of results, and (4) allowing for self-pacing.

VARIATIONS IN PROGRAMS

Skinner's programs are *linear.* The programmer lays out the route or sequence of frames for all students to follow in completing the program. Each frame or segment of the program includes a small piece of knowledge to avoid any error. The frames in linear programs rarely include more than one or two sentences.

Crowder (1960) has developed programs that part ways with Skinner's linear programs. He has built variations into his programs, describing them as "intrinsic programs," or branching programs, in which a student's responses determine the route he follows. Alternative routes called "branches" are predictors of the problems he may have in completing the program. These branches allow the student who has answered a question incorrectly to go back and review pertinent information about a concept and find out why his response was not correct. Students who do not make similar mistakes never see these frames and can skip over material by moving ahead to later frames in the program. The branching program typically presents more information per frame than the linear program: two or three paragraphs per frame, as opposed to one or two sentences per frame. Last, Crowder uses multiple-choice questions as the method of eliciting student responses. Students recognize the correct answer instead of constructing the response as Skinner requires. Each response to a question is keyed to a different page or frame in the program.

Figures 6.2*a* and 6.2*b* are examples of linear and branching programs.

Programmed materials are not limited to pure linear or branching formats. The sole support of some branching programs is the student's answer, while other branching programs have more inputs: other data such as intelligence or achievement test scores as patterns of earlier responses. There are even "discovery programs," which present an experiment or problem followed by a multiple-choice question that calls for the student to derive a conclusion hypothesis or generalization.

Although professional education journals are filled with controversy over the advantages and disadvantages of both linear and branching programs, research has not shown either type of program to be better than the other (Silberman et al., 1961). Therefore, it doesn't appear to matter whether the student writes out his responses (as in the linear program) or identifies them (as in the branching program). In one study (Roe, 1960) a group of students listened to a programmed lecture. These students learned as well as a group that wrote out responses and a group that merely read the program. No one method proved to be better than another. The lecture took the least time. Bugelski (1964) suggests that the ability of teaching machines or programmed-learning textbooks to control attention is one of their more important advantages in learning, because the student cannot advance without attending to the material.

FIGURE 6.2*a*
PART OF A PROGRAM IN HIGH SCHOOL PHYSICS.

SENTENCE TO BE COMPLETED	WORD TO BE SUPPLIED
1. The important parts of a flashlight are the battery and the bulb. When we "turn on" a flashlight, we close a switch which connects the battery with the _____.	bulb
2. When we turn on a flashlight, an electric current flows through the fine wire in the _____ and causes it to grow hot.	bulb
3. When the hot wire glows brightly, we say that it gives off or sends out heat and _____.	light
4. The fine wire in the bulb is called a filament. The bulb "lights up" when the filament is heated by the passage of a(n) _____ current.	electric
5. When a weak battery produces little current, the fine wire, or _____, does not get very hot.	filament
6. A filament which is *less* hot sends out or gives off _____ light.	less
7. "Emit" means "send out." The amount of light sent out, or "emitted," by a filament depends on how _____ the filament is.	hot

FIGURE 6.2*b*

PART OF A BRANCHING PROGRAM ON INSTRUCTIONAL OBJECTIVES.

Page 6: A course *description* tells you something about the content and procedures of a course; a course *objective* describes a desired outcome of a course.

Whereas an objective tells what the learner is to be like as a result of some learning experiences, the course description tells only what the course is about.

The distinction is quite important, because a course description does not explain what will be accepted as adequate achievement; it does not confide to the learner the rules of the game. Though a course description might tell the learner which field he will be playing on, it doesn't tell him where the foul lines are, where the goalposts are located, or how he will know when he has scored.

It is useful to be able to recognize the difference between an objective and a description, so try an example.

Which of the statements below looks most like an *objective?*

To be able to explain the principles for developing reading readiness in the primary grades . . . turn to page 7.

Discusses principles, techniques, and procedures in developing reading readiness in the primary grades . . . turn to page 8.

Page 7: You said "To be able to explain the principles of reading readiness in the primary grades" was a statement of an objective.

You are correct! The statement describes an *aim* rather than a course. It doesn't do a very good job of it, but at least it does attempt to describe a goal rather than a process.

Now let us move on. TURN TO PAGE 10

Page 8: Oh, come on now! The collection of words that led you to this page is a piece of a course description, and not a very good description at that. I hope you are not being misled by the fact that college catalogs are composed of such phrases. They are *not* statements of intended learning outcomes and they are *not* what we are concerned with here.

Let me try to explain the difference this way. A course description describes various aspects of a PROCESS known as a "course." A course objective, on the other hand, is a description of a PRODUCT, of what the learner is supposed to be like as a *result* of the process.

Return to page 6 and read the material again.

PROGRAMMED LESSON PLANS

Deterline (1967) lays out a plan for programming lectures, demonstrations, or classroom exercises. The teacher begins by developing a response outline that includes the specific responses each student is to make during the lecture — giving definitions, making discriminations, solving problems. After these responses are set down, the teacher makes an outline of the material he plans to present to help the students answer each question. At first, the material preceding each question should be relatively short to minimize confusion. As the students become more competent, the discussion and explanation can be longer and more complex.

As the lecture unfolds, the teacher directs information to his students that will guide them to answer a question he has previously anticipated. After the students respond, the teacher discusses the correct answer, asks for further questions, and goes on to the next part of the lesson plan. Providing the students with the questions in advance avoids delays. Otherwise, the teacher will have to write them on the blackboard if he cannot read them aloud without confusion.

Many modifications of this procedure come to mind. The teacher can even prepare lecture notes for his students — a structure for them to build on during note taking. Students will then have some idea of what they should be learning and can spend more time thinking about the lecture rather than simply copying it in their notebooks. Included in the outline are the questions asked during the lecture.

CRITICISMS OF PROGRAMMED INSTRUCTION METHODOLOGY

Many of the criticisms of behavior modification presented earlier in this chapter also apply to programmed instruction. Thatcher (1972) argues that preplanned educational systems produce regimentation and limit creativity. Although students may show achievement gains, the impersonal form of programmed instruction causes the student to experience dehumanization in school. Thatcher questions the assumption that the people who develop their programs take as a fact: that they know what is best for students. He then argues that programmed instruction limits the student's time for reflecting, guessing, and feeling like a person. Many educators are critical of the single-answer approach of programmed instruction, which makes knowledge seem fixed and orderly — an erroneous picture of the universe!

Proponents of programmed instruction respond that nothing is more dehumanizing than sitting in a classroom and failing because the teacher hasn't adequately explained the material or doesn't set aside time to work with individual students or forces all students to learn at the same rate. In Skinner's (1968) words: "In principle, nothing could be more regimental than education as it now stands" (p. 90). He states that programmed instruction can further student freedom in the sense that it reduces the abrasive factors in the classroom and at the same times teaches self-direction.

What other issues about programmed instruction concern you? Under what circumstances would you use the various instructional methods discussed in this chapter?

INDIVIDUALIZED INSTRUCTION PROGRAMS

The principles of programmed instruction have been introduced in various degrees into the regular school program ushered in by individualized instructional programs: Program for Learning in Accordance With Needs (PLAN), developed by the Westinghouse Corporation; Individually Guided Education (IGE), developed at the Research and Development Center for Cognitive Learning at the University of Wisconsin; and Individually Prescribed Instruction (IPI), developed at the Learning Research and Development Center at the University of Pittsburgh. Since their development in the 1960s, these programs have entailed reorganization of entire schools throughout the United States.

I shall now discuss Project PLAN to show you how such a program functions. Project PLAN is a program of individualized instruction in language arts, mathematics, social studies, and science. It is composed of teaching-learning units that identify objectives, materials to be used, and, where possible, alternative ways to attain the objectives. The student has considerable freedom in planning his program of studies and in selecting among alternative modes of instruction.

Each teaching-learning unit begins with a learning objective that tells the student what he is going to learn. Learning activities follow. Included in the learning activities are references for study, self-test questions, and discussion questions. Once the student completes these activities he takes a performance test. If he satisfactorily passes this test, he advances to a new teaching-learning unit; if not, he meets with his teacher to discuss a plan of action. An excerpt from one of Project PLAN's teaching-learning units in science at approximately the seventh-grade level follows (see Figure 6.3).

The PLAN system features a computer that receives and stores records about each student's previous program, his progress, and his performance. Each day the teacher has computer information available to her about what lesson objectives students have completed and

FIGURE 6.3
A PORTION OF A TEACHING-LEARNING UNIT IN SCIENCE AT ABOUT SEVENTH-GRADE LEVEL IN PROJECT PLAN.

LIVING SYSTEMS IN SPACE

Step 1. Objectives

Describe the technological advances for counteracting each of the following conditions in outer space that permit man to establish a closed ecological system in his space craft: (1) lack of gravity, (2) absence of food, (3) decreased air pressure, (4) extremes of temperature, and (5) lack of oxygen.

Use	Do
Today's Basic Science: The Molecule and the Biosphere, Teacher's Edition, John Gabriel Navarra et al. (Harper & Row, 1965).	(*a*) Read pp. 428–429. For use during the next 5 to 10 days, set up a balanced aquarium. See instruction on pp. 430–431. Set up the aquarium now, before going any further with this TLU. You may use any aquarium that may be already set up in the classroom.
	(*b*) From your readings in activity (*a*), list those items that are necessary for the survival of man.
	(*c*) Your list should include all the conditions listed in the objectives, except gravity, and more. Gravity is not really necessary for human survival in space but does cause more problems when there is no gravity.
Life Science, Singer Science Series, Teacher's Edition, Helen Dolman MacCracken et al. (L. W. Singer Co., 1968).	(*d*) Read pp. 302–305, the section "What effect does weightlessness have on man?"
	(*e*) Do the activity on p. 303, "Collect pictures."

what students are now doing. Periodic computer reports on the progress of each student are part of PLAN's provisions.

When using individualized instruction programs, students within the same class can work at various levels. They are not restricted to the objectives at any one particular grade level and they progress according to their own abilities and interests.

TEACHER-MADE LEARNING GUIDES

Teachers can prepare learning guides similar to the one in Figure 6.3. A basic learning guide generally includes the following elements (Gronlund, 1974b):

> *Name of the Unit (topic to be studied)*
>
> *Purpose of the Unit (reason for studying the topic)*
>
> *Statement of Objectives (intended learning outcomes)*
>
> *Pretest (or directions for obtaining it)*
>
> *Learning Activities (materials and methods for achieving the objectives)*
>
> *Self-tests (to aid student in monitoring his learning)*
>
> *Post-test (or directions for obtaining it)*
>
> *Enrichment Activities (learning opportunities beyond the objectives) (p. 44)*

You can reduce these elements as you see fit for your own program. If properly constructed, the learning guide is a self-contained instructional package that enables students to work independently or in groups with minimal teacher guidance. You can develop an entire program by sequencing a series of units.

TASK ANALYSIS

The important components of instruction from the behavioral perspective are the need to (1) state the learning task or objective in behavioral terms, (2) break down the task into prerequisite skills or subtasks, (3) determine the relationship between the prerequisite skills and the logical order in which they should be learned, (4) design materials and procedures for teaching each of the subtasks, and (5) provide feedback to the student about his performance as he completes each of the subtasks and the terminal objectives.

One of the most important functions of the teacher, after the determination of the objective, is the analysis of the task (steps (2) and (3) above). The task analysis enables the teacher to sequence instruction properly which according to the behavioral psychologist leads to more efficient and successful learning. The programmer uses task analysis in her determination of the order of frames in a teaching machine. The curriculum designer welcomes the guidance of task analysis in sequencing learning units in individualized instruction programs.

Let's outline a task analysis for a fairly simple objective in mathematics: "The student will divide any real numbers (including decimal fractions) up to four digits with 90 percent accuracy when presented in the form: NN.N) ddd.d" (Packard, 1975, p. 224).

1. *The first step is to move the decimal point to the proper place.*

   15.2) 1862.4

2. *Then the student estimates the first digit of the quotient and writes the number above the line and the appropriate digit.*

   ```
        1
   152) 18624
   ```

3. *The third step is to multiply the divisor by the estimated quotient (1 × 152) and write the product below the problem as shown here.*

   ```
        1
   152) 18624
        152
   ```

4. *Then the student subtracts the product from part of the quotient and enters the difference below these numbers.*

   ```
        1
   152) 18624
        152
         34
   ```

5. *The fifth step is to "bring down" the next digit in the number being divided.*

   ```
        1
   152) 18624
        152
         342
   ```

After step five the student recommences the procedure of estimating a digit of the answer and repeating the process of multiplying and subtracting until she reaches the desired degree of accuracy.

This outline presumes that the student can discriminate numbers, subtract, and divide. These behaviors are part of the student's entering abilities. If they are not, they will have to be taught before the student can successfully attain the objective. Teachers often overlook important subskills in their teaching and, as a result, find that their students have difficulty meeting requirements.

Subskills cannot be taught at random; some of them are prerequisite to others. In the division problem, addition and subtraction must be taught before multiplication. However, teaching the student to adjust the decimal point or to bring down another number from the quotient can take place at any time, since none of the other skills depends on them.

Developing a task analysis for lessons takes practice. In the process you must estimate the students' entry behavior. If you know which skills they have already mastered before instruction, you will not have to teach them these skills. Sometimes a teacher finds that her task analysis is not detailed enough because she erroneously assumed that her students had certain entry behavior. By pretesting and making modifications in your original task analysis, you can develop a better instructional sequence.

In analyzing the total task, Packard (1975) suggests that

> you decide, on the basis of what you already know about the students, what skills they probably already have, categorizing these as entry or prerequisite behaviors. Then you categorize all the other component skills as intermediate objectives leading to your terminal objective. (p. 230)

An example of a complete task analysis is presented in Figure 6.4.

GAGNÉ'S CONDITIONS OF LEARNING

Gagné (1970) has contributed much theory and research to this area. He arranges eight types of learning in a hierarchy of relationships based on the assumption that the higher levels of learning depend on the lower levels. Each type of learning is distinguished from the others primarily by the conditions required for the specific learning. Table 6.3 summarizes the conditions for Gagné's eight types of learning. You can see that different types of learning require different teaching strategies. Teaching a student to discriminate mathematical symbols (type 5 learning) requires a different strategy than teaching him to solve mathematical problems (type 8 learning).

Gagné stresses the importance of developing a task analysis *before* beginning instruction. This prepares a student for learning something new after he has acquired the necessary capabilities. Higher-order skills or capabilities like problem solving are more easily learned if the student has a foundation of lower or subordinate capabilities (like concepts and rules).

FIGURE 6.4
A SAMPLE TASK ANALYSIS.

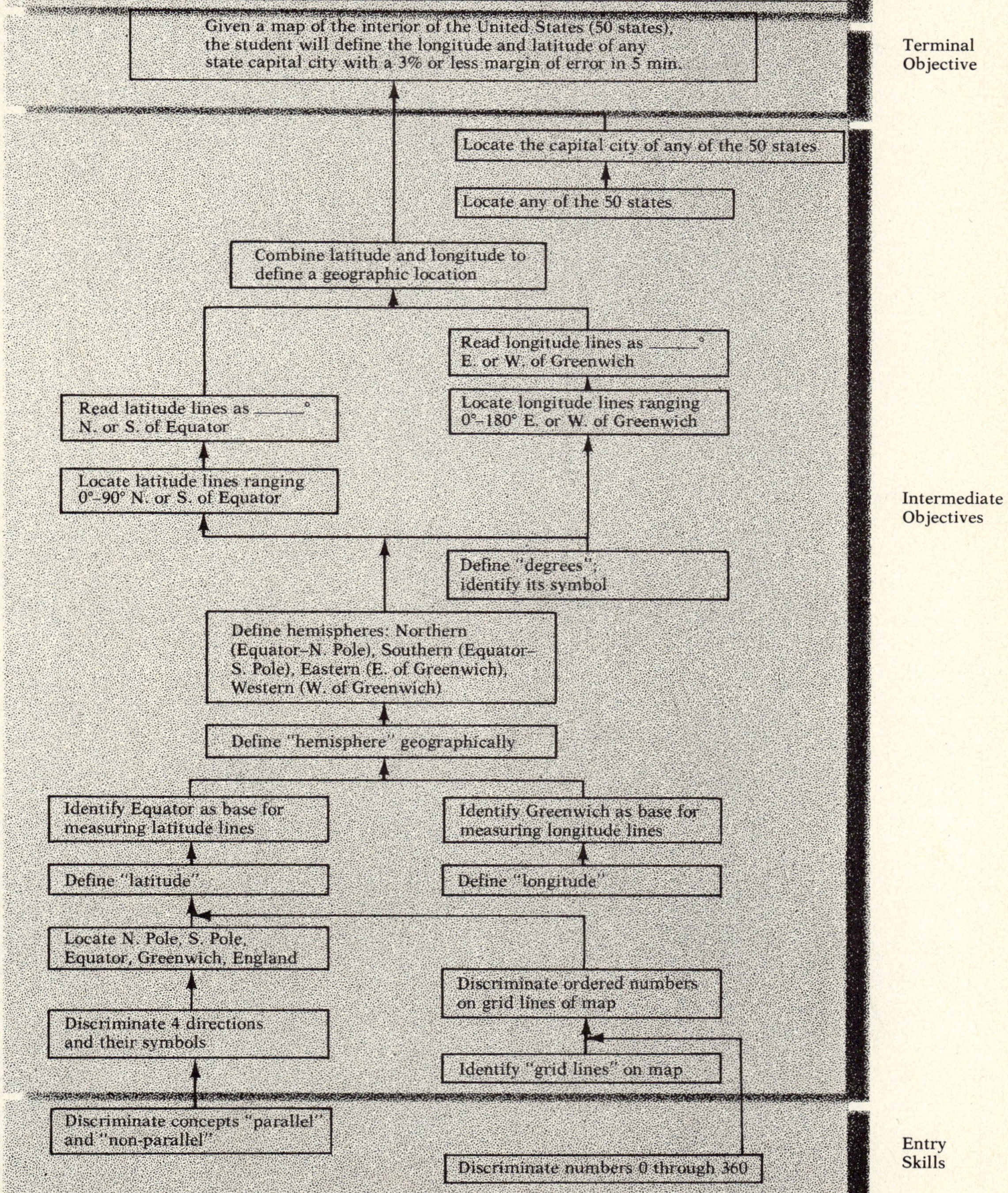

From R. Packard, *Psychology of Learning and Instruction* (Columbus, Ohio: Charles E. Merrill, 1975), p. 233. Reprinted by permission of the publisher.

Table 6.3
The Eight Types of Learning According to Gagné

Type 1: Signal learning — the individual learns to make a *general* diffuse response to a signal. This is the classical conditioning response of Pavlov.

Conditions:
1. The stimulus produces a generalized reaction (contiguity).
2. The stimulus provides the signal.
3. The stimulus must precede the signal.

Type 2: Stimulus-response learning is a type of learning in which a very precise muscular movement in response to a very specific stimulus is formed. It involves operant conditioning, contiguity, and practice.

Conditions:
1. Learning is gradual.
2. Response becomes more sure and precise.
3. Controlling stimulus becomes more sure and precise.
4. Condition 2 plus 3 equals successive approximation.
5. Reinforcement follows the response.

Type 3: Chaining — what is acquired is a chain of two or more stimulus-response connections. (Example: the grip on a bat, the stance and swing in hitting a ball)

Conditions:
1. Individual links must be previously established.
2. There must be contiguity between links.

Type 4: Verbal associations — the learning of chains that are verbal. (Example: English word "match" from the French word "*alum*ette" — illuminate — lum — light — match)

Conditions:
1. Learner must know what the word means.
2. He must make a connection between the words.
3. There must be a coding connection. (E.g., be able to associate *lum* with illuminate.)

Type 5: Multiple discrimination — the individual learns to make *n* different identifying responses to as many different stimuli (learning a French vocabulary list or symbols for the chemical elements). The learning of each stimulus-response connection is a simple Type 2 occurrence; the connections tend to interfere with each other's retention.

Conditions:
1. Individual chains between each stimulus and each response must be learned.
2. Steps must be taken to reduce interference.

Type 6: Concept learning — the learner acquires a capability of making a common response to a class of stimuli which may differ widely in

physical appearance (e.g., classifying a football, tennis ball, basketball, and baseball all as balls).

Conditions: 1. There is initial coding of property (ballness) plus a response capability.
2. Learner must be able to generalize to a variety of conditions.
3. Learning may be a gradual process. Therefore, there must be the possibility of multiple presentations of examples of the concept.

Type 7: Rule learning — the chaining of two or more concepts. (Example: when water freezes, its volume becomes larger. This principle embodies the concepts of freeze, volume, and larger.)

Conditions: 1. All concepts must have been previously learned.
2. Concepts must be brought together (not necessary that the *student* do this).
3. Learning takes place in one trial.

Type 8: Problem solving (thinking) — two or more previously acquired principles are somehow combined to produce a new capability that can be shown to depend on a "higher order" principle.

Conditions: 1. Learner must be able to identify the essentials of a solution.
2. He must be able to recall previously learned principles.
3. He must be able to combine the principles so that a new one is formed.
4. There is a sudden solution — repetition will add nothing.

From Wilson, Robeck, and Michael, *Psychological Foundations of Freedom* (New York: McGraw-Hill, 1974), p. 145.

Gagné cites numerous studies to support this belief. In one study, Weigand (1969) attempted to identify all the prerequisite capabilities for sixth graders to solve a physics problem. Only one student had previously acquired these capabilities. She tested each student on the various subskills needed to perform the task. In some students, two or three skills were missing; in others, many more. Weigand taught students all the subordinate skills to determine whether the students could solve the problem once they had learned the lower skills. She found that nine out of ten students were able to solve the problem after instruction on the subskills.

Gagné suggests that in developing a task analysis the teacher should ask herself: "What is it I want my students to do? What do they need to know to do it?" Once the terminal objective emerges, the teacher works backward to delineate which capabilities students must possess to reach the terminal objective. Remember that some students in the class will need more time on certain subskills, while others can skip one or more of the subskills.

KEY POINTS

OPERANT CONDITIONING IN BEHAVIOR MODIFICATION

1. *Define and state operationally the behavior to be changed.*
2. *Obtain an operant level of the behavior that you are considering changing.*
3. *Arrange the learning or treatment situation so that desirable behavior will occur.*
4. *Identify potential reinforcers.*
5. *Shape and/or reinforce desired behavior and, if necessary, use procedures to weaken inappropriate behavior.*
6. *Maintain records of the desired behavior to determine whether strength or frequency of response has increased.*

OPERANT CONDITIONING IN TEACHING

1. *Specify the desired behavioral objective, structure lessons in small steps, and present them in a sequence.*
2. *Provide for involvement in a lesson by encouraging students to respond to various questions and problems.*
3. *Provide immediate feedback to student responses to all ques-*

tions, quizzes, and homework assignments.

4. *Praise students for correct answers, proper study habits, and other desirable classroom behavior.*

TASK ANALYSIS

1. *Each learner begins a learning task with a different set of previously learned prerequisite skills. To be effective, a lesson must take into account what the learner already knows how to do and what he needs to know.*
2. *Content in a given area should be arranged in a hierarchical fashion so that the student first masters the simpliest abilities and concepts that are necessary for later learning.*
3. *A learner is ready to learn something new when he has mastered the prerequisite skills used in the new task.*

SUGGESTIONS FOR FURTHER READING

The following two books provide good examples of behavior modification in classrooms:

Harris, M. B. *Classroom uses of behavior modification.* Columbus, Ohio: Merrill, 1972.

Klein, R. D., Hapkiewicz, W. G., & Roden, A. H. (Eds.). *Behavior modification in educational settings.* Springfield, Ill.: Charles C Thomas, 1973.

Gagné, R.M. *The conditions of learning* (2nd ed.). New York: Holt, Rinehart and Winston, 1970. This book provides good information on developing task analysis.

Gronlund, N.E. *Individualizing classroom instruction.* New York: Macmillan, 1974. The author describes common classroom procedures for individualizing instruction and provides sources of information on programs and procedures of special interest.

Markle, S. M. *Good frames and bad: A grammar of frame writing.* New York: Wiley, 1964. A good source for writing your own programs.

Skinner, B. F. *Walden two.* New York: Macmillan, 1948. Skinner conceives of a Utopia based on the application of science to human behavior.

______. *Beyond freedom and dignity.* New York: Knopf, 1971. (Condensed in the August 1971 issue of *Psychology Today.)* Skinner calls for a technology of behavior to improve society.

______. *The technology of teaching.* New York: Appleton-Century-Crofts, 1968. This book includes some of Skinner's most important writings.

FOLLOW-UP ACTIVITIES

1 Evaluate the impact of operant conditioning. According to Skinner, we are all products of operant conditioning. To what extent do you agree with this statement? Can you use operant conditioning principles to explain some of your own behavior?

2 Discuss the usefulness of teaching machines and programmed textbooks. How do you regard the use of teaching machines and programmed textbooks? Do they adequately solve the problem of providing efficient individual instruction? In what situations would you prefer to be taught by a machine or a program rather than by a teacher? What factors would influence your decisions?

3 Discuss the advantages and disadvantages of sequencing instruction.

The extent to which the teacher should sequence material is an often-debated learning issue. What are the advantages and disadvantages of sequencing instruction? Discuss the different ways in which material can be sequenced.

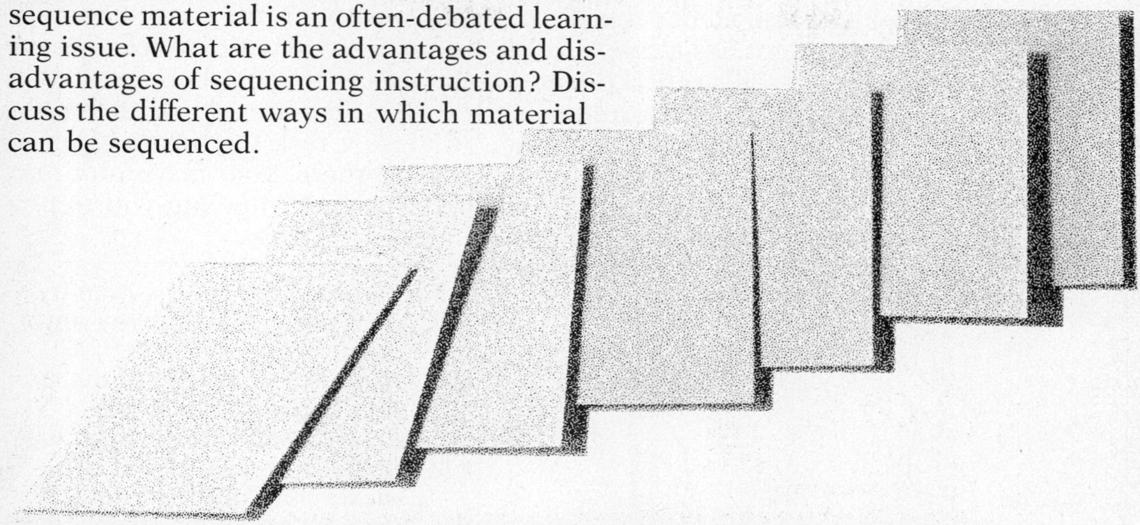

4 Interview students who are using programmed materials.

Observe a class using programmed materials and question students about their reactions to this method. Discuss with the teacher her views regarding programmed instruction and her assessment of the students' progress.

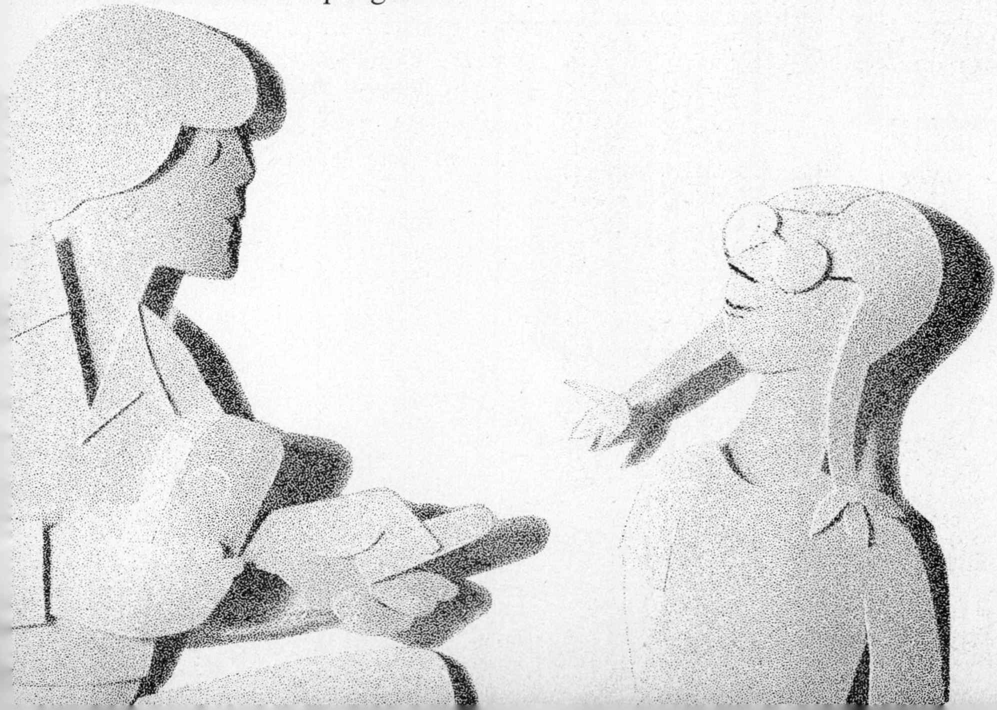

5 Complete a task analysis. In this activity you will have a chance to apply what you have learned in developing a task analysis for a small instructional unit. The activity involves the following basic steps: choosing a task, specifying the entry behavior (skills a student has already mastered before instruction), defining the prerequisite skills (all skills and behaviors that must be mastered prior to attaining the terminal objective), and determining the order in which the skills must be taught. Choose a task in your field of specialization that is relatively small and simple. Your instructor may want to approve Part One of the activity before allowing you to proceed to Part Two.

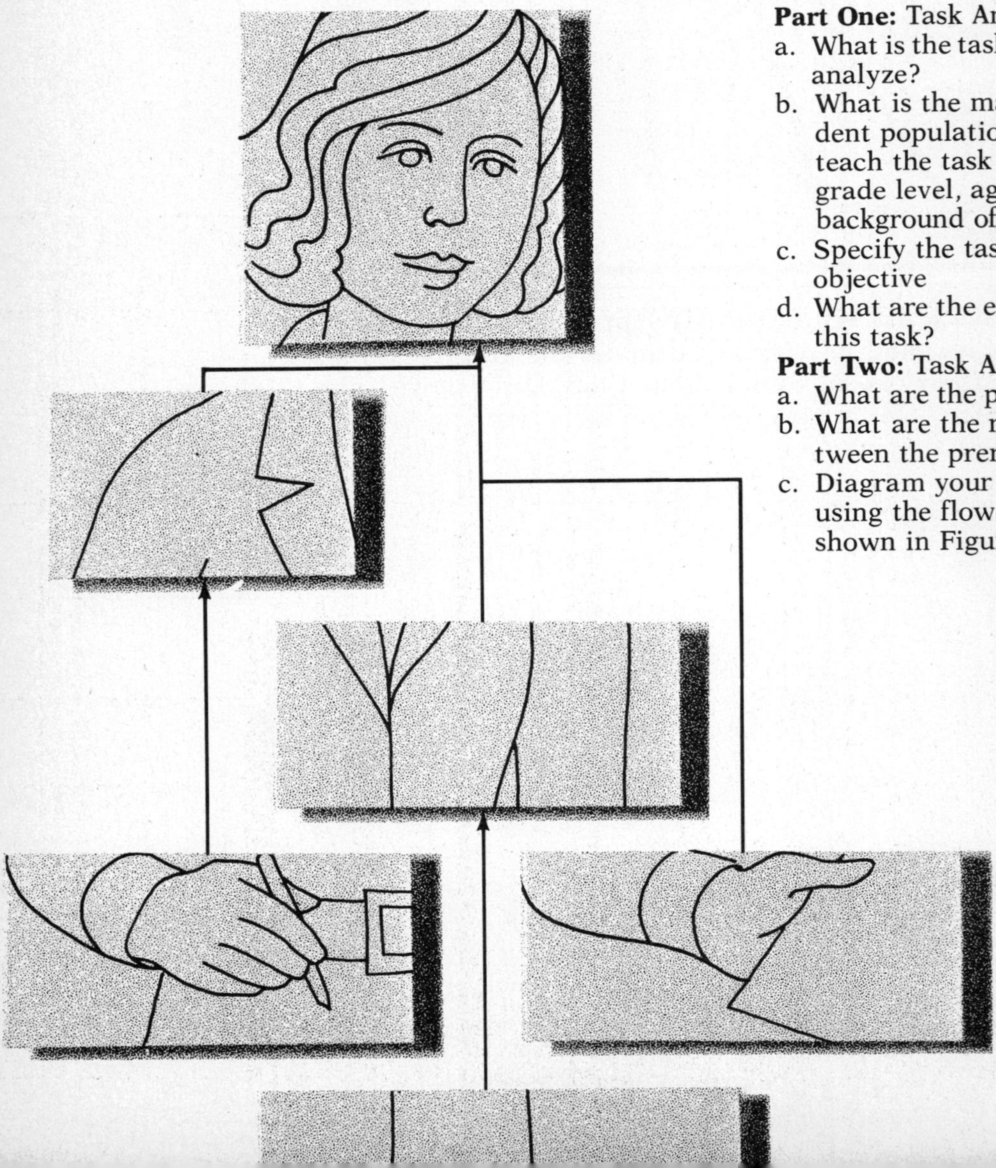

Part One: Task Analysis Activity

a. What is the task you are going to analyze?
b. What is the makeup of the student population you would teach the task to? Identify the grade level, age, and possible background of the students.
c. Specify the task as a behavioral objective
d. What are the entry behaviors for this task?

Part Two: Task Analysis Activity

a. What are the prerequisite skills?
b. What are the relationships between the prerequisite skills?
c. Diagram your task analysis using the flow-chart format shown in Figure 6.4.

6 Experiment with behavior modification. If you have the opportunity to work with students on an individual or group basis, you might try to use behavior modification. Review the principles of learning and basic techniques covered in Chapter 6 before you begin. First, state operationally the behavior to be changed. Next, obtain an operant level of this behavior. Then write a procedure for changing the behavior. Next, try out your plan and maintain records of the reinforced behavior to keep track of whether or not strength or frequency of response has increased. Last, evaluate the effectiveness of your behavior modification program. Use the following checklist as a step-by-step plan.

Description of behavior to be changed
Operant level of behavior (use a graph to chart behavior over a period of time)
Procedure used to change behavior
What happened when you tried out procedure (plot behavior on the graph used in the second step)
Evaluation of behavior modification program

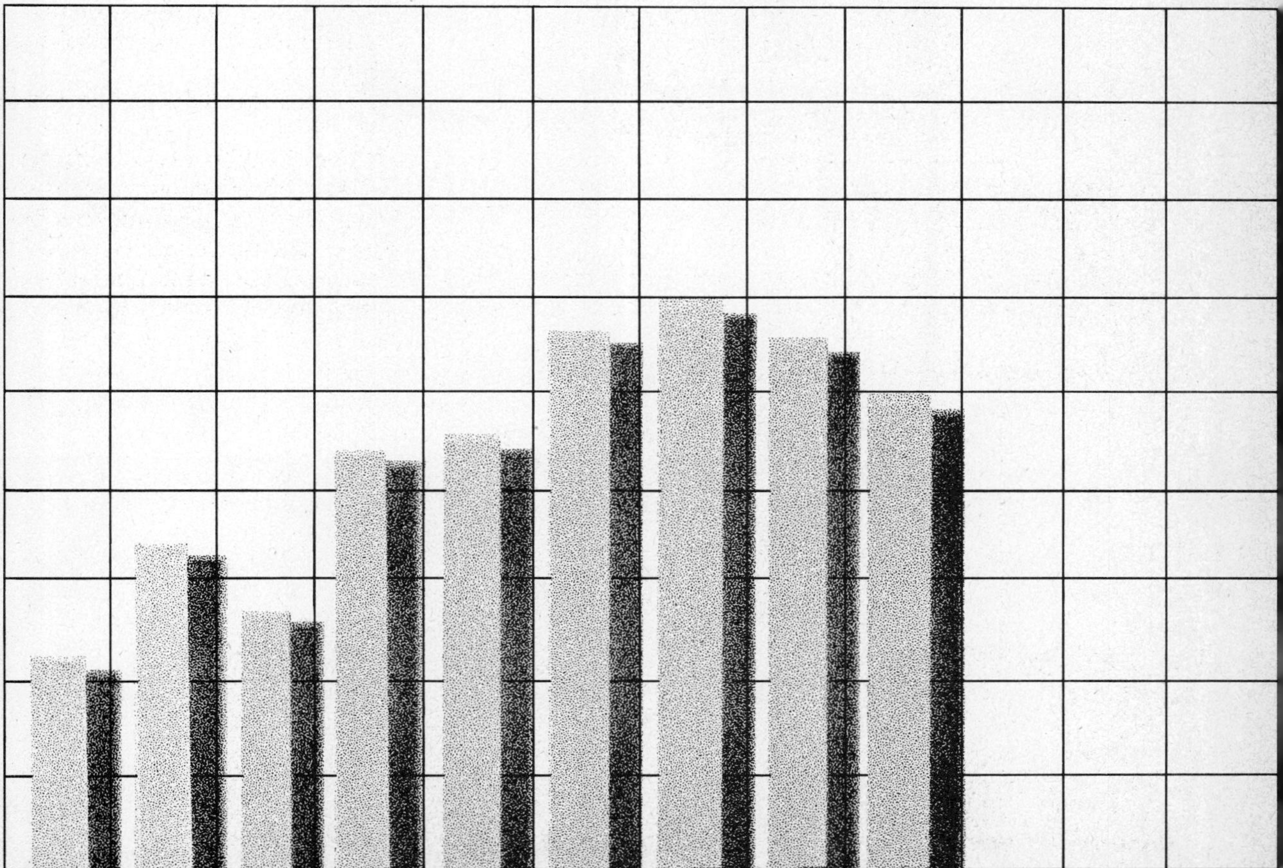

7

COGNITIVE PSYCHOLOGY: LEARNING THEORIES AND APPLICATIONS

ORIENTATION

Can stimulus, response, and reinforcement adequately explain the learning process? Cognitive psychologists are not satisfied with this explanation. Their basic assumption is that a person's behavior is always based on cognition, an act of knowing or thinking about the situation in which behavior occurs. As a result, they are preoccupied with the organization of knowledge, information processing, and decision-making behavior — aspects of the cognitive realm.

Each of the cognitive theorists discussed in this chapter has made important contributions to understanding the teaching-learning process. Piaget is concerned with how children think and how their thinking changes with age. He helps us view behavior from a cognitive-developmental perspective. Bruner and Suchman identify the advantages of discovery or inquiry methods of learning. Finally,

Ausubel suggests that if knowledge is organized and presented properly, students can learn more effectively through textbook and lecture methods.

GESTALT PSYCHOLOGY

Up until the late 1920s and early 1930s behavioristic theories dominated the field of American psychology. During the 1920s a group of German psychologists rejected the process of learning as simply the formation of associations between stimuli and responses and advanced another view. These psychologists were influenced by studies of perception indicating that people respond to whole patterns or situations. They felt that the behavioristic analysis of learning — the reduction of behavior to its smallest parts — was too mechanistic, incomplete, and inadequate for explaining higher mental processes. Their construction of the learning process was in terms of larger, more complex components. To them, learning was restructuring a situation or problem in a new light.

The German term for this view of learning is *gestalt*, a term that roughly translates into English as "form," "pattern," or "configuration." For example, the psychologists noted that a person tends to impose order on a disorganized perceptual field. This is the general law or principle of *pragnanz* (German) or *pregnance* (English). Pregnance denotes clarity, an optimal state of structuring, a stage of consciousness that emphasizes the essential. A tendency toward pregnance means teaching toward a "good gestalt" configuration.

Among the many other laws of perception related to learning, gestalt psychologists have identified the law of *closure*. Operating under this law, a person presented with a series of spaced dots [(. . .), (::), (:.)] will tend to identify them as a line, square, and triangle rather than as simple dots. In other words, he will see them as a totality and not in parts.

Gestalt psychology was advanced by Max Wertheimer (1880–1943), who studied perception and problem solving. He was followed by Kurt Koffka (1886–1941), who described in detail the laws of perception; Wolfgang Kohler (1887–1959), who was noted for his studies of insight using apes; and Kurt Lewin (1892–1947), who contributed greatly to the study of personality and social psychology by developing a cognitive-field psychology, a derivative of gestalt psychology.

An important concept in gestalt psychology is *insight*, the sudden perception of the relationships among elements in a problem situation. Insight is often referred to as the "aha" or "now-I-see" phenomenon and is an alternative explanation to learning by trial and error. Kohler (1927) posed an insight problem to an ape by hanging a bunch of bananas either beyond the ape's reach or outside its cage. In the first situation, the ape had to pile boxes on top of each other to reach the bananas; in the other situation, it had to reach outside the cage with a long stick or, in some cases, assemble two sticks in order to reach the bananas. Kohler found that sometimes the ape solved the problem immediately. Sometimes after an initially unsuccessful attempt to reach the bananas, the ape apparently sat down to think about the problem and then suddenly saw the solution.

Wertheimer (1945) was one of the early gestalt psychologists to deal directly with classroom learning. He deplored the rote memorization methods used in school and wanted children to understand, not memorize, academic content. In one of his problems he required learners to find the area of a parallelogram. He began by explaining the area of a rectangle, not simply giving the students the formula (length × height), but showing them why the formula works: The area is equal to the number of squares in a row times the number of rows (see Figure 7.1, part A). He then presented the learners with a parallelogram cut out of paper (see Figure 7.1, part B) and asked them to find its area.

Many students were stumped and stated that they had never learned the formula; others applied the same procedure used for the rectangle, not knowing whether they were correct or not. One learner, noting that the two projecting ends of the parallelogram made the problem difficult, asked for scissors, cut off one end, and fitted it against the other end, converting the parallelogram into a rectangle (see Figure 7.1, part C). Another learner folded the parallelogram into a ring: She saw that she could cut it anywhere and have a rectangle.

According to Kohler's and Wertheimer's analyses of the learning process, both the apes and the children restructured the problem into a better gestalt. The ape saw another use for the boxes. The children, also, saw another way to construct the problem. Thus, all learning involves the insight or understanding of relationships, particularly the relationships between part and whole.

In gestalt psychology, the degree of ambiguity that the learner perceives in a given situation does more to promote learning than either punishment or reward. The learner is motivated to reduce ambiguity, not by external factors such as reward but by perceptual organization. If a learner sees no ambiguity in a situation or believes that he understands what the teacher is presenting, he is not motivated to learn because he has ordered the situation in his mind.

COGNITIVE-FIELD PSYCHOLOGY

Lewin's interest in perception and motivation encouraged him to de-

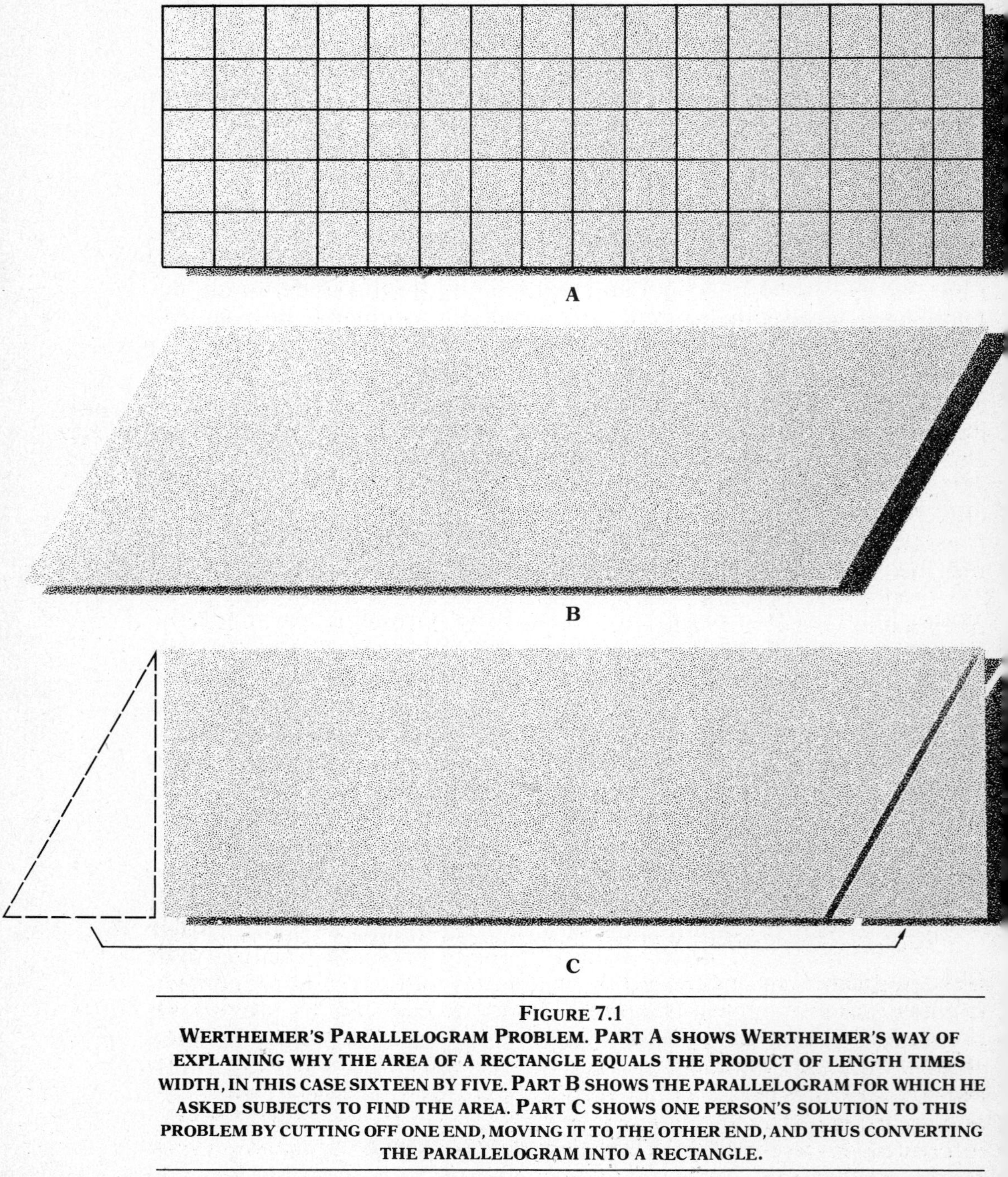

FIGURE 7.1
WERTHEIMER'S PARALLELOGRAM PROBLEM. PART A SHOWS WERTHEIMER'S WAY OF EXPLAINING WHY THE AREA OF A RECTANGLE EQUALS THE PRODUCT OF LENGTH TIMES WIDTH, IN THIS CASE SIXTEEN BY FIVE. PART B SHOWS THE PARALLELOGRAM FOR WHICH HE ASKED SUBJECTS TO FIND THE AREA. PART C SHOWS ONE PERSON'S SOLUTION TO THIS PROBLEM BY CUTTING OFF ONE END, MOVING IT TO THE OTHER END, AND THUS CONVERTING THE PARALLELOGRAM INTO A RECTANGLE.

From W. F. Hill, *Learning: A Survey of Psychological Interpretation* (Scranton, Pa.: Chandler Publishing Co., 1971), p. 104. Reprinted by permission of the publisher.

velop a cognitive-field psychology. A major concept in Lewin's theory is the *life space* or psychological world in which the individual lives. It encompasses both himself and everything that psychologically influences him. An object that is physically close to a person is not a part of his life space if the person is unaware of and unaffected by that object. However, an object that is not a physical fact can exist in someone's life space if it affects his behavior. If a child awakens from a dream hearing "something" in his room, that "something" is a part of his life space despite his parents' reassurance that nothing is there.

Lewin's explanation of behavior — the end product of interaction among the forces and elements of an individual's life space — included the individual's goals, situations he was trying to avoid, and psychological barriers that restricted his movement. Cognitive-field theory, like gestalt psychology, views learning behavior as a reorganization or restructuring. The structure of an individual's life space is determined by his perceptions, and learning occurs as a result of changes in and perceptual reshufflings of this structure.

Lewin's field theory implies that because of a teacher's experience, his life space or cognitive structure may be in another sphere from that of his students. What is meaningful and clear to the teacher may be boring and obscure to his students.

Many of Lewin's concepts can be traced to the writings in phenomenological psychology, a branch of humanistic psychology that deals with the importance of how an individual views his own world. I shall deal with this point of view in the next chapter.

Before leaving the gestalt psychologists, let's briefly compare their ideas about learning with those of the S-R psychologists. We saw that the S-R psychologists emphasize practice and repetition: piecemeal learning that eventually coalesces. The gestalt approach suggests starting from a response to the whole or total situation: learning experiences are then retrospectively divided into separate parts or units.

IMPLICATIONS OF GESTALT PSYCHOLOGY FOR TEACHING

Gestalt psychology organizes learning in patterns, not parts. The gestalt psychologists have advice in this spirit for the teacher faced with problematic teaching situations. To fill students' gaps in information, she should provide them with a good overview of the course and delve into the interrelationships of various topics. Personal understanding and meaning contribute to learning, and gestalt psychologists are not interested in step-by-step instruction, drill, or arbitrary explanations by the teacher.

PIAGET: A COGNITIVE-DEVELOPMENTAL THEORY

Although the gestalt psychologists led the shift toward the internal factors in the learning process, they had limited impact on classroom teaching and curriculum development. We now turn to the Swiss psychologist, Jean Piaget, who, through his analysis of the processes involved in the organization of knowledge, has contributed significantly to a cognitive theory of learning. His theory deals with the thinking process as a gradual shift from concrete to abstract intellectual functioning.

Piaget is actually considered a developmental psychologist because of his study of the "developmental stages" or age-level changes that provide the framework for what children can learn at different ages. The unique aspect of Piaget's theory is that it separates and identifies stages of intellectual or cognitive development. The child's stage of development sets limits for her learning and influences the type of learning that can take place.

Piaget's theory could have been presented in Chapter 2, which took up different cognitive characteristics of students. He is one of the few psychologists who presents a comprehensive theory of the development of intelligence or the thought process. I have decided to treat his theory here because of the important instructional and learning implications that it embodies. The first part of my discussion deals with the development of the stages in the thinking process; the second part derives the instructional and learning implications of the theory.

Piaget reflects an interest in human intelligence not at all like the theoretical positions discussed in Chapter 2. Instead of focusing on the measurement or components of intelligence, his primary interest is in the *development* of intelligence.

Piaget worked in Binet's experimental laboratory standardizing some intelligence tests and became interested not in the determination of correct or incorrect answers but in the child's reasoning processes that led him to his response, especially to incorrect responses. His work ignores the whole basis of conventional IQ testing, which is that intellectual growth is largely a statistical concept developed from test scores obtained at different age levels for the same individual. This method produces a quantitative conception of intelligence: As an individual develops, he acquires more "intelligence," like beads on a string.

From the Piagetian perspective, mental growth means the acquisition of new mental abilities that were not present before. Intel-

lectual growth is not a quantitative but a qualitative situation in which there are significant differences between the thinking of children and adolescents, as well as between preschool and school-age children (Elkind, 1974).

Biologists are hard pressed to explain how structures evolve so that organisms can adapt to their environment. Piaget has explored this same problem in regard to human adaptation and has researched a theory of intellectual or cognitive development based on the premise that intellectual structures — organizational properties of thought — are formed in the individual as he interacts with his environment. The emerging structures better enable him to cope with the increasing demands of his environment.

Piaget uses the term "scheme"[1] almost interchangeably with "structure." A scheme is a repeatable behavior pattern. Initially, scheme relates to inborn reflexes such as the "sucking scheme"; during adolescence schemes are mental, as in the "scheme of classification," "scheme of probability," and "operational schemes," or "operations" for short. The acquisition of a scheme implies that there has been a change in the child's intellectual development.

Although Piaget's overwhelming concern is with the structures of intelligence, he stresses two other aspects of intelligence: content and function. *Content* refers to the child's specific patterns of behavior that surface in the responses he gives to the various problems or situations he faces.

Early in his career (during the 1920s and 1930s), Piaget's research interest focused on the content of children's thoughts, pertaining to such phenomena as changes in reasoning ability from early to late childhood, moral behavior and judgment, the child's conception of the world around him — the origin of trees, dreams, sun, and moon — and his conception of certain natural phenomena — the movement of clouds and rivers. However, for the last three decades, Piaget's research interest has deepened. From the description of the content of children's thoughts he has intensified the analysis of the basic processes underlying and determining the content (Ginsburg & Opper, 1969).

Function refers to the manner in which an organism makes intellectual progress. According to Piaget, all organisms inherit two basic tendencies or "invariant functions": organization and adaptation. Ginsburg and Opper (1969) provide an excellent discussion of these tendencies.

[1]I am using the terminology suggested by Ginsburg and Opper (1969), who state that Piaget's French term "scheme" is usually translated as "schema" (plural: schemata). They suggest that because Piaget has begun lately to use the French word "schema" for another purpose, the retention of the French word "scheme" in English is preferable.

The term "organization" describes the ability of organisms to systematize or to organize their physical or psychological processes into coherent systems. In the physical realm, for example, fish possess a number of structures that allow them to function effectively in water: gills, a circulatory system, and temperature mechanisms. All these structures work together efficiently to maintain fish in their environment. This physical coordination is the result of the organizational tendency.

This same organizational tendency characterizes the psychological level. An infant has separate behavioral structures for visual focusing and grasping. At some point in his development, he is able to organize both of these behavioral structures into a higher-order structure by grasping an object while he looks at it. Organization, then, integrates physical and psychological structures into higher-order systems.

The second aspect of functioning is adaptation. All organisms are born with a tendency to adapt to their environment. The ways in which adaptation takes place differ from organism to organism. Adaptation may be considered in terms of two complementary processes — assimilation and accommodation. Assimilation refers to the process by which an individual uses an existing structure or ability to deal with some problem in his environment. Accommodation is a process by which the individual must change in response to environmental demands. This adaptation necessitates a modification or rearrangement of his existing mental structures.

The following example illustrates the relationship between assimilation and accommodation. A child who has learned to open cabinets by pulling on them will have to develop a new sequence of hand movements in order to open a cabinet with a handle that must be turned to open it — he will have to accommodate to the environment. However, once he has learned this new response, he will be able to recall the sequence of behaviors when opening this particular type of cabinet door — he will have assimilated the new experience. In review, if an individual has an existing behavior pattern for interacting with his environment, he assimilates this behavior; if he does not have an appropriate set of behaviors to deal with a situation, he must change his pattern of response and accommodate to his environment.

To Piaget, adaptation is a balance of assimilation and accommodation. If, in the process of assimilation, the individual cannot adapt to the environment, a state of disequilibrium exists. Accommodation is the result of this disequilibrium, and the individual's present structures are either altered or new ones emerge. Intellectual growth is a continual process of equilibrium-disequilibrium states. However, when equilibrium is restored, the individual is at a higher intellectual level than before (Sullivan, 1967).

Adaptation can also be applied to classroom learning. Cognitive progress depends partly on accommodation for development. The student must enter an area of the unknown in order to learn. He can't study only what he already knows — he can't rely on assimilation. In a situation in which the student's existing cognitive processes are not used, accommodation but no assimilation occurs. In courses that present you with nothing new, you have probably overassimilated; in courses that you don't grasp, you have overaccommodated. Neither situation will facilitate your cognitive growth.

In summary, there are three aspects of intellectual growth: structure, content, and function. As the child develops, his structure and content change but his functions remain the same. The organization and adaptation functions create a series of stages, each possessing particular psychological structures that determine the child's thinking ability. Intelligence for Piaget, then, is the sum of available structures an individual has at his disposal at a particular point in his development.

PIAGET'S DEVELOPMENTAL STAGES

A question often asked about Piaget's stages is "What causes an individual to move from one stage to another?" Piaget (1964) identifies four factors that influence this transition.

One factor is maturation. The development of the central nervous system, brain, motor coordination, and other physical manifestations of growth influence cognitive development. Until the child's motor coordination is developed to a certain extent he cannot walk, and if he is limited in exploring his environment, he will not know much about it. Although maturation is an important factor in intellectual development, it does not sufficiently explain it. If it did, teachers would play a very minor role in influencing intellectual development.

A second transitional factor is physical experience. The child's interaction with his physical environment can increase the rate of his development because observation and manipulation of objects aid the emergence of more complex thinking.

A third factor, social transmission, marks the influence of language, formal instruction, and reading, as well as social interaction with peers and adults.

The fourth factor influencing stage transition is equilibration or self-regulation. This factor incorporates the ability to reestablish equilibrium states during periods of disequilibrium. It is a process by which the individual attains higher levels of cognitive functioning through a step-by-step assimilation and accommodation.

Let us now explore the various stages and corresponding structures identified by Piaget. The stages can be represented as follows:[2]

1. *Sensorimotor Period (0–2 years)*
2. *Preoperational Period (2–7 years)*
3. *Concrete Operations Period (7–11 years)*
4. *Formal Operations Period (11 years and above)*

It should be noted that these age ranges are only approximations. All children proceed through each stage, but at different rates. Thus, it is possible for a six-year-old child to be at the concrete operations stage or an eight-year-old child to still be at the preoperational stage in his thinking. However, the sequence of development is the same for all children. Each successive stage is built in a hierarchical fashion on the preceding stage. Structures belonging to earlier stages become integrated and incorporated as part of the stages that follow.

SENSORIMOTOR PERIOD (0–2 YEARS)

Sensorimotor thought occupies approximately the first two years of life and embodies those behaviors not mediated by signs or symbols. The infant begins life with innate reflexes, schemes that are modified and combined with other schemes to form more complex behavior.

During this time the infant has no conception of "object permanence." When an object is hidden from view, he fails to look for it. As the infant continues to experience the environment, toward the end of the sensorimotor period, he behaves as though he realizes that a hidden object still exists and begins looking for it after he has seen it hidden. Other primitive concepts not present at birth — space, time, causality — develop and become incorporated into the child's behavior patterns (Sullivan, 1967).

Our interest in the school-age child prompts us to move on to the remaining stages in Piaget's theory. We shall spend more time on these later stages.

PREOPERATIONAL PERIOD (2–7 YEARS)

Although the child makes rapid cognitive growth during his first two years of life, his abilities are limited to objects that he can see in his environment. His "thinking" acts on objects that he can perceive directly. However, toward the end of his second year, the child begins using symbols to represent various aspects of his environment. For example, he can use the word "ball" to represent a real ball when it is not in immediate view. This symbolic ability adds a new dimension to

[2]You may encounter slightly different classifications in other readings, especially for middle childhood.

the child's thinking ability (Ginsburg & Opper, 1969).

A great deal of Piaget's research on childhood concerns understanding the nature of a class — a set of objects that are united by some relationship, such as girls, dogs, balls, or red circles. The ability to add classes together, multiply classes, and break down classes into subclasses is necessary for conceptual thinking. The child at this period has a difficult time with such classification tasks and is only capable of formulating primitive concepts referred to by Piaget as "preconcepts."

Phillips (1969) has summarized some of the limitations of preoperational thought under six headings:

1. *Concreteness*
2. *Irreversibility*
3. *Centering*
4. *Egocentrism*
5. *States versus transformations*
6. *Transductive reasoning*

Concreteness. The preoperational child is capable of manipulating symbols and, when compared to the child in the sensorimotor period, is rather abstract in his thinking. Nevertheless, when compared to an adolescent or adult, the preoperational child is still oriented toward the concrete.

Irreversibility. Reversibility is the ability to return to the point of origin, to do and undo, to go in one direction and compensate for it in another direction. Every mathematical or logical operation is reversible: $4 + 8 = 12$, and $12 - 8 = 4$; all boys + all girls = all children, and all children − all girls = all boys. The preoperational child does not have the ability to deal with problems that necessitate reversible thinking.

Phillips (1969) illustrates this limitation from one of his own observations. He asked a four-year-old child: "Do you have a brother?"

"Yes."
"What's his name?"
"Jim."
"Does Jim have a brother?"
"No." (p. 61)

Another example, commonly referred to as the conservation

experiment, further illustrates the lack of reversible thought, or irreversibility. The idea that the amount or quantity of a matter stays the same regardless of any changes in shape or position is incomprehensible to the child. Though he observes two small glasses, A and B, identical in size and shape and each filled with an equal amount of water, and in turn observes as the water from glass A is emptied into another glass, C, which is taller and narrower, he tends to conclude that the quantity of water has changed. C contains more water than A because "it is higher." The child says this even though he readily admits that no water has been added or removed.

In another conservation experiment, two clay balls of equal size are shown to the child. The child is asked if they are the same size, after which one of the balls is rolled into a sausage shape. The child is then asked the same question, the usual response being that the sausage-shaped ball is larger.

A child presented with two rows of pennies states that each row contains the same number of pennies. However, if one row is elongated without any change in the number of pennies, the child usually declares that the rows are no longer equivalent.

Conservation does not take place at the same time in all subject areas. The child usually grasps conservation of numbers (age 5–6) before conservation of substance, or mass (age 7–8), and weight (age 9–10), followed last by conservation of volume (age 11–12).

Centering. This characteristic is also related to the previous problems. The child's tendency is to focus on only one dimension or detail of an event to the neglect of other important aspects. In the water-level problem demonstrating the child's irreversible thinking, one reason for his difficulty is that he focuses on length — the taller glass — and forgets about width. The preoperational child cannot decenter, or focus back and forth between details, and his reasoning is necessarily distorted.

Egocentrism. Many of Piaget's readers have misunderstood the term "egocentrism"; it is not used in a derogatory sense to describe the child's personality. It simply means that the child has difficulty taking another person's point of view. Egocentrism enters the arena of language and communication. Watch any group of preschool children playing together and you will hear egocentric speech. You may hear children repeating words merely for the pleasure of pronouncing them or talking "toward" each other without really expecting each other to listen or reply.

States versus transformations. The preoperational child focuses on the static aspect of an event rather than on the transformations from one state to another. In the water-level problem, the child is intent on the height of the water, not on the act of pouring. In the conservation-of-substance problem with the clay balls, he retains the image of the shape of the clay and ignores the transformations — the change from the round to the sausage shape. In one experiment, the child is asked to "depict the successive movements of a bar which falls from a vertical, upright position to a horizontal one" (Flavell, 1963, p. 158). Although the solution of this problem is obvious to the adolescent, the preoperational child fails to draw the intermediate positions of the bar.

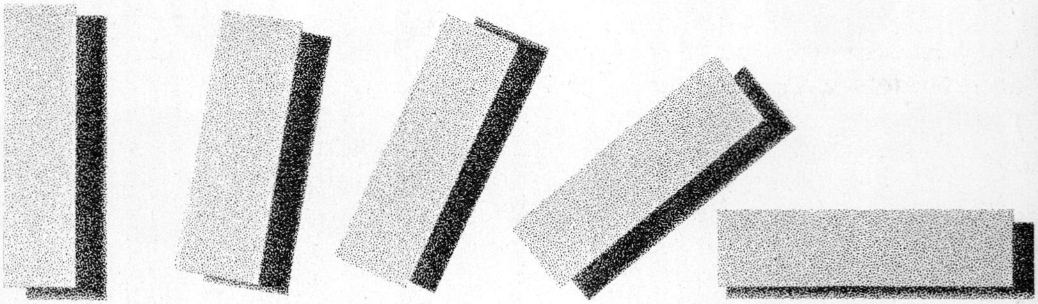

Transductive reasoning. Deduction is reasoning from the general to the specific: Assuming that all children are good, if we see a child we deduce that she is good. Induction proceeds in the opposite direction, establishing generalizations from specific instances: If we meet a large number of good children, we can conclude that they are all good.

According to Piaget, the preoperational child's thinking is somewhere in between, moving from the particular to the particular without touching on the general. The child sees some relationship between particular instances when there is none. Piaget calls this transductive reasoning. The child who walks through the forest, not knowing whether she sees a succession of turtles or the same one is reappearing time and time again, is thinking transductively. This is an example of the preconcept we talked about earlier.

Piaget reported an example of transductive thinking when his daughter failed to take a nap one afternoon. She said to him, "I haven't had my nap, so it isn't afternoon" (Piaget, 1952, p. 232). It is very common for children at this age to see relationships between particular instances, such that if A causes B, then B causes A.

CONCRETE OPERATIONS PERIOD (7–11 YEARS)

This stage marks the beginning of operational thought. That is, the child acquires logical thought processes (operations) that she can apply to concrete problems. When faced with a discrepancy between thought and perception, as in the conservation problems, the child in the concrete operations period opts for logical decisions instead of the perceptual decisions a child in the preoperational period makes.

The following mathematical symbols are examples of operations: = (equal), + (combining), − (separating). Each of these operations has its counterpart in logic; for example, + is equivalent to *and,* − is equivalent to *except* (Phillips, 1969). Piaget uses the structure of logic as a model for explaining the qualitative differences in children's thinking ability during both the concrete and formal operations period.

The operations of this period are tied to personal experience. They are concrete but not formal operations. The child is still unable to deal with abstract material such as hypotheses and verbal propositions.

The following are an important set of concrete operations:

Combinativity, or classification, is an operation by which two or more classes are combined into a larger group: all boys + all girls = all children. Relationships such as $A > B$ and $B > C$ can be combined into a new relationship, $A > C$. For the first time, the child can form a variety of class relationships and understands that some classes can be included in other classes.

Reversibility is the major criterion for operational thought in Piaget's system. It implies that every logical or mathematical operation can be cancelled by an opposite operation. All children − all girls = all boys; or $7 + 3 = 10$ and $10 - 7 = 3$.

Associativity is an operation by which several classes can be combined in any order: $(1 + 3) + 5 = 1 + (3 + 5)$. In reasoning, this operation allows a child to arrive at answers in many different ways.

Identity is an operation in which there exists a null element that, when combined with any element or class, produces no change: $10 + 0 = 10$. Also, a quantity can be nullified by combining it with its opposite: 10 − 10 = 0; or, if I walk three miles east and three miles west I end up where I started from.

It is not that children at the concrete operations stage are "brighter" than preschool children but that they have acquired certain abilities (operations) for solving problems that they could not solve correctly before. Concrete operational thinking is stable as compared to the highly impressionistic and static thinking of the preoperational period.

The concrete operational child can bring these operations to bear on such problems as class relationships. If you ask a preschooler if there are more girls or more children in the class, she will respond that there are more boys than girls, for the young child has difficulty dealing with classes and subclasses at the same time. She cannot conceive that it is possible to belong to two classes at the same time. However, a six- or seven-year-old child will have no difficulty with this problem. He is capable of deducing the following: boys + girls = children (combinativity), since children − boys = girls (reversibility); thus, children ≠ boys (Elkind, 1968).

Using these same operations, the child develops an awareness of the principles of conservation. She can focus on both length and width (decentration), and she recognizes that pouring water into different size beakers does not change the amount of water because the amount of water is the same as in the beginning (identity and reversibility).

The child in this period can now rank a series of objects in order, such as wooden dolls or sticks, according to their size. Piaget refers to this operation as *serializing*. However, the child can do this only as long as the problem is presented concretely; it is not until adolescence that such a problem can be solved mentally using verbal propositions.

Language also changes at this time. The child becomes less egocentric and more sociocentric in her communication. She now makes an attempt to understand other people and communicate her feelings and ideas to adults and peers. Her thought processes also become less egocentric and she can now take another's point of view.

Formal Operations Period (11 Years and Above)

At approximately eleven years of age, a new operations period emerges in which the older child can use his concrete operations to form more complex operations. Inhelder and Piaget (1958), Flavell (1963), and Baldwin (1967) provide excellent detailed discussions of the operations available to the adolescent during this period.

The child's major advance during this period is that he no longer needs to think in terms of objects or concrete events; he now has the ability to think *abstractly*. As I stated earlier, a child in the concrete operations period can arrange a series of objects according to size. But it is not until he reaches the formal operations period that he can solve a similar verbal problem: "Edith is fairer than Susan; Edith is darker than Lilly; who is the darkest of the three?"

Flavell (1963) discusses some characteristics of formal operational thought. First, the adolescent's thinking is hypothetico-deductive. He can formulate many alternative hypotheses in dealing with a problem and check data against each of the hypotheses to make an appropriate decision. The child, however, does not have the ability to confirm or reject hypotheses.

Second, this period is marked by propositional thinking. The adolescent is not limited to concrete objects or events in reasoning; he can deal with statements or propositions that describe these concrete data. The adolescent can even deal with contrary-to-fact propositions. If you ask a child in one of the other developmental stages to pretend that he is the president of the United States and then ask him a question about a hypothetical situation he might encounter as president, the child is likely to say, "But I'm not the president of the United States." The adolescent has no trouble accepting contrary-to-fact propositions and reasoning from them (Elkind, 1968).

Last, the adolescent engages in *combinatorial thinking*. When considering solutions to a problem, he can isolate individual factors and possible combinations of factors that may figure in the solution.

IMPLICATIONS OF PIAGET'S DEVELOPMENTAL STAGES FOR EDUCATION

Some educators suggest that Piaget's developmental-stage observations can aid teachers in the structure and sequencing of subject matter in a curriculum. Hunt (1964) presented a rationale for emphasizing physical experience in preschool enrichment programs based on Piaget's description of sensorimotor and preoperational development. He noted that the traditional emphasis on language skills might not be the most fruitful approach to helping disadvantaged children. Peel (1964) used Piaget's description of the concrete and formal operations period to propose that science education programs in the primary grades focus on "describer thinking" rather than on "explainer thinking." His recommendation is based on the fact that propositional thinking and scientific explanations are only possible during the formal operations period. Adler (1966) used Piaget's stages as an outline for sequencing the teaching of set theory in arithmetic.

It is essential that teachers understand the nature and transition of a child's thinking as he progresses through school. While working with teachers on a science curriculum aimed at developing children's ability to use formal operations, Karplus (1964) stated:

> You will probably all agree that there is a transition between children's preoperational thinking at kindergarten age and some of their thinking in terms of propositions when pupils leave elementary school at twelve or so. It seems to me that in general this transition in children's thinking is not recognized by present educational practice in the United States. Teachers with whom I have been in contact have not seemed to be aware that there is such a change taking place and I would say that most instruction above the kindergarten takes place on what one might call the formal level. As an unfortunate consequence of this fact many students never understand the intent of instruction and become dissatisfied with school by the time they are fourteen or sixteen. (p. 113)

Another important difference between children and adolescents is in their use of language. Teachers can be easily mislead by the verbal facility of their students, especially if they don't question students closely. Children of different ages may use a term correctly, without an equal degree of comprehension. A ten-year-old child may define time as "It is something the watch tells," or "Clock tells time," whereas a fifteen-year-old adolescent may define time as "Time is sort of like an interval of space" (Gesell, Ilg, & Ames, 1956).

Ask a young child what a brother is: "He is someone who lives in my house," or "He is a friend." It is only later in the child's development, after he has acquired the operation of reversibility, that he comprehends the meaning of "brother" as a relational concept. If a teacher takes a child's verbalisms as the main indication of his understanding of concepts, he overestimates the degree of the child's learning. I vividly remember the rapidity with which I could state the definition of "osmosis" in my high school biology course ("the passing of a liquid from a place of high concentration to a place of low concentration through a semipermeable membrane") without really understanding what osmosis was. Such definition dexterity enables many students to get through courses without demonstrating an understanding of basic concepts and principles. Piaget's research signals teachers to carefully examine the language of students, for this examination will certainly lead to a better understanding of the quality of thinking in their class.

Piaget's delineation of the relationship between a child's level of conceptual development and the complexity of the subject matter implies that teachers should heed what and how they teach. Piagetians maintain that the ideal learning situation arises from the match between the complexity of the subject matter and the child's level of conceptual development. A teacher who uses the best textbooks available and develops the most interesting and stimulating lesson plans can still fail to reach a majority of students in his class who do not have the necessary structures (operations) to enable them to "understand" the presented material. This means that the classroom teacher must be able to (1) assess a child's level of cognitive development, and (2) determine the type of abilities the child needs to understand the subject matter.

A teaching strategy developed from Piaget's theory is to "confront the child with the illogical nature of his point of view" (Siegel, 1969, p. 473). During the discussion of the assimilation-accommodation process I mentioned that when assimilation fails, the child is in a state of disequilibrium. He must begin to accommodate in order to adapt to his environment. You create disequilibrium in a child when you question him about some illogical statement he has made. The child's attempts to reconcile this disequilibrium carry him to new plateaus in his cognitive development. The confrontation strategy implies that a student's incorrect answers should receive as much teacher attention as his correct answers.

In reacting to this same confrontation, the child advances from egocentric to sociocentric thought. The child has difficulty conceiving of a point of view different from his own. When he locates other individuals standing at different vantage points, the discovery plays an important role in modifying his point of view (Ginsburg & Opper, 1964).

Confrontation takes many forms, including questions, demonstrations, and/or environmental manipulations. Duckworth (1964) quotes Piaget as having stated:

> Good pedagogy must involve presenting the child with situations in which he himself experiments, in the broadest sense of that term — trying things out to see what happens, manipulating things, manipulating symbols, posing questions and seeking his own answers, reconciling what he finds one time with what he finds at another, comparing his findings with those of other children. (p. 2)

The preceding statement also emphasizes the active role of children in the learning process. The Piagetian-type classroom deemphasizes the transmission of knowledge through the lecture-discussion method and encourages the teacher to act more as a catalyst in situations in which children do their own learning.

Piaget is constantly asked (particularly during his travels in the United States) whether educators can speed up the transition between stages by teaching the operations or structures, such as reversibility,

necessary for logical thinking. His statement makes his position on the matter clear:

> The question comes up whether to teach the structure, or to present the child with situations where he is active and creates the structures himself. The goal in education is not to increase the amount of knowledge, but to create the possibilities for a child to invent and discover. When we teach too fast, we keep the child from inventing and discovering himself. . . . Teaching means creating situations where structures can be discovered; it does not mean transmitting structures which may be assimilated at nothing other than a verbal level (Duckworth, 1964, p. 3)

We know that all children in a class are not at the same point in their conceptual development. Piaget discovered that a student's level of thinking is dependent upon specific subject matter. A student may be able to think at a particular level in mathematics but be unable to think at the same level in social studies. As a beginning teacher you will find this situation especially perplexing.

It would appear, then, that you can exercise sound decision making about instructional problems once you have a greater understanding of the various individual levels of thinking existing in your classroom. Modifications of Piaget's methodology can steer you toward this end. You may want to know:

> (1) When a specific youngster can move from simply looking at concrete perceptual material, to dealing with the more abstract symbols; (2) when he can leave the reality of the immediate and explore possibilities without references to their perceptual realities; (3) when he can combine the variety of symbols and new classes and talk about such things as democracy or patriotism with some understanding of what these terms might imply. (Gordon, 1966, p. 14)

Presently a standardized test series of Piagetian tasks does not exist for assessing an individual's level of cognitive development. However, substantial research is progressing toward this end. New kinds of developmental intelligence scales based on Piaget's theory are being developed at the University of Montreal's Institute of Psychology under the direction of Adrien Pinard. The tests in such areas as number, quantity, space, causality, and logical deduction may make it possible to diagnose children's readiness for certain curricula content. If a first grader is having trouble with mathematics, such a test will determine whether or not he is able to apply conservation theory. How can the child understand addition or subtraction if he believes that the number of objects in a group keep changing every time they are rearranged?

Someday educators may develop a scale of instructional objectives that has a one-to-one correspondence with a scale of reasoning. Until the time comes when such tests are available for teachers, you can either make use of some of the tasks previously discussed or develop original tasks.

THE ISSUE OF READINESS

One of the important issues in learning involves the answer to the question "When is the student ready to learn?" We have found that Piaget's answer is a well laid-out plan. He believes that certain schemes or mental operations are present at different developmental stages, limiting the child's ability to deal with some problems, particularly at the abstract level. He implies that the teacher must correctly match the complexity of the subject matter with the child's developmental level. This often means that the teacher must wait for the proper developmental level to present certain material.

Gagné provides an alternative answer to the question of student readiness. He attributes differences in developmental readiness to previously learned intellectual skills. If a child cannot solve a particular task, the chances are that he has not acquired the prerequisite or subordinate skills related to the task. This explanation does not prevent the elementary-grade child from learning complex rules or solving abstract problems. The child can learn any task if he acquires the intellectual skills that are prerequisites.

The differences in the positions of Piaget and Gagne emerge as they explain the conservation-of-liquid problem described earlier: the young child presented with two rectangular containers of water that he acknowledges are of equal amount, the water poured into a taller and narrower third container, and the child's response that the third container has more water than the first container. Piaget accounts for this behavior by stating that the child in the preoperational stage has to believe his eyes because he cannot make use of the necessary mental operations, especially reversibility, to respond correctly to the problem.

Gagné, on the other hand, feels that the child can acquire the subskills that are related to the problem and then perform the task. The classification of these skills yields a learning hierarchy as shown in Figure 7.2. This hierarchy identifies all the skills (mostly in the form of rules) pertaining to volume, area, length, and height.

FIGURE 7.2
A LEARNING HIERARCHY WHICH SHOWS THE CUMULATIVE LEARNING OF INTELLECTUAL SKILLS LEADING TO THE TASK OF JUDGING EQUALITIES AND INEQUALITIES OF LIQUID VOLUME IN RECTANGULAR CONTAINERS.

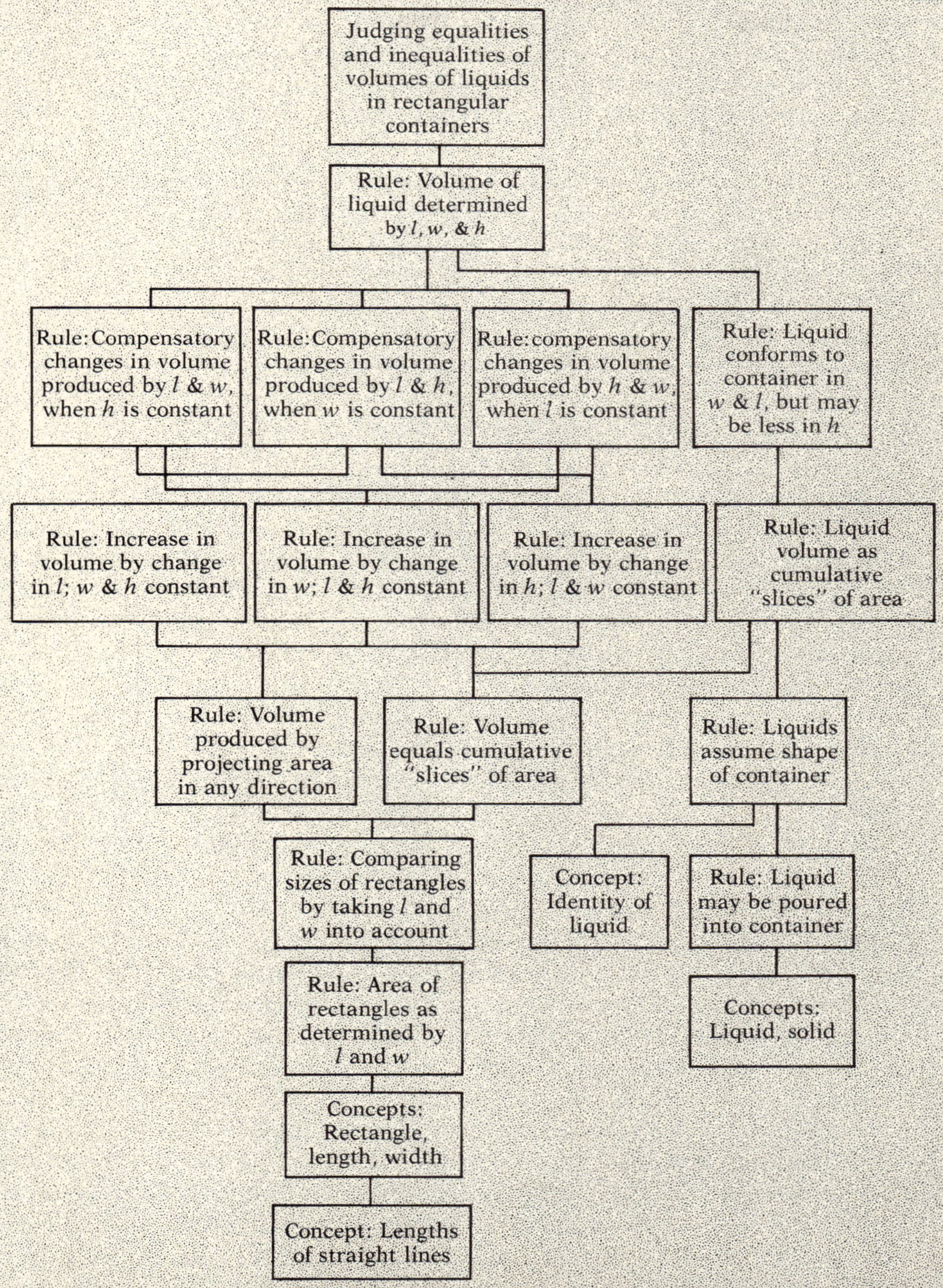

From R. M. Gagné, "Contributions of Learning to Human Development." *Psychological* Review 75 (1968): 184, Figure 3.

According to Gagné, what is lacking in children who cannot solve the water-volume problem is not simply logical processes, such as conservation or reversibility, which *develop over time,* but concrete knowledge, which *can be taught.* Gagné's position implies that the teacher does not have to wait for the child to develop. By following appropriate instructional procedures, the child can attain the objectives Piaget considers unattainable at his particular age or grade level.

Both Gagné's cumulative learning position (Lefrancois, 1968; Bearison, 1968) and Piaget's stage theory (Smedslund, 1961a, b) have empirical support. We will have to await the results of further research before we decide whether Gagné or Piaget can tell us when and what the child is ready to learn.

Bruner: Discovery Learning

Piaget's recommendation for giving children an active role in their classroom learning finds favor with many cognitive psychologists who advocate learning by discovery. The essential criterion for discovery learning is that the learner organize into final form the material to be learned. This procedure differs from reception learning or expository teaching (sometimes referred to as "didactic" teaching), in which the teacher explains to the student all the information he must learn. Discovery learning is like wrapping your own package; reception learning is like having someone open it for you.

Many opinions are offered as to who discovered discovery learning. Dewey (1933) gets a good deal of credit. He analyzed the "complete art of reflective activity" by outlining the modes of thought that spanned the area between a perplexing situation and its solution. Although the writings of Dewey have had a significant impact on public education in America, much of the credit for encouraging the use of discovery learning goes to Jerome Bruner (1960), a Harvard psychologist who came into prominence after the publication of *The Process of Education.* In this book he reported the outcomes of a conference of scientists, scholars, and educators on the teaching of science.

Bruner set down some controversial statements about curriculum development. The following statement is widely quoted and debated: "Any subject can be taught effectively in some intellectually honest form to any child at any stage of development" (p. 52). Bruner's adversaries were quick to point out that a child could *not* learn any subject at a particular age: Could the first grader learn calculus? Bruner's reply to this criticism was that he had phrased his statement in terms of the possibility of teaching meaningful aspects of a subject at a certain age level. Perhaps we can teach some aspect of calculus to a first grader.

The real issue is, how can we develop more effective instructional programs for the young child? Bruner's answer is to coordinate the mode of presentation of the material to the way in which the child can learn it. The child progresses from sensory (enactive) representations to concrete (iconic) representations and, finally, to abstract (symbolic) representations; the teaching sequence should be the same. Curriculum organization should be ordered so that the child first experiences the material, then reacts to a concrete presentation of it, and, finally, symbolizes it (Lefrancois, 1972a).

Another statement in *The Process of Education* emphasizes how subject matter should be taught: "The curriculum of a subject should be determined by the most fundamental understanding that can be achieved of the underlying principles that give structure to that subject" (p. 31). The basic thesis of this statement is that the bare bones of any discipline can and should be exposed to reveal its structure — its most basic elements. Instead of memorizing factual material and isolated content, the student should learn the principles that the disciplines build on. Once the student knows these principles, he can then independently inquire into and solve the problems in the discipline.

Bruner mentions that you must allow the student to become a problem solver, to function in the same way as a scientist, historian, or mathematician. Let students discover meaning for themselves, and you enable them to learn concepts in the language they understand. In "The Act of Discovery," Bruner (1961) discusses four advantages of learning by discovery:

1. *There is an increment in intellectual potency.*
2. *Emphasis is placed on intrinsic rather than extrinsic rewards.*
3. *The student learns how to discover; that is, the student masters the methods of discovery learning.*
4. *The student is more likely to remember information.*

The increment of intellectual potency raises the level of the student's expectation of success. With this growth comes the ability to develop strategies in approaching regularities and irregularities in the environment. By placing emphasis on discovery, the student learns to organize problems rather than attacking them using a hit-and-miss method. Second, intrinsic motivation is the alternative to extrinsic motivation: Self-fulfillment takes precedence over a form of reward from parents, teachers, or peers. Bruner believes that an external reward system precipitates rote learning with little understanding or mastery of the environment. Discovery learning leads to self-reward because the learner achieves satisfaction from finding solutions to problems on his own and is less dependent on extrinsic rewards. Third, a student who has practiced discovery learning can apply these same skills and techniques to work through real problems in his environment. Last, the most important aspect of the conservation of memory is retrieval, and improved memory follows improved organization of knowledge. Bruner finds that the student can more easily retrieve knowledge that he organizes in terms of his individual coding system.

Another important educational practice mentioned in *The Process of Education* is the spiral curriculum, which develops and redevelops topics at different grades. Once a child has learned something at a simplified level, he returns to the topic at a more advanced level. The basic principles of a discipline are studied over and over again at different grade levels, but at higher levels of complexity.

Many educators use the terms "discovery learning," "inquiry training," and "problem solving" interchangeably to classify learning situations that spiral in complexity. These terms can be misleading, since many discovery-learning programs have been developed with slightly different purposes. Few "pure" forms of discovery learning exist because of the variability in the amount of teacher guidance and organization. In this chapter, I am using the term "discovery learning" in its broadest context, which includes inquiry methods.

Taba (1963) outlined a number of steps in discovery learning: First, confront the learner with some problem that creates a feeling of bafflement in him. This starts the process of inquiry. Second, withhold important generalizations. This challenges the student and encourages him to explore the problem individually. Third, the student then grasps the organizing principle of the problem so that he sees the organization of knowledge, understands the causes of the phenomenon, and relates what he sees to his previous knowledge. This is the act of discovery. Fourth, the student demonstrates his understanding of the generalization. Fifth, the student verbalizes the concepts or principles upon which the generalization is based. Taba's process prompts the learner to find things out for himself rather than relying on the teacher for the explanation.

Bruner (1966) provides an example of the discovery method in the following extract. The object of the lesson was to help students learn that, generally speaking, one can reduce a language into what is called types and order:

First write a sentence on the board. Then get the children to form similar sentences as follows:

The	man	ate	his	lunch.
A	boy	stole	a	bike.
The	dog	chased	my	cat.
My	father	skidded	the	car.
A	wind	blew	his	hat.

At this particular point, we have the children provide other sentences *ad libitum.* And they provide them. Sometimes they are wrong. Usually not. We then shift them to the following puzzle: How is it that one can go from left to right across the sentences in practically any row and still come out with a sentence: The boy chased the cat; A father chased a lunch; The man stole my bike; A father stole his hat. Some of the sentences are rather silly, but clearly sentences. Soon they will say things like, There are five places and you can put lots of things in each place. But which kinds of words will fit into each column? Type and token begin to emerge as ideas. Now we reach a very critical point. Ask, for example, whether they can make up some more columns. One child proposed the following, something that put the class on a new level of attitude toward the use of mind. He said that there is a "zero" column that could contain the word "did." I asked what other particular words this column could contain. The children said "did," "can," "has." This was the zero column. Then one of the pupils said that this did not quite fit and that you would have to change the word in the third column too but it would not be very much of a change. They were ready and willing now to get into the syntax of the language, to invent it afresh. They talked about the family of words that would fit and that two columns affected the families each could carry. Only then did we introduce some terminology. We talked about type and order, and that in sentences there were words that were types and they appeared in a certain permissible order. One of the children said of types, "They're called parts of speech. A noun, for example, is a 'person, place or thing.' " To produce a pause, we asked about "dying" and "courage." They were quick to grasp the syntactic distinction of "privilege of occurrence" in a certain position, in contrast to the semantic criterion of person, place or thing and found the idea interesting. They soon began on the alternative ways a sentence could be said and have the same meaning. We were soon building up the idea of productivity. (pp. 106–107)

In another example, Bruner (1960) demonstrated how geography could be taught without having students memorize facts. He gave fifth-grade students blank outline maps and asked them to figure out where the major cities, rivers, and highways were located without referring to books or maps. After completing the exercise, a class discussion began in which the children attempted to justify their selections.

Bruner prefers this type of teaching over expository methods because he feels that the latter method often leads to the memorization of facts without the understanding of concepts and principles involved in the lesson. As a consequence, the students cannot relate their new learning to previous knowledge, nor can they apply it to the solution of new problems. This is static, and sterile, learning.

SUCHMAN: AN INQUIRY METHOD

Richard Suchman (1960) has conducted extensive experiments on inquiry training using biology and physics films developed for intermediate-grade students. These films present events that are "at odds" and that require inquiry to resolve the discrepancy. One such film, *Ball and Ring,* demonstrates what happens when various degrees of heat are applied to a ball and ring, causing their expansion. A brass ball just fits through a brass ring. The ball is then heated and placed on the opening of the ring, which is held in a horizontal position. It does not slip through at once but is held in place by the ring. After some time has passed the ball drops through.

The children viewing the films are required to find out why this phenomenon occurs by asking questions that can be answered only by "yes" or "no." Here is a part of such a session (Suchman, 1960):

Pupil: Were the ball and ring at room temperature to begin with?
Teacher: Yes.
Pupil: And the ball would go through the ring at first?
Teacher: Yes.
Pupil: After the ball was held over the fire it did *not* go through the ring, right?
Teacher: Yes.
Pupil: If the ring had been heated instead of the ball, would the results have been the same?
Teacher: No.

> *Pupil:* If both had been heated would the ball have gone through then?
> *Teacher:* That all depends.
> *Pupil:* If they had both been heated to the same temperature would the ball have gone through?
> *Teacher:* Yes.
> *Pupil:* Would the ball be the same size after it was heated as it was before?
> *Teacher:* No.
> *Pupil:* Could the same experiment have been done if the ball and ring were made out of some other metal?
> *Teacher:* Yes. (p. 42)

Suchman limits the teacher's response to "yes" or "no" to ensure that the student maintains control of the inquiry process. The dialogue illustrates two types of questions: informational and verificational questions — "Were the ball and ring at room temperature to begin with?" — and experimental questions — "If the ring had been heated instead of the ball, would the results have been the same?" If the teacher is not satisfied with the explicitness of the experimental questions he may respond, "That all depends," or "Tell me more."

The teacher tape-records each of the sessions so that he can discuss the student's final solutions and relate them to his questioning behavior. The student learns to improve his questions to become a more effective problem solver.

Suchman's methodology is an example of unguided discovery, the teacher providing neither the principle that applies nor the solution to the problem. In other forms of discovery, often called guided discovery, the teacher may provide the principles relevant to the problem and require the students to find the solution to the problem.

Can you think of some ways to develop discovery learning lessons in your field of specialization? Postman and Weingartner (1969), in their popular book, *Teaching as a Subversive Activity,* describe some important behaviors of the inquiry teacher. When you see such a teacher in action, you observe the following:

> The teacher rarely tells students what he thinks they ought to know.
>
> His basic mode of discourse with students is questioning.
>
> Generally, he does not accept a single statement as an answer to a question.
>
> He encourages student-student interaction as opposed to

> student-teacher interaction. And generally he avoids acting as mediator or judge of the quality of the ideas expressed.
>
> He rarely summarizes the positions taken by students on the learnings that occur. He recognizes that the act of summary or "closure" tends to have the effect of ending further thought.
>
> His lessons develop from the responses of the students and not from a previously determined "logical structure."
>
> Generally, each of his lessons poses a problem for students. (pp. 34–36)

The various discovery methods used in education make it difficult to reach conclusions regarding the effectiveness of discovery learning as a whole with other forms of learning. Most studies have resulted in inconsistent and even contradictory conclusions. Your task is to determine when discovery learning methods work best for you!

AUSUBEL: EXPOSITORY TEACHING

We have seen that most cognitive psychologists favor some form of discovery learning, whereas most behaviorists prefer guided learning or expository teaching. David Ausubel is a cognitive psychologist who favors expository teaching and its correlative, reception learning. In this type of teaching and learning, all the information to be learned is presented to the learner in its final form. This expository-teaching theory explains how lecture and textbook material, when properly organized and presented, can lead to as much understanding and retention as discovery methods.

Some of Ausubel's writings focus on the misconceptions and limitations of discovery learning. In particular, he objects to the view that all discovery learning is meaningful and that all reception learning is rote. Figure 7.3 helps to explain Ausubel's position. It identifies four possible types of learning that include two independent dimensions. The first dimension relates to the way information is presented to the learner (reception or discovery). The second dimension involves the manner in which the learner can incorporate the material into his existing cognitive structure (meaningful or rote). A cognitive structure is the facts, concepts, and generalizations that a learner has already learned and remembers.

In the first stage of learning, information can be communicated to the learner either by some form of reception learning that presents the information in its final form or by some form of discovery learning

Note *

FIGURE 7.3
TYPES OF LEARNING INCLUDED IN MEANINGFUL LEARNING THEORY.

ge I.
rmation to
earned
nade
ilable
he
rner via

Stage II. Received information is incorporated by the learner using means that are

	Meaningful	Rote
Reception	Meaningful reception learning: logically organized information is presented to the learner in final form; he then relates it to his existing knowledge (i.e., incorporates it into his cognitive structure).	Rote reception learning: information of any type is presented to the learner in final form; he then memorizes it.
Discovery	Meaningful discovery learning: information to be learned is ascertained independently by the learner; he then relates it to his existing knowledge (i.e., incorporates it into his cognitive structure).	Rote discovery learning: information to be learned is ascertained independently by the learner; he then memorizes it.

Based on Ausubel and Robinson, *School Learning*, Holt, Rinehart and Winston, (1969) in *Facilitating Student Learning* by William L. Goodwin and Herbert J. Klausmeier, Harper & Row, 1975, p. 187.

that obligates the learner to independently discover part or all of the information.

In the second stage of learning, the learner acts on the information in some way. If he attempts to relate the information to what he already knows, meaningful learning occurs. If he merely attempts to memorize the new information without incorporating it into his cognitive structure, then rote learning occurs. Both the reception/discovery and meaningful/rote dimensions do not describe simple dichotomies but should be thought of as a continuum, along which various degrees of each type of learning exist.

Ausubel states that many educators equate reception learning with rote learning, believing that the only real or meaningful learning takes place when the learner discovers knowledge on his own. He refutes this claim by pointing out that any teaching strategy can lead to rote or meaningful learning. Many of the mathematics and science curricula use discovery-learning methods very effectively in teaching important aspects of the structure of the subject matter.

But even discovery learning can lead to rote learning. When a student discovers an arithmetic formula and then applies it to a particular type of problem without understanding the nature of the problem, she is involved in rote learning. Taba and Elzey (1964) provide an example of this process by demonstrating how an elementary-school child discovered an incorrect rule in arithmetic:

When asked how she decided when to use which process, she

> explained her method as follows: "I know what to do by looking at the examples. If there are only two numbers, I subtract. If there are lots of numbers, I add. If there are just two numbers and one is smaller than the other, then it is a hard problem. I divide to see if it comes out even, but if it doesn't I multiply." Evidently, this child had built a scheme to fit the manner of presentation of problems in the arithmetic book. By applying the scheme, she was also learning an unproductive model of thinking or a "set" which excluded understanding the structure of the problems. (p. 527)

Ausubel makes it clear that he is not opposed to the occasional use of discovery learning, particularly with elementary-school children in the concrete stage of cognitive development. However, the most important function of the school is to impart subject-matter information to students, and once students reach the formal level of cognitive development, they can learn more effectively by reception methods. He asks, "Are students supposed to rediscover every principle in the syllabus?" or "Is the teacher to work until every student discovers a particular principle before moving on?"

Ausubel refutes Bruner's statements supporting the advantages of learning by discovery. Ausubel does not believe that discovery learning alone leads to a more orderly integration and use of knowledge. He attributes the students' organization of knowledge to the structured textbooks, films, and other materials provided by discovery or inquiry programs, as well as to the teacher's questioning and guidance (as suggested by the teacher's handbook in these programs), rather than crediting this organization to the act of discovery.

For this same reason, he believes that problem-solving ability is not transferred to other situations but is limited to the context in which it is learned and the material to which it is applied. Second, concern for "structure" is not unique to discovery learning but is a high priority of reception learning. Third, Ausubel doesn't believe that a discovery approach to learning and intrinsic motivation or a receptive approach to learning and extrinsic motivation are exclusively united. He states that students can easily be turned on by a dynamic instructor who knows how to organize material and relate it to the interests of students.

Ausubel spells out for us the differences between a rote and a meaningful learning situation. Because rote learning entails isolated bits of information that the learner cannot relate to her cognitive structure it is quickly forgotten. Furthermore, she cannot anchor the information to any of her existing conceptual systems. You would be involved in rote learning if, while studying various theories in this book, you could not relate the material to anything you already knew and relied on simply memorizing facts. The ability to relate new information to ideas already possessed by the learner is crucial for retention. As she acquires more knowledge, the new structure of ideas provides a harbor where new information can drop anchor.

The cognitive structure is the foundation for initially relating and subsequently attaching new information. The amount of learning depends, in part, then, on what is already known. Can you see why initial learning in a subject may be more difficult than later learning?

The intent of the learner is a clue to distinguishing between rote and meaningful learning. If the learner tries to make sense out of the material, meaningful learning is more likely to occur. A good strategy for forestalling rote learning is to have the learner constantly rephrase new ideas in his own words, forcing him to determine the substance of the new knowledge. One of the dangers of studying lecture notes verbatim is that the learner often convinces himself that he understands the material. When the instructor's question places the material in a different context, the learner may have difficulty responding to the question.

Ausubel breaks down each academic subject into concepts that are hierarchically arranged. At the "top" of the discipline are the most broad or inclusive concepts, under which are subsumed the less inclusive concepts. Ausubel analogizes the organization of a learner's cognitive structure along similar lines. Figure 7.4 illustrates this pyramidal set of concepts. The process of subsumption of ideas into the cognitive structure is important to understanding meaningful learning.

Ausubel offers a number of organizational principles to help ensure meaningful learning. One is the process of *progressive differentiation.* Both the subject matter and cognitive structure are arranged similarly; therefore, it follows that information should be processed in the same manner. Using this strategy, you teach the most general, inclusive concepts first, the less inclusive concepts second, and only after this do you teach specific information. You might begin a lesson about war by first discussing such concepts as conflict, territoriality, and economic growth, moving on to international treaties, United States-Asian affairs, and finally arriving at the Vietnamese conflict. Many teachers start at the other end of the spectrum by presenting important facts and moving to general concepts. The main advantage of progressive differentiation is the ease of assimilation and retention of new information for the student, because his cognitive structure conveniently provides "hooks" on which to hang, or incorporate, the new material. By the time the teacher reaches the specific information, the student already has in his cognitive structure a place to put

FIGURE 7.4
SCHEMATIC MODELS OF ROTE AND MEANINGFUL LEARNING.

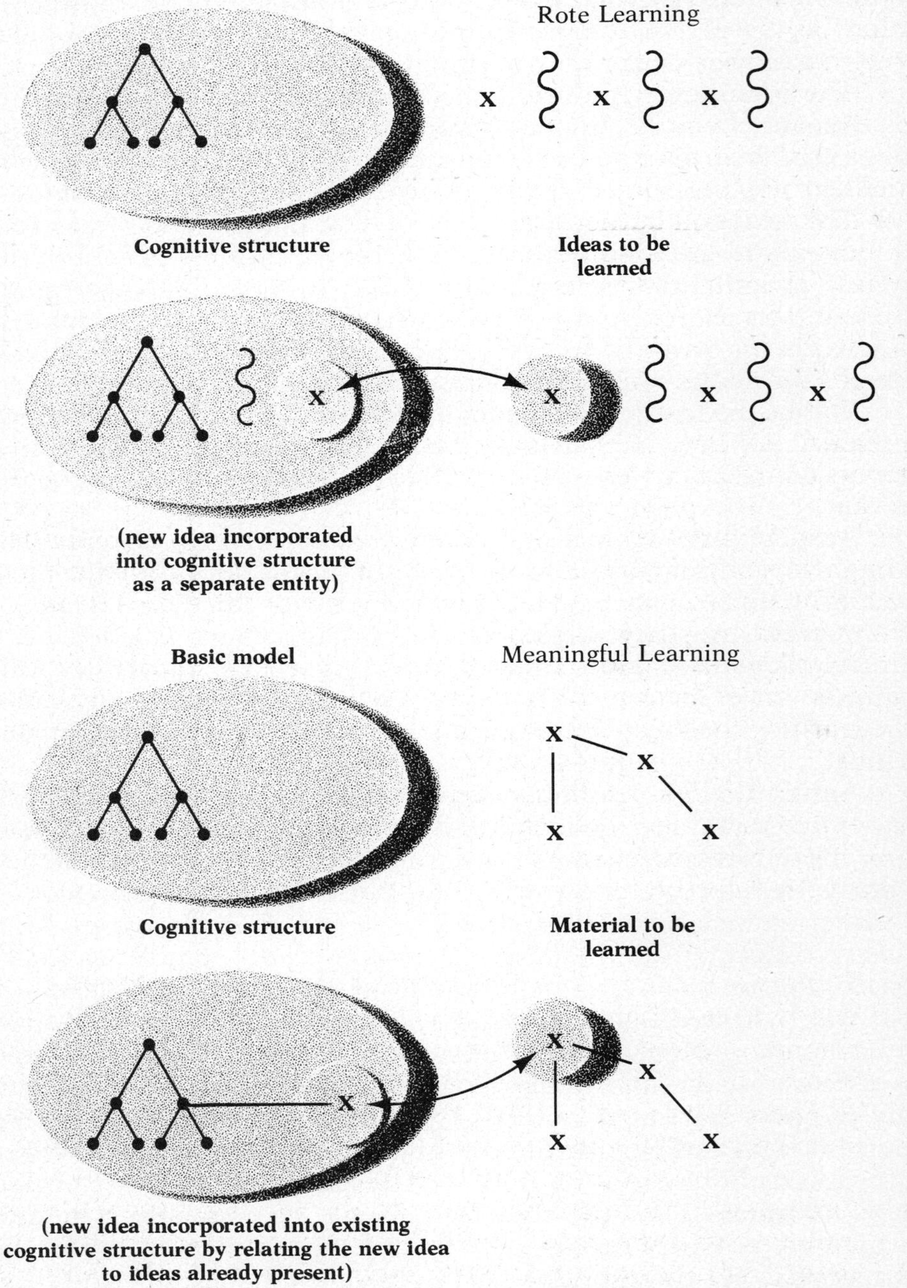

From *Study Guide for Ausubel/Robinson; School Learning: An Introduction to Educational Psychology*, prepared by Floyd G. Robinson.

or relate the information.

If the teacher begins with the most abstract or inclusive ideas, the ideas can include any material that is to follow. But, when a teacher begins with specific information or detailed definitions, the learner may have no place in his cognitive structure to "hang his hat," or to incorporate the ideas. He will soon forget them.

Another principle governing the organization of content in a subject field is *integrative reconciliation.* Ideas must be integrated and reconciled with previously learned ideas in a course. Ausubel contends that textbook authors compartmentalize knowledge into separate homogeneous chapters in which they represent concepts in only one chapter and do not relate them to other ideas presented earlier or later in the course. Books written in this manner make it difficult for the student to explore the similarities and differences between ideas presented throughout the book.

The lack of *integrative reconciliation* in the organization of instructional material creates problems. First, since most authors and lecturers use multiple terms to represent the same concept, the confusion that results encourages rote learning. Second, artificial barriers are erected between the course content and the student who fails to see important relationships in the material. Last, the inadequate use of relevant, previously learned ideas ignores their importance as anchors in learning new material.

Another way to aid the learning process is by the use of *advance organizers,* in the form of introductory material presented in advance of the learning itself but presented at a higher level of abstraction and generality. The organizer provides subconcepts that are reference points to aid the learner in subsuming the new material. I have already stated that one of the conditions for meaningful learning is that the learner possess relevant ideas in his cognitive structure to which he can relate the new material. An advance organizer serves this function.

> The organizer can be a statement, a descriptive paragraph, a question, a demonstration, or even a film. It might be one section or it might be an entire lesson which precedes the other lessons in a unit of work. The form of the organizer is less important than the fact that its solution must be clearly understood and continuously related to the material it is organizing.
>
> The instructor can use organizers at many stages throughout the lesson or unit. As the learner moves to new material, new organizers provide a framework for relating new ideas to information already studied. In this manner, the learner has a framework to organize his information, and relate

and differentiate the many ideas he has learned. (Joyce & Weil, 1972, p. 175)

Before students begin studying the caste system in India, a brief presentation of social stratification as an organizer will help them understand the nature and purpose of the caste system. This more abstract discussion is an organizing outline for relevant information in the lesson. In mathematics, teaching the number line before proceeding to the addition and subtraction of negative numbers is another example of the effective use of an organizer. In teaching literature, the model in Figure 7.5 can be presented as an organizer to explain the derivation of the similarities and differences in various literary forms or to explain the interrelationships of forms within any of the main subdivisions of literature.

Forgetting is an overwhelming impediment to learning. A widely accepted explanation of this phenomenon is interference from previous or subsequent learning. When previous learning interferes with subsequent learning, *proactive* inhibition occurs; *retroactive* inhibition takes place when subsequent learning interferes with previous learning. The child who has learned to spell "relief" may later experience proactive interference when learning to spell "receive." An example of retroactive interference is the difficulty experienced by a

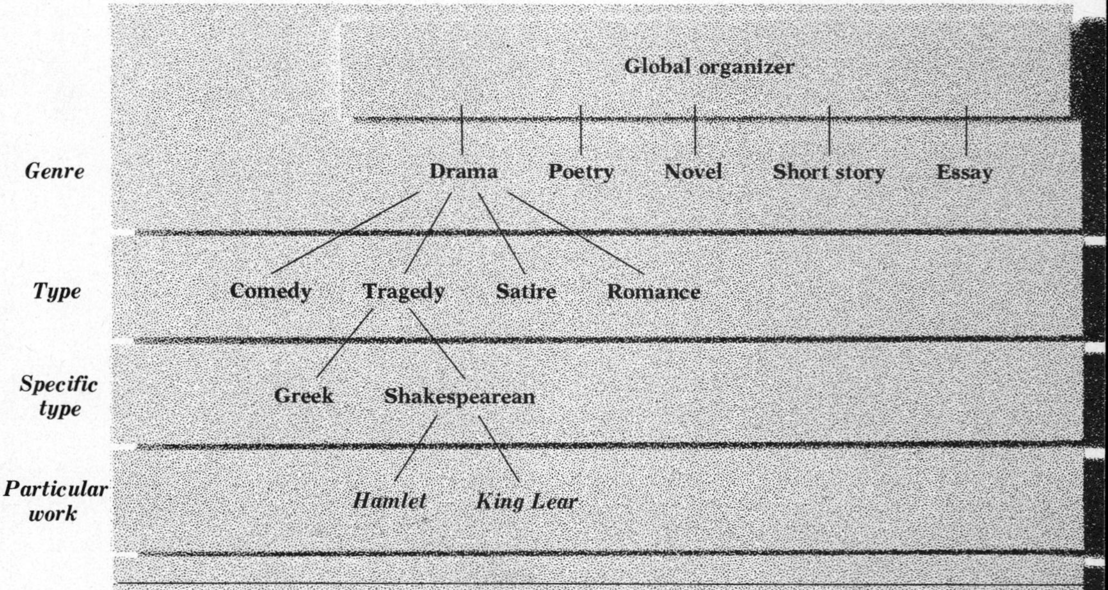

FIGURE 7.5
POSSIBLE MODEL FOR A GENERAL ORGANIZER IN LITERATURE.

From *Study Guide for Ausubel/Robinson; School Learning: An Introduction to Educational Psychology,* prepared by Floyd G. Robinson. Copyright © 1970 by Holt, Rinehart and Winston, Inc. Reprinted by permission of Holt, Rinehart and Winston.

student who finds that his learning in his second-period French class interferes with his learning in his first-period Spanish class. In both of these situations, the use of advance organizers to point out similarities and differences in material can ameliorate the effects of interference.

A number of investigators have studied the effectiveness of advance organizers. In an early study, Ausubel (1960) used an expository organizer to introduce a learning passage on the properties of steel. Some of the principles included in the organizer were the similarities and differences between metals and alloys, their advantages and disadvantages, and the reasons for the production and use of alloys. The organizer provided a framework of background information, but prior testing had already determined that it didn't provide the student with specific information pertaining to what he was to learn about steel. A control group of students received an introductory passage of historical material that did not contain any advanced organizers. Ausubel found that the experimental group performed significantly better than the control group on the final test that measured their knowledge of steel.

In another study, Ausubel and Youssef (1963) used two separate learning passages in sequence, one on Buddhism and the other on Zen Buddhism. The two introductory passages were comparative advance organizers. One pointed out the chief differences and similarities of Buddhist and Christian doctrines. The other did the same for Buddhist and Zen Buddhist doctrines. The control group studied typical introductory material, including historical and biographical data, prior to the learning of each passage. As expected, the use of the organizers produced a significant effect on the learning and retention of the Buddhism material but had less of an impact on the learning of the Zen Buddhism passage.

Investigators have explored the effectiveness of both discovery and reception learning. Unfortunately, the research does not consistently support either approach. One of the problems in the research is that each study has a different definition of discovery and reception methods. Wittrock (1963) advances evidence that reception methods are more effective when the speed of learning is at stake, but Guthrie (1967) has experimented with discovery methods as a more effective teacher of transfer — the application of knowledge to new situations. There also is some evidence that brighter students may profit more from discovery (Hermann, 1971), but the evidence is ambiguous for average and slower students. The decision about which method to use will depend on the instructional objective, the characteristics and abilities of the students, and your own interest and ability to teach in the prescribed manner.

KEY POINTS

PIAGET

1. *Be conscious of the developmental level of the learner.*
2. *Analyze tasks within the curriculum to determine the level of reasoning required for successful solution of each task.*
3. *Motivate learners by emphasizing problems and trying to jolt them out of their ordinary way of looking at things.*
4. *Whenever possible have learners perform some relevant physical action on an object (concrete learning).*

BRUNER

1. *Teach the basic structure of the discipline – the relationships among the most important concepts and principles.*
2. *Use discovery-learning techniques to motivate students, help them retain information, and teach them how to learn.*
3. *Begin a lesson with a problem, and students will learn the basics as they struggle with the problem.*
4. *Gear the instruction to the level of the child's cognitive functioning.*

SUCHMAN

1. *Use puzzling situations to encourage student inquiry into problems.*
2. *Modify your role as a lecturer and allow students greater responsibility for their own learning. Don't dominate discussions or answer questions that students can easily answer themselves.*
3. *Spend time with students analyzing their inquiry strategies and the consequences of particular strategies.*

AUSUBEL

1. *Learning new knowledge will be meaningful to the degree that the learner can relate it to the ideas that she already understands.*
2. *Good intent on the part of the learner ensures the probability that learning will be meaningful.*

3. *A good strategy, for both you and your students, that reduces the possibility of rote learning is to adopt the practice of constantly paraphrasing new ideas. This exercise will encourage you and your students to concentrate on the substance of the material rather than on its literal meaning.*
4. *Organize lessons according to the process of progressive differentiation, moving from the general to the specific.*
5. *Use advance organizers either to activate the student's reception system or to equip him with the necessary receptors he does not have.*
6. *Help the learner discriminate between old and new ideas.*
7. *Relate concepts and principles presented early in the course to those ideas presented later in the course.*

SUGGESTIONS FOR FURTHER READING

The following authors are strong proponents of discovery-learning methods in education:

Ashton-Warner, S. *Teacher*. New York: Simon and Schuster, 1963.

Leonard, G. *Education and ecstasy.* New York: Dell, 1969.

Postman, N., & Weingartner, C. *Teaching as a subversive activity.* New York: Delacorte Press, 1971.

Ausubel, D. P., & Robinson, F. G. *School learning: An introduction to educational psychology.* New York: Holt, Rinehart and Winston, 1969. The major source for more detailed study of Ausubel's theory of learning.

Furth, H. G. *Piaget for teachers*. Englewood Cliffs, N.J.: Prentice-Hall, 1970. Explains how teachers can use Piaget's ideas for enhancing students' cognitive development.

Ginsburg, H., and Opper, S. *Piaget's theory of intellectual development: An introduction.* Englewood Cliffs, N.J.: Prentice-Hall, 1970. A good source for a more detailed study of Piaget's theory.

Morine, H., & Morine, G. *Discovery: A challenge to teachers.* Englewood Cliffs, N.J.: Prentice-Hall, 1973. A practically oriented book that explains and illustrates how discovery methods can be used in the classroom.

FOLLOW-UP ACTIVITIES

1 Teaching students to think. A common complaint heard among teachers is that some students refuse to think. They attempt to memorize information, easily forget concepts taught earlier in the course, and fail to relate previous learning to present situation. Holt (1964) illustrates his concern for this problem in the following description of one of his students:

> What she needs is a broom to sweep out her mind. She has so much junk in there, her filing systems are in such a mess that she can never find anything, and the file drawers and old trunks must be emptied out before they can be put into any kind of order. If she could only forget completely about nine-tenths of the facts and rules she has all mixed up in her head, she might begin to learn something. (p. 112)

How does this problem begin? Does the problem improve or get worse when students reach college? What advice would each of the learning theorists you have studied propose?

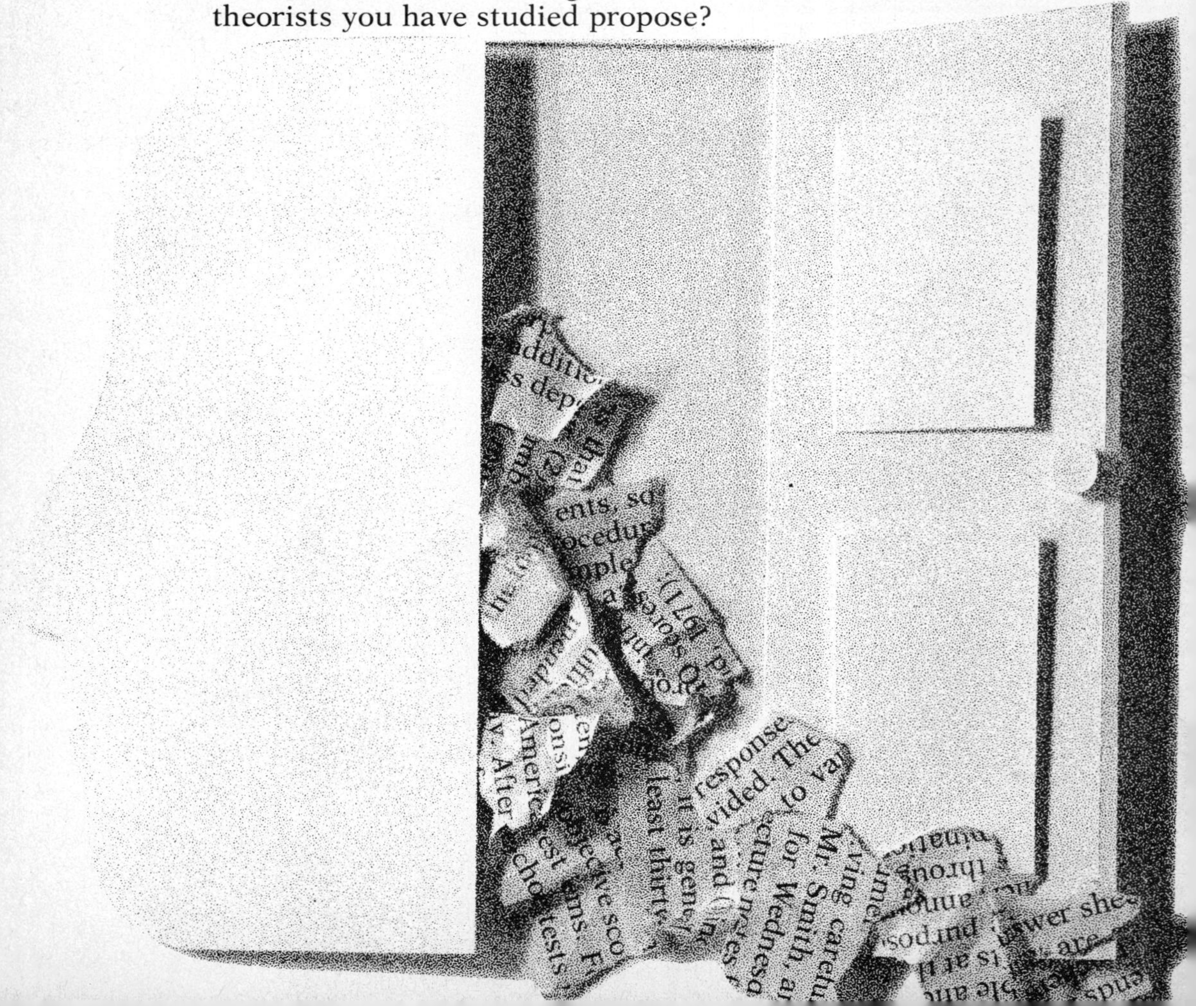

2 Analyze a Piagetian quote.

"The goal in education is not to increase the amount of knowledge, but to create the possibilities for a child to invent and discover. When we teach too fast, we keep the child from inventing and discovering himself. . . . Teaching means creating situations where structures can be discovered; it does not mean transmitting structures which may be assimilated at nothing other than a verbal level" (Piaget, 1964, p. 3).

What does Piaget mean by teaching too fast? Can you relate this statement to your own learning?

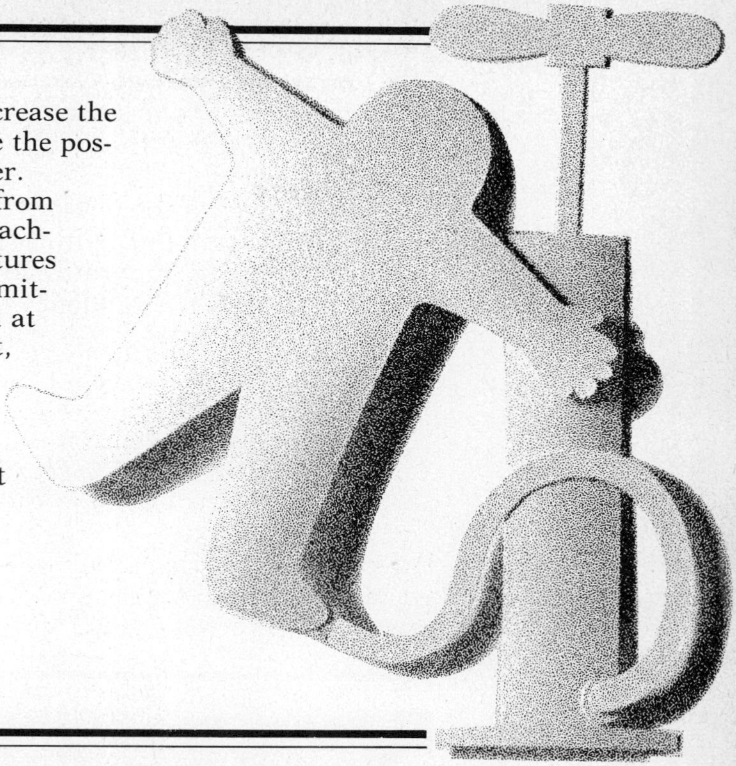

3 **Write an advance organizer.**

Write an organizer to introduce some topic you will be teaching. Explain why your organizer is different from an introduction and how it will facilitate the learning of material in your lesson.

4 Evaluate part of Ausubel's theory.

Try to recall a subject that you studied in the distant past and make a diagram of the relationship among the ideas you have retained. Does the cognitive structure remaining in this subject exhibit properties of pyramidal organization? Is the tendency to forget specifics and remember general ideas in evidence?

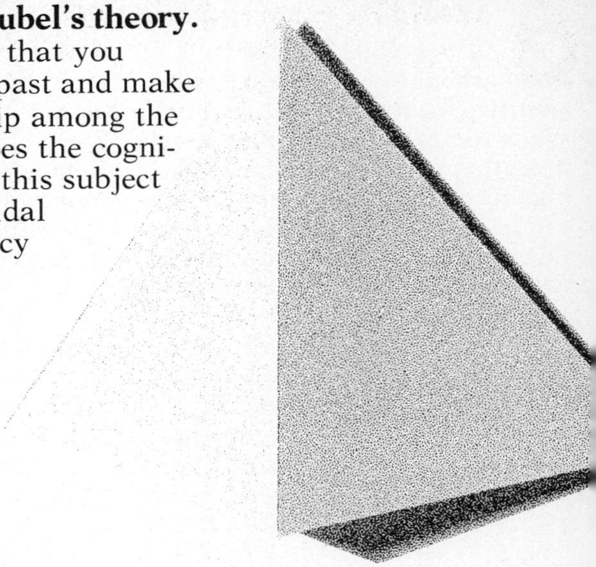

5 Evaluate Bruner's emphasis on structure.

Analyze your own classroom experiences in light of the claims Bruner makes for structure. Recall a course in which the instructor emphasized organization and structure. Did you learn more in that course as compared to another course in which organization and structure was not stressed? Did you retain more knowledge?

6 Try a Piagetian experiment.

Conservation of Quantity

Material:
A ball of clay.

Presentation:
Give the child a ball of clay and ask him to make another exactly like it — just as big and just as heavy.

Activity:
After the child has done the activity, retain one of the balls as a standard of comparison. Change the other one by stretching it into a sausage, flattening it into a cake, or cutting it into smaller pieces. Ask if the amount of clay, its weight, and its volume have changed or remained invariant (conserved) as a result of the transformation. "Do the two pieces of clay have the same amount of clay?"

Justification:
"How do you know?"

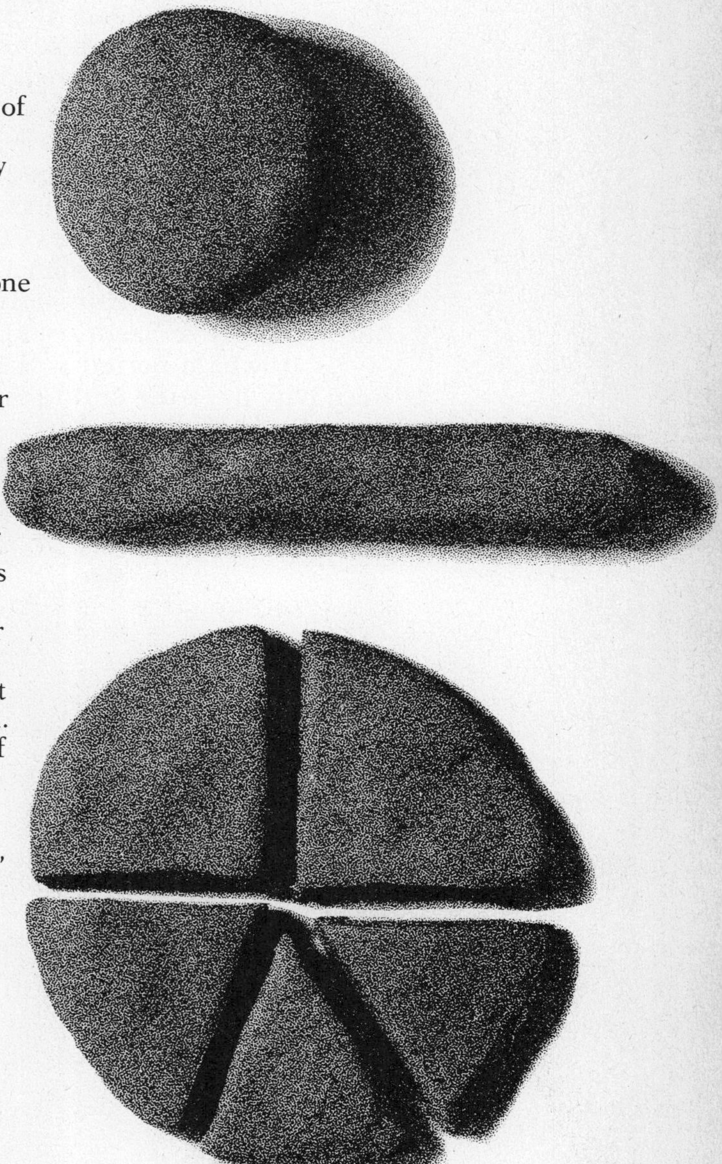

7 Assess a child's level of cognitive development. Piaget places twenty beads (eighteen brown and two white) in a box, the child acknowledging that they all are made of wood. He asks the following question: "In this box, which are there more of, wooden beads or brown beads?" (All the beads are visible.) The child replies that there are more brown beads, "since there were only two white ones." Piaget then asks the child, "Are all the brown ones made of wood?" The child responds, "Yes." Piaget questions further: "If I take away all the wooden beads and put them in a second box, will there be any beads left in the first box?" The child replies, "No, because they are all made of wood." The child is then asked: "If the brown ones are taken away, will there be any beads left?" The child responds, "Yes, the white ones" (Piaget & Szeminska, 1952, p. 165).

In which period is the child? What operation(s) is Piaget testing? Why does the child respond as he does?

8 Use inquiry methods. Using the teacher behavior suggested by Postman and Weingartner in this chapter, teach an inquiry lesson to a small group of students in your class. Ask the students to evaluate your behavior and the success of the lesson.

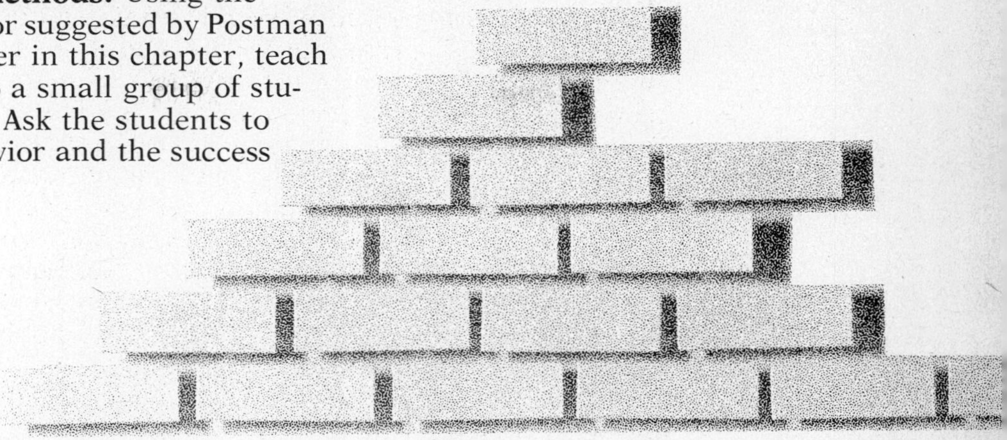

9 Debate operant conditioning and discovery or inquiry methods of teaching. Take the position of an avid proponent of operant conditioning or discovery methods of teaching. Present your arguments and respond to criticisms of your stance.

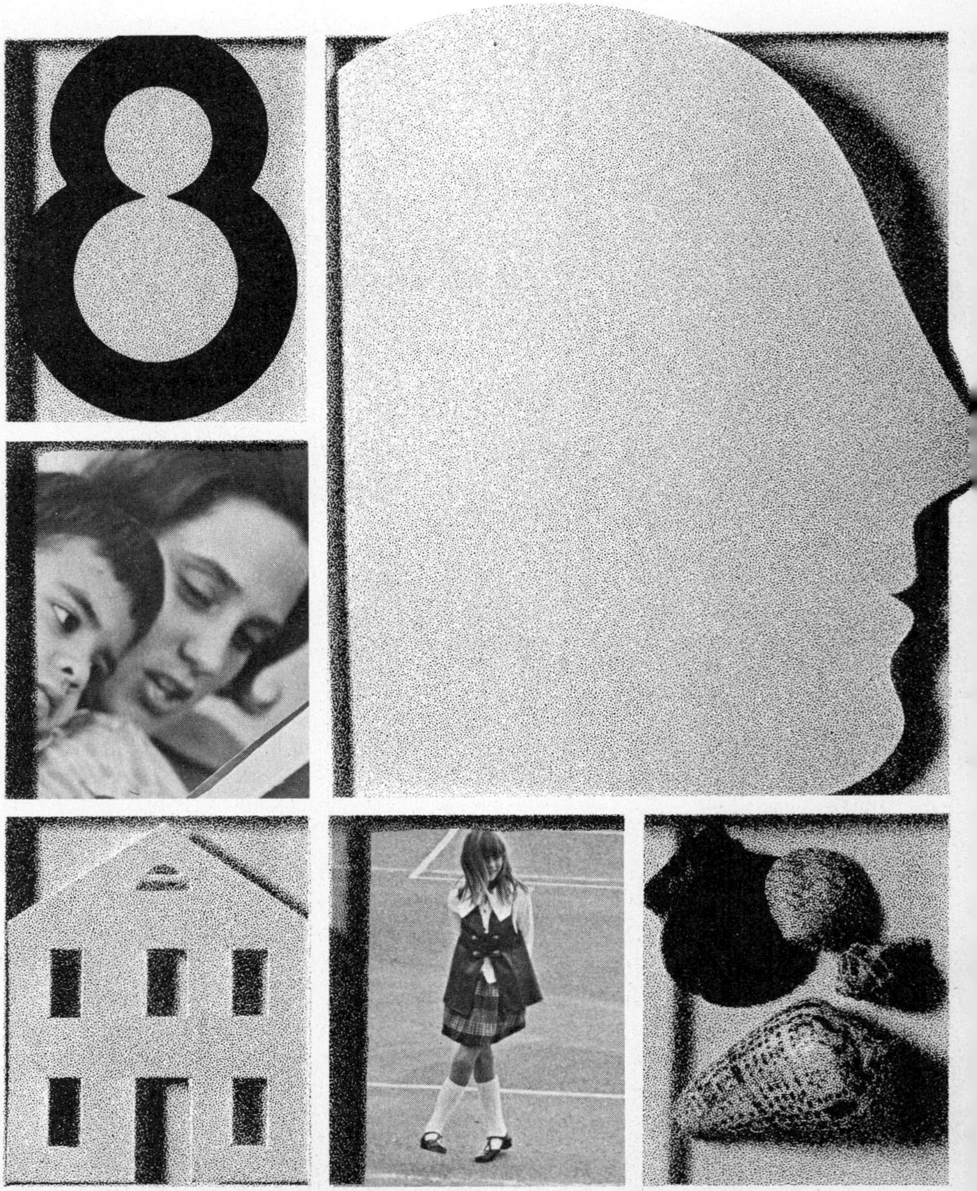
8

HUMANISTIC PSYCHOLOGY: LEARNING THEORIES AND APPLICATIONS

Orientation

Humanistic psychologists and educators place the feelings and concerns of the student on an equal plane with the organization and presentation of material in learning. They believe that if the material lacks personal meaning for the student, there is less likelihood that learning will take place.

Humanistic educators are interested in self-concept development, human relations training, and other affective concerns. As you read this chapter, determine how you can best apply humanistic learning principles in your teaching area.

HUMANISTIC PSYCHOLOGY

During the late 1940s a new psychological perspective emerged from the work of persons engaged in the application of psychology — clinical psychologists, social workers, and counselors — rather than from the work of persons researching the learning process. The movement that grew out of this perspective became known as humanistic, existential, perceptual, or phenomenological psychology and attempted to understand behavior from the point of view of the behaver rather than the observer. We shall see that humanistic psychologists have more in common with the cognitive-field psychologists, Piaget, and Bruner than with the behavioristic psychologists.

Some of the individuals who have contributed significantly to humanistic psychology are Abraham Maslow, Carl Rogers, Erich Fromm, and Arthur Combs. Although these theorists differ among themselves on particular points, they are in agreement on basic principles and assumptions about human behavior.

Combs et al. (1974) explain how humanistic psychologists view behavior:

> To understand human behavior . . . it is necessary to understand the behaver's perceptual world, how things seem from his point of view. This calls for a different understanding of what the "facts" are that we need in order to deal with human behavior; it is not the external facts that are important in understanding behavior, but the meaning of the facts to the behaver. To change another person's behavior it is necessary somehow to modify his beliefs or perception. When he sees things differently, he will behave differently. (p. 15)

This statement is one of the credos of the humanists: concern for the individual's feelings, perceptions, beliefs, and purposes — the inner behaviors that make people different from one another. To understand another person, it is necessary to see the world as the behaver does, to determine how he thinks and feels about himself and his world.

Humanists and behaviorists hold diverging opinions about the success of behavior modification. In Chapter 4 I discussed how self-concept is related to behavior and emphasized that the individual behaves in ways that are consistent with his self-concept. And self-concept influences perception, since we tend to see things that are consistent with the way we view ourselves. This point of view conflicts directly with behaviorism, which tends to deal with the *effects* of behavior rather than its causes. Humanists do not endorse behavior modification as implemented by behaviorists.

Humanistic and behavioral psychologists are poles apart in their view of behavior. The ideological gap is often referred to as the freedom-determinism issue in psychology and has been debated quite extensively by Rogers and Skinner (1956). The behaviorist beholds people as reactive beings who respond to the stimuli in their environment. Past experiences and conditioning shape their behavior. To the humanist, on the other hand, people are determiners of their behavior. They are not subject to their environment but are free to make choices about the quality of their lives.

Humanistic psychologists believe that man's basic motivational tendency is toward self-actualization or self-fulfillment. Maslow (1970) points out that man's other goals center around what he lacks or needs, such as food, safety, and human solidarity. These goals are prerequisites to self-actualization because a person must first satisfy his lower-order needs before he strives for the development of his individuality or the realization of his potentials.

The manner in which self-actualization surfaces in people varies greatly. Developing a hobby, reading a book, driving a truck, raising children, becoming a professor are all paths to self-actualization. Self-actualization is "not so much a matter of what a person does, as how he feels about what he's doing" (Kolesnik, 1975, p. 42). In his choice of action each person wants to improve himself in some way.

Maslow's hierarchy of human needs has important implications that teachers should take into account while teaching children. A teacher may have difficulty understanding why certain children don't do homework, are restless in class, or are completely uninterested in class activities. She assumes that the desire to learn is an important need for all children, but Maslow suggests that interest or motivation for learning may not develop until other basic needs have been met. Children who come to school without breakfast or sufficient sleep, or with personal family problems, anxieties, or fears, are not interested in becoming self-actualized individuals using learning as a means to develop their potentialities.

To understand the behavior of a student you must determine how he perceives the way he acts in a situation. What appears to be strange or unusual behavior to you may not be so from the behaver's (student's) perspective. To the teacher, a student's wanton destruction of school materials is inexplicable. To the student, who can't achieve recognition, status, or prestige in school, his behavior (although improper) is a purposeful act that brings him recognition from his gang.

This is why humanists state that to change behavior one must change an individual's perception. Combs et al. (1971) suggest that misbehavior is "the result of not wanting to do what one knows he should do because something else is more personally satisfying" (p. 96). When a teacher complains that her students are not motivated, she really means that they are not motivated to do what she wants them to do. Yet, if she selected a different activity, she might find a totally different reaction on the part of the students.

Now let's see how a student's internal perspective relates directly to the learning process. Humanists see two parts to learning: the acquisition of new information and the individual's personalization of this information. Teachers make the mistake of assuming that students will learn if subject matter is properly organized and presented. But meaning is not inherent in the subject matter; it is the individual who instills subject matter with its meaning (Combs et al., 1971). The dilemma in teaching is not how to present subject matter but how to help students derive personal meaning from the subject matter. If they can relate it in some way to their lives you have succeeded.

Combs et al. (1971) explain the dominance of personal meaning over a person's information retention by drawing two concentric circles and labeling "perceptions of the self" in the center and "perceptions of the world" in the outer circle. The further events are from the center of the circle (perceptions of the self), the less they will influence the individual. The closer events are perceived to the self, the more they will affect behavior. Now you may understand why so many of the things that we learn are soon forgotten: They have little relation to the self!

I often ask my students to write down main ideas from each of their courses of the previous semester. Every semester many students admit that their list is going to be a brief one because they can't remember many worthwhile ideas from certain courses. Think about your own learning. Do you find a relationship between the amount of your learning and the degree of personal meaning you found in the subject?

Historically, the purpose of education has been to transmit our cultural heritage — knowledge, skills, values, beliefs — from one generation to another. Humanistic educators see broader goals for education than merely passing along knowledge in this manner. Helping students learn more about themselves, helping them relate to others, preparing them for future society, encouraging them to think for themselves and to make their own decisions — these are the goals of education (Kolesnik, 1975).

The goals Kolesnik proposes demand different student-teacher relationships than do the traditional educational goals. In the traditional classroom the teacher makes the decisions concerning what, when, and how the students will learn. The teacher is the center of attention.

The humanistically oriented classroom is more student-centered. The teacher is a facilitator who advises students on how to develop to their full potential. The teacher is responsibile for the educational climate, which should be conducive to learning. At this juncture you may want to return to Chapter 4 and reread Purkey's article, "The Atmosphere the Teacher Creates," which describes the humanistic teacher's behavior in detail.

Humanists give students an important role in determining their own goals and objectives and deciding when they want to work on certain tasks. Students should also participate in the evaluation of their own progress, since they are in the best position to determine what they have learned.

Carl Rogers is one humanistic psychologist whose ideas on education have found their way into various educational settings. The following reading is from his popular book, *Freedom to Learn.* He identifies a number of important humanistic learning principles and describes ways in which teachers can ease the path to learning. As you read the article, compare Rogers' concepts with your own educational experiences.

Regarding Learning and Its Facilitation

> How does a person learn? How can important learnings be facilitated? What basic theoretical assumptions are involved? In this article I have tried to answer these questions in a "bare-bones" fashion, simply stating the core of my views on these questions.

It is customary to begin a presentation with theoretical and general principles, and then to indicate the way in which these principles might be carried out in practice. I have followed the opposite course in this book. I have endeavored to present a wealth of practical experience and descriptions of methods, all of which have been used to set students free of self-initiated, self-reliant learning. Now I would like to make a succinct general statement of some of the principles (or hypotheses) which can reasonably be abstracted, it seems to me, from these and other similar experiences. I will be drawing on my own experience, on the work of many other facilitators of learning who

Reprinted from Carl Rogers, *Freedom to Learn* (Columbus, Ohio: Charles E. Merrill, 1969), pp. 157–166. Reprinted by permission of the publisher.

have sent me accounts of their work and its outcomes, and upon relevant research, some of which has been reported in earlier chapters.

LEARNING

Here are a number of the principles which can, I believe, be abstracted from current experience and research related to this newer approach:

1. *Human beings have a natural potentiality for learning.* They are curious about their world, until and unless this curiosity is blunted by their experience in our educational system. They are ambivalently eager to develop and learn. The reason for the ambivalence is that any significant learning involves a certain amount of pain, either pain connected with the learning itself or distress connected with giving up certain previous learnings. The first type of ambivalence is illustrated by the small child who is learning to walk. He stumbles, he falls, he hurts himself. It is a painful process. Yet, the satisfactions of developing his potential far outweigh the bumps and bruises. The second type of ambivalence is evident when a student who has been absolutely tops in every way in his small town high school enrolls in a superior college or university where he finds that he is simply one of many bright students. This is a painful learning to assimilate, yet in most instances he does assimilate it and goes forward.

This potentiality and desire for learning, for discovery, for enlargement of knowledge and experience, can be released under suitable conditions. It is a tendency which can be trusted, and the whole approach to education which we have been describing builds upon and around the student's natural desire to learn.

2. *Significant learning takes place when the subject matter is perceived by the student as having relevance for his own purposes.* A somewhat more formal way of stating this is that a person learns significantly only those things which he perceives as being involved in the maintenance of or the enhancement of his own self. Think for a moment of two students taking a course in statistics. One is working on a research project for which he definitely needs the material of the course in order to complete his research and move forward in his professional career. The second student is taking the course because it is required. Its only relationship to his own purposes or the enhancement of himself is simply that it is necessary for him to complete the course in order to stay in the university. There can hardly be any question as to the differences in learning which ensue. The first student acquires a functional learning of the material; the second learns how to "get by."

Another element related to this principle has to do with the speed of learning. When an individual has a goal he wishes to achieve and he sees the material available to him as relevant to achieving that goal, learning takes place with great rapidity. We need only to recall what a brief length of time it takes for an adolescent to learn to drive a car. There is evidence that the time for learning various subjects would be cut to a fraction of the time currently allotted if the material were perceived by the learner as related to his own purposes. Probably one third to one fifth of the present time allotment would be sufficient.

3. *Learning which involves a change in self organization – in the perception of oneself — is threatening and tends to be resisted.* Why has there been so much furor, sometimes even lawsuits, concerning an adolescent boy who comes to school with long hair? Surely the length of his hair makes little objective difference. The reason seems to be that if I, as a teacher or administrator, accept the value which he places on nonconformity then it threatens the value which I have placed on conforming to social demands. If I permit this contradiction to exist I may find myself changing, because I will be forced to a reappraisal of some of my values. The same thing applies to the former interest in "beatniks" and the current interest in "hippies." If their rejection of almost all middle class values is permitted to stand, then an individual's acceptance of middle class values as a part of himself is deeply threatened, since to most people it seems that to the degree *others* are right, *they* are wrong.

Sometimes these painful and threatening learnings have to do with contradictions within oneself. An example might be the person who believes "every citizen in this country has equal right to any opportunity which exists." He also discovers that he has the conviction, "I am unwilling for a Negro to live in my neighborhood." Any learning which arises from this dilemma is painful and threatening since the two beliefs cannot openly co-exist, and any learning which emerges from the contradiction involves a definite change in the structure of self.

4. *Those learnings which are threatening to the self are more easily perceived and assimilated when external threats are at a minimum.* The boy who is retarded in reading already feels threatened and inadequate because of this deficiency. When he is forced to attempt to read aloud in front of the group, when he is ridiculed for his efforts, when his grades are a vivid reflection of his failure, it is no surprise that he may go through several years of school with no perceptible increase in his reading ability. On the other hand, a supportive, understanding environment and a lack of grades, or an encouragement of self-evaluation, remove the external threats and permit him to make

progress because he is no longer paralyzed by fear. This is also one of the great advantages of the teaching machine, when properly used. Here the poor reader can begin at his own level of achievement and practically every minute step he makes is marked by reward and a feeling of success.

It is fascinating to me how completely we have tended to disregard the evidence which clearly supports this principle. Nearly forty years ago Herbert Williams, then a teacher, was put in charge of a classroom in which all of the most serious delinquents in a large school system were brought together. They were the "worst boys" in a city of 300,000. He could not hope to carry on much individualized instruction, and the boys were at all levels of school achievement. As might be expected, they were retarded intellectually (average I.Q. 82) as well as in their school achievement. He had very little special equipment. Besides the usual desks and blackboards, there was a large table in the room on which he placed picture books, readers, story books, and textbooks in various subjects, appropriate to all levels of reading achievement. There were also art materials available. There were but two rules. A boy must keep busy doing something, and no boy was permitted to annoy or disturb others. Each child was told, without criticism, of his results on an achievement test. Encouragement and suggestions were given only after an activity had been self-initiated. Thus, if a boy had worked along artistic lines he might be given assistance in getting into a special art class. If activities in mathematics or mechanics had engaged his interest, arrangements might be made for him to attend courses in these subjects. The group remained together for four months. During this period the measured educational achievement (on the Stanford Achievement Test) of those who had been in the group for the major part of this period increased fifteen months on the average, and this improvement was evident in reading, arithmetic, and other subjects. The increase was more than four times the normal expectation for a group with this degree of retardation, and this in spite of the fact that reading and other educational disabilities abounded. This incredible improvement came about through informal, self-directed, activity. It is my belief that studies such as this have been disregarded primarily because they provide a threat to the teacher. Here is evidence that the most unpromising students learn rapidly when they are simply given opportunities to learn and when no attempt is made to teach them. This must seem to many teachers that they might be deprived of their jobs and hence the information is simply not assimilated.

One reason for the success of this highly unorthodox and inexpensive venture must have been the attitude of Mr. Williams himself. He surmises that his interest in each child's home conditions, neighborhood, health, and in each boy individually may have stimulated the youngsters. He states that he wanted to get acquainted with each boy, and spent his time in this sort of activity rather than in teaching. That he had a strong and sympathetic interest in, and belief in, juvenile delinquents is shown by the fact that he went on to become superintendent of a highly progressive institution for delinquents.

5. *When threat to the self is low, experience can be perceived in differentiated fashion and learning can proceed.* In a sense this is only an extension of, or an explanation of, the preceding principle. The poor reader is a good illustration of what is involved in this principle. When he is called upon to recite in class the internal panic takes over and the words on the page become less intelligible symbols than they were when he was sitting at his seat before he was called upon. When he is in an environment in which he is assured of personal security and when he becomes convinced that there is no threat to his ego, he is once more free to perceive the symbols on the page in a differentiated fashion, to recognize the differing elements in similar words, to perceive partial meanings and try to put them together — in other words, to move forward in the process of learning. Any sort of learning involves an increasing differentiation of the field of experience and the assimilation of the meanings of these differentiations. Such differentiations, it seems to me, are most effectively made under two sharply differing kinds of conditions. They may occur when the threat to the *organism* is intense, but such threats are quite different than threats to the *self* as perceived. The combat soldier, for example, learns very quickly to distinguish the shriek of a shell going high overhead from the whine of one which is coming in his direction. He learns to discriminate very readily a normal footpath from one whose surface has been disturbed, since the latter may be a land mine. He is, in these instances, responding to threat of a very serious nature, but this is threat to his organism and not a threat to the self he perceives himself to be. In fact the more quickly he can learn these discriminations the more his self is enhanced. In the ordinary educational situation, however, such realistic life-and-death threats are rare and when these exist pupils respond well to them. Children learn traffic rules, for example, quite readily and comfortably. But humiliation, ridicule, devaluation, scorn and contempt — these are threats to the person himself, to the perception he has of himself, and as such interfere strongly with learning. On the other hand, as described above, when threat to the self is minimized, the individual makes use of opportunities to learn in order to enhance himself.

6. *Much significant learning is acquired through doing.* Placing the student in direct experiential confrontation with practical prob-

lems, social problems, ethical and philosophical problems, personal issues, and research problems is one of the most effective modes of promoting learning. Illustrations range from the class group which becomes involved in a dramatic production, selecting the play and the cast, designing and making the scenery and costumes, coaching the actors, and selling tickets, to much more sophisticated confrontations. I have always been impressed with the fact that brief intensive courses for individuals on the firing line facing immediate problems — teachers, doctors, farmers, counselors — are especially effective because the individuals are trying to cope with problems which they are currently experiencing.

7. *Learning is facilitated when the student participates responsibly in the learning process.* When he chooses his own directions, helps to discover his own learning resources, formulates his own problems, decides his own course of action, lives with the consequences of each of these choices, then significant learning is maximized. There is evidence from industry as well as from the field of education that such participative learning is far more effective than passive learning.

8. *Self-initiated learning which involves the whole person of the learner — feelings as well as intellect — is the most lasting and pervasive.* We have discovered this in psychotherapy, where it is the totally involved learning of oneself by oneself which is most effective. This is not learning which takes place "only from the neck up." It is a "gut level" type of learning which is profound and pervasive. It can also occur in the tentative discovery of a new self-generated idea or in the learning of a difficult skill, or in the act of artistic creation — a painting, a poem, a sculpture. It is the whole person who "lets himself go" in these creative learnings. An important element in these situations is that the learner *knows* it is his own learning and thus can hold to it or relinquish it in the face of a more profound learning without having to turn to some authority for corroboration of his judgment.

9. *Independence, creativity, and self-reliance are all facilitated when self-criticism and self-evaluation are basic and evaluation by others is of secondary importance.* The best research organizations, in industry as well as in the academic world, have learned that creativity blossoms in an atmosphere of freedom. External evaluation is largely fruitless if the goal is creative work. The wise parent has learned this same lesson. If a child is to grow up to be independent and self-reliant he must be given opportunities at an early age not only to make his own judgments and his own mistakes but to evaluate the consequences of these judgments and choices. The parent may provide information and models of behavior, but it is the growing child or adolescent who must evaluate his own behaviors, come to his own conclusions, and decide on the standards which are appropriate for

him. The child or adolescent who is dependent both at school and at home upon the evaluations of others is likely to remain permanently dependent and immature or explosively rebellious against all external evaluations and judgments.

10. *The most socially useful learning in the modern world is the learning of the process of learning, a continuing openness to experience and incorporation into oneself of the process of change.* The point has been made in preceding chapters that a static kind of learning of information may have been quite adequate in previous times. If our present culture survives it will be because we have been able to develop individuals for whom *change* is the central fact of life and who have been able to live comfortably with this central fact. It means that they will not be concerned, as so many are today, that their past learning is inadequate to enable them to cope with current situations. They will instead have the comfortable expectation that it will be continuously necessary to incorporate new and challenging learnings about ever-changing situations.

FACILITATION

So much has been presented in preceding chapters about various methods of facilitating learning and various qualities of the facilitator that only the briefest summary of some of the guidelines which can be abstracted will be presented here.

1. *The facilitator has much to do with setting the initial mood or climate of the group or class experience.* If his own basic philosophy is one of trust in the group and in the individuals who compose the group, then this point of view will be communicated in many subtle ways.

2. *The facilitator helps to elicit and clarify the purposes of the individuals in the class as well as the more general purposes of the group.* If he is not fearful of accepting contradictory purposes and conflicting aims, if he is able to permit the individuals a sense of freedom in stating what they would like to do, then he is helping to create a climate for learning. There is no need for him to try to manufacture one unified purpose in the group if such a unified purpose is not there. He can permit a diversity of purposes to exist, contradictory and complementary, in relationship to each other.

3. *He relies upon the desire of each student to implement those purposes which have meaning for him, as the motivational force behind significant learning.* Even if the desire of the student is to be guided and led by someone else, the facilitator can accept such a need and motive and can either serve as a guide when this is desired or can provide some other means, such as a set course of study, for the student whose major desire is to be dependent. And for the majority of

students he can help to utilize the individual's own drives and purposes as the moving force behind his learning.

4. *He endeavors to organize and make easily available the widest possible range of resources for learning.* He endeavors to make available writings, materials, psychological aids, persons, equipment, trips, audiovisual aids — every conceivable resource which his students may wish to use for their own enhancement and for the fulfillment of their own purposes.

5. *He regards himself as a flexible resource to be utilized by the group.* He does not downgrade himself as a resource. He makes himself available as a counselor, lecturer, and advisor, a person with experience in the field. He wishes to be used by individual students, and by the group, in the ways which seem most meaningful to them insofar as he can be comfortable in operating in the ways they wish.

6. *In responding to expressions in the classroom group, he accepts both the intellectual content and the emotionalized attitudes, endeavoring to give each aspect the approximate degree of emphasis which it has for the individual or the group.* Insofar as he can be genuine in doing so, he accepts rationalizations and intellectualizing, as well as deep and real personal feelings.

7. *As the acceptant classroom climate becomes established, the facilitator is able increasingly to become a participant learner, a member of the group, expressing his views as those of one individual only.*

8. *He takes the initiative in sharing himself with the group — his feelings as well as his thoughts — in ways which do not demand nor impose but represent simply a personal sharing which students may take or leave.* Thus, he is free to express his own feelings in giving feedback to students, in his reaction to them as individuals, and in sharing his own satisfactions or disappointments. In such expressions it is his "owned" attitudes which are shared, not judgments or evaluations of others.

9. *Throughout the classroom experience, he remains alert to the expressions indicative of deep or strong feelings.* These may be feelings of conflict, pain, and the like, which exist primarily within the individual. Here he endeavors to understand these from the person's point of view and to communicate his empathic understanding. On the other hand, the feelings may be those of anger, scorn, affection rivalry, and the like — interpersonal attitudes among members of the group. Again he is as alert to these as to the ideas being expressed and by his acceptance of such tensions or bonds he helps to bring them into the open for constructive understanding and use by the group.

10. *In his functioning as a facilitator of learning, the leader endeavors to recognize and accept his own limitations.* He realizes that he can only grant freedom to his students to the extent that he is com-

fortable in giving such freedom. He can only be understanding to the extent that he actually desires to enter the inner world of his students. He can only share himself to the extent that he is reasonably comfortable in taking that risk. He can only participate as a member of the group when he actually feels that he and his students have an equality as learners. He can only exhibit trust of the student's desire to learn insofar as he feels that trust. There will be many times when his attitudes are not facilitative of learning. He will find himself being suspicious of his students. He will find it impossible to accept attitudes which differ strongly from his own. He will be unable to understand some of the student feelings which are markedly different from his own. He may find himself angry and resentful of student attitudes toward him and angry at student behaviors. He may find himself feeling strongly judgmental and evaluative. When he is experiencing attitudes which are nonfacilitative, he will endeavor to get close to them, to be clearly aware of them, and to state just as they are within himself. Once he has expressed these angers, these judgments, these mistrusts, these doubts of others and doubts of himself, as something coming from within himself, not as objective facts in outward reality, he will find the air cleared for a significant interchange between himself and his students. Such an interchange can go a long way toward resolving the very attitudes which he has been experiencing, and thus make it possible for him to be more a facilitator of learning.

EDUCATIONAL APPLICATIONS OF HUMANISTIC PSYCHOLOGY

As we have "discovered," humanists prefer learning situations that are more student-centered and oriented toward discovery methods of teaching and learning. Generally, they are also less concerned with the methodology of teaching than with personal relations with students and their role as assistants in the learning process.

Narrowing their focus on the establishment of classroom procedures based on humanistic principles, a group of humanistic educators with a wide variety of interests have established special programs and activities under the broad heading of *affective, psychological,* or *humanistic* education. Some of these programs attempt to merge the traditional emphasis on skills and cognitive information with the affective area of feelings, values, and interpersonal behavior. Other programs are exclusively devoted to such affective needs as developing positive self-concepts, values clarification, improving interpersonal relations and self-awareness, and are introduced as special courses apart from the traditional curriculum.

In this section we shall explore some affective programs, along with the open classroom and the free-school movement. This discussion is by no means meant to be an exhaustive survey of humanistic educational procedures. The references at the end of the chapter are a good source list for further investigation in the area.

AFFECTIVE PROGRAMS

George Brown (1971) has established a Center for Humanistic Education at the University of California, Santa Barbara where teachers learn to integrate affective experiences with cognitive learning in the classroom. Brown calls this process *confluent education*, and it is an excellent way to involve students personally in subject matter.

An example of confluent education is a twelfth-grade English unit on Stephen Crane's *The Red Badge of Courage.* Aaron Hillman, the teacher who developed this exercise, wanted his students not only to gain a greater understanding of the novel but also to acquire greater interpersonal awareness by discussing their own concepts of courage, bravery, and fear. Some of the exercises developed for the unit included:

Interviewing someone who has known war

Listening to war music, writing down the freely associated thoughts and feelings evoked, and then sharing them in small groups

Debating whether or not war is inevitable

Comparing Civil War and World War II poetry

As the students participate in these exercises and discuss how Henry Fleming, the hero in the novel, joins and leaves various groups, they also begin to make analogies with their own experiences of social acceptance and rejection. The novel takes on personal meaning when the students start to think about how they might have reacted in a similar situation.

Another example of confluent education is a ninth-grade social studies unit developed by Robin Montz. The unit is based on selected photos from Edward Steichen's picture book, *The Family of Man*, a lecture on theories of the nature of man, and a statement on the self as an example of man. After completing affective exercises toward self-discovery, the students write two essays entitled "Who am I?" and "What is Man?" and list the common elements of the two essays.

In one of the affective exercises the students are asked to write words that describe their character on pieces of paper: "I am pushy," or "I like to help people." Next, they are asked to arrange these words in order, placing the description they like the most on top and the one they like the least on the bottom. Then they are told the following (Brown, 1971):

> Now for a while confine your eyes to the surface of your desk. Don't look at anyone or anything except the top of your desk and the pieces of paper. Take each piece of paper in order and really spend some time with that word. Stay with it for a few minutes and try on the word just as you try on clothes hanging in your closet. Our characters are like a wardrobe. We are sometimes one way, sometimes another. Today we are going through the wardrobe and examining our clothes and trying them on. Really see how they feel. Become the words you see. Accept them as *you* at one time or another, then do with the word and the piece of paper what you want to do. Put it back in your wardrobe, tear it up and throw it away, or whatever you wish. All right, you may begin. (p. 57)

Brown's book, *Human Teaching for Human Learning*, is a storehouse of exercises that have been developed for other units in English and social studies.

Sidney Simon, at the University of Massachusetts, has developed a program called *values clarification* based on the premise that many young people do not know clearly what their values are. They need help in examining their values to direct their insights into how they view choices and make decisions. Simon contends that values clarification does not focus on the content of a person's values but the process of valuing itself.

Simon, Howe, and Kirschenbaum (1972) have organized seventy-nine different values clarification exercises for use in the classroom. One of the first exercises in their book helps a person to realize what activities most enthuse him. Why don't you try the exercise as I explain it? Make a list of ten or fifteen things that give you great pleasure or joy. Write after each pleasure the date you last experienced it. Next, place a dollar sign after each item that costs money. Now go through the list again and place a *P* after those activities that usually require considerable planning. Review your list and place an *S* after amusements that you share with someone or with other people. Last, place an *A* after those thing that you do alone. What does this exercise tell you about your values?

Since the beginning of the 1970s a movement called *psychological education* has encouraged the initiation of courses for the direct promotion of psychological growth in educational settings. Psychological education courses now exist to increase achievement motivation, internal locus of control, creative thinking, interpersonal sensitivity, self-esteem, identity, and other important aspects of human functioning (Alschuler, 1969).

Achievement-motivation courses for adults have been successfully carried out for many years and have now been developed for teachers and students. These courses transmit the behavioral characteristics related to the need to achieve: the steps reaching toward excellence, a set of strong feelings about doing well, and the development of specific action strategies to reach one's goals. The course objective is to teach people to think, talk, and act like people with high achievement motivation. But, most important, individuals are encouraged to evaluate their present actions in the light of their future goals.

The instruction utilizes role playing, discussions, and games to teach achievement behaviors. For example, the concept of "moderate risk" emerges from a ring-toss game. The person with a successful toss at a further distance from the peg scores more points than the person with a successful toss at a closer distance. Two factors, then, determine the winners of this game: the skill of the players and the amount of risk. Standing five or six feet away from the peg ensures a successful toss, but the player only receives 10 to 30 points for his achievement. A riskier approach, but one that would return greater rewards, would be to stand thirteen feet away from the peg and hope for a successful throw of 1,000 points.

The game is a simulation of real-life decision making and risk taking. The teacher or trainer using this game draws a parallel for the students between the way they play the game and the way they make decisions in their own life. McClelland and Alschuler (1971) have shown that students who opt for the easy toss tend to approach other problem-solving situations in the same way. The same is true for the person who plays the long shots. These researchers are confident that if people do not possess the behaviors of successful achievers, they can still learn. Just show them that they can be in control of their own environment by helping them abandon excessive caution or excessive risk taking.

One program, Achievement Competence Training (ACT), developed by Research for Better Schools in Philadelphia, has been used to teach fifth through seventh graders competence in achieving goals and developing more realistic levels of aspiration and a greater sense of internal control. The program consists of the following steps:

1. *Study self*
2. *Get goal ideas*
3. *Set a goal*
4. *Plan*

5. *Strive* 6. *Evaluate*

The preliminary research data from the project, involving over 3,000 students, indicate that the program has been successful in meeting its goals.

Patterson (1973) states that the greatest problem in current approaches to affective education is that they are not based on any systematic theory of human behavior or interpersonal behavior. He suggests that before we can develop affective programs we need to know more about emotional development.

OPEN EDUCATION

The apparent success of the British primary schools and the publication of the Plowden Report (1967), a study advocating the development of the open classroom as a model for elementary education in England, have been important catalysts in the spread of open education in the United States.

Advocates of open education claim that it is both a philosophy and, strongly influenced by Piaget, a theory of human learning. Because of the confusion over what exactly is involved in open education, Walberg and Thomas (1972) have reviewed relevant literature on open education, broken it down into components, and have then sought to verify their descriptions with prominent open educators. They have evolved a list of eight themes, paraphrased as follows:

1. Provisions for Learning. *Manipulative materials supplied in great diversity and range. Children move freely around room. Talking encouraged. No grouping by ability using test scores.*

2. Humaneness, Respect, Openness, and Warmth. *Use of student-made material. Teacher deals with behavior problems by communicating with child, without involving the group.*

3. Diagnosis of Learning Events. *Students correct their own work. Teacher observes and asks questions.*

4. Instruction. *Individualized. No tests or workbooks.*

5. Evaluation. *Teacher takes notes. Individualized. Few formal tests.*

6. Search for Opportunities for Professional Growth. *Teacher uses assistance of someone else. Teacher works with colleague.*

7. Self-perception of Teacher. *Teacher tries to keep all children within sight to monitor their work.*

8. Assumptions About Children and Learning Process. *Classroom climate warm and accepting. Children involved in what they are doing.*

Walberg and Thomas found that open classes differ from traditional classes on five of the eight criteria: Provisions, Humaneness, Diagnosis, Instruction, and Evaluation.

Barth (1973) has investigated the latter criterion — Assumptions About Children and Learning Process — and suggests that before jumping on the bandwagon, teachers should examine whether their assumptions are attuned to those of successful open educators in the United States and England. The following is a partial list of these assumptions. Read each and determine the degree to which you agree with it.

LEARNING

1. *Children are innately curious and will explore their environment without adult intervention.*
2. *The child will display natural exploratory behavior if he is not threatened.*
3. *Play is not distinguished from work as the predominant mode of learning in early childhood.*
4. *Children will be likely to learn if they are given considerable choice in the selection of the materials they wish to work with and in the questions they wish to pursue with respect to those materials.*

INTELLECTUAL DEVELOPMENT

1. *Concept formation proceeds slowly.*
2. *Children pass through similar stages of intellectual development, each in his own way and at his own rate and in his own time.*
3. *Verbal abstractions should follow direct experience with objects and ideas, not precede them or substitute for them.*

EVALUATION

1. *Errors are necessarily a part of the learning process: They are to be expected and even desired, for they contain information essential for further learning.*
2. *Those qualities of a person's learning that can be carefully measured are not necessarily the most important.*

3. *The best way of evaluating the effect of the school experience on the child is to observe him over a long period of time.*

KNOWLEDGE

1. *Knowledge is a function of one's personal integration of experience and therefore does not fall neatly into categories or "disciplines."*

2. *There is little or no knowledge that is essential for everyone to acquire. (pp. 97–99)*

The Walberg and Thomas list of themes brings out that although open educators support students' freedom to move around the room and to select their own learning activities, teacher guidance throughout the process is in evidence. Proponents of open education present this fact to some critics who characterize open education as simply "doing your own thing."

One of the most salient features of an open classroom is the physical environment of the room, where students work individually or in small groups. Figure 8.1 illustrates a typical organization for an open classroom. Most of the individualized instruction is provided by learning or activity centers in the classroom, which allow students to explore particular subject areas, topics, skills, or interests. These centers have the advantages of posting explicit directions for proceeding on a topic without the presence of the teacher and of recording the student's participation and progress for later discussion with the teacher. Figures 8.2*a* and 8.2*b* are examples of typical learning centers.

Good, Biddle, and Brophy (1975) suggest that "openness" be viewed as a continuous set of variables, since classes or schools may be open on some characteristics but closed on others. For example, many teachers use learning or activity centers without adopting other aspects of open education. Some teachers allow students to evaluate their own work but tell them what to learn.

FREE OR ALTERNATIVE SCHOOLS

Another humanistic influence in education, often confused with open education, is the free- or alternative-school movement that grew up in the United States during the mid-1960s. Unlike schools that subscribe to open education, free schools are organized outside the mainstream of traditional public or private education, are less structured, and allow more freedom. They have been established by teachers and parents who reject the compulsory and authoritarian aspects of tradi-

FIGURE 8.1
A TYPICAL CLASSROOM ORGANIZATION FOR AN OPEN CLASSROOM.

From S. Kaplan, J. Kaplan, S. Madsen, and B. Taylor, *Change for Children* (Pacific Palisades, Calif.: Goodyear, 1973), p. 3.

TALL TALES
READING
"NOW" MUSIC
COOKING
ART
legend

FIGURE 8.2*a*
AN EXAMPLE OF A LEARNING CENTER.

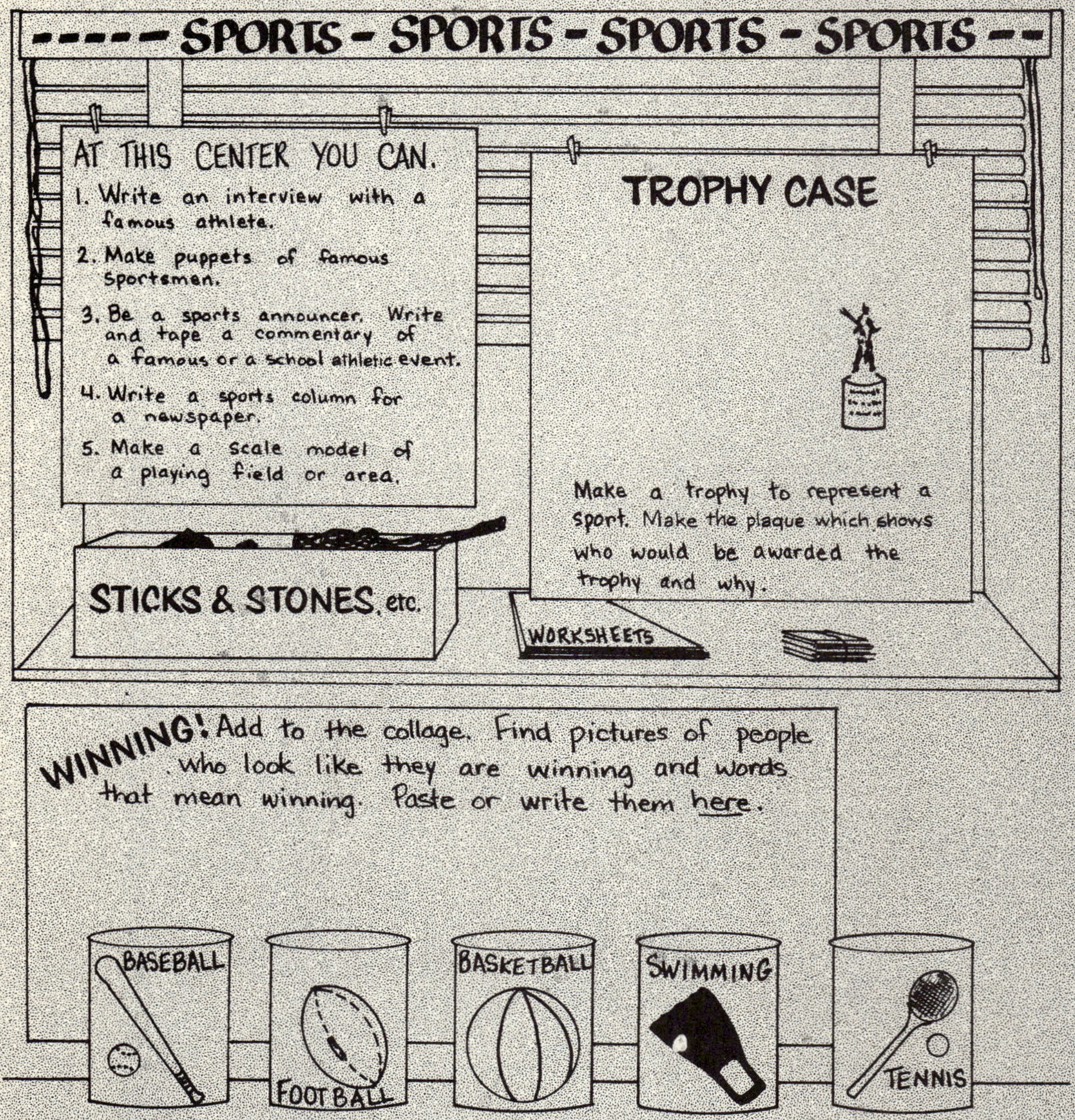

Learning Possibilities

Comparing past and present through the study of sports
Developing the technique of news reporting
Categorizing
Making inferences about people's feelings from their bodily and facial expressions
Using creative thinking to develop original games

From S. Kaplan, J. Kaplan, S. Madsen, and B. Taylor, *Change for Children* (Pacific Palisades, Calif.: Goodyear, 1973), p. 100.

FIGURE 8.2b
AN EXAMPLE OF A LEARNING CENTER.

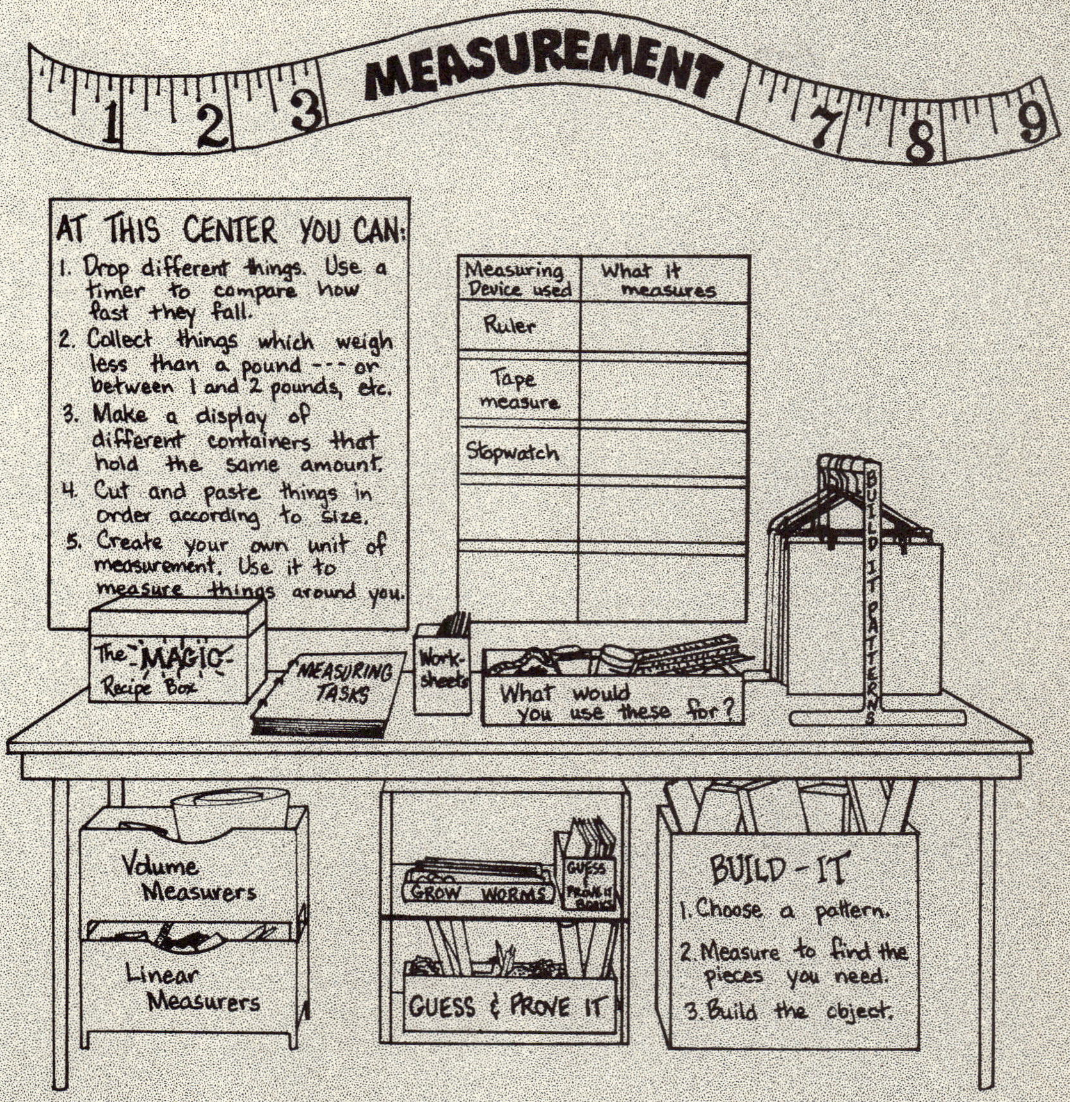

Learning Possibilities

- Developing the concept of the standard unit of measure
- Learning to use different measuring devices appropriately
- Using addition, subtraction, and estimation skills
- Learning about fractional parts
- Learning to follow written directions and diagrams

From S. Kaplan, J. Kaplan, S. Madsen, and B. Taylor, *Change for Children* (Pacific Palisades, Calif.: Goodyear, 1973), p. 68.

tional education: large, formal classes, strict teacher control, emphasis on testing, and rigid curriculum.

Most free schools have eliminated the "restrictive" aspects of education by making attendance voluntary and allowing students to select their own curriculum and participate equally with their teachers in making decisions about the educational program. Generally, free schools attract students whom the traditional educational system has alienated. Because free schools do not set up highly structured curricula, personal feelings and social relationships find expression in such schools.

Many of the proponents of free schools have been influenced by reports of Summerhill, the private coeducational boarding school, founded in England by A. S. Neill (1960), dedicated to the philosophy that the school must fit the child. There, students choose what they wish to learn and how they wish to learn it. They can also decide not to learn.

Both open educators and those who advocate free schools come to a meeting of the minds on the basic motivational assumption that children are naturally curious and motivated to learn by their own interests and desires. Nevertheless, the open educators usually reject many of the approaches of the free school: the laissez-faire attitude toward the curriculum, the absence of attention to cognitive skills, and the unlimited choices for students.

Many of the free schools established in the 1960s have not survived more than a year or two. Deal (1975) found that after the initial euphoric stage, free schools tend to run into organizational problems and, after having departed from the educational status quo, now move closer to conventional schooling by establishing more structure and formal role relationships.

COMPARING THEORIES OF LEARNING

Much of the criticism of humanistic education attacks the belief that students will learn if they are freed from teacher-directed pressure to decide what they want to do in the classroom. Skinner (1973) feels that too many educators delude themselves about what constitutes "freedom": Students are not free simply because their teacher chooses not to exert control over their behavior. He states: "They [students] then simply come under the control of other conditions, and we must look at those conditions and their effects if we are to improve teaching" (p. 13). The teacher who understands the behavioral process, says Skinner, can help students *learn* to be free and happy. This will occur because students will acquire the knowledge and skills of productive and creative individuals.

Although a proponent of humanistic education, Kozol (1972), in his book *Free Schools,* points out that some teachers seek to *force* freedom on students. From his vantage point he sees that although conscious teaching is not always necessary for learning, it is wrong to assume that learning is *never* the result of conscious teaching. (Carl Rogers' writings about teaching have sometimes been so interpreted.) Kozol maintains that when conscious teaching is necessary but "in the name of Joy and Freedom it is not undertaken," parents whose children fail to learn have good reasons to be disturbed with the school and with the teachers who have let them down.

Throughout our discussion of various learning theories we have been confronted with the attempt to reconcile freedom and control in education. Are you now prepared to take a position in this controversy? How much freedom is necessary to learn? To help you think about this issue and the many other issues pertaining to the methods of teaching identified in Chapters 6 through 8, you may refer to Table 8.1, a comparison of the implications of behavioristic, cognitive-developmental, and humanistic psychology for education.

Analyzing Instructional Methods

The instructional methods covered in Chapters 6, 7, and the present chapter were organized by conceptual orientation — behaviorism, cognitivism, and humanism — to better untangle the "pure" assumptions of each theory that underlie common educational procedures. Although you may lean toward a particular theory of learning, you do not have to limit your flexibility by "buying" completely any one position.

The classification of methods under particular theories of learning does not irrevocably wed these methods to one theory. For example, I identified learning guides as a behavioristic method of individualized instruction based on programmed-instruction principles. But suppose a teacher provided students with a large number of activities at various learning centers: Is this a behavioristic or a humanistic teaching strategy, or a combination of both? The open classroom is an example both of Piaget's cognitive-developmental theory and of humanistic theory. My point is that some teaching methods can be used simultaneously for different objectives and can be claimed by more than one theoretical camp.

If it is misleading to confine theories to one field of psychology,

TABLE 8.1
A COMPARISON OF THE IMPLICATIONS OF BEHAVIORISTIC, COGNITIVE-DEVELOPMENTAL, AND HUMANISTIC PSYCHOLOGY FOR EDUCATION.

	BEHAVIORISTIC PSYCHOLOGY	*COGNITIVE-DEVELOPMENTAL PSYCHOLOGY*	*HUMANISTIC PSYCHOLOGY*
INDIVIDUALIZATION	Individualization of task assignment taking the child's level of functioning into account. Individualization of rewards and of discipline.	Adaptation of tasks to child's developmental stage and previous experiences.	Individualization of total approach, according to needs and individuality of child, on an intuitive basis as a consequence of shared experience.
MOTIVATION	The child's interests and needs are not accepted as "given"; they are to be changed and manipulated whenever this seems of advantage. A reward system motivates the child. Motivation is extrinsic. Rewards may be material, social, or fulfill other needs. In contrast to humanism, satisfaction of needs is the consequence and not the precondition of learning.	Interests are the expression of a "drive" toward equilibrium. Knowing is a motive in itself. Motivation is intrinsic. The need for equilibrium is as compelling as physiological needs.	Satisfaction of needs is necessary for optimum learning ability. The child's need for experience, his wish to be helpful and to communicate with others — in short, social motives and need for experience — are emphasized. Motivation is mainly intrinsic.
DEGREE OF SYSTEMATIZATION	Very specific methods of classroom management and teaching are prescribed. Systematization is emphasized. Programmed material is suggested.	Progress in teaching is systematic, but classroom environment is free enough for exploration and discovery. Theory of cognitive development results in definite teaching approaches suitable for the child's developmental level.	A balanced curriculum and balance between freedom and discipline are advocated. Recognition of developmental progression is only one of the factors to be taken into account in adjusting to the child's needs. The teacher must be attuned to the child's intellectual, emotional, and social needs.

Adapted from M. Frostig and P. Maslow, *Learning Problems in the Classroom* (New York: Grune & Stratton, 1973), pp. 97–103. Reprinted by permission.

	Behavioristic Psychology	*Cognitive-Developmental Psychology*	*Humanistic Psychology*
Methodology	Extensive and detailed methods and sequences to develop skills and specific knowledge are advocated. Use of computer and other machine technology to assist teacher.	Materials and curricula to develop basic cognitive skills, such as classification, seriation, conservation, imagery, and problem solving have been developed, as well as specific curricula in science, math, and social studies.	Emphasis on integrated project approach, with particular stress on social studies.
Rote versus Insight Learning	Rote learning and associational learning in small steps are emphasized. Skills are greatly emphasized.	Emphasis is on insight learning and understanding.	Emphasis is on insight learning and understanding, in contrast to mere acquisition of knowledge.
Goals	A person able to fill a job well or to continue with his education because he has mastered skills and knowledge taught on a lower level. Competence is the goal of education.	A person who has optimally developed his cognitive functions and who is innovative and flexible in his thought processes. Most important, he is a person who can decentrate, especially by taking into account the points of view of others, as well as all possible outcomes in making decisions and carrying out actions. Intelligence applied equally well in decisions pertaining both to oneself and to others is the goal of education.	A loving, creative human being with a strong social conscience, aware of the needs of others, feeling fulfilled, and helping others to feel fulfilled. Self-fulfillment and understanding are the goals of education.
Curricular Objectives	Focus on academic knowledge and skills and on socially defined personal and social behavior characteristics.	Focus on total development: sensory-motor, linguistic, and cognitive. Social interaction serves as a tool to develop decentration, intelligence, and logical thought.	Focus on social development, communication skills, sensitivity to beauty, and other humanistic values. The child's sensitivity to group needs as well as to individual needs is to be enhanced. Social influences are more emphasized than biological ones. The goal is optimum interrelationship with the environment, not adjustment.

	Behavioristic Psychology	*Cognitive-Developmental Psychology*	*Humanistic Psychology*
Form of Classroom Management	Teacher-centered. The teacher prescribes curriculum and classroom procedures. Social relationships are not emphasized as goals but utilized as means.	Student-centered. The teacher assists the child and guides him in his learning, explorations, and discovery. The classroom structure permits and fosters self-direction.	Student-centered. The teacher assists child but does not direct him in his learning. The classroom structure permits freedom of choice for the child and fosters creativity and exploration. The importance of human relationships is recognized. The classroom situation permits and should foster social learning.
Making Teaching Meaningful	Emphasis is usually not on integration of topics but rather on a linear progression in teaching content and skills. Behaviorists are not concerned with "meaning" except as meaning is derived from understanding previous steps. Mastery is emphasized in behavioristic terms of specific mastery of subject matter or adjustment to classroom demands. Mastery or attainment of extraneous rewards makes learning meaningful.	Integration of knowledge is emphasized. Integration is not achieved merely by associations between thoughts, or between contents of curricula, or by addition of new knowledge. The hierarchical order of concepts and skills must be grasped to make meaningful what has been learned. Concepts are related to other coordinated, supraordinated, and subordinated concepts.	Meaning derives from integration of topics and relation of the content to child's personal needs. Additional emphasis is placed on human needs in general, on creativity and involvement, and on development of the child's feeling of "being in the world" and awareness of the world around him.
Active Participation	Behaviorists are little concerned with activity, except if the activity is the behavior to be elicited. The child may be a rather passive recipient of knowledge and should follow directions. The behavior is shaped, not guided.	Activity is regarded as the basis of all mental development. The child learns by exploring and experimenting. In new learning, he proceeds from activity to perceptual learning and then to symbolic learning. To make symbolic learning possible, he must learn to read, write, make graphs, use mathematical language, and so on.	Experience requires action. The child needs to relate himself actively to the environment and to share with others in activities. The child's need for play and activity must also be satisfied.

it is also dangerous to make incorrect distinctions between theories. One of my students attempted to summarize the differences between humanism and behaviorism as follows: "The humanists are the 'good' guys who are concerned about students, while the behaviorists are the 'bad' guys who are more interested in technology than people." Of course, behaviorists would take issue with his conceptualization by pointing out that they are not against a teacher's being warm and friendly and that they are strongly people-oriented. However, they don't find these characteristics sufficient for effective instruction. Likewise, although humanists are less interested than behaviorists in the organization of material for instruction, they are not necessarily opposed to planning and using specific teaching techniques.

Reading about so many conflicting educational theories, you may have rightly asked an anguished "What is the best way to teach?" Joyce and Weil (1972) have an excellent response to this question: "There are many kinds of 'good' teaching, and . . . the concept 'good' when applied to teaching, is better stated 'good for what?' and 'good for whom' " (p. 3)?

Presently, the research on teaching and learning indicates that no one method or curriculum finds equal success with all students. You should not conclude from this finding that it does not matter how you teach. The good teacher is one who can continually adjust his behavior to teach in many different ways, depending on the instructional objective of the lesson and the individual differences of the students.

If a teacher analyzes instructional objectives solely in terms of Bloom's *Taxonomy of Educational Objectives* or Gagné's types of learning, it becomes apparent to him that he would have difficulty using any one instructional method or orientation for all types of objectives. Learning hierarchies, behavior modification, discovery learning, values clarification, and other strategies all have their place. If the objective of a lesson is to recall factual material, a structured presentation with drills and repetition is the method to use, not some discovery-learning procedure. A teacher faced with a group reluctant to offer their own ideas needs to select a method with the greatest possibility of altering the students' behavior and encouraging more autonomous learning. A teacher who wants to promote more cooperation in the classroom will not choose programmed instruction over a method emphasizing group interaction.

I reiterate here the importance of considering differences in students when you plan your teaching. Chapters 2 and 3 directed your attention to these student characteristics. Research investigations have concluded that it is advisable to match instructional methods with student characteristics. Dowaliby and Schumer (1973) found that low-anxiety students learned significantly better than high-anxiety students in student-centered discussion groups. High-anxiety students were more relaxed and performed better than low-anxiety students in teacher-centered lecture classes. These results are consistent with other studies matching highly anxious students with more structured learning situations such as programmed instruction (Gaudry & Spielberger, 1971). In an investigation of discovery and expository methods with students of different reasoning skills, Kropp, Nelson, and King (1967) found that children strong in deductive reasoning profited more from exposition than from discovery. Children strong in inductive reasoning learned more from discovery than from exposition.

Hunt and Sullivan's (1974) book, *Between Psychology and Education*, is a consideration of learning within the framework of student ability and educational approach. In one area of study they identify students according to their conceptual levels. Low CL students are dependent on external standards and have difficulty taking on different points of view. High CL students react to internal standards, can process more information, and are capable of considering an experience from different viewpoints. Hunt and Sullivan write that low CL students profit from structured situations, whereas high CL students are adaptable to varied environments. In educational practices a less structured situation is highlighted by student-centered activities such as discovery learning and open classroom procedures that delegate the responsibility for organizing the material to the student. A highly structured approach is teacher-centered, the teacher organizing the lectures and programmed instruction. Using the Hunt and Sullivan model, McLachlan and Hunt (1973) found that low CL students learned much better after listening to a lecture than after trying a discovery approach, while high CL students were able to glean knowledge from both conditions. In another study, Hunt (1972) reported that when students were given a choice to attend either a highly structured or a less structured high school, 70% of the students who had a great need for structure chose the highly structured school.

Dunn and Dunn (1974) suggest that before placing students in instructional programs you match their learning styles with how the program will require them to learn. Table 8.2 compares some of the required skills and learning-style characteristics of the traditional classroom with those of the open classroom. These authors deem an instructional program unsuitable for a student if it demands skills and abilities that he does not yet possess. Can you identify students who are (or were) unsuccessful in a traditional classroom because of limitations in their learning style?

In analyzing instructional methods, let us not forget the

TABLE 8.2
THE RELATIONSHIP BETWEEN REQUIRED STUDENT SKILLS AND LEARNING-STYLE CHARACTERISTICS IN TRADITIONAL AND OPEN CLASSROOMS.

REQUIRED STUDENT SKILLS	*LEARNING-STYLE CHARACTERISTICS*
TRADITIONAL CLASSROOM	
1. To pay attention for consecutive intervals of twenty to fifty minutes.	Is motivated.
2. To sit still for consecutive intervals of one to three hours.	Does not require mobility.
3. To retain information by listening.	Is an auditory learner.
4. To accept that what is taught is necessary, valuable, and interesting.	Is authority-oriented.
5. To learn whenever a subject is being taught.	Time is not a factor.
6. To keep working at an item until it is mastered.	Is persistent.

OPEN CLASSROOM	
1. To learn without continuous direction and supervision.	Is motivated.
2. To avoid an essentially social, rather than academic, experience.	Is responsible.
3. To discipline oneself to concentrate and to learn self-selected ideas, data, and values.	Is motivated and responsible.
4. To study in the midst of movement, discussion, and varied activities.	Sound, structure, and the mobility of others are not factors.
5. To interact positively with other children.	Is peer-oriented.
6. To retain information without drill reinforcement.	Is not in need of imposed structure.

Adapted from R. Dunn, and K. Dunn, "Learning Styles as a Criterion for Placement in Alternative Programs," *Phi Delta Kappan* 55 (1974): 275-278. Reprinted by permission of *Phi Delta Kappan* and the authors.

teacher's behavior and personality. Some teachers cannot tolerate a low degree of structure and organization or find it difficult to relinquish authority over what goes on in the classroom. These teachers often have difficulty reconciling the use of student-centered teaching-learning activities with their teaching style. Do you have any strong biases or preferences that might limit your flexibility in teaching?

Before moving on to the last two chapters on measurement and evaluation, take some time to review the teaching-learning model identified in Chapter 1. We have now discussed student differences, teacher-student interaction, instructional objectives, learning theories, and methods of teaching. Do you have a better understanding of how these variables influence a teacher's decision making?

Key Points

1. *Humanistic psychologists are concerned with a person's feelings and perceptions as the clues to his actions.*

2. *Humanistic psychologists believe that a person determines his or her own behavior.*
3. *Humanistic psychologists see a person's motivational tendency as moving toward self-actualization or self-fulfillment.*
4. *Maslow places the satisfaction of lower-order needs such as food and safety before people's drive to develop their individuality or to realize their potential.*
5. *The student's perception of his actions is the key to understanding his behavior.*
6. *Humanistic psychologists identify two parts to learning: the acquisition of new information and the individual's personalization of this information.*
7. *The closer the individual perceives events are to himself, the more likely he will be to react to them.*
8. *Humanistic educators value educational goals that help students learn more about themselves, relate to others, and make independent decisions.*
9. *Humanistic educators prefer learning situations that are more student-centered and oriented toward discovery methods of teaching and learning.*
10. *Confluent education stresses the importance of integrating affective experiences with cognitive learning in the classroom.*
11. *Values clarification aids young people in examining their value system so that they can arrive at better decisions.*
12. *Open education gives the student freedom to select his activities and encourages the teacher to act more as an assistant or facilitator of learning than as one who wields knowledge.*
13. *Free schools allow students to select their own curriculum and to collaborate with teachers in making decisions about the educational program.*
14. *The determination of how much freedom students need to learn effectively is an unresolved issue in education.*
15. *Not all instructional methods can be pigeonholed in one theory of learning.*
16. *The decision of how to teach takes into account the variables of individual differences of students, teacher behavior, instructional objectives, and principles of learning.*

Suggestions for Further Reading

The following books set forth the points of view of critics of the open classroom:

Meyers, D. A., & Meyers, L. *Open education reexamined.* Lexington, Mass.: Heath, 1973.

Troost, C. J. (Ed.). *Radical school reform: Critique and alternatives.* Boston: Little, Brown, 1973.

Read the following two books for specific information on how to establish an open classroom:

Blitz, B. *The open classroom: Making it work.* Boston: Allyn & Bacon, 1973.

Stephens, L. S. *The teacher's guide to open education.* New York: Holt, Rinehart and Winston, 1974.

Combs, A., Blume, R., Newman, A., & Wass, H. *The professional education of teachers* (2nd ed.). Boston: Allyn & Bacon, 1974. This book covers what humanistic teachers are like and how they should be prepared for their professional role.

Johnson, D. W., & Johnson, R. T. *Learning together and alone.* Englewood Cliffs, N.J.: Prentice-Hall, 1975. Compares competitive, cooperative, and individualized learning environments and demonstrates how each can be used most effectively in achieving cognitive and affective objectives.

Kolesnik, W. B. *Humanism and/or behaviorism in education.* Boston: Allyn & Bacon, 1975. The author presents a clear discussion of the main differences between humanism and behaviorism.

Maslow, A. *Toward a psychology of being.* New York: Van Nostrand, 1962. A leading humanistic psychologist presents his views.

Neill, A. S. *Summerhill.* New York: Hart, 1970. An example of a school based on student needs.

Rogers, C. *Freedom to learn.* Columbus, Ohio: Merrill, 1969. A discussion of how humanistic principles can be applied to learning.

FOLLOW-UP ACTIVITIES

1 Remember your teachers. Select a teacher you had who used humanistic principles in interacting with students and another whose behavior tended toward the opposite continuum. How successful were they in motivating and gaining respect from students, attaining educational objectives, and encouraging independent learning?

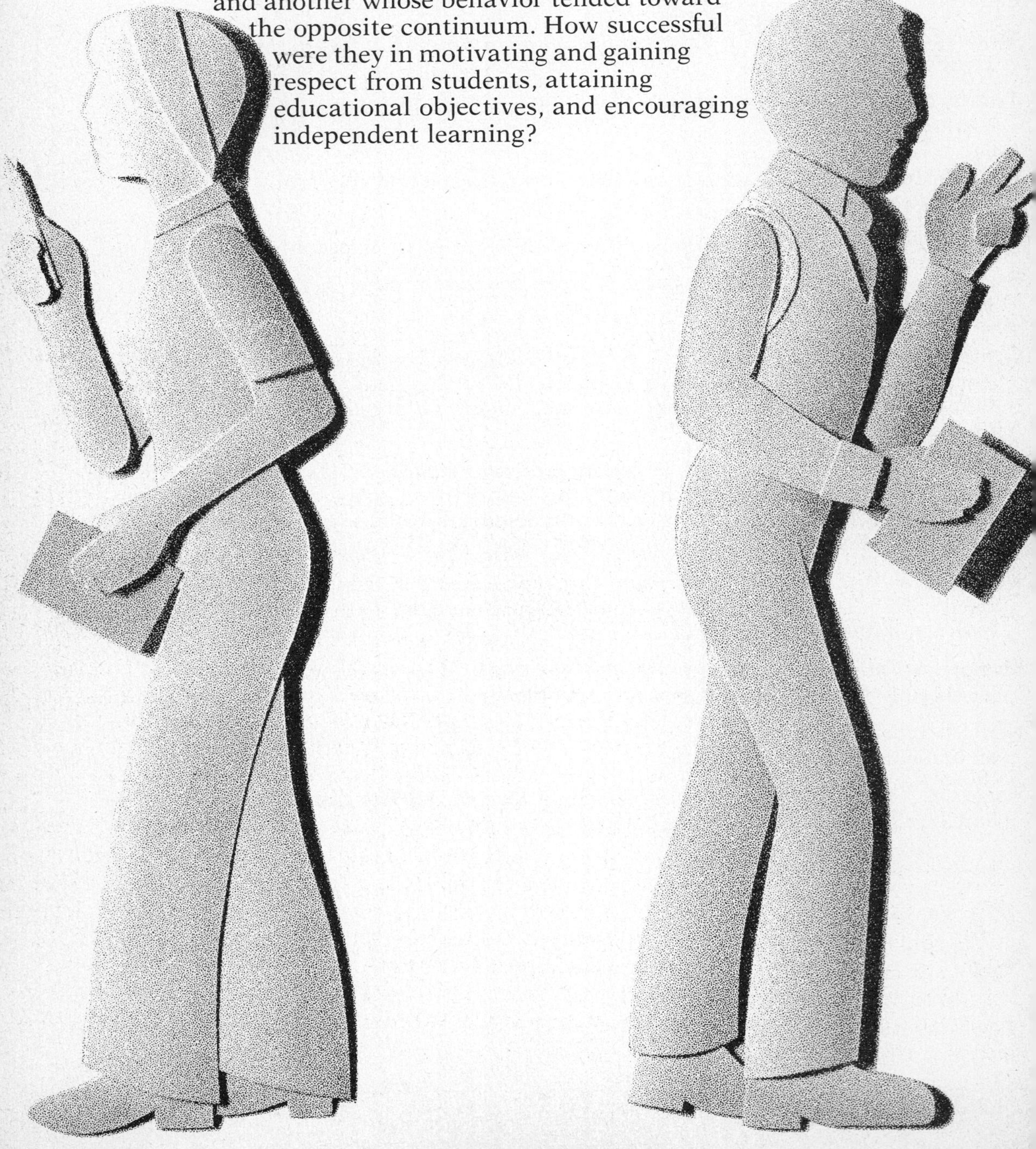

2 Apply open-classroom concepts to the high school. How can open-classroom concepts be applied to a high school? Describe open-classroom procedures and explain how they can help the high school student.

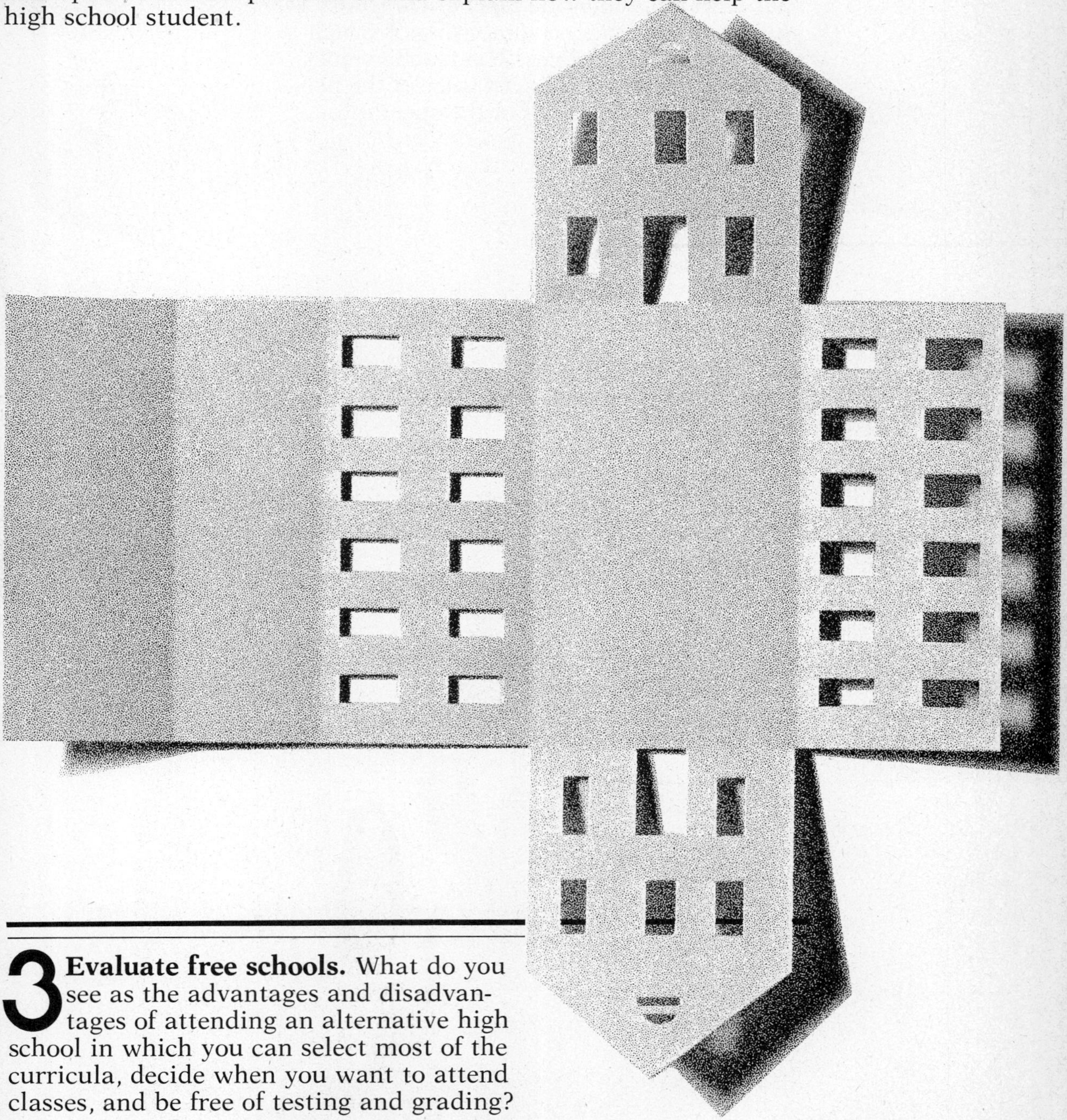

3 Evaluate free schools. What do you see as the advantages and disadvantages of attending an alternative high school in which you can select most of the curricula, decide when you want to attend classes, and be free of testing and grading?

4 **Role playing: acceptance.** Work with a small group of students. Let one student volunteer to role play a student in a situation in which the teacher confronts a student who has done something of which the teacher disapproves. The teacher must demonstrate both his acceptance of the person and his disapproval of the specific behavior.

5 **Read "Intelligence From a Perceptual Point of View."** Combs (1952) offers an interesting view of the nature and growth of intelligence in this article. His theory is that one's intelligence is an amalgam of the richness and variety of perceptions possible to a person at a given moment: Perceptions determine "intelligence." Read the article and compare Combs' view of intelligence with those discussed in Chapter 2. To what extent does Combs afford meaningful information for a teacher?

6 Evaluate a newspaper editorial on open classrooms. Read the following newspaper editorial and discuss the extent to which you agree or disagree with the editor. See the Suggestions for Further Reading section for books by critics and proponents of the open classroom.

Old vs. New

The Wurtsboro elementary school was featured as a traditional educational institution in a CBS news special on Tuesday night. The program, in documenting the differences between "old-fashioned" and open classroom concepts, was slanted in favor of the latter. Somehow the Wurtsboro school came out smelling like a rose.

Open classrooms, which have been seriously under consideration if and when Ellenville has a new school, are the current rage in educational circles. Apparently the powers-that-be in Albany, anxious to prove themselves as innovators, came up with an idea to leave out partitions and open up classrooms around a central core.

The contention is that open classrooms stress self-guidance and a more relaxed student-teacher relationship. Traditional schools are accused of fostering boredom, anxiety and indifference.

Practical application appears to prove just the opposite. In a great many places where open classrooms have been tried, discipline has evaporated, and concentration by teacher and student alike has disintegrated. Teacher preparation time has doubled. Several schools have given up — adding partitions or closing.

Further relaxing of discipline could be a dangerous precept. Vandalism in schools is appalling, here and everywhere. Parental and educational permissiveness has backfired by producing a generation interested only in doing their own thing, at the expense of others. How then can self-guidance be expected of those who have never known any? They have no guidelines.

The closed classroom concept seems eminently preferable — there may be boredom, or indifference, but with no distractions and firm ground rules by the teacher, learning processes can proceed in an orderly way.

Despite the evident bias shown on the TV screen Tuesday, many viewers felt the Wurtsboro system came out ahead. Learning by rote in an atmosphere of calm may just be the best method of education after all.

—*Ellenville Journal*
Ellenville, New York
April 20, 1972

7 Using teaching methods in affective education. Write a report on one of the affective educational procedures and then demonstrate its methods and techniques in class. The following references will be helpful: Lyon (1971); Miller (1976); Simon, Howe, and Kirschenbaum (1972); and Brown (1971).

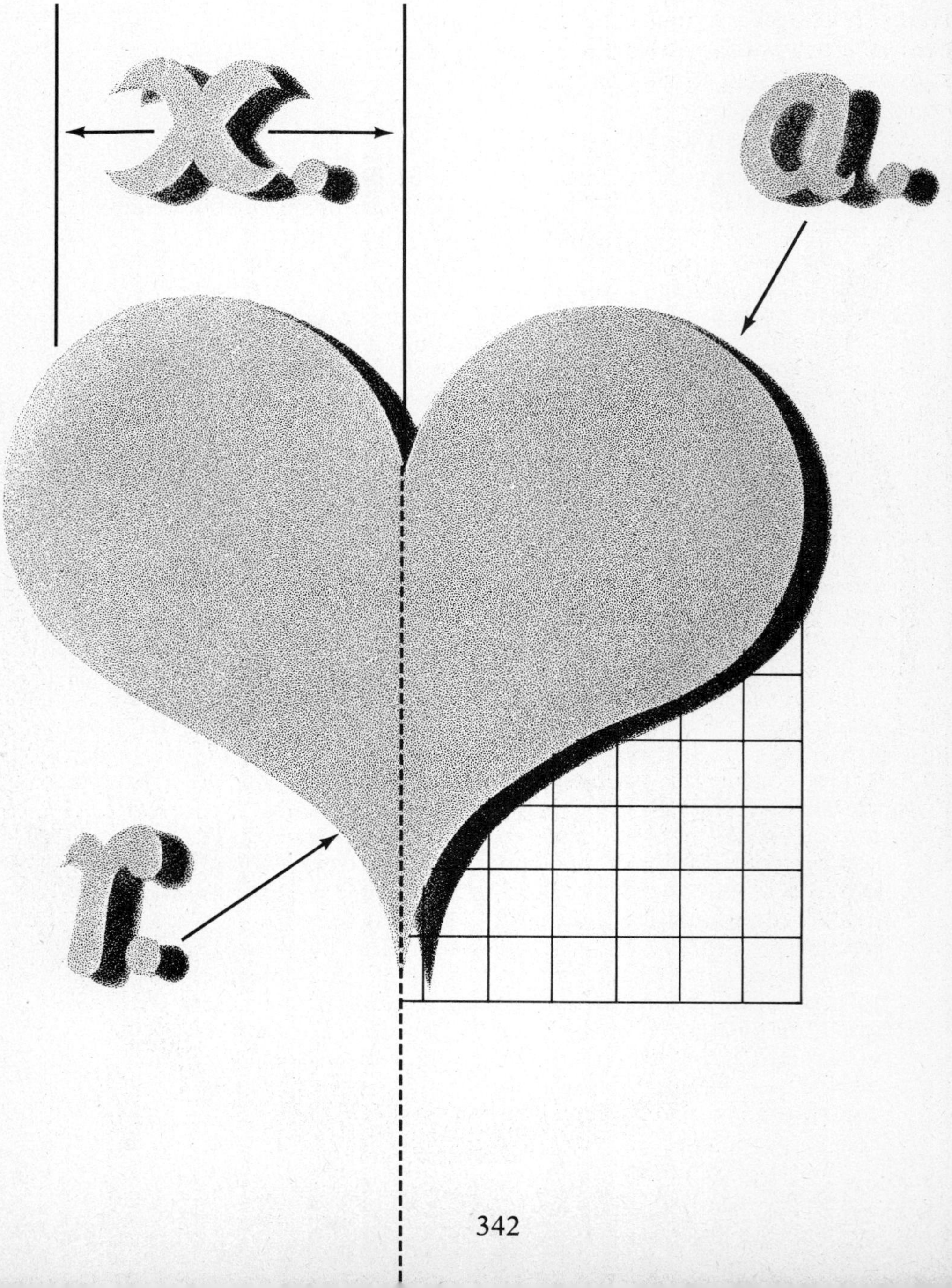

8 Reevaluate a teacher's lesson. In the fifth follow-up activity of Chapter 1 I asked you to evaluate a lesson. Go back to the same lesson and reevaluate it. Compare your first and second evaluations. How do they differ? If you did not select this activity in Chapter 1, visit a classroom and evaluate the teacher's lesson based on the suggested criteria from Chapter 1.

STANDARDIZED AND TEACHER-MADE EVALUATION INSTRUMENTS

ORIENTATION

When a person hears the term "evaluation," the first thought that often comes to mind is tests or grades. By the time a student reaches college, she has taken thousands of examinations. She has welcomed some of these examinations and feared others. Unfortunately, most of us probably remember more of the anxiety engendered by examinations than we do the joys. Can you remember how you felt as a young child waiting for the teacher to return a test paper from a difficult examination? What about the sleepless night before an important examination in college or the wait for a postcard reporting a final grade?

Although the teacher gives many tests to measure how well the student has attained the objectives and to assign her a final grade, evaluation plays a role in many other teacher decisions. Before beginning instruction, teachers often need to assess the students' backgrounds or entry behavior to set the appropriate level for instruction. During instruction it is sometimes necessary to diagnose stu-

dents' strengths and weaknesses to discover why they may be having difficulty in a particular subject. The teacher may have to assess students' attitudes about classroom procedures and perhaps change his behavior to accommodate them. These are just a few of the reasons for obtaining evaluation information.

TenBrink (1974) identifies evaluation as "the process of obtaining information and using it to form judgments which in turn are to be used in decision making" (p. 8). For teachers to evaluate properly they must know what kinds of judgments and decisions are called for and how to gather information for their decisions. Chapter 9 is directed toward garnering information. Chapter 10 identifies ways to interpret and report test scores. These last two chapters will help you make the transition from raw material to finished product.

HOW SHOULD YOU JUDGE STUDENT LEARNING?

The degree of student learning can be interpreted in one or both of two ways: (1) in terms of performance relative to a group or (2) in terms of performance relative to a behavioral criterion of proficiency. The first method is called *norm-referenced* measurement. The second method is called *criterion-referenced* measurement.

Norm-referenced measurement is the most common method of testing used by teachers and will receive the most attention in this book. A student's score on most tests reflects his performance as compared to that of his classmates. Grading on a curve is an example of norm-referenced measurement.

In recent years criterion-referenced measurement has entered the grading arena. With this method the performance of a student is couched in terms of the learning outcomes or objectives of the course. The statement that "Lisa did better than 80% of the students on a test of biological terminology" is a norm-referenced evaluation. In criterion-referenced measurement, we might say that "Lisa got 80% of the items correct on a test of biological terminology."

In criterion-referenced testing, the teacher concentrates on a limited number of specific objectives. Explicit instructional objectives are necessary because each test item must correspond to a particular objective or criterion. The following setup is an example of this relationship.

In criterion-referenced testing the teacher is primarily concerned with how many items of a set of specific objectives a particular

Objective	*Sample Test*
A. Discriminates between +, −, =, ×	A. Draw a circle around the sign which means "to add." + − = ×
B. Names the instrument used for measuring each weather unit.	B. The instrument used to measure the amount of precipitation in a city is called a(an) ______ .

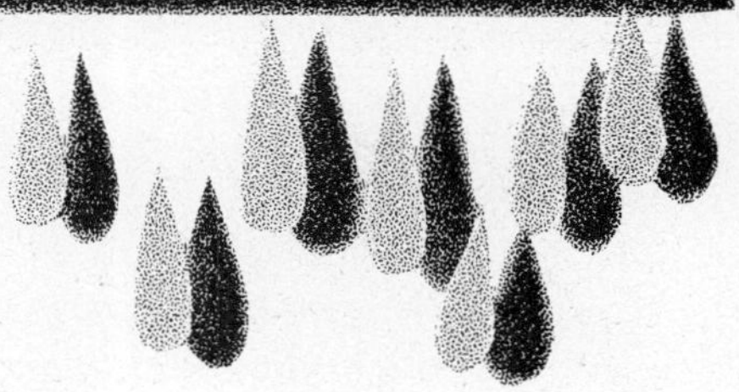

student has mastered. In norm-referenced testing the test items are written to reflect the objectives and content in a more diffuse manner and result in a large spread of scores, which is necessary to reliably rank students in order of achievement. Criterion-referenced testing does not aim for a wide range of scores because the purpose is to have all students master the objectives. Gronlund (1973) states: "If none of the students (or only a few) can answer an item before instruction but all of them can answer it after instruction, both the test items and the instruction have been effective" (p. 15).

The actual construction of norm-referenced and criterion-referenced tests is very similar, using both essay and objective items. The difference lies in the purpose of the tests.

Criterion-referenced testing is a part of individualized programs like Project PLAN (see Chapter 6) and other mastery learning programs when the instructional intent is to raise almost all students to a specified level of achievement. Presently, classroom instruction uses this testing to greatest advantage when the learning outcomes are cumulative and progressively more complex, as in mathematics, reading, and foreign language, and when minimum levels of mastery can be established. When the subject matter is not cumulative, when the student does not need to reach some specified level of competency, as in social studies, and when tests measure success in comparative steps, norm-referenced testing is in its element.

A MASTERY LEARNING APPROACH

Bloom (1968) believes in fixing a mastery level of learning for students. He states that "most students (perhaps over 90%) can master what we have to teach them" (p. 2). The following is an outline of his mastery learning strategy (Bloom, 1971):

1. *The course is broken down into small units covering one or two weeks of instruction.*
2. *The instructional objectives are clearly specified for each unit.*
3. *The learning tasks within each unit are taught using regular group instruction.*
4. *Diagnostic progress tests (formative tests) are administered at the end of each learning unit to determine whether each student has mastered the unit and, if not, what he still has to do to master it.*
5. *Specific procedures for correcting learning deficiencies, such as working with other students in small groups, rereading specific pages, and using programmed materials and audio-visual aids, as well as additional learning time are prescribed for those who did not achieve unit mastery. Retesting may be done after the corrective study.*
6. *When the units are completed, a final test (summative test) is administered to determine course grades. All students who perform at or above the predetermined mastery level receive a grade of A in the course. However, grades are also assigned on the basis of absolute standards that have been set for the course.*

Bloom's strategy differs from conventional classroom instruction in (1) its emphasis on mastery of small learning units, (2) its use of diagnostic progress test to inform students of what impediments still bar their mastery of the subject, and (3) its emphasis on corrective procedures for helping students overcome learning difficulties. The additional learning time provided helps maintain a high level of achievement for all students.

Block (1973) has advanced evidence that mastery learning programs develop positive interests in and positive attitudes toward the subjects in which they are used. Perhaps even more important, students show greater confidence in their ability to learn under the mastery learning approach.

Would you like to be in a course using a mastery approach? Do you see any problems in this approach to learning?

CHARACTERISTICS OF A GOOD TEST

Norm-referenced instruments satisfy certain criteria. The most crucial of these criteria are *validity* and *reliability*.

VALIDITY

Test validity is concerned with the question, Does the test measure what it is supposed to measure? Tests have high, moderate, or low degrees of validity. Because a test can be valid for some purposes but invalid for others, validity does not only refer to the test itself but also to the question, Valid for which purposes? For example, a mathematics test may have high validity for measuring mathematical reasoning but have low validity for measuring computational skills.

Tests are constructed and given for different purposes, causing variations in the actual approach to validity. However, the basic idea subsists. Three types of validity have been identified in educational and psychological measurement: *content* validity, *criterion-related* validity, and *construct* validity. Classroom teachers are most concerned with the first two types of validity.

Content validity aims for an adequate sampling of a specified universe of content. In constructing a test, the teacher should include test items that sufficiently represent the instructional objectives of the unit and the subject-matter content. Many students, after analyzing the test questions in their courses, often remark that some material was not even tested on the examination. Such a test may have low content validity. I will sketch out some guidelines for constructing teacher-made tests later in this chapter.

Criterion-related validity is concerned with two questions: How well does the test judge present ability? and How well does the test judge future ability? The teacher validates the results of a test by comparing the test scores with one of these two criteria.

Let us take two examples of tests. A typing test determines an applicant's ability as a secretary; the Scholastic Aptitude Test (SAT) predicts a student's future academic performance in college. In the

first example, we want to estimate present ability and we obtain the relationship between the test score and present performance at the same time. A high correlation in this case would indicate that the typing test is a good indicator of typing skills on the job. This type of criterion-related validity is often called *concurrent* validity. In the second example, we are interested in prediction, and we extend the criterion related to the test scores over a period of time. This type of criterion-related validity is called *predictive* validity. Time is the variable in the two types of criterion-related validity. The typical procedure for reporting criterion-related validity is by the use of a validity coefficient, which reveals the correlation or relationship between the test and criterion.

The third type of validity is construct validity. Psychologists develop tests to measure traits and abilities such as intelligence, anxiety, creativity, and social adjustment. These traits are also called constructs. The tests determine the "amount" of the trait or construct a person possesses.

Although a test may exhibit more than one type of validity, some tests are constructed with one type of validity in mind. Content validity is an earmark of teacher-made tests and standardized achievement tests. Criterion-related validity is the main factor in intelligence and scholastic aptitude tests used to predict school or college success. Construct validity justifies the use of a test for measuring specific psychological traits or abilities.

RELIABILITY

Reliability is a qualitative judgment about the *consistency* of test scores or other evaluation results from one measure to another. It is difficult to make good judgments based on unreliable test scores. The different methods available for determining reliability are evidence of the recognition that there are different types of consistency. Two important types of reliability are consistency over time and consistency over different forms of an evaluation instrument.

Consistency over time is often referred to as *test-retest* reliability. In this procedure, an individual takes the same test at two different times and the results of the tests are compared by using a correlation coefficient. If the results are very stable — students who score high on the first administration score high on the second administration and low-achieving students score low both times — this consistency will be indicated by a high correlation coefficient.

Consistency over different, but equivalent, forms of the *same* test is determined by administering these forms to the same students in close succession and correlating the resultant scores. This correlation coefficient provides a measure of equivalence indicating the degree to which both forms of the test measure the same aspects of student behavior. A high correlation coefficient would indicate that either test could be used to measure students' knowledge of the material. A low correlation coefficient would indicate that both forms of the test *do not* measure the same material. This type of reliability can measure the growth of students over a period of time. If they are tested at the beginning of the year with form A and at the end of the year with form B, they will be measured by a yardstick of the same behavior.

Teachers can improve the reliability of their tests by (1) including items that discriminate among students, so that almost no one gets all the items correct or incorrect, (2) using objective scoring procedures, and (3) including a sufficient number of test items. For example, it is generally recommended that multiple-choice tests include at least thirty-five to forty items.

STANDARDIZED TESTS

Standardized tests are commercially prepared by measurement experts who have carefully studied all test items. These tests measure various aspects of human behavior under uniform procedures. They each embody a fixed set of questions with the same directions, timing constraints, and scoring procedures. A reference or norm group usually takes a standardized test first so that the teacher can compare his students' performances with those of other students in the nation.

The two types of standardized tests most used in school evaluation programs are aptitude and achievement tests. An aptitude test measures a student's potential for success in learning. Individual and group intelligence tests are the most widely used aptitude tests in school. An achievement test measures how much of the academic content for his grade level a student has absorbed.

Other standardized tests used to a lesser degree in school are interest, attitude, and personality inventories. Guidance counselors use interest inventories to help them in vocational counseling. Attitude and personality inventories identify factors that may influence study habits, motivation, and adjustment in school and are helpful in furthering teachers' understanding of their students.

Since most of the standardized tests used in school are aptitude and achievement tests, I will only be describing these two tests. If your interests lie also with the other types of standardized tests, you can find a discussion of interest, attitude, and personality inventories in books on educational measurement (Sax, 1974; Payne, 1974; Gronlund, 1971).

Aptitude tests help educators in predicting success for students in various educational programs. A common use these test results are put to is organizing groups that are similar in learning abilities. Aptitude tests can identify students needing special attention: the gifted, the mentally retarded, the learning-disabled, and other exceptional children. They are also useful in comparing a student's actual achievement, in the form of school grades, with his potential achievement. Very often the results of an aptitude test indicate that a student has the potential to attain a higher achievement level. Educators often call this student an underachiever. In such a case, the teacher and guidance counselor should investigate the possible reasons for the student's low academic achievement.

Achievement tests serve many functions. A school district can check up on its instructional program by comparing students' test results with those of other students in the nation. If, in the comparison, the students in a high school score consistently lower in mathematics, the school district should evaluate the curriculum and instructional methods in the light of this deficiency. By examining achievement test scores in September, a teacher can determine the achievement level of her students and more accurately plan to stress needed areas during the year. Diagnostic achievement tests are particularly helpful in identifying specific errors of learning that are handicapping a student. For example, difficulty in reading can stem from many causes: comprehension, speed, auditory skills, syllabication, and vocabulary. A diagnostic test will zero in on the specific areas of weakness for remediation.

APTITUDE TESTS

INDIVIDUAL TESTS OF INTELLIGENCE

I discussed the theory and issues of intelligence under the subject of individual differences in Chapter 2. Now I shall enumerate the different types of tests used in schools. When educators mention individual intelligence tests, they are usually referring to the Stanford-Binet and Wechsler tests. They are administered to a single student at a time by a *trained* examiner, usually a school psychologist.

The Binet, as it is often called, yields a single IQ score. It employs a separate set of items for different age levels. Examples of tasks at the six-year level are presented below (Biehler, 1974a):

Six-year level

First test: Defining at least six out of a list of forty-five vocabu-

> lary words. (These are arranged in order of difficulty. Testing stops after six consecutive failures.)
>
> Second test: Explaining the differences between two objects, such as wood and glass. Must get two out of three.
>
> Third test: Telling which feature is missing in a series of "mutilated pictures." Must get four out of five.
>
> Fourth test: Picking out three, ten, six, nine, and then seven cubes from a pile of twelve, to demonstrate the ability to count. Must count at least four of the five trials correctly.
>
> Fifth test: Completing analogies such as "A bird flies, a fish . . ." Must get three out of four.
>
> Sixth test: Solving two out of three simple pencil mazes by tracing the proper pathway. (p. 585)

From these examples it is evident that verbal skills play an important role in success on this test. Since schools emphasize verbal abilities, we find that the Binet correlates well with academic achievement.

Another of the individually administered intelligence tests are the Wechsler Intelligence Scales: Wechsler Preschool and Primary Scale of Intelligence (WPSSI), the revised Wechsler Intelligence Scale for Children (WISC-R), and the Wechsler Adult Intelligence Scale (WAIS). They differ from the Stanford-Binet test on two counts. First, the tests are not constructed by specific age levels but consist of different subtests given to each examinee. Second, the tests yield scores from two sections — verbal and performance — as well as a combined IQ for the whole test.

The WISC-R consists of twelve main tests. The verbal score is measured by the following subtests: General Information, General Comprehension, Arithmetic, Similarities, and Vocabulary, with Digit Span included as an alternate test. The performance score is determined by Picture Completion, Picture Arrangement, Block Design, Object Assembly, and Coding, with Mazes as an alternate test. The total IQ is computed from the combination of the verbal and performance subtests.

If a student took both the Stanford-Binet and WISC-R intelligence tests, she would probably come out with a slightly different score for each. As you might expect, the verbal section of the WISC-R relates more closely to the Stanford-Binet score than does the performance section. In general, the Stanford-Binet is more heavily weighted with verbal ability questions. Bilingual children, children from homes in which English is seldom spoken, and poor readers may have trouble with the Stanford-Binet. The WISC-R covers a broader range of abilities than the Stanford-Binet and is more useful in clinical evaluation, especially in the diagnosis of brain and neurological disorders.

The Test Report. After an examiner administers an individual intelligence test, he scores the responses in the test booklet, computes the subject's IQ, and prepares a report of the subject's test-taking behavior. This last bit of information is sometimes more helpful to the teacher than the reported IQ score. The child's attitude toward the testing situation is telling: Did he pay attention to the examiner's directions? Did he answer the questions immediately, or did he ponder over them? Did he become easily frustrated when difficult questions were asked? Did he appear to be anxious during the testing session? The answers to these questions may answer the teacher's questions about academic placement and remedial help. At the very least, they will help the teacher understand classroom learning problems (Mueller, 1974).

GROUP INTELLIGENCE OR SCHOLASTIC APTITUDE TESTS

Most of the testing in school is done on a group basis. Group intelligence tests, like achievement tests, are usually administered to a large number of students at one time by persons with relatively little training in test administration.

Group tests above the first two or three grades require that the students be able to read the questions and the choice of responses, and indicate their responses on a special answer sheet provided. The type of test items and their level of difficulty are appropriate to various ages and grade levels.

Some group intelligence tests provide a single score similar to the Stanford-Binet, whereas others provide two or more scores based on separate types of mental ability. Examples of single-score tests are the Henmon-Nelson Tests of Mental Ability (grades 3–12) and the Otis-Lennon Mental Ability Test (grades K–12).

Tests representative of a two-factor approach are the Lorge-Thorndike Intelligence Tests (grades 3–13), the California Test of Mental Maturity (CTMM) (grades K–16), and the Kuhlman-Anderson Measure of Academic Potential (grades K–12). Figures 9.1*a* and 9.1*b* include sample test items from the Lorge-Thorndike Intelligence Tests. The verbal battery of tests is composed of five subtests: (1) vocabulary, (2) sentence completion, (3) arithmetic reasoning, (4) verbal classification, and (5) verbal analogy. The nonverbal battery consists of three subtests: (1) pictorial classification, (2) numerical relationships, and (3) pictorial analogy.

In order to clarify the purpose and function of these tests, many

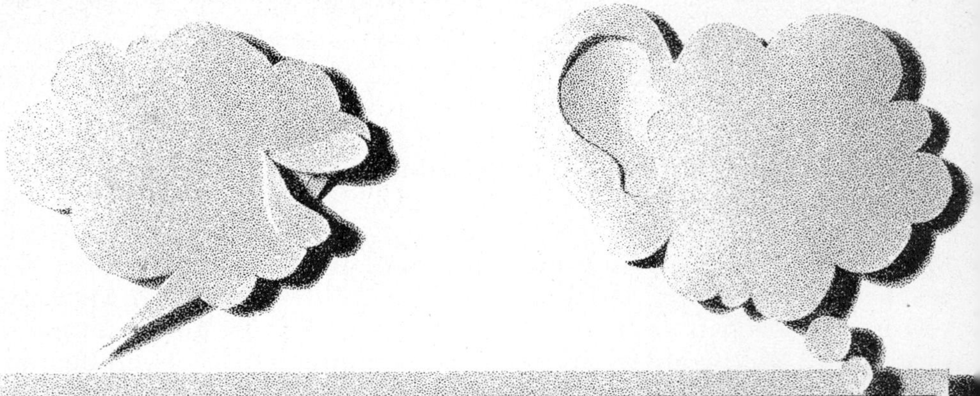

Figure 9.1*a*
Sample Items From the Lorge-Thorndike Intelligence Tests, Verbal Battery.

VOCABULARY (Choose the word that has the same meaning or most nearly the same meaning as the word in dark type.)

loud A quick B noisy C hard D heavy E weak

SENTENCE COMPLETION (Choose the word that will make the best, the truest, and the most sensible complete sentence.)

The sun always rises in the

A east B wind C night D rain E water

ARITHMETIC REASONING (Work the problem and select the answer.)

A boy bought a pencil for 10 cents and some paper for 10 cents. How much did he spend?

A 5 cents B 10 cents C 15 cents D 20 cents E none of these

VERBAL CLASSIFICATION (Choose the word that belongs with the words in dark type.)

go run walk move

A think B dream C march D sing E seem

VERBAL ANALOGIES (Choose the word that is related to the third word in the same way that the second word is related to the first.)

laugh → happy : cry →

A wonder B sad C hide D lost E rough

FIGURE 9.1b

SAMPLE ITEMS FROM THE LORGE-THORNDIKE INTELLIGENCE TESTS, NONVERBAL BATTERY.

FIGURE CLASSIFICATION (Find the drawing at the right that goes with the first three.)

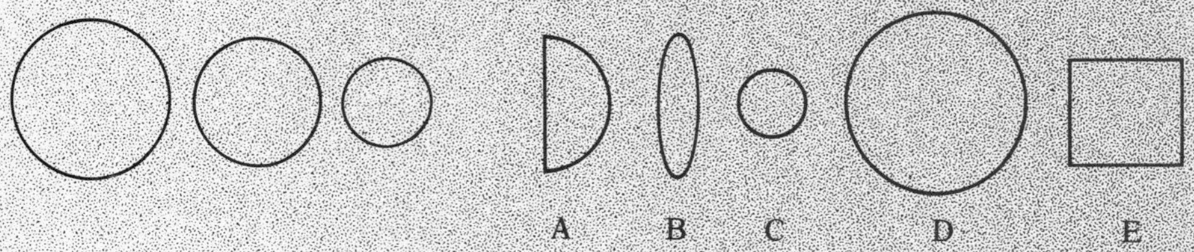

NUMBER SERIES (Find the number at the right that should come next in the series.)

5 5 4 4 3 → A 1 B 2 C 3 D 4 E 5

FIGURE ANALOGIES (Find the drawing at the right that goes with the third drawing in the same way that the second drawing goes with the first.)

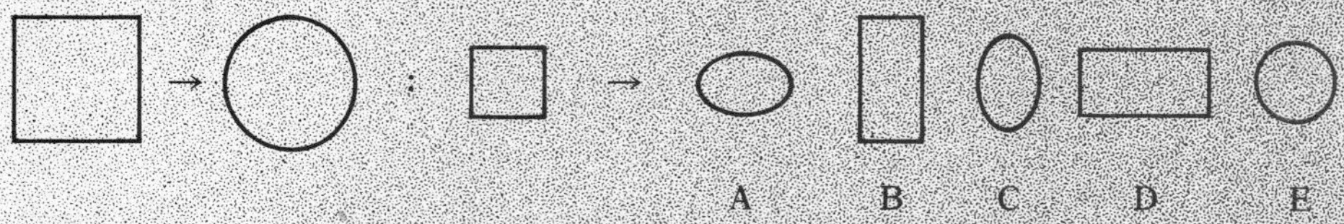

authors have redesignated group intelligence tests as tests of scholastic aptitude or academic aptitude, emphasizing that the tests do not measure inherited capacity but learned abilities or school success. The names of different group tests often cause confusion over what they measure. The names of some achievement tests sound like they should be intelligence tests, and vice versa. Don't make a decision to use a test on its name alone, for it may turn out to measure something entirely different from what you intended it to.

Although group tests are more economical and easier to administer, they have some disadvantages. First, the uninterested and unmotivated student may score lower on a group test than on an individually administered test because he does not have his own examiner to focus specifically on his responses. Second, group tests rely heavily on paper-and-pencil items and emphasize speed, verbal ability, and reading comprehension to a much greater extent than individual tests. Last, the scoring is completely objective and allows no room for judgment of test-taking behavior. It is not uncommon for a teacher to ask for the administration of an individual intelligence test when her information about a student appears to be inconsistent with the group test result.

Cautions in Interpreting IQ Tests. Many problems in IQ testing have arisen from the false belief that test scores are static. Even in the most perfect testing situations, test scores on the same individual can fluctuate many points. The following are some guidelines for interpreting individual test scores (Gronlund, 1971):

1. *An IQ score from the same test can be expected to fluctuate from 5 to 10 points. Given a student's score, say 100, his performance can be most safely interpreted as a band of IQ scores ranging from 95 to 105.*
2. *IQ scores from different tests can be expected to vary. Hieronymus and Stroud (1969) found that this difference could be as large as 8 points in verbal IQ's and less for nonverbal IQ's. Also, since each test measures different aspects of mental ability and is standardized on different populations, the IQ's are not directly comparable. In interpreting IQ scores, we should know the test from which it was derived.*
3. *Greater variation in IQ scores can be expected for elementary school pupils than for high school pupils. This can be accounted for largely by the fact that abilities tend to be less stable during their formation. Be very cautious in making decisions about young children based on IQ scores. (p. 319)*

The above variations occur in normal testing situations. However, greater problems in interpreting and using IQ scores occur when outside factors introduce additional possibilities of error in scores. In general, IQ scores are less dependable for the following types of pupils (Gronlund, 1971):

1. *Students from environments that have denied them full opportunity to learn the types of tasks included in the test*
2. *Students who are not motivated by school-related tasks*
3. *Students who are weak in reading skills or have language handicaps*
4. *Students who have poor emotional adjustment (p. 319)*

ACHIEVEMENT TESTS

The test battery of a standardized achievement test generally consists of individual tests all standardized on the same representative group. The teacher can then compare test scores on the separate subtests to determine the relative strengths and weaknesses of students in the different areas covered by the test (Gronlund, 1971).

Elementary school achievement tests focus on the basic skills taught in school: reading, language, arithmetic, and study skills. Some tests also include measures of achievement in social studies and science.

High school curricula vary more than elementary school curricula, and it is more difficult to develop achievement test batteries with high content validity throughout high schools. Therefore, in addition to using test batteries, high school teachers can select separate tests from specific content-oriented tests to measure achievement in English, social studies, science, or mathematics. Another approach is to use tests that measure general educational development and do not depend on any particular courses for their questions. One such test battery is the Sequential Tests of Educational Progress (STEP). The unique aspect of this test is that it emphasizes application, interpretation, and evaluation of academic content to a greater extent than tests that measure basic skills. Since the questions are not derived from specific course content this test provides a fairer measure of achievement for students with different educational experiences.

Select your achievement tests with care. First, although the tests have similar titles, they often differ in how much emphasis they place on the various skills measured. For example, the specific arithmetic skills tested on two different achievement tests may differ. One might emphasize computational skills and the other, problem-solving abilities. Second, standardized achievement tests measure only a portion of the knowledge and skills taught in school, so be sure to choose the most appropriate test for your school's curriculum.

Teachers can locate information about any standardized test from Buros' *Tests in Print* and *Mental Measurements Yearbook*. The latter source provides reviews of tests by measurement experts. You can order specimen sets of the examinations that appear in Buros from test publishers. These sets include a copy of the actual examination booklet and test manuals that evaluate the validity and reliability of the test. Check the test items against the course content in the areas to be tested to determine whether the test adequately measures the objectives of the school.

The following are some achievement tests commonly used in schools:

California Achievement Tests (grades 1–14)

Iowa Tests of Basic Skills (grades 3–9)

Comprehensive Tests of Basic Skills (grades 2–12)

Metropolitan Achievement Tests (grades 1–12)

SRA Achievement Series (grades 1–9)

Stanford Achievement Tests (grades 1–12)

A special type of achievement test used in schools is the diagnostic test, designed to assess those skills and abilities that are important in learning a particular subject, usually reading and mathematics. The Durrell Analysis of Reading Difficulty, for example, covers student performance in silent and oral reading, listening, comprehension, word analysis, phonetics, pronunciation, writing, and spelling. The teacher can recommend remedial instruction to overcome the learning problems signaled by the Durrell tests.

Beatty, Madden, and Gardner (1966) point out two important differences between a diagnostic and a general achievement test. First, the diagnostic test analyzes knowledge in a single subject area in depth, while the general achievement test collects information on the distribution of knowledge across many subject areas. Second, the diagnostic test includes a larger proportion of items that are relatively easy to answer, the better to assess below-average performance, while the achievement test includes a wider range of items from very easy to very difficult, the better to assess a greater ability span for different grade levels.

CRITICISMS OF STANDARDIZED TESTING

Not all educators are pleased with the extensive use of standardized testing in our nation's schools. In Chapters 2, 4, and 9, I have identified some of the criticisms they have brought to bear on the validity and utilization of tests: Tests discriminate against some individuals, tests presumably measure innate characteristics, and test scores may influence teacher expectations and, of course, behavior regarding student potential and achievement.

In the following article, Holmen and Docter (1974) discuss five criticisms that are independent of test validity. The authors have discussed this topic at greater length in their book, *Educational and Psychological Testing: A Study of the Industry and Its Practices* (New York: Russell Sage Foundation, 1972). Can you identify with any of the authors' concerns?

Criticisms of Standardized Testing

Tests have a harmful effect on the shaping of cognitive styles. The widespread use of mutiple-choice test items, matching items, and other test components with a single correct answer is said by some critics of testing to contribute to undesirable styles of thinking. Some claim that the young student is carefully taught that all problems must have a right or wrong answer, and thus the student is led to think in this manner about all questions.

Tests shape school curriculums and restrict educational change. When teachers know that the evaluation of their students will be based on a particular kind of test of some more or less predictable content, they make extensive efforts to assist their students to perform well on these tests. The proponents of statewide testing programs would probably argue that this is exactly what they have in mind — that teachers ought to be encouraged to cover material which their colleagues consider essential. "What's wrong with this?" they ask.

Critics of testing say that experimentation with new ways of teaching, the introduction of new subject matter, and the whole process of individualizing instruction in terms of the needs and interests of individual students are hamstrung by a slavish adherence to standardized achievement testing. The question seems to come down to finding an acceptable balance between the need to know what has

Adapted from M. Holmen and R. Docter, "Criticisms of standardized testing." *Today's Education* (January–February 1974): 58, 60. Reprinted by permission of the National Education Association and authors.

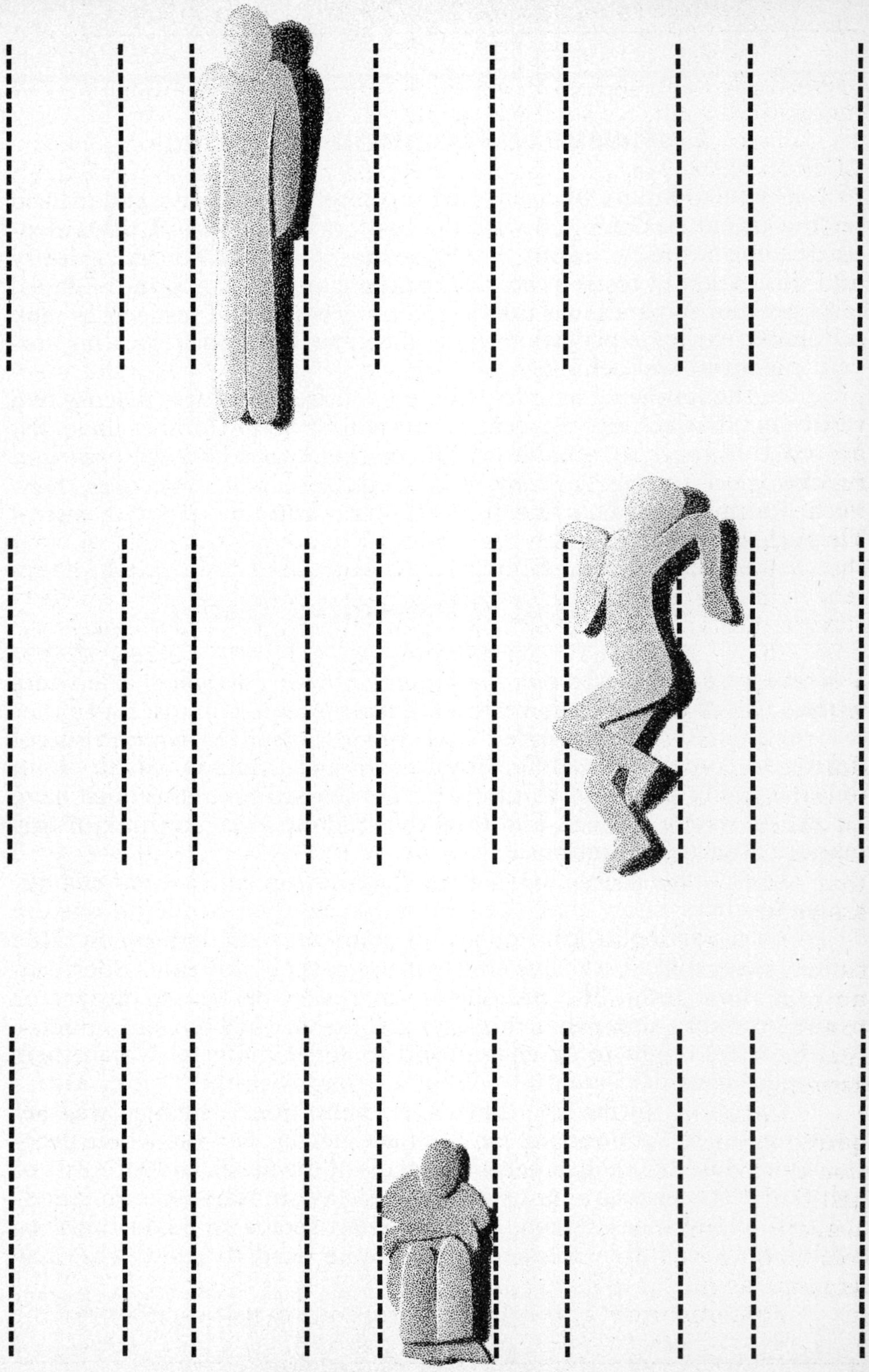

been learned during a given period of time and the encouragement of innovation, change, and experimentation in the classroom.

Tests distort the individual's self-concept and level of aspiration. Of all the criticisms of tests, one of the most penetrating and difficult to dismiss is that young persons may generalize from test results and make conclusions about themselves which are not warranted or intended. For example, consider the teenager who may be struggling to establish a more positive and more realistic self-concept. How helpful is it for him to be shown his low test scores, which may make him conclude that he is far less capable than his classmates?

How many high school students have received brief and inappropriate counseling recommendations, usually based in part on test results, and have concluded from these recommendations that they are not "college material"? One large school district, for example, regularly presents junior high school students with test result summaries printed on cards that the students take home to their parents. These cards offer a lucid and easily understandable summary of what the various achievement and aptitude scores mean. Although the intent is to make information available to parents, there are obviously risks in terms of shaping the attitudes of students toward themselves.

In our view, the proper handling of test results calls for neither a strategy of silence and secrecy nor for open distribution of data without discussion, clarification, and interpretation of meanings.

Tests select homogeneous educational groups. A common procedure in organizing a school is to assign students to classes on the basis of estimates of learning ability. Very often these estimates are based on ability testing. It is a short step to conclude that tests have determined the organizational style of schools, and it may surely be argued that tests do indeed contribute to the way in which students are assigned.

Critics of the ability-track system, as this arrangement is often called, frequently see educational testing as the bad guy. But, were no test data available, an educational administrator dedicated to ability-track grouping could find numerous criteria, such as grades, teachers' ratings of ability, and so forth, for making these assignments.

Concerns about homogeneous grouping in schools have acquired strength with recent research which suggests that this allocation procedure tends to do more harm to the low groups than can be justified. The proponents of heterogeneous assignment to classes argue that children with lower ability need the stimulation and the role models provided by higher-ability students if they are to achieve as much as they possibly can.

Contemporary approaches to school organization stress the

importance of providing a program of individual instruction for each child, regardless of the range of competencies within a class. Educators are now stressing the positive influences of heterogeneous grouping, with the result that the track system is generally thought to be on the way out. But for the parents of children who are assigned to low groups, the track system is an unpleasant reality based primarily on test results. Hence, since tests are often painted as the villain in the situation, it is assumed that banning tests will eliminate the track system.

However, with regard to a school district set on the perpetuation of homogeneous ability grouping, the problem is not so much one of testing or not testing, but rather one of adherence to a questionable concept of educational organization.

Tests invade privacy. School attendance is mandatory for young children. Once in school, the children are generally required to participate in activities, including testing, which some parents consider to be invasions of privacy.

Certainly few would argue against allowing schools to give tests to determine what a student has learned in some course of study, but should schools be allowed to require students to take intelligence tests? What good is such information to a school? Can data from some tests be used to the disadvantage of a student without his knowledge that such information even exists? How can the line be more clearly established between information that a school requires to help reach a legitimate decision and information that it has no business acquiring in the first place? The right to privacy is precious to the citizens of a free society; only when there is compelling justification should tests invading privacy be used.

TESTS AS GATEKEEPERS: THE CENTRAL CRITICISM

At the heart of the criticisms about tests and testing programs is one fact that is likely to help perpetuate at least some of the criticism: Tests are often used as tools for the allocation of limited resources or opportunities. Put another way, educational and psychological tests are frequently designed to measure differences among individuals so that one person receives a reward or privilege which another is then denied.

For example, we see this in the assignment of elementary school children to classes for the gifted or in the selection of students for college admission or for advanced professional study. Tests, therefore, are likely to stir strong emotions, for they serve in many different ways as gatekeepers, opening and closing pathways of human opportunity.

Are tests necessarily the kind of gatekeepers we want? This is a question involving individual values, organizational goals, and, increasingly, laws and regulations designed to assure equal access to educational and employment opportunities. One thing is certain: Tests are no longer granted any immunity or magical status, nor are they assumed to be good simply because of their objectivity or psychometric purity. The lawmaker as well as the man on the street has a skeptical eye on educational and psychological testing.

There have been too many serious lapses of professional judgment, not only by those who are using tests without the proper qualifications, but also by professionals who should know better. And minority groups' intense concern for fair play relative to testing is not going to evaporate; indeed, it will probably be expressed with increasing vehemence.

However, while we may anticipate continued criticism of tests for a variety of reasons, testing programs that measure up to high professional standards and can be shown to make constructive contributions to human assessment may well be regarded as beneficial by most people.

TEACHER-MADE TESTS

Although standardized tests play an important role in measurement and evaluation in education, most tests used in school are developed by classroom teachers. Standardized tests will seldom fit the specific content and objectives in any given course. If Mr. Jones wants to measure student learning at the end of a unit on the Civil War, he will have to construct his own test.

Standardized tests are useful for determining how local achievement compares to national norms. The teacher-made test is more useful for measuring local classroom instruction. Table 9.1 presents the comparative advantages of teacher-made and standardized tests of achievement.

Teacher-made achievement tests are usually divided into two categories: (1) the objective tests, which are highly structured and limit the type of response a student can make. The answer key designates a response as either correct or incorrect. These tests include multiple-choice, completion, matching, and true-false items; (2) the subjective or essay tests, which allow a student to impose his own organization on the material and present it in his own words. In scoring an essay test, the teacher must make qualitative decisions about how close a student's answer is to the model answer.

There are no definite rules for using an objective or subjective

TABLE 9.1
COMPARISONS BETWEEN TEACHER-MADE AND STANDARDIZED ACHIEVEMENT TESTS.

CHARACTERISTIC	*TEACHER-MADE ACHIEVEMENT TESTS*	*STANDARDIZED ACHIEVEMENT TESTS*
Directions for administration and scoring	Usually no uniform directions specified	Specific instructions standardize administration and scoring procedures
Sampling of content	Both content and sampling are determined by classroom teacher	Content determined by curriculum and subject-matter experts; involves extensive investigations of existing syllabi, textbooks, and programs; sampling of content done systematically
Construction	May be hurried and haphazard; often no test blueprints, item tryouts, item analysis or revision; quality of test may be quite poor	Uses meticulous construction procedures that include constructing objectives and test blueprints, employing item tryouts, item analysis, and item revisions
Norms	Only local classroom norms are available	In addition to local norms, standardized tests typically make available national, school district, and school building norms
Purposes and use	Best suited for measuring particular objectives set by teacher and for intraclass comparisons	Best suited for measuring broader curriculum objectives and for interclass, school, and national comparisons

test other than the considerations of what the teacher wants to measure and the available time for the task. Many teachers use combinations of both types of tests, since each has its merits and limitations. A comparison of essay and objective tests appears in Table 9.2.

Taking time to plan a test pays dividends in a more reliable and valid measurement instrument. Too often, teachers whip up tests at the last minute without giving careful consideration even to the purpose of the examination. Mr. Smith, an American history teacher, announces on Monday a test for Wednesday. After school he skims through the textbook and his lecture notes for information for the examination. He writes test items until he is satisfied that he has a sufficient number for the test.

Mr. Smith's strategy raises a number of questions. First, does he know what learning outcomes he is measuring? If he spent most of the class time on the *analysis* of political parties' influence on foreign policy, his examination should emphasize this learning outcome and not the *recall* of factual material about the parties. Second, did he adequately cover the content of the entire unit? Perhaps he completed his test items before reaching the last chapter in the book and failed to include any questions from an important section of the material. The first question asks the teacher to think about the cognitive level of the test item. The second question shows concern for adequate coverage of the material. Taken together, the answers to these questions evaluate the content validity of the measuring instrument.

Think about the tests you have taken during your school experience. Can you identify situations in which "important" lecture information or required readings were not even included in the examination? What about the level of questions? Have you taken examinations that asked for an almost total regurgitation of factual material? Make a list of some characteristics of teacher-made tests that have irritated you at some time during your academic career. Maybe *your* instructor would like to see your list!

PLANNING THE TEST

Before beginning to write any test items, the teacher should perform three tasks. These steps can alleviate many problems in the nature and scope of the examination.

1. Identify the learning outcomes to be measured by the test. *Here is where instructional objectives and the* Taxonomy of Educational Objectives *come in handy. If you have written objectives before instruction, you should have little difficulty in completing this planning phase. If you had no specified objec-*

TABLE 9.2
A COMPARISON OF ESSAY AND OBJECTIVE TESTS.

	ESSAY	*OBJECTIVE*
ABILITIES MEASURED	Requires the student to express himself in his own words, using information from his own background and knowledge.	Requires the student to select correct answers from given options, or to supply an answer limited to one word or phrase.
	Can tap high levels of reasoning such as required in inference, organization of ideas, comparison and contrast.	Can also tap high levels of reasoning such as required in inference, organization of ideas, comparison, and contrast.
	Does not measure purely factual information efficiently.	Measures knowledge of facts efficiently.
SCOPE	Covers only a limited field of knowledge in any one test. Essay questions take so long to answer that relatively few can be answered in a given period of time. Also, the student who is especially fluent can often avoid discussing points of which he is unsure.	Covers a broad field of knowledge in one test. Since objective questions may be answered quickly, one test may contain many questions. A broad coverage helps provide reliable measurement.
INCENTIVE TO PUPILS	Encourages pupils to learn how to organize their own ideas and express them effectively.	Encourages pupils to build up a broad background of knowledge and abilities.
EASE OF PREPARATION	Requires writing only a few questions for a test. Tasks must be clearly defined, general enough to offer some leeway, specific enough to set limits.	Requires writing many questions for a test. Wording must avoid ambiguities and "giveaways." Distractors should embody most likely misconceptions.
SCORING	Usually very time-consuming to score.	Can be scored quickly.
	Permits teachers to comment directly on the reasoning processes of individual pupils. However, an answer may be scored differently by different teachers or by the same teacher at different times.	Answer generally scored only right or wrong, but scoring is very accurate and consistent.

TABLE 9.3
A TEST PLAN FOR A UNIT ON TEST CONSTRUCTION.

	CHARACTERISTICS OF A GOOD TEST	*PLANNING A TEST*	*WRITING TEST ITEMS*
EVALUATION			
SYNTHESIS			
ANALYSIS			
APPLICATION			
COMPREHENSION			
KNOWLEDGE			

tives for the unit, this initial step will take you more time and effort.

2. Outline the subject-matter content to be measured by the test. *This step is taken to ensure that you identify all important content.*

3. Prepare a test plan or table of specifications. *A table of specifications is a two-dimensional table on which the learning outcomes are listed along one side and the subject-matter topics along the other side. The intersecting cells in the table allow the teacher to fill in the proportion of test items devoted to each learning outcome and each subject-matter topic. An example of a table of specifications for a short unit on test construction is presented in Table 9.3.*

As the teacher writes a test item, she makes a tally in the corresponding cell in the table. This procedure directs the teacher's attention to the assessment of instructional outcomes other than those at the knowledge level and ensures that she draws test items from the different topics or readings in the unit. By examining the table, the teacher can easily determine whether the items adequately measure the nature of the instruction.

Regardless of the type of test items written for an examination, there are some general guidelines about writing tests that are always applicable (Chase, 1974):

1. *Avoid replication of the textbook in writing test items.*
2. *Begin writing items well in advance of the test, and allow time for test revision.*
3. *Avoid trick items and procedures.*
4. *Make sure the directions are clear.*

The last two guidelines are expecially important. Some teachers forget that the purpose of examinations is to assess students and not to outwit them.

WRITING TEST ITEMS

I shall now examine commonly used types of objective test items — multiple-choice, matching, completion, and true-false — and then go on to essay items. You will learn about the physical makeup of these items and how to write your own. I will also present the pros and cons of their use.

MULTIPLE-CHOICE ITEMS

The multiple-choice item contains a *stem,* which identifies a problem situation, and several *alternatives* or *options,* which provide possible solutions to the problem. The alternatives include a correct answer and several plausible wrong answers, or distractors. The stem may be stated as a direct question or an incomplete statement. The student's task is to select the correct (or best) response from the list of alternatives provided. The following are examples of multiple-choice items with the two types of stems:

Question variety

Stem: What is the most important type of validity in teacher-made tests?

Responses: A. predictive
B. content
C. construct
D. concurrent

Incomplete statement variety

Stem: The arithmetic average is the same as the
Responses: A. median
B. mode
C. mean
D. variance

Some items are more easily written in one format than in the other. The question format is generally easier to write and encourages the item writer to pose a clear problem, but it often results in a longer stem.

Most multiple-choice items offer four or five choices to reduce the student's chances of obtaining a correct response by guessing. There is no reason for all items on the test to include the same number of alternatives; some items generate more plausible distractors than others.

The quality of a multiple-choice item is a combination of the clarity of the stem and the skill with which the various alternatives are written. Here are some suggestions for writing multiple-choice items:

1. *Make all alternative responses grammatically consistent with the stem and parallel in form. Suppose the test item presented earlier was written as follows:*

   The type of validity of major concern in teacher-made tests is
   1. predictive and concurrent
   2. content
   3. construct and content
   4. predictive and construct

   Since the item asks for type, *a student could eliminate alternatives 1, 3, and 4 because they include more than one type.*

2. *Avoid making the correct response consistently longer or shorter than the others.*
3. *Underline negative wording whenever it is used in the stem of an item.*
4. *Avoid overuse of the alternatives "all of the above" and "none of the above."*

5. *Vary the position of the correct answer in a random manner.*
6. *Make certain each item is independent of the other items in the test.*

The multiple-choice item has numerous merits. First, it can measure objectives from the entry knowledge level to the most complex level. Second, the teacher can sample a great deal of information in a relatively short time. Third, scoring is completely objective; the correct answer is not open to interpretation. Last, as I have already stated, the four or five choices reduce the possibility of obtaining a correct answer through guessing.

The main problems with multiple-choice items are the difficulty of writing test items and students' complaint that there is more than one defensible "correct" answer. You can remedy the latter problem by carefully writing items (Sax, 1974).

Students often discuss the advisability of changing answers on multiple-choice tests. Students commonly believed that they should stick with their first answer. However, research evidence does not support this position. The research studies on this issue find that students who change their responses to test items raise their score (Reiling & Taylor, 1972; Lynch & Smith, 1972). One explanation for this finding is that students taking examinations are aided by information from other test items as they go along, so that careful reconsideration can result in a correct response. Does this finding appear inconsistent with your own experience?

Lynch and Smith (1972) think that when students go over a corrected examination, they are more concerned with why they got a question wrong than with why they got certain questions right. They are more likely to notice right-to-wrong changes and conclude that changing responses lowers test scores. Thus, many students do not change responses. A good rule to follow if you understand a question better or recall additional information: Change your answer!

MATCHING ITEMS

The matching item is a modification of the multiple-choice form. A series of stems appear in one column and the responses in another. The student must select the option that is correctly associated with the stem. The following is an example of such an item:

In the left-hand column are terms associated with different psychologists and educators. For each term, choose a name from the right-hand column and place the letter identifying it on the line preceding the number of the term.

___1. self-actualization	a) Skinner
___2. mastery learning	b) Maslow

__3. operant conditioning	c) Thorndike
__4. assimilation	d) Bloom
__5. learning hierarchy	e) Gagné
	f) Binet

The following are some suggestions for constructing matching tests:

1. *Include only homogeneous material in each matching exercise.*
2. *Indicate clearly the basis on which the matching is to be done.*
3. *The questions should contain at least five and not more than fifteen items.*
4. *The items in the response column should be arranged in systematic order. Dates should be in chronological order, whereas names of people, terms, and so on should be in alphabetical order. This reduces the amount of time needed to search for the correct response.*
5. *All the items should be on a single page, not as shown above!*

The matching item is most appropriate for assessing associations. It is not readily adaptable for measuring complex levels of learning.

COMPLETION ITEMS

A completion, or fill-in-the-blank, item confronts the individual with a statement for which he must supply a missing word or phrase. This type of item emphasizes *recall* of previously learned material rather than recognition.

The Stanford-Binet is an example of a(n) ______ test.

The following are some suggestions for construction of completion items:

1. *Omit key words and phrases rather than trivial details.*
2. *Avoid overmutilated statements, such as the ______ and ______ were ______ in World War II.*
3. *If possible, items should require a single-word answer.*
4. *Avoid lifting statements directly from the text.*
5. *Make the blanks of uniform length.*
6. *Avoid grammatical clues to the expected answer.*
7. *Arrange the test with the answers in a column for easier scoring.*

8. *Prepare a scoring key that contains all acceptable answers.*

The completion item is relatively easy to construct. It requires recall of information, so it reduces the possibility of guessing the correct answer from the correct response.

The completion item has its limits. Scoring completion items is difficult because constructing them for only one answer is difficult. Second, answers are restricted to a few words and the items tend to measure recall of specific facts rather than more complex learning outcomes.

TRUE-FALSE ITEMS

The true-false item is a declarative sentence that the test taker must decide is correct (true) or incorrect (false).

T F A table of specifications is used to plan for teacher-made tests.

The following are some suggestions for constructing true-false items:

1. *Include only one central idea in each statement.*
2. *Word the statement so precisely that it is unequivocally true or false.*
3. *Keep the statements short and use simple language.*
4. *Use negative statements sparingly and avoid double negatives.*
5. *Avoid use of specific determiners such as "always," "never," and "seldom."*
6. *Attribute statements of opinion to a source.*
7. *Avoid a disproportionate number of either true or false statements.*
8. *Explain the desired method of marking before the student begins the test. You may have him write out the words "true" or "false" or circle the correct letter.*

The advantage of the true-false item is that it tends to be brief. The teacher can ask questions covering a great deal of material and can score the items in a short time. Because true-false items emphasize memorization of facts and are open to guesswork they have their limits, too.

ESSAY QUESTIONS

Essay questions are used to their best advantage in measuring higher-order mental processes — application, analysis, synthesis, and evaluation — and should not be used to measure knowledge of facts or principles. They provide an opportunity for the student to use his own words, style, and organization in dealing with the subject matter of a course.

Teachers should be aware of at least three limitations of essay questions. First is the problem of content validity. An adequate sampling of the content and objectives of a unit or course by essay questions is impossible. These questions take more time to answer than objective items, limiting the number of questions that can be asked and thus limiting the content coverage of the examination.

Second, subjective scoring makes essay test results lower in reliability than objective tests, which use more precise scoring. A number of extraneous factors can influence a teacher's scoring of an essay question. Handwriting, the use of pen rather than pencil, and spelling and grammatical errors will probably disincline the teacher toward the student. A "halo effect," which occurs when a teacher's general impression of the student affects the evaluation of the paper, is an unfortunate possibility. This effect can be either positive or negative.

Last, although essay questions take less time to write than objective questions, they relinquish this gain in the scoring. For this reason, teachers with large classes often limit essay testing to very specific objectives.

The following are some suggestions for constructing essay questions:

1. *Use essay questions to measure complex learning outcomes only.*

2. *Relate the questions as directly as possible to the learning outcomes being measured. Gorman (1974) suggests some key words that relate to specific types of learning you may wish to measure:*

words	define, what is the meaning
facts	state, identify, describe
concepts	explain, distinguish between
relations	explain giving reasons, examples
structures	explain the interrelationships, show how it is organized
comprehension	give the meaning, summarize
creativity	write a theme, develop a plan, suggest
problem solving	what was the cause

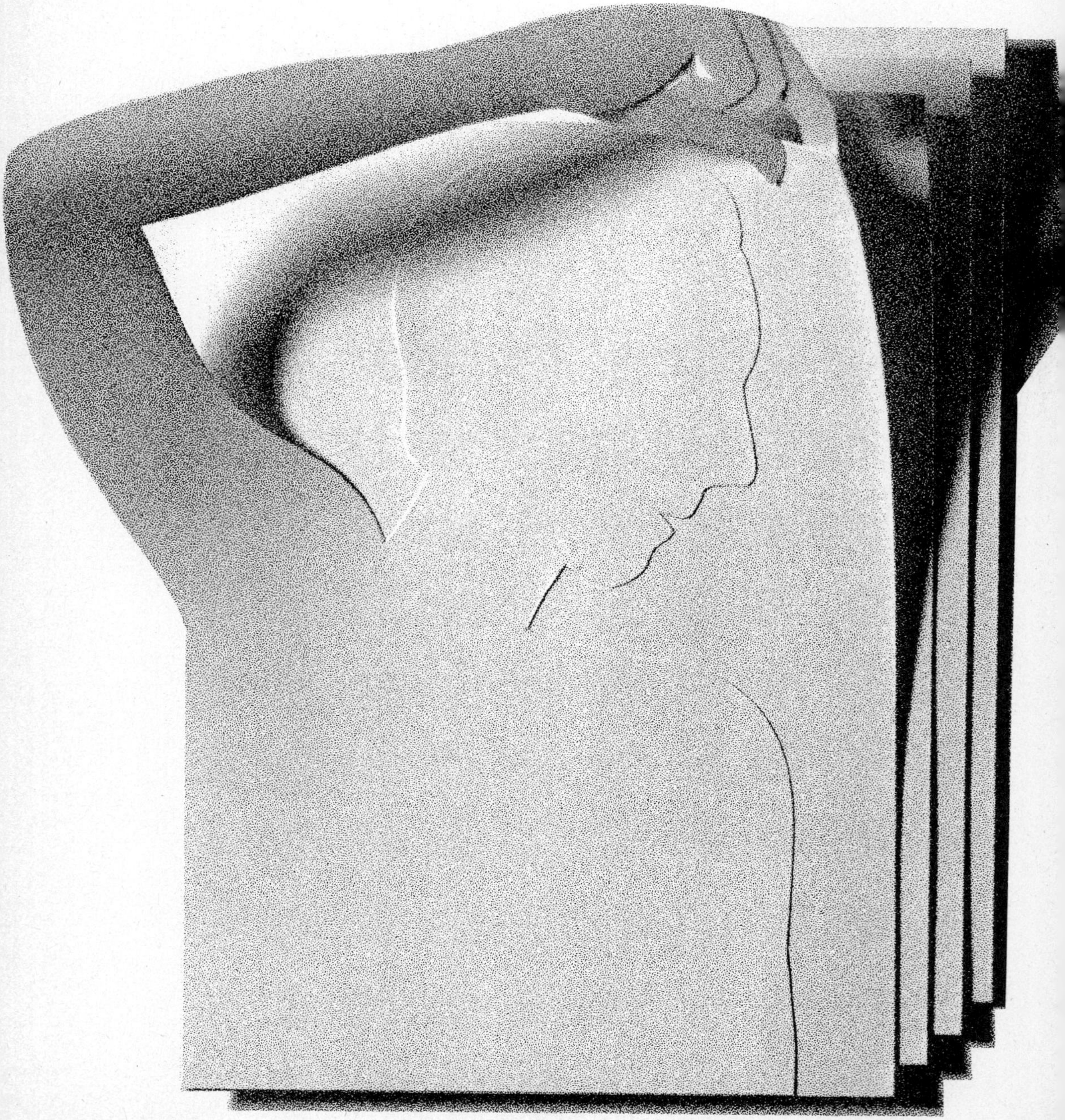

analysis	compare, contrast, distinguish
critical thinking	criticize (on the basis of . . .), evaluate
application, transfer	(given an example or case) explain in terms of . . . (p. 422)

3. *Formulate questions that present a clear, definite task to the student. For example, look at the following questions:*
   a) Discuss essay tests.
   b) Discuss the merits and limitations of essay tests.
   The first question is too general because it allows the student to write whatever he wants. The second question focuses specifically on the particular response requested of the student.
4. *Provide ample time for answering and give suggested time limits for each question.*

Since subjectivity in scoring is one of the major limitations of the essay question, the following guidelines for uniform standards in scoring are suggested to reduce (although not totally alleviate) this problem (Gronlund, 1971):

1. Prepare in advance a model answer and the number of credit points allowed for each question. *You have now set a standard against which all students will be judged. By determining the number of points for each question, you can further subdivide the points for various parts of the answer.*
2. Grade all papers without knowledge of the "author." *This procedure attempts to counteract the halo effect. You can implement it in two ways. One method is to ask each student to write his name on the back of the examination booklet so that the teacher won't know which student he is evaluating. A second method is to pass a sheet of paper containing a series of numbers and ask each student to write his name on the sheet opposite one of the numbers. The students place their number instead of their name on the examination booklet. After all the students have signed the sheet, take it and file it until all the examinations are scored. Only then are the students' names matched with their numbers for recording the grades. Of course, if a teacher is familiar with the handwriting of his students, these procedures would not reduce the halo effect.*
3. Grade only one question at a time for all papers. *By grading the first question for all students before moving on to the next question, the teacher is more likely to use the same standard for every student. When you switch from one model answer to*

another in grading each question in one paper, you will probably modify the standard. This question-by-question procedure can also limit the halo effect. Suppose a student does poorly on the first three questions of an examination but does very well on the fourth question. If the teacher had graded each student's complete paper, he might be prejudiced by the student's poor start. His expectations would preclude his adequately crediting the student's response to question four.

4. Write comments as well as grades on the paper. *Students frequently hear that examinations are learning experiences. If this is to be true, the teacher should briefly explain deficiencies in the student's responses for his benefit. Students also like to be praised for their good work. If they only receive criticism, they might develop anxiety about writing. Can you remember any personal experiences, bad or good, with teacher evaluations of your essays or term papers?*

MEASURING AFFECTIVE OUTCOMES

When teachers need to measure the outcomes of affective objectives or to learn more about the personal concerns of their students, they can construct their own surveys. Open-ended questions and questionnaires are useful formats for eliciting such information.

OPEN-ENDED QUESTIONS

Open-ended or incomplete sentences require the student to complete a statement in any way she chooses, thereby revealing what feelings and attitudes the topics arouse in her. The following examples illustrate stimuli that will evoke student responses:

My teacher . . .
What I want most . . .
I am happiest when . . .
The thing I like most about this class . . .
The thing I like least about this class . . .
Other boys (girls) . . .

QUESTIONNAIRES

Questionnaires can be designed to obtain a wide variety of responses regarding student problems, attitudes, and interests. The following are some of the different forms questionnaires can take:

A. *On the next social studies unit*
   1. *I want to work alone.*
   2. *I want to work with one or two friends.*
   3. *I want to work with a group.*

B. *Forty minutes of science is*
   1. *too much.*
   2. *about right.*
   3. *not enough.*

	Always	Sometimes	Never
C. *Does the teacher give you enough time to finish tests?*			
Does the teacher listen to you when you have a problem?			
Does time go quickly in this class?			

D. *For each activity listed below, circle the choice that best represents how you feel about the activity in question. SL means "strongly like"; L means "like"; I means "indifferent to"; D means "dislike"; and SD means "strongly dislike."*
   1. *Spending time in a library*
      SL   L   I   D   SD
   2. *Listening to the top musical hits of the week*
      SL   L   I   D   SD

KEY POINTS

1. *Norm-referenced measurement interprets student performance relative to a group.*
2. *Criterion-referenced measurement interprets student performance with respect to a specified behavioral criterion of proficiency.*
3. *In mastery testing, the teacher wants to find out whether the student has or has not satisfactorily mastered the objectives.*
4. *Validity and reliability are two important criteria for evaluating the quality of tests.*
5. *Validity determines whether the test measures what it is supposed to measure. A test may be valid for one purpose but not for another.*
6. *Content validity involves how well the items on a test sample a defined universe of tasks.*
7. *Criterion-related validity involves the ability of a test to either*

verify or predict an individual's status in relation to a criterion.

8. *Construct validity justifies the use of a test for measuring specific psychological traits or constructs.*
9. *Reliability refers to the consistency of test scores or other evaluation results from one measure to another.*
10. *Test-retest reliability is a measure of the consistency of test results for the same test over time.*
11. *Equivalent-forms reliability is a measure of the consistency of test results over different but similar forms of the same test.*
12. *Standardized tests are commercially prepared by measurement experts and measure behavior under uniform procedures.*
13. *Achievement tests measure a student's knowledge in a particular academic area at some point in time.*
14. *Diagnostic achievement tests, usually used in reading and arithmetic, analyze student strengths and weaknesses in detail.*
15. *Aptitude tests predict the student's probability of success in various educational programs.*
16. *Intelligence tests are the most common aptitude tests used in school.*
17. *The Stanford-Binet and Wechsler are two individually administered intelligence tests.*
18. *Group intelligence or scholastic aptitude tests are the most widely used measures of academic aptitude.*
19. *Teachers must not be hasty in interpreting IQ scores of students who have not had an opportunity to learn tasks included in the test, are unmotivated, have poor reading skills, or are not well adjusted emotionally.*
20. *Information on standardized tests can be located in Buros'* Tests in Print *and* Mental Measurements Yearbook.
21. *Standardized achievement tests usually include a test battery of individual tests all standardized on the same representative group.*
22. *Many educators criticize standardized tests. These criticisms pertain to both the validity and use of the tests.*

23. *The main advantage of teacher-made classroom tests over standardized tests is their greater relevance to the local curriculum.*

24. *The development of a table of specifications (a two-way grid integrating content and behavioral outcomes) can make test development easier for the teacher.*

25. *Teacher-made tests include objective and essay items.*

26. *The multiple-choice test can be used to measure objectives at all levels of complexity.*

27. *Essay tests are most appropriate for measuring the higher-order mental processes of application, analysis, synthesis, and evaluation.*

SUGGESTIONS FOR FURTHER READING

Bloom, B., Hastings, T., & Madaus, G. *Handbook on formative and summative evaluation of student learning.* New York: McGraw-Hill, 1971. This book includes a good chapter on affective evaluation methods.

Gronlund, N. *Preparing criterion-referenced tests for classroom instruction.* New York: Macmillan, 1973. This book provides a concise discussion of the construction of criterion-referenced tests.

Samuda, R. J. *Psychological testing of American minorities: Issues and consequences.* New York: Dodd, Mead, 1975. A discussion of important issues in the testing of minority students.

Smith, R. M. (Ed.). *Teacher diagnosis of educational difficulties.* Columbus, Ohio: Merrill, 1969. A good source for diagnostic testing in various specific areas.

TenBrink, T. D. *Evaluation: A practical guide for teachers.* New York: McGraw-Hill, 1974. An evaluation text based on a decision-making model.

FOLLOW-UP ACTIVITIES

1 Identify your position on the importance of standardized tests. Which of the following statements comes closest to representing your position on standardized tests? Defend your selection.

Pro: Standardized tests serve an important function by helping the school assess a student's achievement, assisting in academic and vocational guidance, and determining placement in appropriate classes. Without these tests teachers and administrators would make greater errors in their decisions.

Con: Schools spend too much time testing students. Most tests have little impact on student learning and should be abolished. Better decisions can be made without these tests.

2 **Use Buros' *Mental Measurements Yearbook*.** Select two or three standardized tests that a school district could use for a subject area or grade level of interest to you. Use Buros' *Mental Measurements Yearbook* to report on the merits and limitations of each test.

3 **Evaluate teacher-made tests.** What types of teacher-made tests have given you the greatest aggravation in the past? Why? Obtain a copy of a teacher-made test and analyze it for examples of faulty test construction. If you cannot obtain a copy of a test, report on faulty items in a test you have recently taken. Discuss the modifications you would make in the items.

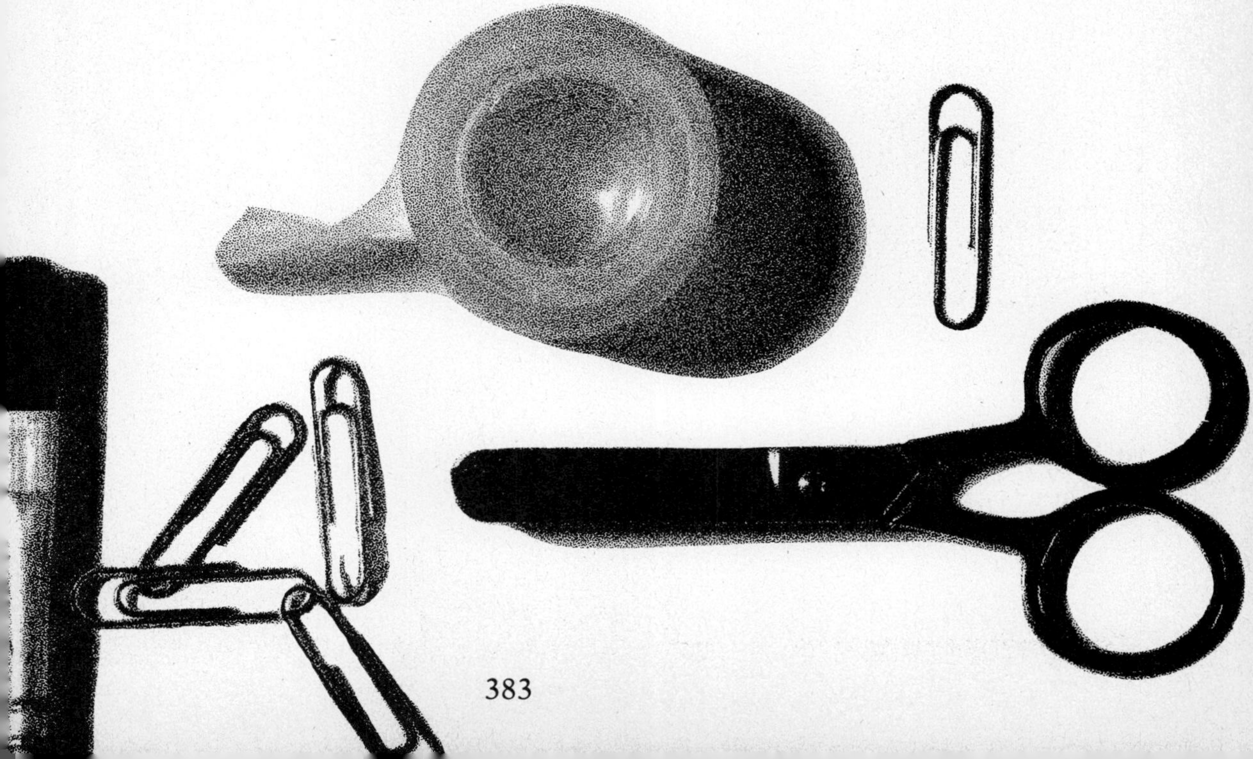

4 **Write exam questions.** Write one exam question on material covered in Chapter 9. Adapt your question to true-false, completion, four-item matching, multiple-choice, and short-answer formats. Ask a classmate to answer them. The response to the short-answer item should be two to four sentences long. Evaluate the answers, provide feedback, and ask for criticisms and suggestions.

5 Analyze test questions. Obtain a copy of a teacher-made test and classify each question according to both the *Taxonomy of Educational Objectives: Cognitive Domain* and Guilford's (1959) description of intellectual operations. Does one type of thinking dominate the test?

Taxonomy of Educational Objectives: Cognitive Domain
Knowledge
Comprehension
Application
Analysis
Synthesis
Evaluation

Guilford's Intellectual Operations
Cognition
Memory
Convergent production
Divergent production
Evaluation

ANALYZING TEST SCORES AND REPORTING STUDENT PROGRESS

ORIENTATION

Now that you know how to use the various tests in school, you need to know how to interpret the test results. This chapter describes some elementary statistical procedures used to determine the meaning of a test score.

After tests are scored, it is the teacher's responsibility to summarize and interpret the meaning of the scores and to compare performances among students. The basic statistical methods outlined here will be your tools for evaluating and reporting test results.

Toward the latter part of the chapter, I will ask you to think about the importance of grades in education. To what extent do they help or hinder academic achievement?

FREQUENCY DISTRIBUTION

One of the first steps in analyzing test scores is the construction of a *frequency distribution* of the scores. This is simply a table that summarizes how often each score occurs. By inspecting this table, the teacher can determine the distribution of test scores in his class.

MEASURES OF CENTRAL TENDENCY

As part of the analysis of a distribution of scores we often need to calculate various measures of the average or typical performance of the group as a whole. These averages are called *measures of central tendency*, most familiar of these being the mean, the median, and the mode. Let's use the following small distribution of scores to determine the three measures: 8, 10, 12, 13, 16, 16, 23.

The mean is the arithmetic average of a set of scores, the result of adding the scores and dividing this sum by the number of scores.

$$\text{Mean} = \frac{\sum X}{N} = \frac{98}{7} = 14.$$

$\sum$ signifies "sum" whatever follows. The letter X stands for any score value, and N equals the number of scores. The symbol M or X is often used to denote the mean.

The median is another measure of central tendency representing the middle score in a distribution. The median in the sample distribution is 13. In an even number of scores (8, 10, 20, 32), there are two middle values; in this case, the median is the mean of the two middle scores ($[10 + 20] \div 2 = 15$).

The third measure of central tendency is the mode, or the score with the highest frequency of occurrence. The mode in the sample distribution is 16. When a distribution has two most frequently occurring scores, it is a bimodal distribution.

All three of these measures provide an indication of the average, but their usefulness often hinges on the character of the score distribution. The mean generally gives the best average of test scores. However, when there are extreme scores in the distribution, the median can better describe the average. Look at the following distribution of scores: 90, 43, 40, 30, 22. The mean is 45 and the median is 40. Four of the five scores are less than the mean because of the one extreme score. In this case the mean gives a false impression of the actual central tendency of scores and the median is a better indicator of the average. The mode is not used as often as the mean and median but is appropriate when there are a large number of common scores.

VARIABILITY

Although the measures of central tendency provide helpful information for interpreting test scores, they don't take into consideration an important characteristic of test scores. Look closely at the following distribution:

	GROUP A	GROUP B	
	96	82	
	98	90	
Mean = 100 Median = 100	100	100	Mean = 100 Median = 100
	102	110	
	104	118	

Although the two distributions exhibit the same mean and median, the variability or dispersion of the scores differ. One indicator of the variability is the range of scores. In group A, the range is 8 (104 − 96); the range for group B is 34 (118 − 82).

Range tells us the variability between the highest and lowest scores in a distribution, but it doesn't tell us anything about the variability between the mean and the rest of the distribution. For this reason, the *standard deviation* is the most important measure of variability because it provides a measure of how dispersed or spread out the scores are around the mean. The more spread out from the mean, the larger the standard deviation. The more scores clustering around the mean, the smaller the standard deviation. The standard deviation for the scores in group A and group B are 10 and 14, respectively.

The formula for determining the standard deviation is

$$s = \sqrt{\frac{\sum (X-M)^2}{N}}$$

It reads like this: "The standard deviation is equal to the square root of the sum of the squared deviation from the mean divided by the number of scores." Figure 10.1 provides a step-by-step illustration for computing the standard deviation.

INTERPRETING TEST SCORES

The number of items answered correctly on a test is the *raw score.*

If a test has a number of subtests, each test engenders a separate raw score. The teacher cannot interpret the meaning of these scores or compare them with other scores if all they represent is the number of correct items. Suppose both Vivian and Doreen answer correctly twenty-three items on their French and Spanish examinations, respectively. Who performed the best? First, we don't know the number

FIGURE 10.1
COMPUTATIONAL GUIDE FOR STANDARD DEVIATION.

s = standard deviation of a set of scores
Σ = the sum of
X = one score
M = the mean of a set of scores
N = the number of students with scores
$\sqrt{\ }$ = the square root of

Problem: Compute the standard deviation of the following scores: 4, 6, 8, 14.
Step 1: Prepare four columns of figures as follows: X, M, $(X-M)$, and $(X-M)^2$.
Step 2: List the scores under Column X, and determine M. ($M = 8$)
Step 3: Subtract the mean from each score to obtain figures for column $(X-M)$ as follows:

X	M	$(X-M)$	$(X-M)^2$
4	8	−4	16
6	8	−2	4
8	8	0	0
14	8	6	36

Step 4: Square each of the differences in column $(X-M)$ to obtain the figure in column $(X-M)^2$ as shown above.
Step 5: Add column $(X-M)^2$ to obtain $(X-M)^2 = 56$.
Step 6: Substitute the numbers in the formula as follows:

$$s = \sqrt{\frac{56}{4}} = \sqrt{14}$$

Step 7: Find the square root of 14:

$$s = \sqrt{14} = 3.74$$

of items on each test. Second, if we are to evaluate their performance relative to other students, we don't know how they performed in relation to other students.

To simplify the interpretation of test scores, test makers provide ways to make comparisons among test scores by converting raw scores to *derived* scores. The derived scores most frequently used in schools are *percentile ranks, grade equivalents,* and *standard scores.*

One of the easiest ways to compare an individual's score to others in a group is to rank all the scores. The disadvantage of this method is that it doesn't make distinctions between the size of groups. A rank of 14 in a group of fourteen is quite different from a rank of 14 in a group of forty. In the first case the rank is the lowest in the group, whereas in the second it is considerably higher.

One way to alleviate the problem is to use *percentile ranks.* Percentile ranks indicate a person's group rank in terms of the percentage of individuals at or below his score. If Bob's score on a science test gives him a rank of 10 in a class of forty, we can say that ¾ or 75% of the class made a lower score than Bob on the science test. Thus, 75 is his percentile rank. Another way of stating his performance is that he scored at the 75th percentile. By using percentages, the ranks of individuals in groups of unequal size can be compared.

Very often the beginning student in measurement confuses percentile ranks with the percentage of correct items on the test. These are two entirely different scores. Getting 85% of the items correct on an easy test may place a student at the 50th percentile. On a more difficult test, getting 85% of the items correct may place him at the 95th percentile.

Another precaution to take with percentile ranks is not to average or add them because they do not form equal intervals at all points along the scale. In most distributions, the distance between percentiles is less near the middle and greater at its extremes: More people tend to score in the middle range of a test. Therefore, in terms of actual points scored on a given test, a difference of four percentile ranks at the upper extreme — say, percentile 90 to 94 — may mean a difference of fifteen points on the test. On the other hand, a difference of four percentile ranks near the center of a distribution — say, percentile 50 to 54 — may mean a difference of only two or three points.

Another type of derived score is the *grade equivalent.* The grade equivalent for a raw score indicates the grade placement of students for whom the given score is the average or norm. A table for grade-equivalent scores is included in the test manual for most standardized achievement tests. If a score of 60 on a reading test has a grade equivalent of 4.9 (read "four years, nine months"), 60 would be the average score of students in the ninth month of the fourth grade. Since the school year is comprised of ten months, grade-equivalent scores range from .0 to .9.

Grade-equivalent scores have been very popular in the elementary grades because of their apparent ease of interpretation. If a sixth-grade student takes a test in September (6.0) and scores 6.3, it is obvious that the student has scored higher than the average student in the first month of the sixth grade. His score is the average score obtained by students in the third month of the sixth grade.

Test specialists have been concerned about the misinterpretations that grade-equivalent scores are often subject to. The units are not equal along the scale, so an increase from 5.5 to 5.6 may very well require more items correct than an increase from 5.8 to 5.9. A second circumstance open to misinterpretation is when a student scores two or more grade levels above her grade level. Can a fourth grader who receives a grade-equivalent score of 6.8 on a mathematics examination do sixth-grade mathematics? This would depend on the curriculum in the sixth grade. The only thing we can be sure of is that the student scored well above the average fourth grader taking the test.

Another way to interpret raw scores is by the use of *standard scores* expressed in terms of standard deviation units. These scores indicate how far away a given score is from the mean of the distribution. A big plus in their favor is that they are based on equal units of measurement throughout the distribution.

A typical type of standard score is the *z score.* This score represents the number of standard deviation units a raw score is from the mean. It is based on a mean of 0 and a standard deviation of 1. A negative z score indicates that a student scored below the mean. For example, if Debbie made a raw score of 27 in a distribution with a mean of 30 and a standard deviation of 5, her z score would be −.6. She is three raw-score points, or −.6 standard deviations, below the mean. Mathematically, a z score is defined as

$$z = \frac{X-M}{s} = \frac{27-30}{5} = \frac{-3}{5} = -.6.$$

If Debbie had a score equal to the mean, her z score would be zero:

$$z = \frac{35-35}{5} = \frac{0}{5} = 0.$$

Since many individuals find negative numbers and decimals troublesome to work with, many test publishers convert z scores to *T scores.* This is done by multiplying by 10 and adding 50:

$$T = \left(\frac{X-M}{s}\right) \times 10 + 50, \text{ or } T = 10z + 50.$$

By multiplying each z by 10, you eliminate the decimal; by adding 50 points to the product, you eliminate the negatives. The T score scale has a mean of 50 and a standard deviation of 10.

Another of the common standard scores are the College Examination Board Scores. On this scale, z scores are multiplied by 100, and 500 points are added to the product. Thus, a z score of 0 (mean) is equivalent to 500, and a z score of −1 is equivalent to 400.

Many intelligence tests convert raw scores to deviation IQ's, another type of standard score. Deviation IQ's have a mean of 100 and standard deviations of 15 or 16 (depending on the particular test). As a result, a deviation IQ of 130 always represents a score falling two standard deviations from the mean (assuming $s = 15$).

To understand the relationship between the various derived scores discussed in this section, examine the normal distribution and related scales in Figure 10.2. In a normal distribution, for example, a z score of −1 is the same as a T score of 40 or a percentile rank of 16.

A "normal" distribution or curve is a mathematical model that represents the way in which many human characteristics are distributed. It is bell-shaped, symmetrical, and the mean, median, and mode all fall at the same point. Because of this precise definition, it is possible to determine the proportion of scores falling under any area of the curve.

Several features of the normal curve are of special interest in interpreting scores. For example, approximately 34% of the scores fall one standard deviation above and below the mean. This means that approximately 68% of normally distributed scores are within one standard deviation of the mean. Approximately 14% of the scores fall between one and two standard deviations above and below the mean; approximately 2% of the scores fall between two and three standard deviations above and below the mean.

By identifying how far a score is from the mean in a normal distribution, you can determine the percentage of scores above or below any given score. A student who receives a 600 on the Scholastic Aptitude Test (SAT) is one standard deviation above the mean ($M = 500$). Therefore, he scored higher than approximately 84% of all students taking the test. In other words, a SAT score of 600 is equivalent to a percentile rank of 84.

Many school districts report test scores by *stanines*. This type of scale divides the normal curve into nine parts. Scores are expressed along a scale ranging from 1 (low) to 9 (high), with 5 representing the average performance for students in the reference group. The percentage of students at each stanine level is shown below.

Stanine	1	2	3	4	5	6	7	8	9
Percentage	4	7	12	17	20	17	12	7	4

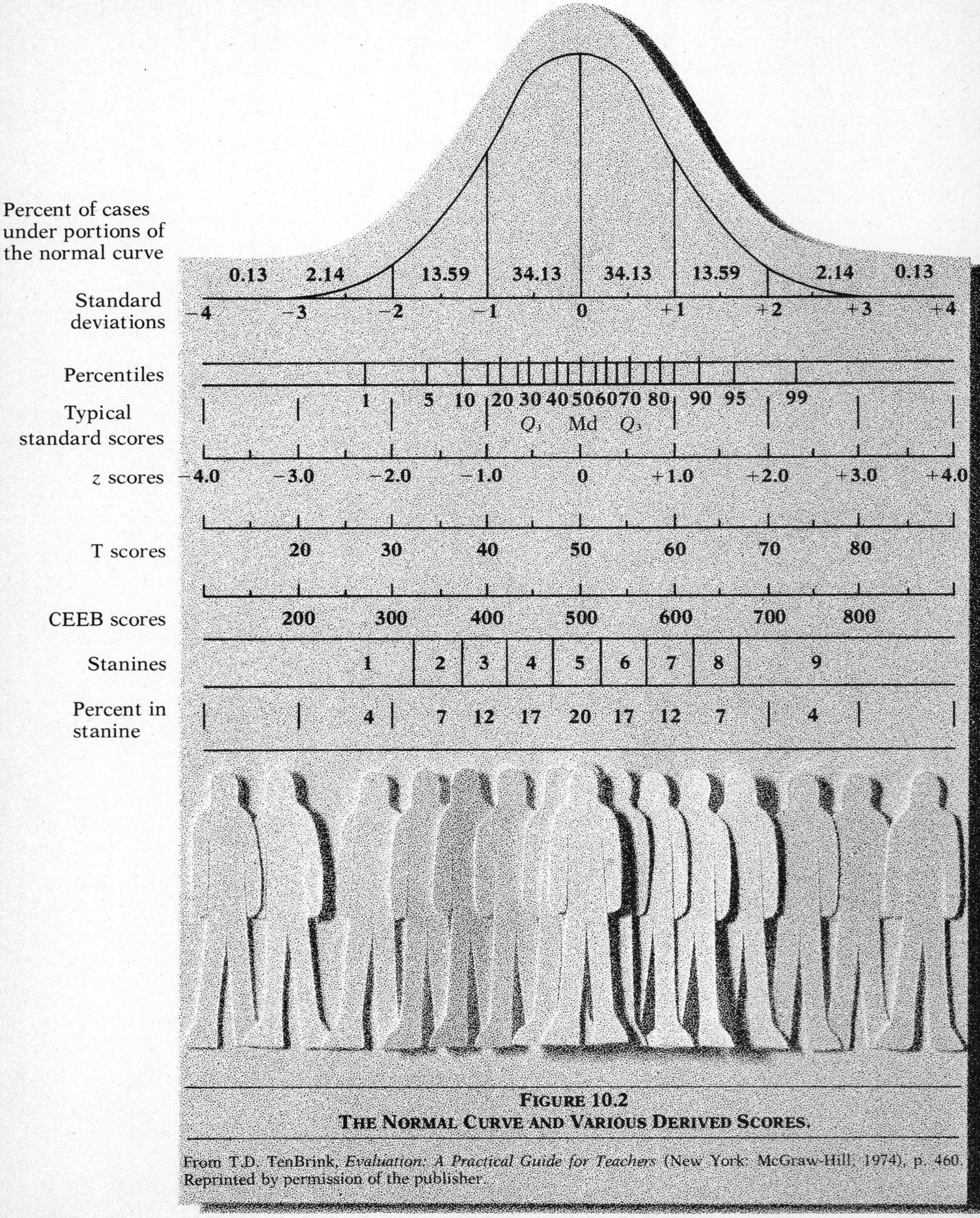

Figure 10.2
The Normal Curve and Various Derived Scores.

From T.D. TenBrink, *Evaluation: A Practical Guide for Teachers* (New York: McGraw-Hill, 1974), p. 460. Reprinted by permission of the publisher.

A stanine represents a percentage of scores; it is not a point. Therefore, in a given distribution of scores, the lowest 4% receives a stanine of 1, the next highest 7% a stanine of 2, and so on until the highest 4% receives a stanine of 9.

Most standardized tests have tables that convert raw scores to various derived scores. The teacher must record these scores on a profile sheet for each student and interpret their meaning. Figure 10.3 is a profile used in reporting scores on the Metropolitan Achievement Test. If Mrs. Williams asked for a conference to discuss her son James' scores, what would you tell her? Remember, grade scores (equivalents), percentile ranks, and stanines are different ways of representing the same test results.

STANDARD ERROR OF MEASUREMENT

It would suit everyone if a test score were a precise measure of a student's true ability or achievement. Unfortunately, even the best tests have some degree of error in the scores they produce. As a result, measurement experts believe that it is often desirable to record a test score as a band or interval rather than as a single point or score.

Most standardized test manuals report the *standard error of measurement* of a particular test. This statistic is an estimate of the amount of error in a test score. Suppose the standard error of measurement of a test is 4. If a student who makes a raw score of 40 on the test takes the test many times, about two thirds of her scores will fall between 36 and 44 (40 ± 4).

The standard error of measurement keeps us aware of the inaccuracy of test scores and helps us compare students. If a principal decides to offer a special class for bright students, he might use an aptitude test to select the composition of the class. Suppose the standard error of measurement of this test is 5. The principal decides that all students who score 70 or above on the test can select the course. Mary scores 68 and wants to take the course. On the basis of her academic record, she appears to be someone who could benefit from such a course. Since the standard error of measurement of the aptitude test is 5, Mary's actual ability is probably between 63 and 73 (68 ± 5). Thus, it would be quite possible for Mary to obtain a score above the cut-off score if she was tested again. There is strong support for including Mary in the class. This example illustrates the importance of considering test scores as intervals rather than as static scores.

FIGURE 10.3
METROPOLITAN ACHIEVEMENT TESTS PROFILE.

Pupil Information Box

Name	James Williams
Date of Test	April 15
Boy	
Date of Birth (Day / Month / Year)	
Girl	
School	
City	
State	
Grade	8
Teacher	

Score Summary Box

TEST	RAW SCORE	STANDARD SCORE	GRADE EQUIVALENT	PERCENTILE RANK	STANINE
1 Word Knowledge	29	88	7.5	36	4
2 Reading	27	91	7.8	44	5
1 + 2 Total Reading	56	90	7.6	40	5
3 Language	60	98	9.3	54	5
4 Spelling	30	94	8.1	38	4
5 Mathematics Computation	19	92	6.7	24	4
6 Mathematics Concepts	22	90	7.3	36	4
7 Mathematics Problem Solving	17	92	7.0	30	4
5–7 Total Mathematics	58	96	6.9	28	4
8 Science	49	92	7.6	36	4
9 Social Studies	64	102	9.5	60	6

ADVANCED METROPOLITAN ACHIEVEMENT TESTS

Grading and Reporting Student Progress

Various methods are used to grade students and report their progress, including letter grades based on comparative and absolute standards, behavioral mastery reports, pass-fail, and parent-teacher conferences. Many schools use combinations of methods, such as letter grades and parent-teacher conferences. This section presents material on the advantages and limitations of these procedures.

BASING GRADES ON THE NORMAL DISTRIBUTION

In norm-referenced evaluation, grades are assigned for different levels of achievement. A certain percentage of students get A's, B's, C's, D's, and F's. Letter grades are easily understood by parents and students and are easy and convenient in maintaining school records. These advantages aside, the meaning of letter grades varies from teacher to teacher and the grades do not indicate a student's learning strengths and weaknesses.

The most rigid form of letter-grade evaluation is grading on the curve. In this procedure the grades are arranged to approximate the shape of a normal distribution. This distribution is illustrated in Figure 10.4. The largest proportion of students receive C grades, and the percentage of A and B grades is matched by an equivalent percentage of D and F grades. When a teacher grades on a curve, the percentage of students receiving each grade is predetermined. The grading is based on the assumption that the students in a typical class will fall into a normal distribution on achievement because they are normally distributed on aptitude.

The assumptions underlying the letter-grading system have been abundantly criticized. The size of many classroom groups is often too small to expect a normal distribution, and teachers' achievement tests seldom yield normally distributed scores. The homogeneous-grouping system, used in many schools, of placing students with similar abilities in classes negates the normal-distribution assumption from the beginning (Terwilliger, 1971). Finally, even if students were normally distributed in terms of aptitude, will achievement be distributed in the same way? We discussed earlier the notion of mastery learning, which attempts to ensure that almost all students can master the material in a given course. You should think carefully about these criticisms before grading on the curve.

FIGURE 10.4
NORMAL CURVE WITH A TYPICAL DISTRIBUTION OF GRADES.

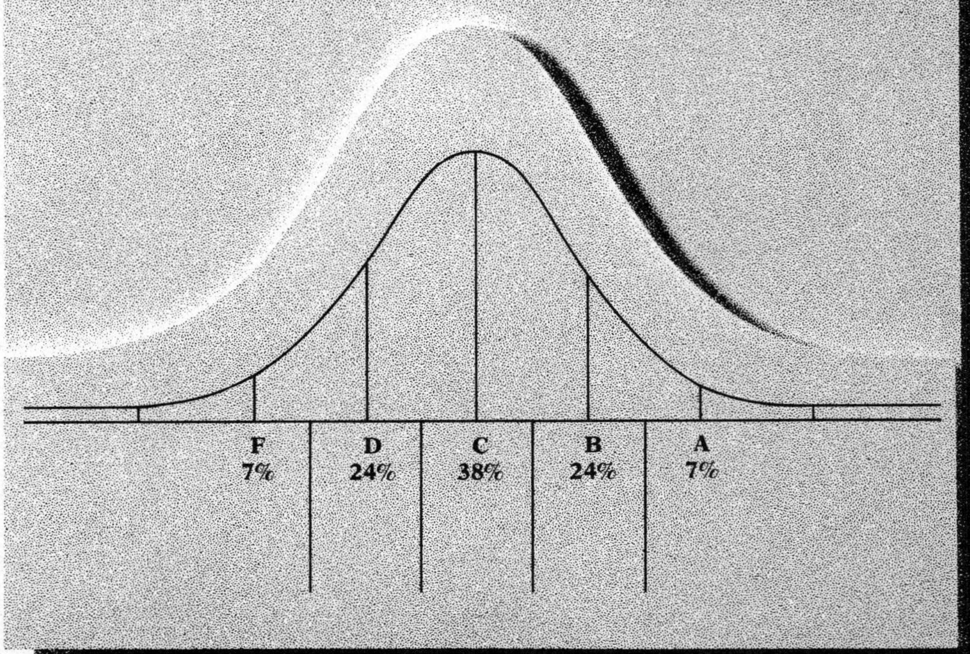

THE INSPECTION METHOD

Smith and Adams (1972) support a visual-inspection method of grading. With this method the teacher grades students on a norm-referenced system but experiences greater flexibility in the percentages of letter grades assigned.

The procedure is quite simple. After the scores have been obtained, the teacher establishes a frequency distribution (see Figure 10.5). The following are some guidelines for determining letter grades:

1. *The large group of scores around the median should be assigned C.*
2. *The lines drawn at* Q_1 *and* Q_3*, the 25th and 75th percentiles, can be used to indicate the limits of the C group.*
3. *The groups just above and below the C group are assigned B and D, respectively. The groups at either extreme are assigned A or F.*

If the test is too easy or too difficult, the scores will pile up at

FIGURE 10.5
GRADES ASSIGNED BY VISUAL INSPECTION OF SCORES.

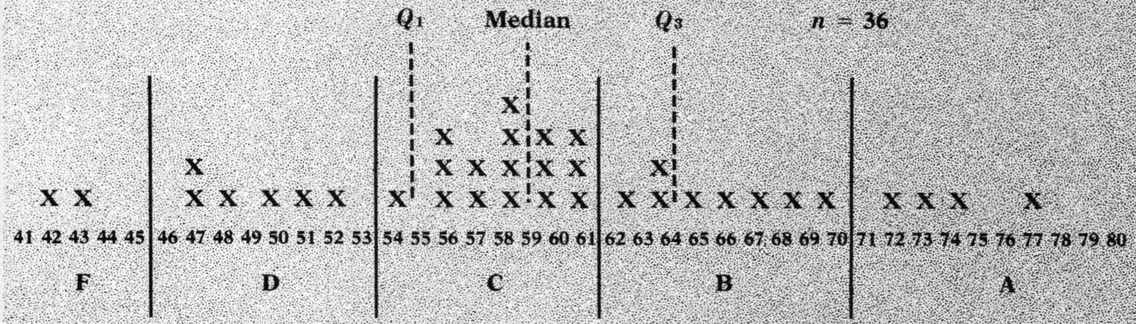

From Figure 4 (p. 239) in *Educational Measurement For the Classroom Teacher*, 2nd Edition, by Fred M. Smith and Sam Adams. Copyright © 1966, 1972 by Fred M. Smith and Sam Adams. By permission of Harper & Row Publishers, Inc.

one end of the distribution, making a clear separation of achievement levels difficult. If everyone does well, there may be no need to assign F's. In other distributions, no one may do well enough to receive an A. In distributions with gaps above or below the median, the teacher may not assign any B's or D's.

BASING GRADES ON PREDETERMINED LEVELS OF ACHIEVEMENT

Sometimes grades are assigned on the basis of predetermined levels of achievement, such as the following:

A = 90 – 100%
B = 80 – 89%
C = 70 – 79%
D = 60 – 69%
F = Below 60

With this system the student receives a grade based on the percentage of questions answered correctly. There are no limitations on the percentage of letter grades given. At first glance, this system of grading appears very fair: No one receives a low grade just because he is at the bottom of the class distribution. The drawback lies with the teacher, who through the difficulty of the tests can control the percentage of students receiving high or low grades. If scores are too high, the teacher may begin to grade a little tougher to bring them down. If they are too low, he may grade a little easier.

BEHAVIORAL MASTERY REPORTS

Dissatisfaction with traditional grading and reporting systems has led to the development of behavioral mastery reports. This report consists of a list of behavioral objectives with indications of the extent to which the student has met or mastered each objective. Figure 10.6 is a report card with such a list of objectives.

A behavioral report permits a degree of communication to the parent not possible with other systems. By specifically identifying those skills and abilities the student has attained, the report puts the parent in a better position to judge the quality of his child's education.

The use of this approach drives home its limitations. In highly structured subjects like mathematics, it is possible to identify and report student progress in a specific domain of learning outcomes; in loosely defined subjects like social studies, the domain of learning outcomes is difficult to assess and there is no clear hierarchical structure. A second deficiency in behavioral mastery reports is the problem of identifying all instructional objectives in terms of specific student outcomes. Third, it is difficult to specify meaningful standards of performance for many objectives: What is mastery? How does one establish a minimal level of competency (Gronlund, 1974a)?

PASS-FAIL

Pass-fail grading removes the competitive pressures of letter grading and permits students to explore new subject areas without fear of receiving low grades. In some pass-fail procedures, the instructor doesn't know who is in his course on the pass-fail basis and who is in on a regular grading system. He submits letter grades for all students to the registrar, who then converts all passing grades to P for the pass-fail students.

This system is limited in that it provides little information about student learning. In addition, students may not do assigned readings or do just enough to get by in lieu of attempting to attain a high level of competency in the course.

PARENT-TEACHER CONFERENCES

The parent-teacher conference is most effective for reporting student progress at the elementary school level and for dealing with special

Figure 10.6
Report Card Based on a System of Criterion-Referenced Measurement.

Grade Two

Skill	*Date*
Concepts	
Understands commutative property of addition (e.g., 4 + 3 = 3 + 4)	______
Understands place value (e.g., 27 = 2 tens + 7 ones)	______
Addition	
Supplies missing addend under 10 (e.g., 3 + ? = 5)	______
Adds three single-digit numbers	______
Knows combinations 10 through 19	______
Adds two 2-digit numbers without carrying	______
Adds two 2-digit numbers with carrying	______
Subtraction	
Knows combinations through 9	______
Supplies missing subtrahend—under 10 (e.g., 6 − ? = 1)	______
Supplies missing minuend—under 10 (e.g., ? − 3 = 4)	______
Knows combinations 10 through 19	______
Subtracts two 2-digit numbers without borrowing	______
Measurement	
Reads and draws clocks (up to quarter hour)	______
Understands dollar value of money (coins up to $1.00 total)	______
Geometry	
Understands symmetry	______
Recognizes congruent plan figures—that is, figures which are identical except for orientation	______
Graph Reading	
Knows how to construct simple graphs	______
Knows how to read simple graphs	______

From J. Millman, "Reporting Student Progress: A Case for a Criterion-Referenced Marking System," *Phi Delta Kappan* 52 (1970): 226–231. Reprinted with permission.

problems at the secondary level. It improves the teacher's communication with parents and can provide the teacher with a source of more detailed information about the student. The limitations of the parent-teacher conference are the amount of time needed to conduct the interviews and the special counseling skills needed to communicate productively with the parent.

These conferences require thorough planning. Before the conference the teacher should carefully read the student's permanent record and summarize the information on a sheet for easy reference. Some school districts have available parent-teacher conference report forms that teachers complete prior to meeting with parents.

The following do's and don'ts are helpful pointers for conducting conferences with parents (Smith & Adams, 1972):

> 1. *Do allow enough time (about thirty minutes), and start and terminate the conference promptly.*
> 2. *Do use a positive rather than a negative approach.*
> 3. *Do use specific examples of a child's behavior rather than vague generalities.*
> 4. *Do use open-ended questions to draw out the parent to discuss his child.*
> 5. *Do accept and consider carefully all the suggestions made by the parent.*
> 6. *Do not enter a conference with inadequate data about a child.*
> 7. *Do not monopolize the conference; give the parent time to react.*
> 8. *Do not compare a parent's child with others in the class.*
> 9. *Do not "talk down" to the parent.*
> 10. *Do not become defensive and argue with the parent. (p. 253)*

TO GRADE OR NOT TO GRADE?

The last section of this chapter includes two readings with opposing positions on the use of grades in school. After reading the two papers, determine which position comes closest to your point of view. Are there other issues not identified by the authors that should be considered?

Should School Marks Be Abolished?

School marks of some kind are a significant element in almost all formal programs of education. Yet there are few educational practices that have been attacked more persistently, or for which a wider variety of remedies have been proposed. Clearly, the problem of marking is one that merits careful consideration, not only by school administrators but also by teachers, students, and all others concerned with the processes of education.

WHAT IS A SCHOOL MARK?

For the purposes of this discussion it may be helpful to define the term "school mark" rather specifically. *A school mark is a number or a letter that is used to express the level of a student's achievement in some subject of study.* At the beginning of this century numerical marks were prevalent. Usually the numbers purported to express the percent a student had learned of what he was expected to learn. Often a mark somewhere in the vicinity of 70 was regarded as the minimum passing mark.

Somewhat later, letter marks began to replace numerical marks in many schools and colleges. The system that became most popular made use of five letters, defined approximately in these terms:

A—excellent
B—good
C—average
D—poor
F—failing

This system, or some variant of it, is prevalent today.

THE NEED FOR PERIODIC REPORTS

The case for school marks, as here defined, rests primarily on the validity of two propositions. Here is the first.

It is educationally useful to determine, and to report periodically, the level of a student's achievement in each of the major subjects he is studying.

This proposition simply asserts that some kind of a determination of educational achievement should be made from time to time, and reported in some fashion to those who need to know it. It implies

From R.L. Ebel, "Should School Marks Be Abolished?" *Michigan Journal of Secondary Education* 6 (1964): 12–18. Reprinted with permission of the publisher.

that if superior educational achievements are desired they must be defined, identified and rewarded. The proposition suggests that those concerned with the processes of education ought to pay attention, systematically, to the results they are getting.

This seems to be a reasonable suggestion. Formal education is a purposeful activity. It is directed toward the attainment of certain goals. It requires the skillful management of complex processes. Things can go wrong, so that students sometimes fall far short of the desired levels of achievement. If these deficiencies are to be corrected, the first requirement is that they be clearly recognized. Periodic reports of levels of student achievement permit this recognition.

Formal education is an important activity. Communities go to a great deal of trouble to establish and maintain schools. Laws are passed, taxes are assessed, buildings are built, teachers are employed, courses are planned and taught, all for the purpose of promoting student learning. Is it reasonable to provide excellent facilities for learning without making some effort to assess what is being learned? Reports of student achievement provide one basis for this assessment.

Formal education is a cooperative activity. It requires the coordinated efforts, not only of students and teachers but also of school administrators and parents. All of them have a legitimate interest in the outcome of their efforts. They have a real need to know to what extent educational goals are being achieved, for if those goals are being attained badly they may need to change the nature and magnitude of their efforts. Reports on levels of student achievement can help to provide them with this knowledge.

Some Apparent Exceptions

Can not education occur in the absence of periodic evaluations? Indeed it can. A great deal of a person's education is gained informally or incidentally, not as a result of purposefully planned and carefully organized educational programs. While the extent and quality of a person's informal education will affect his success in formal schooling, it is not feasible or necessary to assess informal educational attainments separately and directly. The situations in which periodic determinations and reports of levels of achievement are most useful are those in which the educational experiences are planned and organized most purposefully to help students attain definite goals.

There are a few notable examples of educational programs, such as Sunday School programs, and certain educational-recreational programs for adults, in which formal efforts to evaluate student achievement are rare or absent altogether. In some of these no very definite goals for attainment are set. Continued attendance and participation is valued more highly than the achievement of any particular kinds or levels of competence. Learning unquestionably goes on, and in some instances it may go on very well. In other instances it appears to go very badly. Specific data on average levels of achievement are necessarily lacking. If no attempt is made to assess levels of achievement precisely and formally, no very specific or dependable data are likely to exist to show how good or poor the average level of achievement may be.

SOME LOGICAL DILEMMAS

Those who claim that learning proceeds better in the absence than in the presence of systematic determinations of achievement encounter an interesting logical problem. They cannot provide evidence to support the claim without doing what they say ought not to be done. They must measure achievement to prove that learning is facilitated by not measuring achievement. It is impossible in principle to show that more will be learned when no attempt is made to determine how much has been learned. And there is something patently absurd in the assertion that the best progress will be made when no attention is paid to progress. It is like suggesting that a business will prosper best if it keeps no financial accounts, or that a driver will reach his destination most certainly if he drives with his eyes closed.

Somewhat the same logic applies to the suggestion that informal procedures for assessing and reporting student achievement provide better information than formal procedures. The only difference between the two is that the formal procedures are planned more carefully and purposefully, and executed more systematically. Surely careless, incidental, unsystematic determinations and reports cannot in the long run provide more useful information than can be obtained from purposeful, painstaking procedures. In almost all human activities, painstaking effort is a better recipe for success than casual indifference.

SCHOOL MARKS AND PUPIL ADJUSTMENT

Thus far in this discussion our attention has been directed toward educational achievement, toward cultivation of the student's knowledge and development of his abilities. But what of his feelings? What of his adjustment? Is there no danger that our periodic reports of levels of achievement may have the effect of destroying self-confidence and discouraging educational efforts?

There is indeed, and recognition of this danger has been largely responsible for suggestions that precise, systematic reports on achievement ought to be abolished, or at least de-emphasized. But the suggestions are unsound. If adopted they tend to impair achievement without contributing much to improved adjustment. Let us explain.

A rational person living in a real world is bound to experience failure as well as success. What he regards as success, and what as failure, depends largely on his own self-concept, and his own level of aspiration. If that level is much too high, he may experience failure rather consistently. But if he has come to terms with himself, and with the demands of the world, most of his days will seem to be reasonably satisfactory. The occasional stunning defeats will be balanced by about an equal number of glorious success.

Anyone who expects his own performances to be consistently above average *for him* is expecting the impossible. Anyone who expects to excel others in all lines of endeavor is expecting the improbable. Most of us manage to find a few things we can do a little better than most other people, and we concentrate on doing those things. We settle for near average performance in most other activities.

These considerations are relevant to educational programs too. A school that strives to avoid experiences of failure is not helping students to come to terms with themselves or with life. A school that tries to shield a student from knowledge that he does some things better than others, and that some others can do many things better than he can, is not contributing much to his adjustment either. On the other hand, a school whose programs offer nothing but a high probability of failure to some of its students in anything they attempt to learn can hardly qualify as a good school. But in such cases it is the school's program, not the reports of achievement, that should be blamed and corrected. The reports did not create the failure, and the failures would still be there, whether reported or not. In fact, systematic reports of student achievement can contribute to the solution of problems like this, by calling attention to their existence.

Thus even when the primary goal is adjustment rather than achievement, a good case can be made for periodic reports of student levels of achievement. To ignore differences in attainments, or to withhold information about them from those most concerned, the students and their parents, really solves no problems and helps no one in the long run. Ignorance is a poor ally to education, and the encouragement of ignorance has no place in the process of education. We need to know, and periodic determination and reporting of achievements help us to know, how well our efforts are succeeding and in what ways they need to be redirected.

THE CASE FOR SYMBOLIC MARKS

The second major proposition supporting the case for school marks is this.

A standard set of symbols, such as conventional letter or numeri-

cal marks, can provide a satisfactory means for reporting levels of student achievement.

Symbols such as these have the useful virtues of simplicity, conciseness, and convenience. If properly used they can have the essential virtue of unequivocal meaningfulness. Of course, they cannot communicate all that might be useful about a student's strong and weak points, or the reasons for his successes or deficiencies. They provide only a single over-all index of the general level of achievement. But this is by all odds the most important thing to communicate in the first instance. It provides an excellent starting point and stimulus for more detailed investigations of attainments, deficiencies, and possible corrective actions.

The two chief rivals of symbolic marks are individually written descriptive reports and oral interviews. Both of these are much more time-consuming than symbolic marks to prepare or conduct. While they permit communication of many more different items of information, each of these items tends to be less specifically stated, and to be less well supported by specific evidence. In these reports and interviews teachers try to say mainly pleasing, general things, in the interests of good interpersonal relations. Many of the same things can be said, without serious falsification, of almost all their students. Hence it is not surprising that teachers sometimes report difficulty in finding different ways to express the same impressions they have about many of their pupils.

The time required to write reports and conduct interviews raises other serious questions. It may impose an extra burden on the teachers. In some schools classes are dismissed for half a day over a two-week period to allow the teacher time to interview the parents of each child separately. Whether a child's educational development is promoted enough, as a result of one half-hour interview, to make up for the loss of ten half-days of school work may be open to question.

THE MEANINGFULNESS OF MARKS

But, actually, how much meaning does a symbolic mark have? What does an A in first-year French, or a D in beginning algebra, really signify?

To begin with, such marks have very little to say directly about how much French or how little chemistry the student knows. What they can say is that the student who got the A in French showed outstanding achievement, in comparison with his peers, all of whom were presumably seeking to attain the same goals. The D in chemistry reflects below-average achievement. On the assumption that a reasonably good course was fairly well taught to moderately capable students, a well-informed educator can make some pretty good guesses as to how much French or chemistry has been mastered in each case. But the meaning of the mark is essentially relative meaning, expressing the achievement of one student in relation to that of his classmates.

This is clearly limited meaning, but it is far from meaninglessness. It is about all the meaning one can reasonably ask of a standard set of symbols applied to all kinds of course content. Somewhat surprisingly, it may signify more with respect to actual content mastery than can be gleaned from the typical written report or oral interview.

To make a quantitative measure of achievement (i.e., a mark) *completely* meaningful with respect to content mastered, one would need a *complete* inventory of that content and all of its possible applications. This is a task so great as to be practically impossible of completion. The best one can hope for, ordinarily, is to approximate such an inventory with a sample of the items of knowledge and ability it ought to include. A good objective achievement test may provide such a sample. If one has a copy of the test before him, and knows what score a particular student made on it, he can form a reasonably accurate impression of what the student can or cannot do in that area of achievement.

The achievements of a group can often be reported meaningfully by indicating what proportion of its members can successfully complete each of a small number of representative tasks. During World War II, Admiral Nimitz used this technique effectively to report on the mathematical competence (or lack of it) of naval recruits. He presented a list of sixteen problems requiring fundamental arithmetical operations with whole numbers, common fractions and decimals, and reported that the average recruit could solve less than half of those problems correctly.

Limitations of Marks

The second proposition said that symbolic marks *can* be satisfactory. Often, it must be admitted, they are not. In some cases the school faculty has not taken the trouble to define the marks clearly, and to supervise the use of the marking system so as to maintain the defined meanings. In other cases, and for various reasons, teachers do not secure enough reliable data on levels of student achievement to make the marks they issue reasonably accurate. But the logical remedy for these deficiencies is to correct them, not to abolish marks.

School marks have a limited but an important function. They sometimes need to be supplemented by written reports and oral interviews. On the grounds of convenience and meaningfulness, however, they have definite advantages over other forms of periodic

AB
CD
F

reports. They merit the widespread use that is currently made of them in an overwhelming majority of schools and colleges.

Carefully weigh Ebel's analysis of the importance of grades because the following position takes a completely different point of view. You may want to debate these positions in class.

It's Time for Schools to Abolish the Marking System

The marking system is damaging in its impact on the education of our children. It should go the way of the hickory stick and dunce cages. It should be abandoned at all levels of education.

Our marking system is no longer relevant to the needs and educational programs of our society. It says nothing meaningful about a pupil. It glosses over exceptional effort on the part of some pupils and lack of effort on the part of others. It says nothing about the most important outcomes of education. It leads us to measure the outcomes of our educational programs in terms of what people know, when we ought to be measuring them in terms of what people are and are in the process of becoming. It tells us a little about what the pupil has done to the subject he studies but nothing about what his study of the subject has done to him. We think we must use this worn-out system to motivate pupils, but all the studies I have seen show that marks have no motivating effect.

But the marking system is not only irrelevant and mischievous. It is destructive. It destroys the self-concepts of millions of children every year. Note the plight of the deprived child. He often enters school at six with few of the preschool experiences that the middle-class children bring to school. We ask him to learn to read. He is not ready to read. We give him a low mark — we repeat the low mark for each marking period — often for as long as the child remains in school. At the end of perhaps the ninth grade, the child drops out of school. What has he learned? He has learned he cannot learn. We have told him so several dozen times. Why should he think otherwise?

We have lied to him. He can learn. If we were worth our salt as teachers and as a school, we should have taught him he can learn. We should have asked him to do things he can do, not what we know he can't do. Every day we should have sent him home with more confidence in himself, liking himself better than when he came in.

E.O. Melby, "It's Time for Schools to Abolish the Marking System." From *Nation's Schools* 77 (1966): 104. Reprinted with permission of the publisher.

But don't tell me it's only the deprived who suffer from our marking system. All children are injured. They are injured because they are induced to seek the wrong goals — to be satisfied when their performance reaches a given level, rather than when they have done their best. They are injured because they develop a dislike for subjects in which they get a low grade, literature for example. Often these dislikes are lifelong. Think of all the college graduates and high school graduates who dislike mathematics for example. The low grade they received told them they were deficient in mathematical ability when most often they were merely the victims of bad teaching.

When I say these things about our obsolete marking system, someone always asks "What shall we tell the parents about the child?" "What shall we report to the university?" My answer is let us be both informative and conducive to the growth of the pupil's self-concept. Let us describe his growth in meaningful terms that are really descriptive of the pupil's effort, unique qualities, interests, attitudes, and behaviors. As for standards, we should evaluate each pupil in terms of his own capacity and growth, not in comparison with others, who are very different. A slow learner may become a better self-actualizing person than a fast learner.

We should be engaged with parents in the joint undertaking of helping the pupil to grow as a self-actualizing person. Our marking system injures the self-concepts of many children and is an obstacle to self-actualization. As for university entrance, from four years of high school experience, we should be able to decide what kind of post high school education the student should undertake. We either recommend him to a state university or junior college. On what basis?

When you go to a doctor for a history and physical check-up, the doctor writes constantly as you talk, describing your condition. He accumulates your medical history. He does not give you an "A" or a "C." He does not use meaningless terms which blot out your individuality. He uses descriptive language which, when he reads it, causes you to come alive as a unique person — in health terms.

Why can't we in education do the same? Why do we bury the observations of a pupil's teachers over a dozen years in meaningless symbols? Why do we ignore the specific judgments of all the teachers who worked hard with the pupil and had much to pass on both to parents and the next teacher?

In American schools today perhaps a third of the children get very little in effective education. What is worse, their experience in school destroys their self-confidence. On a nationwide basis we are belatedly coming to grips with the problem. We are trying many plans. But, unless we abandon our crude and destructive marking system, nothing else we do will have much value.

KEY POINTS

1. *A frequency distribution for a test is a table summarizing how often each score occurs.*
2. *The mean is the arithmetic average of a set of scores.*
3. *The median is the middle score in a distribution.*
4. *The mode is the score with the highest frequency of occurrence.*
5. *The standard deviation is a measure of the dispersion or variability of the scores from the mean.*
6. *A raw score is the number of items answered correctly on a test.*
7. *A percentile rank indicates a person's rank in a group in terms of the percentage of individuals at or below his score.*
8. *A grade-equivalent score indicates the grade placement of students for whom the given score is the average or norm.*
9. *Percentile ranks and grade-equivalent scores cannot be added or averaged because they do not form equal intervals at all points along the scale.*
10. *Standard scores represent test scores that have fixed means and standard deviations.*
11. *The basic standard score is the z score, which is calculated by dividing the standard deviation into the difference between a given raw score and the mean of all the scores.*
12. *A T score is obtained by multiplying a z score by 10 and adding 50.*
13. *A normal or bell-shaped curve is a mathematical model that symbolically represents the way in which many human characteristics are distributed.*
14. *A normal curve is often used to interpret standardized test results.*
15. *Stanines are scores that represent the normal curve divided into nine parts. Each part is a stanine.*
16. *The standard error of measurement estimates the amount of error in a test score.*

17. *Grades can be based on comparative or absolute standards.*
18. *Some methods used to grade students and report their progress are letter grades, behavioral mastery reports, pass-fail, and parent-teacher conferences.*

SUGGESTIONS FOR FURTHER READING

Hoffman, B. *The tyranny of testing.* New York: Crowell-Collier, 1962. A critical analysis of multiple-choice testing.

Kirschenbaum, H., Simon, S., & Napier, R. *Wad-Ja-Get? The grading game in American education.* New York: Hart, 1971.

Lyman, H. B. *Test scores and what they mean.* Englewood Cliffs, N.J.: Prentice-Hall, 1973. A detailed discussion of the interpretation of test scores.

The following references discuss alternative procedures for grading:

Gronlund, N. E. *Improving marking and reporting in classroom instruction.* New York: Macmillan, 1974.

Terwilliger, J. S. *Assigning grades to students.* Glenview, Ill.: Scott, Foresman, 1971.

FOLLOW-UP ACTIVITIES

1 Evaluate grading methods and procedures.

a. What effect do grades have on you? Think about the courses you had in high school or those that you are now taking. Would you have behaved differently had you not been graded in any of them? In which courses would you not have altered your performance, regardless of whether or not you had been graded?

b. What experiences have you had with pass-fail and absolute standards (A = 90–100%, B = 80–89%, and so on)? What do you consider the advantages and disadvantages of each? How did these grading priorities dispose you toward learning?

c. Discuss what you believe was an unfair grading system used by a teacher. Defend your position and point out how the system could be improved.

d. Should a grade represent student achievement only, or should it also include the student's effort and work habits?

2 **Interpret a grade summary sheet.** Given the grade summary sheet below for a sample of students in an eighth-grade social studies class, determine the teacher's primary basis for assigning grades. Are there inconsistencies in grading priorities? If so, how would the teacher defend them? What are some possible sources of teacher bias? Could the grading system be made more equitable? If so, how?

Grade Summary Sheet

Grade/Subject: Eighth Grade/Social Studies *Grading Period:* First Six Weeks

Name	*Pre-Test*	*Post-Test*	*Grades on Group Reports*	*Individual Project Reports*	*Student Self-Evaluation*	*Final Grade*
Ames, Sally	90%	89%	A–	A	A	A
Brooks, Sid	42	67	B+	C+	A	B
Colton, Billy	72	82	A–	A+	B	A
Courtes, Sally	86	86	B+	B	A	B
Debs, Sam	54	57	B	C	B	C
Williams, Tom	70	80	B	B+	A	B
Young, John	70	80	B	B+	A	B
Zimmer, Alice	62	72	A–	B+	B	A

3 Interpret achievement test scores. Your school system has administered the Elementary Reading Test for grades 3 and 4 from the Elementary Battery of the Metropolitan Achievement Tests to all third-grade students in October, and you now have the scores for each student. A portion of the score sheet is provided below. What does it mean?

		Word Knowledge	Reading
Sims, Fred	Grade equivalent	4.8	4.4
	Percentile rank	95	85
	Standard score	55	53
	Stanine	8	7
Simmons, Tom	Grade equivalent	3.2	3.1
	Percentile rank	60	45
	Standard score	44	41
	Stanine	6	5

Which boy does each of the following statements describe?

a. Scored close to the average third grader in the October testing.
b. More than a year above third-grade level in Word Knowledge.
c. Scored very well in Reading; only 15% of the standardization group did better than he.
d. About 40% of the students in the country scored lower than he in Word Knowledge.
e. With the total score scale divided into nine segments, he scored the second from the top in Word Knowledge.

4 Interpret information from a cumulative record. In June, Billy North's parents make an appointment with you, his English teacher, to discuss his academic progress. They want him to become a doctor but are afraid that he will not get into college if his academic work continues to decline. Given the information from a part of his Cumulative Record below, how would you start this meeting? What would you tell his parents about his potential and academic progress? What recommendations would you make? You may want to consult reference materials for information about the standardized tests used by the school.

CUMULATIVE RECORD
CENTRAL JUNIOR HIGH SCHOOL

Name: Billy North
Age: 13
Grade: 7

Test Record

Intelligence tests		IQ	Grade Level
Group			
California Test of Mental Maturity	Language	77	6th
	Performance	96	
Individual			
Wechsler Intelligence Scale for Children	Verbal	81	6th
	Performance	99	
	Full Scale	88	

Achievement tests		Grade equivalent scores	7th
California Achievement Tests (taken in October)	Total reading	5.6	
	Total arithmetic	7.3	
	Total language	6.1	

Academic Record

Subject	Final Grades	Grade Level
English	C−	7th
Mathematics	C+	7th
Social Studies	D	7th
Science	B	7th

Work habits: below average.

References

Adams, D. M. Some questions concerning behavioral objectives. *Journal of Teacher Education,* 1972, *23*, 25–26.

Adler, I. Mental growth and the art of teaching. *The Arithmetic Teacher,* 1966, *13*, 576–584.

Alschuler, A. S. Psychological education. *Journal of Humanistic Psychology,* 1969, *9*, 1–16.

Anderson, H. H. The measurement of domination and of socially integrative behavior in teachers' contacts with children. *Child Development,* 1939, *10*, 73–89.

Arnold, R. The achievements of boys and girls taught by men and women teachers. *Elementary School Journal,* 1968, *68*, 367–371.

Aronson, E. Busing and racial tension: The jigsaw route to learning and teaching. *Psychology Today,* 1975, *8*, 43–50.

Aspy, D. N. An investigation into the relationship between teachers' actual knowledge of learning theory and their classroom performance. *Journal of Teacher Education,* 1972, *23*, 21–24. (a)

Aspy, D. N. *Toward a technology for humanizing education.* Champaign, Ill.: Research Press, 1972. (b)

Atkinson, J. W. The mainsprings of achievement-oriented activity. In J. Krumboltz (Ed.), *Learning and the educational process.* Chicago: Rand McNally, 1965.

Atkinson, J. W., & Feather, N. T. *A theory of achievement motivation.* New York: Wiley, 1966.

Ausubel, D. P. The use of advanced organizers in the learning and retention of meaningful verbal material. *Journal of Educational Psychology,* 1960, *51*, 267–272.

Ausubel, D. P., & Robinson, F. G. *School learning.* New York: Holt, Rinehart and Winston, 1969.

Ausubel, D. P., & Youssef, M. The role of discriminability in meaningful verbal learning. *Journal of Educational Psychology,* 1963, *54*, 331–336.

Baldwin, A. L. *Theories of child development.* New York: Wiley, 1967.

Bandura, A. Social learning through imitation. In N. R. Jones (Ed.),

Nebraska symposium on motivation. Lincoln: University of Nebraska Press, 1962.

Bandura, A. Behavioral psychotherapy. *Scientific American,* March 1967, pp. 78–86.

Bandura, A. *Principles of behavior modification.* New York: Holt, Rinehart and Winston, 1969.

Bandura, A., & Walters, R. H. *Social learning and personality development.* New York: Holt, Rinehart and Winston, 1963.

Barron, F. *Creative person and creative process.* New York: Holt, Rinehart and Winston, 1969.

Barth, R. S. So you want to change to an open classroom? *Phi Delta Kappan,* 1971, *53*, 97–99.

Barth, R. S. *Open education and the American school.* New York: Agathon, 1972.

Battle, E., & Rotter, J. Children's feelings of personal control as related to social class and ethnic group. *Journal of Personality,* 1963, *31*, 482–490.

Bearison, D. J. *The role of measurement operations in the acquisition of conservation.* Paper presented at the annual meeting of the Eastern Psychological Association, 1968.

Beatty, L. S., Madden, R., & Gardner, E. F. *Manual for administering and interpreting the Stanford Diagnostic Arithmetic Test.* New York: Harcourt Brace Jovanovich, 1966.

Becker, W. C., Engelmann, S., & Thomas, D. R. *Teaching: A course in applied psychology.* Chicago: Science Research Associates, 1971.

Becker, W. C., Madsen, C. H., Arnold, C. R., & Thomas, D. R. The contingent use of teacher attention and praise in reducing classroom behavior problems. *Journal of Special Education,* 1967, *1*, 287–307.

Bernstein, B. Language and social class. *British Journal of Sociology,* 1960, *11*, 271–276.

Bettelheim, B. The problem of generations. In E. Erickson (Ed.), *The challenge of youth.* New York: Doubleday, 1965.

Bickham, S. The educational implications of Arthur Jensen's research. *Intellect,* 1974, *103*, 161–164.

Biehler, R. F. *Psychology applied to teaching.* Boston: Houghton Mifflin, 1971.

Biehler, R. F. *Psychology applied to teaching* (2nd ed.). Boston: Houghton Mifflin, 1974. (a)

Biehler, R. F. *Study guide: Psychology applied to teaching* (2nd ed.). Boston: Houghton Mifflin, 1974. (b)

Birney, R. C., Burdick, H., & Teevan, R. C. *Fear of failure.* Princeton, N. J.: Van Nostrand, 1969.

Bissell, J., White, S., & Zivin, G. Sensory modalities in children's learning. In G. S. Lesser (Ed.), *Psychology and educational practice.* Glenview, Ill.: Scott, Foresman, 1971.

Blackham, G. J., & Silberman, A. *Modification of child behavior.* Belmont, Calif.: Wadsworth, 1971.

Bledsoe, J. C. Self-concept of children and their intelligence, achievement, interests, and anxiety. *Journal of Individual Psychology,* 1964, *20*, 55–58.

Bledsoe, J. C. Self-concept of children and their intelligence, achievement, interests, and anxiety. *Childhood Education,* 1967, *43*, 436–438.

Block, J. H. *Mastery learning in the classroom: An overview of recent research.* Paper presented at the annual meeting of the American Educational Research Association, New Orleans, February 1973.

Bloom, B. S. *Stability and change in human characteristics.* New York: Wiley, 1964.

Bloom, B.S. Learning for mastery. *Evaluation Comment.* Los Angeles: University of California, Center for the Study of Evaluation, May 1968.

Bloom, B. S. Replies to Dr. Jensen's article. *ERIC Clearinghouse on Early Childhood Education,* 1969, *3*, 50.

Bloom, B. S. Mastery learning. In J. H. Block (Ed.), *Mastery learning: Theory and practice.* New York: Holt, Rinehart and Winston, 1971.

Bloom, B. S., Engelhart, N. D., Furst, E. J., Hill, W. H., & Krathwohl, D. R. *Taxonomy of educational objectives. Handbook I: Cognitive domain.* New York: McKay, 1956.

Bluming, M., & Dembo, M. *Solving teaching problems: A guide for the elementary school teacher.* Pacific Palisades, Calif.: Goodyear, 1973.

Boocock, S. S. *An introduction to the sociology of learning.* Boston: Houghton Mifflin, 1972.

Broadbent, F., & Cruickshank, D. *The identity and analysis of first-*

year teachers, 1965. (ERIC Document Reproduction Service No. ED 013 786)

Brodsky, C. M. *A study of norms for body form – Behavior relationships.* Washington, D.C.: Catholic University of America Press, 1954.

Brookover, W. B., Patterson, A., & Thomas, S. Self-concept of ability and school achievement. *Sociology of Education,* 1964, *37*, 271–278.

Brookover, W. B., Patterson, A., & Thomas, S. *Improving academic achievement through students' self-concept enhancement, self-concept of ability, and school achievement* (Project No. 1636). Washington, D.C.: U.S. Department of Health, Education, and Welfare, Office of Education, 1965.

Brophy, J. E., & Good, T. L. Teachers' communication of differential expectations for children's classroom performance: Some behavioral data. *Journal of Educational Psychology,* 1970, *61*, 365–374.

Brophy, J. E., & Good, T. L. *Teacher-student relationships: Causes and consequences.* New York: Holt, Rinehart and Winston, 1974.

Brown, G. I. *Human teaching for human learning.* New York: Viking, 1971.

Bruner, J. *The process of education.* Cambridge: Harvard University Press, 1960.

Bruner, J. The act of discovery. *Harvard Educational Review,* 1961, *31*, 21–32.

Bruner, J. Some elements of discovery. In L. S. Shulman and E. R. Keislar (Eds.), *Learning by discovery: A critical appraisal.* Chicago: Rand McNally, 1966.

Bugelski, B. K. *The psychology of learning applied to teaching.* Indianapolis: Bobbs-Merrill, 1964.

Carin, A. A., & Sund, R. B. *Developing questioning techniques: A self-concept approach*. Columbus, Ohio: Merrill, 1971.

Carlton, L., & Moore, R. H. The effects of self-directive dramatization on reading achievement and self-concept of culturally disadvantaged children. *Reading Teacher*, 1966, *20*, 125–130.

Carter, R. How valid are marks assigned by teachers? *Journal of Educational Psychology*, 1952, *43*, 218–228.

Chafetz, J. S. *Masculine/feminine or human?* Itasca, Ill.: F. E. Peacock, 1974.

Chambers, J. A. College teachers: Their effect on creativity of students. *Journal of Educational Psychology*, 1973, *65*, 326–334.

Charters, W. W. The social background of teachers. In N. Gage (Ed.), *Handbook of research on teaching*. Chicago: Rand McNally, 1963.

Chase, C. I. *Measurement for educational evaluation*. Reading, Mass.: Addison-Wesley, 1974.

Christensen, C. M. Relationships between pupil achievement, pupil affect-need, teacher warmth, and teacher permissiveness. *Journal of Educational Psychology*. 1960, *51*, 169–174.

Claiborn, W. Expectancy effects in the classroom: A failure to replicate. *Journal of Educational Psychology*, 1969, *60*, 377–383.

Clarizio, H. F. Toward positive classroom discipline. New York: Wiley, 1971.

Cogan, M. The behavior of teachers and the productive behavior of their pupils. *Journal of Experimental Education*, 1958, *27*, 89–124.

Cohen, R. A. Conceptual styles, culture conflict and nonverbal tests of intelligence. *American Anthropologist*, 1969, *71*, 828–856.

Cohen, S. Educational psychology: Practice what we preach! *Educational Psychologist*, 1973, *10*, 80–86.

Coleman, J. S. *The adolescent society*. New York: Free Press, 1961.

Coleman, J. S. *Equality of educational opportunity*. Washington, D.C.: U.S. Department of Health, Education, and Welfare, Office of Education, Government Printing Office, 1966.

Coleman, W., & Cureton, E. E. Intelligence and achievement: The "jangle fallacy" again. *Educational and Psychological Measurement*, 1954, *14*, 347–351.

Combs, A. W. Intelligence from a perceptual point of view. *Journal of Abnormal and Social Psychology*, 1952, *47*, 662–673.

Combs, A. W., Avila, D. L., & Purkey, W. W. *Helping relationship: Basic concepts for the helping professions*. Boston: Allyn & Bacon, 1971.

Combs, A. W., Blume, R. A., Newman, A. J., & Wass, H. L. *The professional education of teachers* (2nd ed.). Boston: Allyn & Bacon, 1974.

Combs, A. W., & Snygg, D. *Individual behavior* (2nd ed.). New York: Harper & Row, 1959.

Conant, J. B. *The American high school today*. New York: McGraw-Hill, 1959.

Coopersmith, S. *The antecedents of self-esteem*. San Francisco:

Freeman, 1967.

Coopersmith, S., & Feldman, R. Fostering a positive self-concept and high self-esteem in the classroom. In R. H. Coop & K. White (Eds.), *Psychological concepts in the classroom*. New York: Harper & Row, 1974.

Costello, C. G. Ego involvement, success and failure: A review of the literature. In H. J. Eysenck (Ed.), *Experiments in motivation*. New York: Macmillan, 1964.

Cote, R. W. Behavior modification: Some questions. *The Elementary School Journal*, 1973, *24*, 45–47.

Crandall, V. C. Sex differences in expectancy of intellectual and academic reinforcement. In C. P. Smith (Ed.), *Achievement-related motives in children.* New York: Russell Sage Foundation, 1969.

Crandall, V. C., Katkovsky, W., & Crandall, J. J. Children's beliefs in their own control of reinforcement in intellectual-academic situations. *Child Developement*, 1965, *36*, 91–109.

Cropley, A. J. *Creativity*. London: Logmans, 1967.

Crowder, N. A. Automatic tutoring by intrinsic programming. In A. A. Lumsdaine & R. Glaser (Eds.), *Teaching machines and programmed learning*. Washington, D.C.: National Education Association, 1960.

Datta, L., Schaefer, E., & Davis, M. Sex and scholastic aptitude as variables in teachers' ratings of the adjustment and classroom behavior of Negro and other seventh-grade students. *Journal of Educational Psychology*, 1968, *59*, 94–101.

Davidson, H. H., & Lang, G. Children's perceptions of their teachers' feelings toward them related to self-perception, school achievement, and behavior. *Journal of Experimental Education*, 1960, *29*, 107–118.

Davis, W., & Phares, E. Parental antecedents of internal-external control of reinforcement. *Psychological Reports*, 1969, *24*, 427–436.

Deal, T. E. An organizational explanation of the failure of alternative secondary schools. *Educational Researcher*, 1975, *4*, 10–16.

deHirsch, K., Jansky, J., & Langford, W. S. *Predicting reading failure*. New York: Harper & Row, 1966.

Dellas, M., & Gaier, E. L. Identification of creativity: The individual. *Psychological Bulletin*, 1970, *73*, 55–73.

Deterline, W. A. Practical problems in program production. In P. C. Lange (Ed.), *Programmed instruction*. The Sixty-sixth Yearbook of the National Society for the Study of Education (Part II). Chicago: University of Chicago Press, 1967.

Deterline, W. A. The secrets we keep from students. *Educational technology*, 1968, *8*, 7–10.

Dewey, J. *How we think: A restatement of the relation of reflective thinking to the educative process*. Boston: D. C. Heath, 1933.

DiStefano, J. J. *Interpersonal perceptions of field-independent and field-dependent teachers and students*. Unpublished doctoral dissertation, Cornell University, 1969.

Dittes, J. E. Effects of changes in self-esteem upon impulsiveness and deliberation in making judgments. *Journal of Abnormal and Social Psychology*, 1959, *58*, 348–356.

DiVesta, F. J., & Thompson, G. G. *Educational psychology*. New York: Appleton-Century-Crofts, 1970.

Dowaliby, F. J., & Schumer, H. Teacher-centered versus student-centered modes of college classroom instruction as related to manifest anxiety. *Journal of Educational Psychology*, 1973, *65*, 125–132.

Doyle, W., Hancock, G., & Kifer, E. Teachers' perceptions: Do they make a difference? *Journal of the Association for the Study of Perception*, 1972, *7*, 21–30.

Duckworth, E. Piaget rediscovered. In R. E. Ripple & V. N. Rockcastle (Eds.), *Piaget rediscovered: A report of the conference on cognitive skills and curriculum development.* Ithaca, N.Y.: Cornell University, School of Education, 1964.

Duell, O. K. Effect of type of objective, level of test questions, and the judged importance of tested materials upon posttest performance. *Journal of Educational Psychology,* 1974, *66*, 225–232.

Dunn, R., & Dunn, K. *Practical approaches to individualizing instruction*. West Nyack, N.Y.: Parker, 1972.

Dunn, R., & Dunn, K. Learning styles as a criterion for placement in alternative programs. *Phi Delta Kappan*, 1974, *55*, 275–278.

Ebel, R. L. What are schools for? *Phi Delta Kappan*, 1972, *54*, 3–7.

Educational Policies Commission. *The central purposes of American education.* Washington, D. C.: National Education Association, 1961.

Eisner, E. W. Instructional and expressive educational objectives: Their formulation and use in curriculum. In W. J. Popham, E. W.

Eisner, H. J. Sullivan, & L. L. Tyler (Eds.), *Instructional objectives* (AERA Monograph Series on Curriculum Evaluation, *3*, 1–31). Chicago: Rand McNally, 1969.

Elkind, D. Adolescent cognitive development. In J. F. Adams (Ed.), *Understanding adolescence: Current developments in adolescent psychology*. Boston: Allyn & Bacon, 1968.

Elkind, D. *Children and adolescents: Interpretive essays on Jean Piaget* (2nd ed.). New York: Oxford, 1974.

Erlenmeyer-Kimmling, L., & Jarvik, L. F. Genetics and intelligence: A review. *Science,* 1963, *142*, 1477–1478.

Eysenck, H. J. *The IQ argument*. New York: The Library Press, 1971.

Farnham-Diggory, S. *Cognitive processes in education: A psychological preparation for teaching and curriculum development*. New York: Harper & Row, 1972.

Feshback, N. Student teacher preferences for elementary school pupils varying in personality characteristics. *Journal of Educational Psychology*, 1969, *60*, 126–132.

Finn, J. Expectations and the educational environment. *Review of Educational Research*, 1972, *42*, 387–410.

Flanagan, J. C. The PLAN system for individualizing education. *Measurement in Education*, 1971, *2*, 1–8.

Flanders, N. A. *Analyzing teacher behavior*. Reading, Mass.: Addison-Wesley, 1970.

Flavell, J. H. *The developmental psychology of Jean Piaget*. Princeton, N. J.: Van Nostrand, 1963.

Fleming, E., & Anttonen, R. Teacher expectancy or My Fair Lady. *American Educational Research Journal*, 1971, *8*, 241–252.

Franc, L. H. *Problems perceived by seventy-five beginning school teachers*, 1973. (ERIC Document Reproduction Service No. ED 073 064)

Frazier, B. H. *Design of a microeconomy system for correcting delinquent behavior patterns in institutionalized children*. Paper presented at the Conference of Behavioral Engineering in Therapeutic Environments, Walter Reed Army Medical Center, Washington, D. C., 1969.

Frazier, N., & Sadker, M. *Sexism in school and society*. New York: Harper & Row, 1973.

French, E. The effects of the interaction of motivation and feedback on task performance. In Atkinson, J. W. (Ed.), *Motives in fantasy, action and society*. Princeton, N. J.: Van Nostrand, 1958.

Friedman, H., & Friedman, P. *Frequency and types of teacher reinforcement given to lower- and middle-class students*. Paper presented at the annual meeting of the American Educational Research Association, New Orleans, 1973.

Fuller, F. F. Concerns of teachers: A developmental conceptualization. *American Educational Research Journal*, 1969, *6*, 207–226.

Gage, N. L. I.Q., heritability, race differences, and educational research. *Phi Delta Kappan*, 1972, *53*, 308–312.

Gage, N. L., & Berliner, D. C. *Educational psychology*. Chicago: Rand McNally, 1975.

Gagné, R. M. *The conditions of learning* (2nd ed.). New York: Holt, Rinehart and Winston, 1970.

Gall, M. D., & Ward, B. A. *Critical issues in educational psychology*. Boston: Little, Brown, 1974.

Gardner, W. I. *Children with learning and behavior problems: A behavior management approach*. Boston: Allyn & Bacon, 1974.

Gaudry, E., & Spielberger, C. D. *Anxiety and educational achievement*. Sidney: Wiley, 1971.

Gentile, J. R., Frazier, T. W., & Morris, M. C. *Instructional applications of behavior principles*. Monterey, Calif.: Brooks/Cole, 1973.

Gesell, A., Ilg, F. L., & Ames, L. B. *Youth: The years from ten to sixteen*. New York: Harper & Row, 1956.

Getzels, J. W., & Jackson, P. W. *Creativity and intelligence*. New York: Wiley, 1962.

Ginsburg, H., & Opper, S. *Piaget's theory of intellectual development: An introduction*. Englewood Cliffs, N. J.: Prentice-Hall, 1969.

Giusti, J., & Hogg, S. Management in instruction. *Journal of Teacher Education*, 1973, *24*, 41–43.

Givner, A., & Graubard, D. S. *A handbook of behavior modification for the classroom*. New York: Holt, Rinehart and Winston, 1974.

Goertzel, V., & Goertzel, M. *Cradles of eminence*. Boston: Little, Brown, 1962.

Goldberg, M., Passow, A., & Justman, J. *The effects of ability group-*

ing. New York: Teachers College Press, 1966.

Good, T.L. Which pupils do teachers call on? *Elementary School Journal,* 1970, *70,* 190–198.

Good, T. L., Biddle, B. J., & Brophy, J.E. *Teachers make a difference*. New York: Holt, Rinehart and Winston, 1975.

Good, T. L., & Brophy, J. E. Behavioral expression of teacher attitudes. *Journal of Educational Psychology*, 1972, *63*, 617–624.

Good, T. L., & Brophy, J. E. *Looking in classrooms*. New York: Harper & Row, 1973.

Good, T. L., & Grouws, D. *Reaction of male and female teacher trainees to descriptions of elementary school pupils* (Tech. Rep. No. 62). Columbia, Mo.: University of Missouri, Center for Research in Social Behavior, 1972.

Goodwin, W., & Sanders, J. *An exploratory study of the effect of selected variables upon teacher expectation of pupil success*. Paper presented at the annual meeting of the American Educational Research Association, Los Angeles, April 1969.

Gordon, I. J. *Studying the child in school*. New York: Wiley, 1966.

Gordon, I. J. *A test manual for the How-I-See-Myself Scale*. Gainesville: University of Florida, Florida Educational Research and Development Council, 1968.

Gorman, R. M. *The psychology of classroom learning*. Columbus, Ohio: Merrill, 1974.

Greenberg, H. M. *Teaching with feeling: Compassion and self-awareness in the classroom today*. New York: Macmillan, 1969.

Gronlund, N. E. *Stating behavioral objectives for classroom instruction*. New York: Macmillan, 1970.

Gronlund, N. E. *Measurement and evaluation in teaching* (2nd ed.). New York: Macmillan, 1971.

Gronlund, N. E. *Preparing criterion-referenced tests for classroom instruction*. New York: Macmillan, 1973.

Gronlund, N. E. *Improving marking and reporting in classroom instruction*. New York: Macmillan, 1974. (a)

Gronlund, N. E. *Individualizing classroom instruction*. New York: Macmillan, 1974. (b)

Guilford, J. P. Three faces of intellect. *American Psychologist*, 1959,

14, 469–479.

Guskin, J. *The social perception of language variations: Black dialect and expectations of ability*. Paper presented at the annual meeting of the American Educational Research Association, Minneapolis, March 1970.

Guthrie, E. R. *The psychology of learning* (Rev. ed.). New York: Harper, 1952.

Guthrie, J. T. Expository instruction versus a discovery method. *Journal of Educational Psychology*, 1967, *58*, 45–49.

Hadley, S. A school mark — fact or fancy? *Educational Administration and Supervision*, 1954, *40*, 305–312.

Hall, E. T. Listening behavior: Some cultural differences. *Phi Delta Kappan*, 1969, *50*, 379–380.

Hamachek, D. E. Characteristics of good teachers and implications for teacher education. *Phi Delta Kappan*, 1969, *50*, 341–345.

Hamachek, D. E. *Encounters with the self*. New York: Holt, Rinehart and Winston, 1971.

Harrow, A. J. *A taxonomy of the psychomotor domain: A guide for developing behavioral objectives.* . New York: McKay, 1972.

Havighurst, R. J. Minority subcultures and the law of effect. *American Psychologist*, 1970, *25*, 313–322.

Heckhausen, H. *The anatomy of achievement motivation*. New York: Academic Press, 1967.

Henry, J. *Culture against man*. New York: Random House, 1963.

Hermann, G. D. Egrule vs. ruleg teaching methods: Grade, intelligence, category of learning. *Journal of Experimental Education*, 1971, *39*, 22–33.

Herrnstein, R. I.Q. *The Atlantic*, 1971, *228*, 43–64.

Hess, R., Shipman, V., Brophy, J., & Bear, R. (in collaboration with A. Adelberger). *The cognitive environments of urban preschool children: Follow-up phase.* Chicago: University of Chicago, 1969. (Mimeo. final report)

Hewett, F. M. Educational engineering with emotionally disturbed children. *Exceptional Children*, 1967, *23*, 459–467.

Hieronymus, A. N., & Stroud, J. B. Comparability of I.Q. scores on five widely used intelligence tests. *Measurement and Evaluation in*

Guidance, 1969, *2*, 135–140.

Hill, K., & Sarason, S. B. A further longitudinal study of the relationship of test anxiety and defensiveness to test and school performance over the elementary school years. *Child Development Monographs*, 1966, *31*, 1–76.

Holmen, M. G., & Docter, R. F. Criticisms of standardized testing. *Today's Education*, January–February 1974, *63*, 50–58; 60.

Holt, J. *How children fail*. New York: Pitman, 1964.

Honzik, M. P. Environmental correlates of mental growth: Prediction from the family setting at 21 months. *Child Development*, 1967, *36*, 337–364.

Horner, M. Women's will to fail. *Psychology Today*, 1968, *3*, 36–38.

Hoy, W. K. The influence of experience on the beginning teacher. *School Review*, 1968, *76*, 312–323.

Hunt, D. E. *Alternative approaches in two York County secondary schools* (Grants-in-aid project) Toronto: Ontario Department of Education, 1972.

Hunt, D. E., & Sullivan, E. V. *Between psychology and education*. Hinsdale, Ill.: Dryden Press, 1974.

Hunt, J. McV. *Intelligence and experience*. New York: Ronald Press, 1961.

Hunt, J. McV. The psychological basis for using preschool enrichment as an antidote for cultural deprivation. *Merrill-Palmer Quarterly*, 1964, *10*, 209–248.

Hunter, M. C. The teaching process. In D. Allen and E. Seifman (Eds.), *The teacher's handbook*. Glenview, Ill.: Scott, Foresman, 1971.

Hunter, M. C. Appraising teaching performance: One approach. *National Elementary Principal*, 1973, *52*, 60–62.

Husén, T., & Svennson, N. Pedagogic milieu and development of intellectual skills. *School Review*, 1960, *68*, 36–51.

Inhelder, B., & Piaget, J. *The growth of logical thinking from childhood to adolescence*. New York: Basic Books, 1958.

Jackson, P. *Life in classrooms*. New York: Holt, Rinehart and Winston, 1968.

Jackson, P., & Lahaderne, H. Inequalities of teacher-pupil contacts.

Psychology in the Schools, 1967, 204–211.

Jackson, P., Silberman, M., & Wolfson, B. Signs of personal involvement in teachers' descriptions of their students. *Journal of Educational Psychology*, 1969, *60*, 22–27.

James, C. D. *A cognitive-style approach to teacher-pupil interaction and the academic performances of black children*. Unpublished master's thesis, Rutgers University, 1973.

Jencks, C. S. *Inequality: A reassessment of the effect of family and schooling in America*. New York: Basic Books, 1972.

Jenkins, B. *Teachers' views of particular students and their behavior in the classroom*. Unpublished doctoral dissertation, University of Chicago, 1972.

Jenkins, J., & Deno, S. Influence of student behavior on teachers' self-evaluation. *Journal of Educational Psychology*, 1969, *60*, 439–442.

Jensen, A. R. How much can we boost IQ and scholastic achievement? *Harvard Educational Review*, 1969, *39*, 1–123.

Johnson, D. *An investigation of sex differences in reading in four English-speaking nations* (Tech. Rep. No. 209). Madison: University of Wisconsin, Research and Development Center for Cognitive Learning, 1972.

Johnson, D. W., & Johnson, R. T. *Learning together and alone: Cooperation, competition, and individualization*. Englewood Cliffs, N. J.: Prentice-Hall, 1975.

Jourard, S. M., & Secord, P. F. Body-cathexis and personality. *British Journal of Psychology*, 1955, *46*, 130–138. (a)

Jourard, S. M., & Secord, P. F. Body-cathexis and the ideal female figure. *Journal of Abnormal and Social Psychology*, 1955, *50*, 243–246. (b)

Joyce, B., & Weil, B. *Models of teaching*. Englewood Cliffs, N. J.: Prentice-Hall, 1972.

Kagan, J. Reflection-impulsivity and reading ability in primary grade children. *Child Development*, 1965, *36*, 609–628.

Kagan, J. Understanding the psychology of mental growth. *Grade Teacher Magazine*, 1966, pp. 79; 123–130.

Kagan, J. Check one: Male, female. *Psychology Today*, 1969, *3*, 39–41.

Kagan, J., Pearson, L., & Welch, L. Conceptual impulsivity and inductive reasoning. *Child Development*, 1966, *37*, 583–594.

Kagan, J., Rosman, B. L., Day, D., Albert, J., & Phillips, W. Information processing in the child: Significances of analytic and reflective attitudes. *Psychological Monographs*, 1964, *78*, (1, Whole No. 578).

Kaplan, S., Kaplan, J., Madsen, S., & Taylor, B. *Change for children: Ideas and activities for individualizing learning*. Pacific Palisades, Calif.: Goodyear, 1973.

Karplus, R. The science curriculum improvement study. In R. E. Ripple & V. N. Rockcastle (Eds.), *Piaget rediscovered: A report of the conference on cognitive skills and curriculum development*. Ithaca, N. Y.: Cornell University, School of Education, 1964.

Katkovsky, W., Crandall, V. C., & Good, S. Parental antecedents of children's beliefs in internal-external control of reinforcements in intellectual achievement situations. *Child Development*, 1967, *38*, 765–776.

Katz, L. Developmental stages of the preschool teacher. *The Elementary School Journal*, 1970, *73*, 50–54.

Kelly, E. A study of consistent discrepancies between instructors' grades and term-end examination grades. *Journal of Educational Psychology*, 1958, *49*, 328–334.

Kendall, E. We have men on the staff. *Young Children*, 1972, *27*, 358–362.

Kibler, R. J., Cegala, D. J., Barker, L. L., & Miles, D. T. *Objectives for instruction and evaluation*. Boston: Allyn & Bacon, 1974.

Kirk, S. A. *Educating exceptional children (2nd ed.)*. Boston: Houghton Mifflin, 1972.

Klein, S. Student influence on teacher behavior. *American Educational Research Journal*, 1971, *8*, 403–421.

Kleinfeld, J. *Instructional style and the intellectual performance of Indian and Eskimo students* (Final Report, Project No. 1-J-027). Washington, D. C.: Department of Health, Education, and Welfare, Office of Education, 1972.

Kogan, N. Educational implications of cognitive style. In G. Lesser (Ed.), *Psychology and educational practice*. Glenview, Ill.: Scott, Foresman, 1971.

Kohler, W. *The mentality of the apes*. New York: Harcourt, Brace & World, 1927.

Kolesnik, W. B. *Humanism and/or behaviorism in education*. Boston: Allyn & Bacon, 1975.

Komarovsky, M. *Women in the modern world: Their education and their dilemmas*. Boston: Little, Brown, 1953.

Kounin, J. *Discipline and group management in classrooms*. New York: Holt, Rinehart and Winston, 1970.

Kowitz, G. T. Test anxiety and self-concept. *Childhood Education*, 1967, *44*, 162–165.

Kozol, J. *Free schools*. Boston: Houghton Mifflin, 1972.

Krathwohl, D. R., Bloom, B. S., & Masia, B. *Taxonomy of educational objectives. Handbook II: Affective domain*. New York: McKay, 1964.

Kranz, D., Weber, W., & Fishell, K. *The relationships between teacher perception of pupils and teacher behavior toward those pupils*. Paper presented at the annual meeting of the American Educational Research Association, Minneapolis, March 1970.

Kropp, R. P., Nelson, W. H., & King, F. J. *Identification and definition of subject-matter content variables related to human aptitudes*. Tallahassee: Florida State University, 1967.

Krumboltz, J. D. & Krumboltz, H. B. *Changing children's behavior*. Englewood Cliffs, N. J.: Prentice-Hall, 1972.

Kryspin, W. J., & Feldhusen, J. F. *Analyzing verbal classroom interaction*. Minneapolis: Burgess, 1974.

Labov, W. Academic ignorance and black intelligence. In M. D. Gall & B. A. Ward (Eds.), *Critical issues in educational psychology*. Boston: Little, Brown, 1974.

Leacock, E. B. *Teaching and learning in city schools: A comparative study*. New York: Basic Books, 1969.

Lee, P. C. Male and female teachers in elementary schools. *Teachers College Record*, 1973, *75*, 79–98.

Lefcourt, H. Internal versus external control of reinforcement: A review. *Psychological Review*, 1966, *65*, 206–220.

Lefrancois, G. R. A treatment hierarchy for the acceleration of conservation of substance. *Canadian Journal of Psychology*, 1968, *22*, 277–284.

Lefrancois, G. R. *Psychology for teachers*. Belmont, Calif.: Wadsworth, 1972. (a)

Lefrancois, G. R. *Psychological theories and human learning: Kongor's report.* Belmont, Calif.: Brooks/Cole, 1972. (b)

Lembo, J. M. *The psychology of effective classroom instruction*. Columbus, Ohio: Merrill, 1969.

Leonard, G. B. *Education and ecstasy*. New York: Dell, 1968.

Lesser, G. S., Fifer, G., & Clark, D. H. Mental abilities of children from different social-class and cultural groups. *Monographs of the Society for Research in Child Development*, 1965, *30* (4, Serial No. 102).

Lewin, K., Lippitt, R., & White, R. K. Patterns of aggressive behavior in experimentally created "social climates." *Journal of Social Psychology*, 1939, *10*, 271–299.

Long, J. D., & Huck, S. W. *The effect of behavioral objectives on student achievement*. Paper presented at the annual meeting of the American Educational Research Association, Chicago, 1972.

Ludwig, D. J., & Maehr, M. L. Changes in self-concept and stated behavioral preferences. *Child Development*, 1967, *38*, 453–467.

Lynch, D. O., & Smith, B. C. *To change or not to change item responses when taking tests: Empirical evidence for test takers*. Paper presented at the annual meeting of the American Educational Research Association, Chicago, April 1972.

Lyon, H. C. *Learning to feel – Feeling to learn*. Columbus, Ohio: Merrill, 1971.

Maccoby, E. E. (Ed.). *The development of sex differences*. Stanford, Calif.: Stanford University Press, 1966.

Maccoby, E. E., & Jacklin, C. N. *Sex differences revisited: Myth and reality*. Paper presented at the annual meeting of the American Educational Research Association, Chicago, 1974.

Madsen, C. H., Becker, W. C., Thomas, O. R., Koser, L., & Plager, E. An analysis of the reinforcing function of "sit down" commands. In R. K. Parker (Ed.), *Readings in educational psychology*. Boston: Allyn & Bacon, 1968.

Maehr, M. L., & Sjogren, D. D. Atkinson's theory of achievement motivation: First step toward a theory of academic motivation. *Review of Educational Research*, 1971, *41*, 143–161.

Mager, R. F. *Preparing instructional objectives.* Palo Alto, Calif.: Fearon, 1962.

Mager, R. F., & McCann, J. *Learner-controlled instruction.* Palo Alto, Calif.: Varian Associates, 1961.

Mahone, C. H. Fear of failure and unrealistic vocational aspiration. *Journal of Abnormal and Social Psychology*, 1960, *60*, 253–261.

Maslow, A. H. *Motivation and personality* (2nd ed.). New York: Harper & Row, 1970.

Mathis, B. C., & McGaghie, W. C. From theories for learning to theories for teaching. In L. J. Stiles (Ed.), *Theories for teaching*. New York: Dodd, Mead, 1974.

McCandless, B. R. *Children: Behavior and development* (2nd ed.). New York: Holt, Rinehart and Winston, 1967.

McCarthy, J. J., & McCarthy, J. F. *Learning disabilities*. Boston: Allyn & Bacon, 1969.

McClelland, D. C., & Alschuler, A. S. *The achievement motivation development project* (Final report to United States Office of Education, Project No. 7-1231). Washington, D. C.: Bureau of Research, 1971.

McDonald, F. *Educational psychology* (2nd ed.) Belmont, Calif.: Wadsworth, 1965.

McKeachie, W. J. Motivating teaching methods and college learning. In M. R. Jones (Ed.), *Nebraska Symposium on Motivation*. Lincoln: University of Nebraska Press, 1961.

McKeachie, W. J., Lin, Y., & Mann, W. Student ratings of teacher effectiveness: Validity studies. *American Educational Research Journal*, 1971, *8*, 435–445.

McLachlan, J. F. C., & Hunt, D. E. Differential effects of discovery learning as a function of student conceptual level. *Canadian Journal of Behavioural Science*, 1973, *5*, 152–160.

Meeker, M. N. *The structure of intellect: Its interpretation and uses*. Columbus, Ohio: Merrill, 1969.

Mendoza, S., Good, T., & Brophy, J. *Who talks in junior high classrooms?* (Report Series No. 68). Austin: University of Texas, Research and Development Center for Teacher Education, 1972.

Mercer, J. R. Sociocultural factors in labeling mental retardates. *Peabody Journal of Education*, 1971, *48*, 188–203.

Messer, S. Reflection-impulsivity: Stability and school failure. *Journal of Educational Psychology*, 1970, *61*, 487–490.

Miller, H. L., & Woock, R. R. *Social foundations of urban education*.

Hinsdale, Ill.: Dryden Press, 1970.

Miller, J. P. *Humanizing the classroom: Models of teaching in affective education*. New York: Praeger, 1976.

Mouly, G. J. *Psychology for effective teaching* (3rd ed.). New York: Holt, Rinehart and Winston, 1973.

Moustakas, C. *The authentic teacher: Sensitivity and awareness in the classroom*. Cambridge, Mass.: Doyle, 1966.

Mueller, R. J. *Principles of classroom learning and perception*. New York: Praeger, 1974.

Neill, A. S. *Summerhill*. New York: Hart, 1960.

Newman, H. H., Freeman, F. N., & Holzinger, K. J. *Twins: A study of heredity and environment*. Chicago: University of Chicago Press, 1937.

Nolan, J. D. The true humanist: The behavior modifier. *Teachers College Record*, 1974, *76*, 335–343.

O'Connor, P., Atkinson, J. W., & Horner, M. Motivational implications of ability grouping in school. In J. W. Atkinson & N. T. Feather (Eds.), *A theory of achievement motivation*. New York: Wiley, 1966.

Ogilvie, B. C., & Tutko, T. A. Sport: If you want to build character, try something else. *Psychology Today*, 1971, *5*, 63–69.

Packard, R. G. *Psychology of learning and instruction*. Columbus, Ohio: Merrill, 1975.

Page, E. B. Teacher comments and student performance: A seventy-four classroom experiment in school motivation. *Journal of Educational Psychology*, 1958, *49*, 173–181.

Palardy, J. What teachers believe — What children achieve. *Elementary School Journal*, 1969, *69*, 370–374.

Parnell, D. The Oregon walkabout. *Phi Delta Kappan*, 1974, *56*, 205–206.

Patterson, C. H. *Humanistic education*. Englewood Cliffs, N. J.: Prentice-Hall, 1973.

Payne, D. A. *The assessment of learning: Cognitive and affective*. Lexington, Mass.: D. C. Heath, 1974.

Peel, E. A. Learning and thinking in a school situation. In R. E. Ripple & V. N. Rockcastle (Eds.), *Piaget rediscovered: A report of the conference on cognitive skills and curriculum development*. Ithaca,

N. Y.: Cornell University, School of Education, 1964.

Phillips, B. N., Hindsman, E., & McGuire, C. Factors associated with anxiety and their relation to the school achievement of adolescents. *Psychological Reports*, 1960, *7*, 365–372.

Phillips, B. N., Martin, R. P., & Meyers, J. Interventions in relation to anxiety in school. In C. D. Spielberger (Ed.), *Anxiety: Current trends in theory and research*. New York: Academic Press, 1972.

Phillips, J. L. *The origins of intellect: Piaget's theory*. San Francisco: Freeman, 1969.

Piaget, J. *The child's conception of number*. London: Humanities Press, 1952.

Piaget, J. Development and learning. In R. E. Ripple & V. N. Rockcastle (Eds.), *Piaget rediscovered: A report of the conference on cognitive skills and curriculum development*. Ithaca, N. Y.: Cornell University, School of Education, 1964.

Piaget, J., & Szeminska, A. *The child's conception of number* (C. Gattegno & F. M. Hodgson, Trans.). New York: Humanities Press, 1952.

Plowden, Lady B., et al. *Children and their primary schools: A report of the Central Advisory Council for Education*. London: H. M. Stationery Office, 1967.

Plowman, P. D. *Behavioral objectives*. Chicago: Science Research Associates, 1971.

Popham, W. J., & Baker, E. L. *Systematic instruction*. Englewood Cliffs, N. J.: Prentice-Hall, 1970.

Postman, N., & Weingarten, C. *Teaching as a subversive activity*. New York: Delacorte Press, 1969.

Poteet, J. A. *Behavior modification: A practical guide for teachers.* Minneapolis: Burgess, 1973.

Premack, D. Toward empirical behavior laws: 1. Positive reinforcement. *Psychological Review*, 1959, *66*, 219–233.

Prescott, D. A. *The child in the educative process*. New York: McGraw-Hill, 1957.

Pressey, S. L. A simple apparatus which gives tests and scores — And teaches. *School and Society*, 1926, *23*, 373–376.

Preston, R. Reading achievement of German and American children. *School and Society*, 1962, *90*, 350–354.

Purkey, W. W. *The self and academic achievement*. Englewood Cliffs, N. J.: Prentice-Hall, 1970.

Ramírez, M., & Castañeda, A. *Cultural democracy, bicognitive development, and education*. New York: Academic Press, 1974.

Ramírez, M., & Price-Williams, D. R. Cognitive styles of children of three ethnic groups in the United States. *Journal of Cross-Cultural Psychology*, 1974, *5*, 212–219.

Reed, H. B. Implications for science education of a teacher competence research. *Science Education*, 1962, *46*, 473–486.

Reiling, E., & Taylor, R. A new approach to the problem of changing initial responses to multiple-choice questions. *Journal of Educational Measurement*, 1972, *9*, 67–70.

Reissman, F. The strategy of style. *Teachers College Record*, 1964, *65*, 484–495.

Rist, R. Student social class and teacher expectations: The self-fulfilling prophecy in ghetto education. *Harvard Educational Review*, 1970, *40*, 411–451.

Roe, A. *Automated teaching methods using linear programs* (Report No. 60-105, Automated Research Project). Los Angeles: University of California, Department of Engineering, 1960.

Rogers, C. R. *Freedom to learn*. Columbus, Ohio: Merrill, 1969.

Rogers, C. R., & Skinner, B. F. Some issues concerning the control of human behavior. *Science*, 1956, *124*, 1057–1066.

Rohwer, W. D. Learning, race, and school success. *Review of Educational Research*, 1971, *41*, 191–210.

Rosen, B., & D'Andrade, R. The psychosocial origins of achievement motivation. *Sociometry*, 1959, *22*, 185–218.

Rosenshine, B., & Furst, N. Research on teacher performance criteria. In B. Smith (Ed.), *Research in teacher education: A symposium*. Englewood Cliffs, N. J.: Prentice-Hall, 1971.

Rosenthal, R., & Jacobson, L. *Pygmalion in the classroom: Teacher expectation and pupils' intellectual development*. New York: Holt, Rinehart and Winston, 1968.

Rotter, J. Generalized expectancies for internal versus external control of reinforcement. *Psychological Monographs*, 1966, *80* (1, Whole No. 609).

Rowe, M. Science, silence, and sanctions. *Science and Children*, 1969, *6*, 11–13.

Ryan, K. The first year of teaching. In K. Ryan (Ed.), *Don't smile until Christmas*. Chicago: University of Chicago Press, 1970.

Sadker, M. Elements of sex bias in schools. In M. Gall & B. Ward (Eds.), *Critical issues in educational psychology*. Boston: Little, Brown, 1974.

Sanders, N. M. *Classroom questions: What kinds?* New York: Harper & Row, 1966.

Sarason, I. G. The effects of anxiety and threat on the solution of a difficult task. *Journal of Abnormal and Social Psychology*, 1961, *62*, 165–168.

Sarason, S.B., Davidson, K.S., Lighthall, F.F., Waite, R.R., & Ruebrush, B.K. *Anxiety in elementary school children*. New York: Wiley, 1960.

Sarason, S. B., Hill, K. T., & Zimbardo, P. G. A longitudinal study of the relation of test anxiety to performance on intelligence and achievement tests. *Monographs of the Society for Research on Child Development*, 1964, *29*, (7, Serial No. 98).

Sax, G. *Principles of educational measurement and evaluation*. Belmont, Calif.: Wadsworth, 1974.

Schmuck, R. A., & Schmuck, P. A. *A humanistic psychology of education*. Palo Alto, Calif.: National Press Books, 1974.

Seaberg, D. I. *The four faces of teaching: The role of the teacher in humanizing education*. Pacific Palisades, Calif.: Goodyear, 1974.

Sears, P. S. Levels of aspiration in academically successful and unsuccessful children. *Journal of Abnormal and Social Psychology*, 1940, *35*, 498–536.

Sherman, J. A. *On the psychology of women: A survey of empirical studies*. Springfield, Ill.: Charles C Thomas, 1971.

Shockley, W. Negro IQ deficit: Failure of a "malicious coincidence" model warrants new research proposals. *Review of Educational Research*, 1971, *41*, 227–248.

Shumsky, A. Individual differences in learning styles. In A. Shumsky (Ed.), *In search of teaching style*. New York: Appleton-Century-Crofts, 1968.

Siegel, I. E. The Piagetian system and the world of education. In D.

Elkind & J. H. Flavell (Eds.), *Studies in cognitive development: Essays in honor of Jean Piaget*. New York: Oxford, 1969.

Sigel, I. E., & Coop, R. H. Cognitive style and classroom practice. In R. H. Coop & K. White (Eds.), *Psychological concepts in the classroom*. New York: Harper & Row, 1974.

Silberman, H. R., Melaragno, R. J., Coulson, J. E., & Estavan, D. Fixed sequence versus branching autoinstructional methods. *Journal of Educational Psychology*, 1961, *52*, 166–172.

Silberman, M. Behavioral expression of teachers' attitudes toward elementary school students. *Journal of Educational Psychology*, 1969, *60*, 402–407.

Silverman, S., & Kimmel, D. The effects of immediate feedback on the behavior of teachers-in-training. *School Applications of Learning Theory*, 1972, *4*, 16–23.

Simon, A., & Boyer, E. G. (Eds.). *Mirrors for behavior: An anthology of observation instruments*. Philadelphia: Research for Better Schools, 1970.

Simon, S. B., Howe, L. W., & Kirschenbaum, H. *Values clarification: A handbook of practical strategies for teachers and students*. New York: Hart, 1972.

Skeels, H. M. Adult status of children with contrasting early life experiences: A follow-up study. *Child Development Monographs*, 1966, *31* (3, Serial No. 105).

Skeels, H. M., Updegraff, R., Wellman, B. L., & Williams, H. M. *A study of environmental stimulation: An orphanage preschool project*. Des Moines: University of Iowa Studies in Child Welfare, 1938.

Skinner, B. F. *Science and human behavior*. New York: Macmillan, 1953.

Skinner, B. F. The science of learning and the art of teaching. *Harvard Educational Review*, 1954, *24*, 86–97.

Skinner, B. F. *The technology of teaching*. New York: Appleton-Century-Crofts, 1968.

Skinner, B. F. The free and happy student. *Phi Delta Kappan*, 1973, *55*, 13–16.

Smedslund, J. The acquisition of conservation of substance and weight in children. II. External reinforcement of conservation of weight and of the operations of addition and subtraction. *Scandina-*

vian Journal of Psychology, 1961, *2*, 71–84. (a)

Smedslund, J. The acquisition of conservation of substance and weight in children. III. Extinction of conservation of weight acquired normally and by means of empirical controls on a balance scale. *Scandinavian Journal of Psychology*, 1961, *2*, 85–87. (b)

Smith, B. O. A concept of teaching. *Teachers College Record*, 1960, *61*, 229–241.

Smith, C. P. Relationships between achievement-related motives and intelligence, performance level, and persistence. *Journal of Abnormal and Social Psychology*, 1964, *68*, 523–532.

Smith, C. P. (Ed.). *Achievement-related motives in children*. New York: Russell Sage Foundation, 1969.

Smith, F. M., & Adams, S. *Educational measurement for the classroom teacher* (2nd ed.). New York: Harper & Row, 1972.

Smith, I. M. *Spatial ability*. San Diego: Knapp, 1964.

Snow, R. Unfinished Pygmalion. *Contemporary Psychology*, 1969, *14*, 197–199.

Soares, A. T., & Soares, L. M. Self-perceptions of culturally disadvantaged children. *American Educational Research Journal*, 1969, *6*, 31–45.

Solomon, D., & Oberlander, M. I. Locus of control in the classroom. In R. H. Coop & K. White (Eds.), *Psychological concepts in the classroom*. New York: Harper & Row, 1974.

Spaulding, R. L. *Achievement, creativity, and self-concept correlates of teacher-pupil transactions in elementary schools* (U.S. Office of Education, Cooperative Research Report No. 1352). Urbana: University of Illinois, 1963.

Spearman, C. *The abilities of man: Their nature and measurement.* New York: Macmillan, 1927.

Spears, H. Kappans ponder the goals of education. *Phi Delta Kappan*, 1973, *55*, 29–32.

Spencer, E. F., & Smith, R. M. Arithmetic skills. In R. M. Smith (Ed.), *Teacher diagnosis of educational difficulties*. Columbus, Ohio: Merrill, 1969.

Sperry, L. *Learning performance and individual differences: Essays and readings*. Glenview, Ill.: Scott, Foresman, 1972.

Spicker, H. H. Intellectual development through early childhood education. *Exceptional Children*, 1971, *37*, 629–640.

Spielberger, C. D., & Katzenmeyer, W. G. Manifest anxiety, intelligence, and college grades. *Journal of Consulting Psychology*, 1959, *23*, 278.

Sprinthall, R. C., & Sprinthall, N. A. *Educational psychology: A developmental approach*. Reading, Mass.: Addison-Wesley, 1974.

Staffieri, J. R. A study of social stereotype of body image in children. *Journal of Personality and Social Psychology*, 1967, *7*, 101–103.

Stanchfield, J. *Sex differences in learning to read*. Bloomington, Ind.: Phi Delta Kappa Educational Foundation, 1973.

Stein, A. The effects of sex-role standards for achievement and sex-role preference on three determinants of achievement motivation. *Developmental Psychology*, 1971, *4*, 219–231.

Stein, A., Pohly, S., & Mueller, E. *Sex typing of achievement areas as a determinant of children's motivation and effort*. Paper presented at the meeting of the Society for Research in Child Development, 1969.

Stephens, M. J., & Evans, E. D. *Development and classroom learning*. New York: Holt, Rinehart and Winston, 1973.

Stodolsky, S. S., & Lesser, G. S. Learning patterns in the disadvantaged. *Harvard Educational Review*, 1967, *37*, 548–593.

Suchman, J. R. Inquiry training in the elementary school. *Science Teacher*, 1960, *27*, 42–47.

Sullivan, E. V. *Piaget and the school curriculum: A critical appraisal* (Bulletin No. 2). Toronto: Ontario Institute for Studies in Education, 1967.

Sutter, E. M. *Individual differences and social conditions as they affect learning by computer-assisted instruction*. Unpublished doctoral dissertation, University of Texas, 1967.

Taba, H. Learning by discovery: Psychological and educational rationale. *The Elementary School Journal*, March 1963, pp. 310–315.

Taba, H. *Teaching strategies and cognitive functioning in elementary school children*. San Francisco: San Francisco State College, 1966.

Taba, H., & Elzey, F. Teaching strategies and thought processes. *Teachers College Record*, 1964, *65*, 524–534.

Tanner, L. N., & Lindgren, H. C. *Classroom teaching and learning: A mental health approach*. New York: Holt, Rinehart and Winston, 1971.

TenBrink, T. D. *Evaluation: A practical guide for teachers*. New York: McGraw-Hill, 1974.

Terman, L. M., & Merrill, M. A. *Stanford-Binet intelligence scale: Manual for the third revision, form L-M*. Boston: Houghton Mifflin, 1960.

Terman, L. M., & Oden, M. *Genetic studies of genius: Mental and physical traits of a thousand gifted children*. Stanford, Calif.: Stanford University Press, 1925.

Terman, L. M., & Oden, M. *Genetic studies of genius: The gifted group at mid-life. Thirty-five years' follow-up of the superior child*. Stanford, Calif.: Stanford University Press, 1954.

Terwilliger, J. S. *Assigning grades to students*. Glenview, Ill.: Scott, Foresman, 1971.

Thatcher, D. A. Ask not what you can do for the machine. . . . *Phi Delta Kappan*, 1972, *53*, 509–511.

Thomas, A., & Stewart, N. Counselor's response to female clients with deviate and conforming career goals. *Journal of Counseling Psychology*, 1971, *18*, 352–357.

Thorndike, E. L. *Educational psychology*. New York: Columbia University, Teachers College, 1913.

Thorndike, E. L. *The measurement of intelligence*. New York: Columbia University, Teachers College, 1927.

Thorndike, R. Review of Pygmalion in the classroom. *American Educational Research Journal*, 1968, *5*, 708–711.

Thurstone, L. L. *Primary mental abilities*. Chicago: University of Chicago Press, 1938.

Torrance, E. P. *Guiding creative talent*. Englewood Cliffs, N. J.: Prentice-Hall, 1962.

Torrance, E. P. *Rewarding creative behavior*. Englewood Cliffs, N. J.: Prentice-Hall, 1965.

Torrance, E. P. *Encouraging creativity in the classroom*. Dubuque, Iowa: Brown, 1970.

Torrance, E.P. Creative kids. *Today's Education*, 1972, *61*, 22–29.

Trickett, E. J., & Moos, R. Social environment of junior high and high school classrooms. *Journal of Educational Psychology*, 1973, *65*, 93–102.

Tuckman, B., & Oliver, W. Effectiveness of feedback to teachers as a function of source. *Journal of Educational Psychology*, 1968, *59*, 297–301.

Vairo, P. D. Wanted: 20,000 male first-grade school teachers. *Education*, 1969, *89*, 222–224.

Waite, R. R., Sarason, S. B., Lighthall, F. F., & Davidson, K. A. A study of anxiety and learning in children. *Journal of Abnormal and Social Psychology*, 1958, *57*, 267–270.

Walberg, H. J. Changes in the self-concept during teacher training. *Psychology in the Schools*, 1967, *4*, 14–21.

Walberg, H. J. Teacher personality and classroom climate. *Psychology in the Schools*, 1968, *5*, 163–169.

Walberg, H., & Thomas, S. Open education: An operational definition and validation in Great Britain and the U.S. *American Educational Research Journal*, 1972, *9*, 197–208.

Wallach, M. A., & Kogan, N. *Modes of thinking in young children: A study of the creativity-intelligence distinction*. New York: Holt, Rinehart and Winston, 1965.

Walsh, A. M. *Self-concepts of bright boys with learning difficulties*. New York: Columbia University, Teachers College, Bureau of Publications, 1956.

Walters, R. H., Parke, R. D., & Cane, V. A. Timing of punishment and the observation of consequences to others as determinants of response inhibition. *Journal of Experimental Child Psychology*, 1965, *2*, 10–30.

Wattenberg, W. W., & Clifford, C. Relation of self-concepts to beginning achievement in reading. *Child Development*, 1964, *35*, 461–467.

Weigand, V. K. *A study of subordinate skills in science problem solving*. Unpublished doctoral dissertation, University of California, Berkeley, 1969.

Weiner, B. Implications of the current theory of achievement motivation for research and performance in the classroom. *Psychology in the Schools*, 1967, *4*, 164–171.

Wertheimer, M. *Productive thinking*. New York: Harper, 1945.

Williams, F. Psychological correlates of speech characteristics: On sounding "disadvantaged." *Journal of Speech and Hearing Research*, 1970, *13*, 472–488.

Williams, F., Whitehead, J., & Miller, L. Relations between language attitudes and teacher expectancy. *American Educational Research Journal*, 1972, *9*, 263–277.

Williams, H. D. Experiment in self-directed education. *School and Society*, 1930, *31*, 715–718.

Williams, R. L. Danger: Testing and dehumanizing black children. *Clinical Child Psychology Newsletter*, 1970, *9*, 5–6. (a)

Williams, R. L. Black pride, academic relevance, and individual achievement. *Counseling Psychologist*, 1970, *2*, 18–22. (b)

Wilson, J. A., Robeck, M. C., & Michael, W. B. *Psychological foundations of learning and teaching*. New York: McGraw-Hill, 1974.

Winterbottom, M. R. *The relation of childhood training in independence to achievement motivation*. Unpublished doctoral dissertation, University of Michigan, 1953.

Witkin, H. A. A cognitive style approach to cross-cultural research. *International Journal of Psychology*, 1967, *2*, 233–250.

Witkin, H. A. *The role of cognitive style in academic performance and in teacher-student relations*. Princeton, N. J.: Educational Testing Service, 1973.

Witkin, H. A., & Moore, C. A. *Cognitive style and the teaching-learning process*. Paper presented at the annual meeting of the American Educational Research Association, Chicago, April 1974.

Wittrock, M. C. Verbal stimuli in concept formation: Learning by discovery. *Journal of Educational Psychology*, 1963, *54*, 183–190.

Wrightsman, L. S. The effects of anxiety, achievement, motivation, and task importance upon performance on an intelligence test. *Journal of Educational Psychology*, 1962, *53*, 150–156.

Wylie, R. C. *The self-concept: A critical survey of pertinent research literature*. Lincoln: University of Nebraska Press, 1961.

Yamamoto, K. Relationship between creative thinking abilities of teachers and achievement and adjustment of pupils. *Journal of Experimental Education*, 1963, *32*, 2–25.

Yando, R., & Kagan, J. The effect of teacher tempo on the child. *Child Development*, 1968, *39*, 27–34.

Yee, A. Interpersonal attitudes of teachers and advantaged and disadvantaged pupils. *Journal of Human Resources*, 1968, *3*, 327–345.

Zimmerman, B. J., & Dialessi, F. Modeling influences on children's creative behavior. *Journal of Educational Psychology*, 1973, *65*, 127–134.

INDEX